A CENTURY OF JUDGING

A Political History of the Washington Supreme Court

Charles H. Sheldon

UNIVERSITY OF WASHINGTON PRESS
Seattle and London

This book is published by the University of Washington Press as part of its celebration of the Washington Centennial.

Manufactured in the United States of America

This book was published with the assistance of grants from the National Endowment for the Humanities and the Andrew W. Mellon Foundation.

Library of Congress Cataloging-in-Publication Data

Sheldon, Charles H., 1929–
A century of judging.

Bibliography: p.
Includes indexes.
1. Washington (State). Supreme Court—History.
2. Judges—Washington (State)—Selection and appointment—History. 3. Political questions and judicial power—Washington (State)—History.
I. Title.
KFW512.S53 1988 347.797′03534 87-16081
ISBN 0-295-96524-X 347.97073534

To Pat

Contents

Illustrations

Acknowledgments

My debt to others is heavy. The greatest is owed to the subjects of this study, the judges of the Washington State Supreme Court. Over the past dozen years I have had the pleasure and honor of talking to all of the sitting and retired judges about their lives, their jobs, their colleagues, and the court. Whatever insights I have gained are derived from their sharing of their knowledge, thoughts, and hopes; whatever inaccuracies I have recorded are due to my own carelessness. A special debt which can never be repaid is owed to the late Justice Frank P. Weaver. His support and enthusiasm for the project was especially poignant in that he knew he would never see the final results.

Many of the former law clerks to the judges also contributed to my understanding of the court. Although they readily talked about their short stay with the court, none violated that trust between clerk and judge that makes their roles so useful.

The earlier interviews with the jurists were conducted under a grant from the American Philosophical Society (1977). Funding from the National Endowment for the Humanities (1978) permitted a review of archival materials and a continuation of the judicial interviews. The National Science Foundation, Law and Social Science Program (1982), funded the research on law clerks. Finally, the Dean's research fund of the College of Sciences and Arts of Washington State University supported the preparation of the manuscript and provided funds for student assistants. Ann Frey and Jean Austin served admirably as research assistants during the data gathering stages of the project.

Professor Kermit L. Hall of the University of Florida, Dean of Faculty and Academic Vice President David J. Danelski of Occidental College, Professor Emeritus Jack B. Gabbert of Washington State University, and John N. Rupp, Esq., of Schweppe, Krug & Tausend read versions of the manuscript and shared their considerable knowledge. The editing advice of Julidta Tarver and Jack Whelan at the University of Washington Press was invaluable.

The leading collaborator in this project, however, was my wife, Pat. She served as my research companion, taking accurate notes at interviews, patiently tabulating case data, and reviewing files in various archives and libraries. This book is as much hers as mine.

During the years in which I worked on this study, I have gained a much deeper appreciation for those who occupy our state court benches. I hope this book allows others to realize a similar appreciation.

Earlier versions of parts of the book have appeared in the *Gonzaga Law Review* and the *Willamette Law Review*.

A Century of Judging

Introduction

This is a study of the judicial process, centering on the Washington State Supreme Court. It is political as well as historical in its approach. It is historical simply because it records events over time and identifies the persons responsible for those events. However, the meanings to be attached to the sequence of events and the significance given the motives of the persons involved are provided through an understanding of politics.

The study of politics is the "study of the authoritative allocation of values for a society."[1] Courts are political agencies because judges authoritatively allocate values among members of society. This study is about one such agency: the Washington State Supreme Court. The judges of the state's court of last resort, wittingly or unwittingly, have been making public policy. Nonetheless, the judges have not been exclusively or primarily concerned with either changing or maintaining the particular balance of values in society. Others, such as the state legislators, the governor, and those who are part of the state's bureaucracy, are involved even more directly in making public policy and authoritatively allocating values. The Supreme Court is simply one among several agencies that behave politically.

In stable democratic systems "authority" is usually equated with government. Governmental officials make decisions that affect all or a major part of society. These decisions are clothed with authority when those who make them are regarded as having the "right" to make such decisions. The decisions are then considered legitimate. Judges are clearly in such positions of authority. On many matters they have a right to allocate or reallocate values between or among members of society. In one sense, however, their authority is tentative. The judges of the Supreme Court, like other public officials, must exercise care in their decisions concerning public policy lest perceived abuses of their authority result in members of society withdrawing their approval by questioning the court's "right" to

1. David Easton, *The Political System* (New York: Knopf, 1953), 129.

decide on particular matters.[2] Efforts may be mounted to replace one or several members of the bench, or, when possible, appeals can be made to the United States Supreme Court. But unlike other public officials, the justices of the Washington Supreme Court are placed in a somewhat more tenuous position precisely because of the very nature of the authority that they exercise.

The Persistent Dilemma: Accountability vs. Independence

Members of all courts (and no less the Washington Supreme Court) are confronted with a particular dilemma. Ultimately, they must strike a balance between the demands of public accountability implied in policy decisions in a democracy and the requirements of judicial independence associated with the concept of the "rule of law." When judges resolve disputes between litigating parties, they are expected to remain aloof from the parties and the interests they represent. Judicial independence, or the rule of law, demands no less. Justice would suffer should this independence not be observed. In the process of resolving a dispute between litigants, judges reaffirm, change, or on occasion, establish a new public policy. In deciding for the plaintiff or the defendant, trial judges as well as appellate jurists may tentatively (and sometimes definitively) establish precedents that affect the public. They make public policy and, in democratic societies, must be held accountable to the public for that policy; majoritarian rule demands no less. Democracy would suffer should accountability not be observed. Thus, the unique dilemma confronting judges is the inherent tension between judicial independence and public accountability. This tension has been a feature of state and federal judiciaries since the beginnings of the Republic.[3]

Judicial independence is maintained by a variety of informal traditions and formal rules, all of which are designed to allow judges to render decisions free from the distractions of public opinion, the pressures of special interests, and the temptations of personal preferences. For example, Canon 1 of the Code of Judicial Conduct asserts that an "independent and honorable judiciary is indispensable to justice in our society," and then details the specific rules to be observed.

Two characteristics separate judges from their political counterparts and enhance their independence. First, the judges base their

2. See Charles H. Sheldon, *The American Judicial Process: Models and Approaches* (New York: Dodd Mead, 1974), 1–9.

3. G. Edward White, *The American Judicial Tradition* (New York: Oxford, 1979), 2.

decisions upon the results of the adversary process. Advocates for the contending parties urge upon the judges their particular version of the correct resolution of the dispute. According to the late Judge Frederick G. Hamley of the Ninth Circuit Court of Appeals and formerly of the Washington Supreme Court, the adversary process is the very essence of the appellate system.

> The appellate lawyer [must] be a pleader for and upholder of his clients's interest. He must be a partisan for the cause he espouses. Consistent with a high standard of the ethical and fair conduct, his every choice of plan or action must be dictated by its supposed tendency to bring acceptance of his view. It is expected that the attorneys for both sides will follow this course in preparing their briefs and presenting their oral argument. If they do so, the court of review, in whom the judging process is lodged, will be able to reach the right and just decision. This, at least, is the theory of our adversary system, as applied to appellate review.[4]

Although on occasion the proceedings of the legislature or of an administrative agency assume the appearance of an adversary hearing, neither legislators nor executives are, like judges, obligated to remain aloof from the contending parties. Judges, however, must always conduct their proceedings within the adversary structure. This supposedly assures that the parties to the dispute are equally represented, encouraging an independent and objective resolution by the judges.

A second feature which distinguishes the justices from both legislators and executives is their passivity. That is, the lower courts' cases selected for review have been initiated by others and already have been tentatively decided.

When issues of public policy are involved—usually as the result of a challenge to a statute or an administrative rule—the review by the justices can be accelerated. For example, the court can take directly from the trial level a "case involving a fundamental and urgent issue of broad public import which requires prompt and ultimate determination."[5] However, the justices must still wait until others petition them for consideration of their legal grievances. This passivity removes the justices from the divisive events that gave rise to the dispute and helps to preserve a degree of independence. Because judges remain aloof from the contending parties in the adversary hearing, and because they must wait for disputes to be brought

4. Frederick G. Hamley, "Appellate Advocacy," *Arkansas Law Review* 12 (1958): 131.

5. *Rules of Appellate Procedure* (RAP) 4.2 (1983).

to them, the public generally tends to regard them as above society's conflicts and consequently dispensers of evenhanded justice.

Several other formal and informal practices also isolate (and insulate) the jurists. The tenure of the justices of the Supreme Court, at least, is longer than that of other public officials (six years as compared to four or two); their terms are staggered so that only one-third can be replaced at any one time; and partisanship has been removed from the nomination and election of the judges. Although they must be licensed members of the legal profession, upon selection they are dropped from the rolls of the bar association in order to assure the desired separation between advocacy and judging. Judges and practicing attorneys attend each others' meetings by invitation, not by right. The decisional process of the supreme court has traditionally remained obscure, with only the oral arguments and the end product, the written opinion, subject to public scrutiny. Canons of Judicial Conduct also are designed to a great extent to keep the judges insulated from the political world that surrounds them. Of course, judicial self-restraint—a respected tradition of state as well as federal benches—is practiced to keep courts out of the political limelight.

Public accountability, on the other hand, is synonymous with democracy and takes several forms, all for the purpose of keeping judges in check. Election campaigns, outcries from the public, pressures from special groups, resolutions from legislators, complaints from bar associations, and reactions both from law schools and from other judges all make their contributions to accountability.

One major feature of the American judiciary which many would argue necessitates accountability is the power of judicial review. Since 1803, the U.S. Supreme Court has been bestowed with this power through which the laws of the land and the actions of public officials are measured against the Constitution.[6] Should the justices find a discrepancy between a law and the Constitution, the law is pronounced null and void. This power of judicial review is also exercised by state courts and, in fact, antedates that of the U.S. Supreme Court.[7] The Washington Supreme Court enjoys such power and has not been reluctant to exercise it.[8]

The third branch of government, endowed with such awesome

6. Of course I speak of John Marshall's ruling in *Marbury* v. *Madison* (1 *Cranch* 137, 1803).

7. See, for example, *Holmes* v. *Walton* (New Jersey, 1780); *Trevett* v. *Weeden* (Rhode Island, 1786); *Bayard* v. *Singleton* (North Carolina, 1787); and *Rutgers* v. *Waddington* (New York, 1784).

8. See Chapter 1.

power, may actually be "more equal" than the other two branches. Given this power, the issue of independence vs. accountability is brought sharply into focus. The members of the state's court of last resort must decide constitutional issues independent of the immediate preferences of the lawmakers, the executives in state government, or even the public. But similarly, because of the responsibility involved in having the final say in constitutional issues, the judges must be held accountable for their interpretations of the fundamental law. Constitutional government means government by consent. When giving content to the constitution, the justices must confirm that consent in some manner or other.

Constitutions are compacts between the government and the people through which the government is granted certain powers to perform clearly defined duties. At the same time, however, limits are placed upon these grants of power. Article I, Section I, of the Washington constitution states that "All political power is inherent in the people, and governments derive their just powers from the consent of the governed, and are established to protect and maintain individual rights." The Judicial Article (Article IV) of the state constitution also contains both a grant of power and limits on that power.

> The judicial power of the state shall be vested in a supreme court, superior courts, justices of the peace, and such inferior courts as the legislature may provide.
>
> The Supreme Court shall consist of five judges, a majority of whom shall be necessary to form a quorum, and pronounce a decision. In the determination of causes all decisions of the court shall be given in writing and the grounds for the decision shall be stated. The legislature may increase the number of judges of the Supreme Court from time to time and may provide for the separate departments of said court. . . .
>
> The judges of the Supreme Court shall be elected by the qualified voters of the state at large at the general state election. . . . If a vacancy occurs in the office of a judge of the Supreme Court the governor shall appoint a person to hold the office until the election and qualification of a judge to fill the vacancy, which election shall take place at the next general election, and the judge so elected shall hold the office for the remainder of the unexpired term.

Thus, although the judicial power is assigned to the courts, means are provided whereby members of the judiciary are held accountable. Supreme court justices must disclose the reasons for their decisions. If these reasons should prove unacceptable, the public may withdraw its "consent" by replacing the errant justice or justices at the next general election.

Several formal and informal features of the constitution and of statutes are designed to ensure further accountability. Although Washington judges are not subject to recall, two provisions in the constitution can be invoked to remove jurists from office. Impeachment proceedings can be instituted under Article V (Sec. 2), and Article IV (Sec. 9) also allows the removal of judges of courts of record by means of a joint resolution of both houses of the legislature. But Article V has never been invoked against judges, and the joint resolution procedure of Article IV has been attempted only once (in 1899) when superior court judge Sachs was absolved of an accusation of bringing the judiciary into disrepute by gambling and frequenting local drinking establishments in Port Townsend. The record shows no other serious attempts to remove judges through the constitutionally provided means. But the possibility nevertheless remains. Mandatory retirement (at age 75), rotation of the chief justiceship among the senior members of the bench, public hearings, and gubernatorial appointments, as well as bar association involvement in the selection process have all tended to clothe the judges of the Supreme Court with the mantle of democratic accountability.

The push and pull between independence and accountability has continued through the history of the Washington Supreme Court. Perhaps the struggle itself gave direction to that history. The details may have changed, but more often than not the changes were wrought because of a perceived imbalance. The synthesis between independence and accountability, however temporary, was most often forged by fluctuations in the method by which judges were brought to the Supreme Court. The manner in which judges were selected provided the principal means for striking a balance. For example, the nonpartisan electoral system constitutes such an attempt at balancing:

> The idea on an elective judiciary, prevailing throughout the state and local governments of this country, brings into confrontation two conflicting *desiderata*—democratic accountability and judicial independence.
>
> In an attempt to enjoy a system of "rule of law" as well as "popular government" American political institution builders have fashioned a composite notion of "nonpolitical" but elective judiciaries. This composite conception dictates that judges ought to be elected by the

> people, but that such elections should be carried on somewhat differently from those for other elective offices.[9]

Much of the history of the Washington judiciary has been dictated by this tension between public accountability and judicial independence. Two major aspects of that history are analyzed in this study. Judicial recruitment illustrates quite sharply the important role elections and appointments have played in the push and pull between these two antithetical but meritorious features. Actually, the evolution of recruitment from a highly partisan system in early statehood to the present complex nonpartisan system can be best explained by examining the concerns of judges, lawyers, the bar, politicians, and the public for balancing the two contradictory desiderata. Today judicial selection has achieved perhaps an ideal balance—for the moment—between the needs of the judges for independence and the demands of the public for accountability.

Also, the decisions of the judges often reflect this dilemma as they render opinions of public import. As dictated by the state constitution, the justices must substantiate their rulings by written opinions made public in the official *Washington Reports*. Perhaps because of fear of voter retaliation, criticisms from the legal profession, threats from legislators, or personal commitments to public responsibility when policy is considered, the judges often address the issue of independence vs. accountability in their written opinions. An analysis of those opinions can often reveal the judges' thinking on this issue that goes well beyond simply the law they enunciate and the litigants' arguments which they have supported or rejected.

Judicial Philosophies

The antagonists in the struggle between accountability and independence usually have carried the identifying colors of judicial activists or restraintists.[10] The question being addressed by the jurists is: "What should be the policy role of the court in relation to the other branches of government?" The court, as it weighs the wisdom of accountability or independence, can either exercise restraint and leave policy decisions to the politically more accountable branches—

9. Nicholas P. Lovrich, Jr., and Charles H. Sheldon, "Voters in Contested, Nonpartisan Judicial Elections: A Responsible Electorate or a Problematic Public?" *Western Political Quarterly* 36 (June 1983): 241.

10. Stephen Halpern and Charles Lamb, *Supreme Court Activism and Restraint* (Lexington, Mass.: Lexington Books, 1982).

the legislature and the executive—or judges can assume an activist stance and render a decision without regard for, or even in defiance of, the other political departments. The power of judicial review gives judges these options. A restraintist would respond that to remain accountable the judges must grant deference to the policies established by those political leaders who are more directly accountable to their political party, the electorate, and to public opinion. Judges should only reaffirm policies made elsewhere when forced to confront public issues. This aloofness from the politics of the moment permits the jurists to render fair and objective decisions and to administer evenhanded justice in resolving disputes. Policy is for others to make. The activist, on the other hand, would argue that the court is responsible to the law and not to the legislature or the governor. Judges should not avoid changing or making public policy if, in their view, it is warranted. Because of training, commitment to the law, and because of their authority, judges are obligated to ascertain and announce what is best for the community.[11] An activist would allocate values more quickly and more decisively than would a restraintist judge. The debate over activist or restraintist roles has been waged since statehood and likely will endure well into the future. Accountability vs. independence sets the parameters for the debate.

However, those justices may also be committed to a particular philosophical stance or values quite apart from these issues of restraint or activism. Also confronting the judges is the question: "What should be the role of government in our society?" A liberal would suggest that the state, usually in the person of a judge, has a responsibility to act positively in protecting the individual from governmental abuse. The individual also must be helped if he or she is unable to compete fairly in the economic or social struggle. In other words, government must play an active role in the lives of people. In contrast, a conservative would only most reluctantly assign to government any sort of role in the relations among individuals. The state should intervene in private concerns only to keep opportunities open and the rules of competition fair. The economic and social struggle must be allowed to be waged freely (albeit within some limits), with those better able to compete and those who work harder being allowed to enjoy the rewards of their efforts. Only then will persons be motivated to improve their lot and, eventually, that of society generally. The question of accountability arises when

11. Richard Neely, *How Courts Govern America* (New Haven: Yale University Press, 1980).

judges are confronted with deciding for either more or less governmental intervention in defiance of the preferences of either a majority of the citizenry or at least a large, well-organized, and vocal segment thereof, while the majority remains apathetic or ambivalent. To what degree should judges be accountable to the majority or should their commitment to liberal or conservative values take precedence over majoritarian demands?

What makes these manifestations of the perennial debate even more problematic is that they may cut across each other, either canceling one or the other or blunting the thrust of each. A liberal-restraintist judge may, for example, be compelled to give the benefit of a doubt to a conservative piece of legislation in order to remain true to his or her view of the proper role of the courts. On the other hand, a liberal-activist may or may not defer to the legislative version of policy, depending on whether that policy coincides with his or her liberal values. The same dilemma confronts the conservative-activist or conservative-restraintist jurists. Perhaps the persistence of these dilemmas crowds a judge toward the middle in terms of roles (activism-restraint) and values (liberal-conservative). In the long run, this push to the center prevents drastic action from courts of last resort and maintains their authority. The resolution of the accountability vs. independence struggle is largely determined by the mitigating result of judges having to choose between either their values or their role. A court achieves a balance because of the mix of values and roles of its several members. A judge achieves a balance by often having to compromise between his role and his values. Perhaps the evidence that follows in our study will confirm this pluralistic view of those forces that underlie judicial decisions.

An Outline

The logic holding the ensuing study together is, of necessity, fairly loose. First, a short review of the context in which we find the Supreme Court of 1889 is clearly in order (Chapter 1). The court's journey was not instantly chartered upon statehood but had been nudged along by the frontier and territorial experiences and by trends in other states. Gradually does the court begin to fashion Washington law, and even then, of course, it does so only partially. Of necessity, this review of the context must include a discussion of the state's experience with constitution making, which established the springboard from which state government was launched, and which also provided the fundamental materials from which the judges of the state's high court drew for their rulings.

In order to follow and understand the unfolding of the accountability vs. independence drama, an analysis is made of the recruitment of judges to the high court (Chapters 2–7). Next, the kinds of individuals who have survived the excluding process of elections and appointments since 1889 are examined and patterns identified (Chapter 8). Then the variety of disputes that have been brought to the justices and the nature of the decisions rendered are analyzed (Chapter 9). Finally, the behavior of what has been termed "representative" courts is studied (Chapters 10–15). Thus, the structure of the study assumes that when we understand the context within which the court was placed, how judges get to the bench, who they are, what they do when they get there, and why they behave as they do, we will have a fairly comprehensive view of the Washington State Supreme Court and its role in the public affairs of the state.

The history of the recruitment of the judges and justices to the Supreme Court sets the framework for the book. The study of the evolution of recruitment reveals that court elections and appointments progressed through five distinct periods, each with its own characteristic resolution to the independence/accountability conflict. Accountability suggests, of course, being accountable *to* someone or *to* some group, just as independence suggests being independent *from* some person or persons. Generally, as accountability increases, independence correspondingly suffers. From statehood until 1912, judicial candidates were held accountable to political parties and their loyal voters (this meant invariably the Republican Party). During the following twenty years, the parties shared this role with and then were replaced by governors as they gradually provided stability to judicial selection through their appointments. From 1934 to 1950, bar associations brought their particular brand of professional accountability to bear on the jurists. The next two decades experienced an unpredictable mix of recruitment actors pressing their often conflicting versions of accountability on the judges. On occasion the voters, political parties, interest groups, bar associations, and governors intervened in the recruitment sequence. Finally, the 1970s witnessed these various recruitment actors settling into fairly predictable roles in the selection of supreme court justices, sometimes cooperating, competing, or conflicting to retain or remove incumbents. Because the demands for accountability were so dispersed among a number of participants, independence was enhanced. A stable balance was achieved by this pluralistic system.

This study is not meant to put an end to scholarly interest in the Washington Supreme Court. Quite the contrary, one purpose is to generate interest in, and study of, individual members of the bench, particular groups of judges sitting at certain times, the various political climates that generated certain legal disputes, electoral or appointive procedures and results, and the inner workings of courts. The research framework is meant to apply to the study of other states' courts as well. The author wishes to encourage more scholarly studies of judges because so much more needs to be done. New justices will be placed on the high bench, and different value allocations will be made by the court. Students of the judiciary ought to scrutinize the bench as it matures and changes. As public figures the justices of the Supreme Court should be of interest to the student of public affairs, but they should as well always be subject to close public scrutiny. If this study contributes to the latter and adds to the former, it will have been a successful enterprise.

1

The Beginnings of the Judiciary

History doesn't simply "begin" and "end." Antecedents are infinite and consequences are innumerable. Those who have been presumptuous enough to assume the task of recording and explaining the past must arbitrarily select a time to begin. But beyond this, they are confronted with a record that is too often incomplete, with evidence that is contradictory, and with documentation that has disappeared. Clearly, explanations must remain tentative.

To understand the beginnings of the Washington State Supreme Court it is necessary to examine the context into which it was thrust in 1889. Three fairly distinct threads held the legal fabric of the state together when the new Supreme Court was put into place in 1889. First, Washington had its own history to be accounted for, a record which, for our purposes, began when Washington gained its own identity after its separation from the Oregon Territory in 1853. Secondly, despite its isolation at the far northwest corner of the nation, Washington had to confront the judicial developments in other sections of the country. Finally, these two threads were woven together with, if not by, a third in the consummation of the territorial experience in the constitutional convention in the summer of 1889 and statehood the following November. The seventy-five men who met in July in the small city of Olympia to fashion the state's governmental structure attempted to blend their territorial experience with what they knew of trends elsewhere, and to adjust these to their own ideas of a proper form of state government, including the judiciary.

The Territorial Judicial Experience: 1853–89

The early residents of "Northern Oregon" (those who lived north of the Columbia River were estimated in 1853 to number only 3,965) began to agitate for separate territorial status in the first few years of the 1850s. They were motivated in part, of course, by local pride and by the not altogether erroneous belief that the territorial government in Salem was dominated by the residents south of the Columbia. But they also felt that the cumbersome size of the Oregon Territory would itself be an obstacle to statehood.[1] In 1852 a small group of citizens in the north petitioned Congress for the establishment of the "Territory of Columbia." The request was well-received and, with but a name change to "Washington" (because of the possible confusion with the District of Columbia), the bill splitting the Oregon Territory was passed by Congress and signed by the President on March 2, 1853.[2]

The structure of the territorial judiciary was dictated by the politics of the nation's capital and by the geography of the region. Other than local justices of the peace and some probate judges, the judicial business of the territory was in the hands of three judges appointed by the President. Politics usually dictated the choices with only the required confirmation by the Senate as a potential check.[3]

Each of the three territorial judges was responsible for conducting trials in one of the three judicial districts. These district courts were in session twice a year, in the spring and fall, although on different dates in order to accommodate attorneys who had cases in more than one district. Usually the justice responsible for the First District heard cases in Walla Walla, for the Second in Vancouver and for the Third in Olympia, although on occasion cases were also tried in Port Townsend, Seattle, and Steilacoom. The judges were required to reside in their respective districts. Once a year they traveled to Olympia to sit as the Supreme Court to hear appeals from their decisions as district judges.[4] This obvious conflict of interest of a justice reviewing his own trial decision was corrected when a fourth judicial district and judge were added in 1884, allowing the three-judge Supreme Court to rotate membership when a

1. The Oregon Territory embraced approximated 341,000 square miles with over six hundred miles of coastline. It included parts of present day Montana and Wyoming and all of Idaho, Oregon, and Washington.

2. For a review of the politics of the 1853 session, see Edmond S. Meany, *The History of the State of Washington* (New York: Macmillan, 1924), 155–59.

3. Later, as dissatisfaction with the territorial judges and with the delay in hearing cases grew, the locally selected justices of the peace and probate judges assumed more responsibility for litigation. See Earl S. Pomeroy, *The Territories and the United States, 1861–1890* (1947) (reprint ed.; Seattle: University of Washington Press, 1969), 59. See also John R. Wunder, *Inferior Courts, Superior Justice* (Westport: Greenwood Press, 1979).

4. For a brief account of territorial government see Thomas W. Prosch, "Washington Territory Fifty Years Ago," *The Washington Historical Quarterly* 4 (April 1913), 96.

Table 1.1
Territorial Judges

Judge	*Term*	*Judge*	*Term*
Edward Lander	1853–58	James K. Kennedy	1870–73
Victor Monroe	1853–54	Roger S. Greene	1871–87
William Strong	1853–54	J. R. Lewis	1873–79
O. B. McFadden	1854–61	S. C. Wingard	1875–79
F. A. Chenowith	1854–58	John P. Hoyt	1879–87
William Strong	1858–61	George Turner	1884–87
E. C. Fitzhugh	1859–61	W. G. Langford	1887–89
C. C. Hewitt	1861–69	Richard A. Jones	1887–88
J. E. Wyche	1861–70	Frank Allyn	1887–89
E. P. Oliphant	1861–67	L. B. Nash	1887–89
C. B. Darwin	1867–68	C. E. Boyle	1888
B. F. Dennison	1868–70	Thomas Burke	1888–89
Orange Jacobs	1868–75	Cornelius H. Hanford	1889
William L. Hill	1870–71	W. H. Calkins	1889

trial decision of one of the justices was being reviewed. The addition of a fourth justice was also prompted by a crowded docket.[5]

A total of twenty-eight appointees served on the territorial Supreme Court between 1853 and 1889. Despite the important role politics played in their selection and the unattractiveness of serving in such large jurisdictions with inadequate traveling accommodations[6] as well as poor working conditions and pay, territorial judges were not always the incompetent political hacks portrayed in history.[7] Actually, as a group the judges were not all that different from their counterparts on the federal district court benches. The territorial judges, including Washington's, were ambitious, successful, middle-class lawyers who were among the educated elite. Their territorial service was often regarded as the culmination of a judicial

5. The territorial legislature had appealed to Congress for the additional judge in 1882 citing geography and docket pressures as reasons: "That the existing state of the Districts and the courts of this Territory consequent on an allowance of three judges only, and the immense territory forming each district, for the holding of the Court, works a grievance to the people tantamount to a denial of justice" (*Washington Sessions Laws* [9th Sess., 1861–62], 162. Quoted in Pomeroy, *Territories*, 53).

6. Traveling to trials in the districts could be hazardous. For example, "no term of the [Washington] Supreme Court was held in the year 1856, on account of the Indian war" (1 W.T.12, 1885).

7. E.g., Lawrence M. Friedman, *A History of American Law* (New York: Simon and Schuster, 1973), 326.

career rather than merely a stepping stone toward higher political or judicial office.[8]

Despite the relative merits of the judges, local expressions of dissatisfaction with territorial justice were not uncommon. Since territorial courts were legislative courts and thus at the mercy of Congress, the incumbents could be removed from office for purely political reasons. At least seven of the twenty-eight Washington justices suffered such a fate, and others may well have resigned under threats of removal. Angry with at least two of the three judges, the territorial legislature resorted to gerrymandering in 1868. "They put pretty much all the Territory into one judicial district with the design to legislate so far as practicable the other judges out of office."[9] However, the dissatisfaction with territorial supreme courts stemmed less from the kinds of individuals selected and more from the procedure by which they were appointed. The territorial judges were "selected with no more deference to local feeling" than were the governors and secretaries of the territories. (Half of the Washington judges were from out of state when appointed.) The judicial system "failed to allow for distances, costs, and other peculiarities of the high plain and mountain west. Territorial courts did not suit because the territories were of the West."[10] Residents were also very resentful of the absenteeism of the territorial judges.[11] It was widely believed that statehood would correct this and other real and perceived faults in territorial status.

8. Kermit Hall studied the backgrounds of all the judges who had ever served on territorial courts since 1789 and concluded that "the collective backgrounds of the judges reveal that they were seldom the hacks and derelicts described by [some historians] and that the political and legal cultures associated with the frontier environment of the territories produced a rich and complex selection process" (Kermit L. Hall, "Hacks and Derelicts Revisited: American Territorial Judiciary, 1789–1959," *Western Historical Quarterly* 12 [July 1981], 289). Among the several respected products of the territorial selection process who served on the Washington courts were Judges Edward Lander, John P. Hoyt, W. Lair Hill, Orange Jacobs, and Thomas Burke. Often the appointees were experienced in territorial affairs. Elwood Evans, who had been nominated but not confirmed, had served as secretary of the territory betewen 1862 and 1867; Orange Jacobs was a delegate to Congress (1875–79); Joseph R. Lewis had served on the Idaho and New Mexico Territorial Supreme Courts (1869–71 and 1871); Samuel C. Wingard had been U.S. Attorney; and John P. Hoyt had served as secretary and governor of the Arizona Territory (1876–79) and was nominated as governor of the Idaho Territory (1878).

9. *Congressional Globe*, 40th Congress, 2nd Sess., 3709. Quoted in Pomeroy, *Territories*, 57. In some territories the practice was for the legislature to create a vast, arid, largely uninhabited jurisdiction, called a "Sage Brush District," and to assign the undesirable judge to ride circuit throughout the area.

10. *Ibid.*, 61.

11. For example, Justice Wyche missed all of the district court dates for 1865. His

Statehood, the Constitution, and the Judiciary

Because a constitutional democracy requires government by consent, and because the United States Constitution insists upon divided government, that is, federalism, each state was compelled to fashion its own constitution, a contract between public officials and the citizens of the state.[12] The government of the State of Washington, no less than that of the United States, was the product of such a contract. The opening statement of the state's basic law reads: "We the people of the State of Washington, grateful to the Supreme Ruler of the Universe for our Liberties, do ordain this constitution," and the first section of the Declaration of Rights (Article I) reaffirmed that "All political power is inherent in the people, and the governments derive their just powers from the consent of the governed, and are established to protect and maintain individual rights." Clearly, the state's founding fathers regarded the constitution as a contractual agreement between citizens and their government.

By 1889 experimentation with constitution writing by the states was largely exhausted. Except for minor details, the constitutions of the states entering the Union around the turn of the century had much in common. This commonality was largely due to the fact that drafters of the new constitutions borrowed provisions from earlier fundamental laws. Separation of powers was assumed if not explicitly referred to. Each new constitution had a bill of rights, usually as the first article of the document. Courts were assumed to possess the power of judicial review. The needs for public education were anticipated, and municipal entities, not altogether trusted, were held in bondage to the legislature. Corporations, especially railroads, were suspect, and restrictions were often written into the basic law. Perhaps the most obvious concern expressed by the new constitutions was with the legislature. Many of the detailed limitations on government were directed toward the lawmaking branch.

---

excuse was that he "had held all courts for four years, two years for Chief Justice C. C. Hewitt who was in the East. Hewitt and Justice E. P. Oliphant . . . had . . . been absent longer than he" (Wilfred J. Airey, "A History of the Constitution and Government of Washington Territory" [Ph.D. diss., University of Washington, 1945], 272).

12. The ideas of consent and divided government were expressed much earlier in several of Chief Justice John Marshall's opinions. For example, in *Barron* v. *The Mayor and City Council of Baltimore* (7 *Pet.* 243, 1833), he wrote: "The constitution was ordained and established by the people of the United States for themselves, for their own government, and not for the government of the individual states. Each state established a constitution for itself, and, in that constitution, provided such limitations and restrictions of the powers of its particular government as its judgment dictates."

As a consequence of these multiple concerns of constitution writers, the documents were longer, more detailed, and laden with what we today would regard as relatively mundane matters more appropriate for inclusion in statutes than in the state's fundamental law.

The character of these state constitutions both encouraged and discouraged the rôle of courts. On the one hand, the details of state documents appeared to lock state judges out of the interpreting function enjoyed by federal judges as they read meanings into the ambiguous and sparse wording of the U.S. Constitution. On the other hand, the "wordy, excessive texts of the state constitutions were made to order for an aggressive judiciary." For example, the constitutions were detailed and technical in their attempt to control the excesses of legislative behavior, and the legislatures often responded with "sloppy, corrupt, and selfish legislation." Who would enforce the checks on the part-time, untrained, susceptible citizen legislators? "Either no one or the courts."[13] At the same time, the constitutional limitations placed on corporations and county-municipal entities invited considerable creativity in the art of circumvention; consequently, there were a considerable number of court tests in response. Washington's experience was no exception.

The Washington Supreme Court, like its esteemed counterpart at the federal level, had available the power of judicial review if, in its view, the separation of powers became distorted, or a citizen's rights were threatened by governmental action, or some of the details of the constitution were transgressed. Although the power of judicial review was not mentioned outright in Article IV or elsewhere in the constitution, by 1889 its exercise had become traditional among state and federal benches. Also, with twenty-two of the seventy-five members of the constitutional convention being attorneys, it seems unlikely that the delegates were unaware of this potentially powerful and essential role for the courts. If the constitution makers failed to discuss the issue (the records are incomplete),[14] they had to have assumed judicial review to be implied in the words "judicial powers" found in Section 1 of Article IV.[15] Judge Theodore L. Stiles, who

13. Friedman, *History*, 312, 316.

14. The convention had hired professional secretaries to keep the records of the debates. Claiming that they had not been paid for their efforts, the recorders destroyed their minutes of the convention proceedings. Thus, historians are limited largely to newspaper accounts of the details of day-to-day proceedings. Edmond S. Meany wrote: "The convention engaged the two best stenographers in the Territory . . . to keep records. A resolution was adopted requesting the Legislature to appropriate money to pay the stenographers and to secure the publication of the records . . . but . . . it was defeated. Twelve years later the stenographers stated that they would no longer think of trying to transcribe their shorthand notes." (Meany, *History*, 24).

15. But see *Bellingham Bay Improvement Co.* v. *New Whatcom* (20 WASH 53, 1898).

had been a delegate to the constitutional convention and was one of the five original members of the Supreme Court, delivered the 1899 presidential address before the annual gathering of the Washington State Bar Association in which he asserted:

> The courts are, and in the nature of things, must be the appellate body, and their power of review extends over the entire domain of public and private right. Once it is conceded, as it now is, universally, that a statute may be declared void as unconstitutional, there is no denying the proposition of judicial supremacy. Whenever the Legislature enacts a law it thereby assumes and asserts that it is constitutional; and whenever the court declares to the contrary, the judgment of the court prevails, and there is no power except that of the people in constitutional convention that can reverse it.[16]

Washington's high court has exercised its power of judicial review sparingly but without hesitation since 1890.[17] If not setting public policies, the court has, on occasion, vetoed those set by the legislature.[18]

Sources of the Washington Constitution

The delegates to the constitutional convention in Olympia had the benefit of several sources to guide their deliberations. First, in an earlier attempt at gaining statehood, the citizens of the territory had sent delegates to Walla Walla in 1878 to design a basic law which they hoped would be accepted by Congress and the President. Interestingly, the issue of calling a constitutional convention and petitioning Congress for statehood was on every territorial ballot from 1869

16. Theodore L. Stiles, "Legislative Encroachments upon Private Rights," *Proceedings of the Washington State Bar Association* (1899), 66. Earlier, in an article in the *Tacoma Daily Ledger*, Stiles had written: "In its operation upon the executive, and especially the legislative branches of government, the constitution is an instrument of limitation, and both of these departments have been pressed hard upon, and as many people believe, over, the lines lain down by their fundamental law, without being checked by the judicial department, unless compelled to do so by unmistakably binding statute. A few more words or some different words, had they been employed by the constitution, would, in every instance which now occurs to me, have served to express a meaning which would have been more satisfactory to the people, and which, I am convinced, was the understanding and intention of that body" (Theodore L. Stiles, "The Constitution of the State and Its Effects Upon Public Interest," reprinted in *The Washington Historical Quarterly* 4 [October 1913], 282).

17. The Territorial Supreme Court had considered the constitutionality of territorial legislative enactments in twelve cases and in half of these found them wanting.

18. See chapter 9 for a tabulation of cases involving judicial review. Approximately two hundred cases over a ten year period posed questions of constitutionality to the justices, and roughly 20% of these failed to pass constitutional muster.

to 1874 and each time the voters rejected the call. However, in 1874 the call for a convention was accepted by a vote of 5,698 to 1,530, largely because of the fear that the Walla Walla region would be annexed to Oregon. Fifteen delegates from Washington Territory and three nonvoting representatives from the Idaho panhandle traveled to Walla Walla and labored for forty days in the summer of 1878 to produce a fairly detailed document which met the approval of the electorate by a 6,537 to 3,236 vote. However, the statehood bills introduced in Congress became lost in committee, and although subsequent bills were also introduced, little interest was then displayed in statehood for Washington. Nonetheless, the Walla Walla constitutional draft was available to the 1889 delegates for study.[19]

Additionally, they were familiar with a number of state constitutions, namely those of Oregon, California, Wisconsin, Missouri, Colorado, and Indiana. Perhaps equally important for the delegates were the efforts of W. Lair Hill, a prominent attorney, former territorial judge, and newspaper man from Portland, Oregon, who had then just taken up residency in Seattle. He was commissioned by his former newspaper, *The Portland Oregonian*, to prepare a draft of a model constitution. A copy of his draft (which relied heavily on the Oregon and California constitutions) was placed on the desks of the delegates and provided a working paper for the convention.[20] The judicial article (Article IV) was largely a product of Hill's draft.

Judicial Selection and the Constitutional Convention

The most obvious means of addressing the independence-accountability issue is through manipulations of judicial recruitment and tenure. The recruitment of state judges has had a mixed past. The federal model, with its lifetime security after initial executive appointment leans heavily toward independence. The short-term popular electron of jurists, often used for trial judges, assures a

19. For a more detailed discussion of the movement toward statehood and the Walla Walla and Olympia conventions, see Paul L. Beckett, *From Wilderness to Enabling Act: The Evolution of the State of Washington* (Pullman: Washington State University Press, 1968), and Beckett, "The Constitutional Framework," in W. F. Mullen et al., *The Government and Politics of Washington State* (Pullman: Washington State University Press, 1978), 19.

20. Knapp quotes from a newspaper account of the Convention: "The admirable draft of a State Constitution by W. Lair Hill, which appeared in the *Oregonian* of the 4th inst., has been the theme of many of the members, who look upon it in the main as just such a constitution as is needed for the new state. The *Oregonian* of that date has been largely in demand by the members ever since its issue" (Quoted in Lebbeus J. Knapp, "Origin of the Constitution of the State of Washington," *The Washington Historical Quarterly* 4 [October 1913], 253).

high degree of accountability. Nonetheless, even with the variety of methods used and the number of changes wrought by the states, certain patterns are evident which provide some explanation for the Washington system adopted in 1889.[21]

Generally, states moved from selecting judges by gubernatorial or legislative appointment with life tenure to popular and partisan election of judges with terms varying from two to fifteen years. Legislatures and governors (who were most often creatures of the legislature) were viewed favorably as having provided some resistance against the crown's representatives and thus could be trusted, initially, with the recruitment of judges.[22] However, by the mid-1800s popular elections had gained favor. "Between 1846 and 1912 every new state entering the Union embraced" popular elections, and many of the earlier appointive states changed to this mode of recruitment.[23]

Several forces were at play in other states and in Washington accounting for the attraction of popular but partisan elections of state judges. The most often recognized cause was the aftermath of Jacksonian Democracy with its emphasis on the abilities of the common people to select and to run government, although it was not expected that virtually anyone could be a judge.[24] After the initial romance with the Jacksonian revolution cooled, "imitation and sentiment" continued to infatuate the newer states with an elected judiciary.[25] For example, California had an elected bench, so did Oregon, and so would Washington.

In conjunction with the Jacksonian influence, the views of the legal profession played significant roles in many constitutional conventions. Attorneys were present in the conventions and always dominated the judiciary committees of those conventions. The concern of the moderates among them was that an appointive system led to suspicion and often to abuses. An elected judiciary would have its own constituency and be clothed with an authority based upon the ballot box. The judges then could play an equal role in the political struggles between governor, legislature, and courts. Especially legislative power would be resisted by a separate and powerful

21. Evan Haynes, *The Selection and Tenure of Judges* (Newark: National Conference of Judicial Councils, 1944), 30–50.

22. James Willard Hurst, *The Growth of American Law: The Lawmakers* (Boston: Little, Brown, 1950), 122.

23. Kermit L. Hall, "Progressive Reform and the Decline of Democratic Accountability: The Popular Election of State Supreme Court Judges, 1850–1920," *American Bar Foundation Research Journal* (Spring 1984), 346–47.

24. Hurst, *Growth*, 140 and Friedman, *History*, 111.

25. Hurst, *Growth*, 140.

supreme court bench. "Popular election also promised to make judicial review more credible."[26]

The debates in the Olympia constitutional convention fail to suggest that the members of the judiciary committee or the convention delegates were concerned with electing judges so that they would be blessed with sufficient authority to deal with the legislature. But the judicial department committee was composed of attorneys, many of whom were respected professionals.[27] They may have simply assumed that a strong judiciary was necessary and that a discussion of the issue was unimportant.

Clearly the delegates and members of the judiciary committee were concerned with gaining partisan advantage. The Republicans dominated the convention and would most likely win the privilege of governing should statehood be granted. Any attempt by the Democrats to dilute the Republican's advantage was quickly and decisively turned aside. Actually, the debates over the judicial article largely followed the respective party lines.

Also the attraction of their own elected judiciary to the founding fathers was in part due to their dissatisfaction with having had the destiny of their territorial judiciary determined by politicians far off in Washington, D.C. Outsiders were appointed by outsiders and imposed on the territory. Judicial services were curtailed, and judges absented themselves returning to or remaining in the East. The residents had more confidence in their own elected local justices of the peace and probate judges.[28] Consequently, from the perspective of the delegates in Olympia, the election of judges was an acceptable and actually desirable means of holding judges more accountable.[29] A closer review of the various alternatives voiced and debated at the Olympia convention is instructive. (See table 1.2.)

26. Hall, "Progressive Reform," 348. See also Kermit L. Hall, "The Judiciary on Trial: State Constitutional Reform and the Rise of an Elected Judiciary, 1846–1860," *The Historian* 44 (May 1983): 353–54.

27. Twelve of the thirteen members of the Committee on the Judicial Department were attorneys and the other member "practiced law." The members and their party affiliation were: George Turner (R), Chairman; Thomas C. Griffitts (D); John R. Kinnear (R); Austin Mires (R); B. L. Sharpstein (D); Theodore L. Stiles (R); Robert F. Sturdevant (R); J. J. Weisenburger (?); D. J. Crolley (R); Ralph O. Dunbar (R); M. M. Godman (D); John F. Gowey (R); and George H. Jones (?). A number of the members were subsequently elected to the Supreme Court (Stiles, Dunbar) or were candidates for that bench (Sharpstein, Godman).

28. Wunder, *Inferior Courts*, 81.

29. This same preference for an elected judiciary had been shown by other states as a result of their experiences with the territorial judiciary. Residents of other territories had also "chafed under the restraining hand of federal judicial appointees" and saw an elected bench as a means of maintaining public accountability (Hall, "Judiciary on Trial," 339).

Table 1.2
Convention Debates on Accountability Provisions of the Constitution

Proposition or Amendment	*Arguments*	*Outcome*
Appointment by governor with confirmation by two-thirds Senate.	In order to prevent "subservience to a corrupt political ring and the whims of the rabble."	"Was lost by a decided vote"
	Would not conform to a republican form of government	
Initial Election: "two shall hold office for terms of three years, three for five years" and each elector shall vote for three "and no more."	Divest politics from the bench, protect the minority, and protect individuals from majorities. (Proposed by Democrats)	Lost by 44 to 23 (or 43-24)
	Political parties should be responsible for courts as well as other agencies, introduce politics into court, to the victors go the spoils. (Republicans) Abridges "Citizen's Right to Vote."	
Elect two from each of two districts: Eastern and Western Washington with chief justice from at-large	Voters would know judges better. (Democrats)	"Motion lost"
	All voters should have a voice.	
Elect judges every six years in April at special election.	Remove judges from partisan politics. (Democrats)	"Motion lost"
	Costs too much and destroys rotation in office.	
Increase from three to five judges and ten year terms when population 1 million.	—	Proposition only
Governor appoint and select chief justice.	—	Proposition only
Increase size from three to five judges	Territorial Court had only three judges who rendered poor decisions and were behind six months; smaller court controlled	Passed by 44 (nayes unrecorded)

Table 1.2 (*continued*)

Proposition or Amendment	*Arguments*	*Outcome*
	by corporations; expedite business; avoid one-man power; broader knowledge	
	Not needed and costs too much; quality more important than quantity; legislature could increase when needed; five no faster than three.	
Allow legislature to increase size and separate departments	Could add when caseload requires; flexibility; separate election possible.	"Motion carried"
	Fear of court-packing and legislative control.	

SOURCES: Beverly Paulik Rosenow (ed.), *The Journal of the Washington State Constitutional Convention, 1889*. Seattle: Book Publishing Company, 1962. Lebbeus J. Knapp, "Origin of the Constitution of the State of Washington," *Washington Historical Quarterly* 4 (October 1913):277.

The commitment to Jacksonian democracy and a belief in partisanship flavored the debates over the size of the supreme bench, the selection of the justices, and their terms of office.[30] Proposals for an appointed judiciary vied, albeit briefly, with an elective system. The judiciary committee considered the two alternatives and quickly adopted election as the means which best coincided with republican (representative) government.

Later in the proceedings, the Democrats proposed that if five justices were to be initially elected to the bench, voters should be limited to casting their ballots for only three of the five. Thus, the minority party could possibly overcome the straight ticket voting prevalent then and gain one if not two of the seats on the bench. Actually, the Democrats argued that this would "divest politics from the bench" and protect the minority and individuals from the dominance of majorities.[31] However, the Republicans countered by sim-

30. The Republican delegates outnumbered the Democrats by 43 to 29. Three delegates were independents.

31. According to an account of the proposal: "The object of the motion was to secure a minority representation on the bench for the Democratic party. At a caucus the evening of July 17, the party had determined to take the stand. The arguments in

ply arguing that the victorious political party should be as much responsible for the courts as it is for the other political agencies of government. They also pointed out that allowing the minority to have representation would actually introduce politics into the court.

Democrats also suggested holding judicial elections separately from the partisan balloting in November. But again, the motivation was to enhance the slim chance Democrats might have had to gain seats on the state's high bench rather than to separate the selection of judges from pressures of accountability implied in partisan elections. The Democrats also attempted, unsuccessfully, to gain partisan advantage by proposing two electoral districts from which the four associate justices would be elected and the chief justice would be elected at large.[32] But the Republicans were in control and tolerated no threat to their anticipated victory when statehood came. After some debate on supreme court jurisdiction and on the salaries of the judges, the delegates moved to consideration of other more contentious articles of the proposed document.

The final approval of the constitution came on August 22, 1889, when seventy-two of the seventy-five delegates signed the final version. On October 1, the constitution was overwhelmingly approved by the electorate by a vote of 40,152 in favor and 11,879 against. The consent of the people had been received, and with the approval of President Benjamin Harrison on November 11, Washington was awarded statehood. At the same October balloting, the people had elected the officials who would assume the responsibilities of the new government, including five supreme court justices. It is this and subsequent elections (and appointments) to the state's court of last resort that will illustrate the persistent conflict between democratic accountability and judicial independence, and these elections will provide a framework for understanding the evolution of the Washington State Supreme Court.

---

the committee of the whole were strictly along party lines" (Beverly Paulik Rosenow, ed., *The Journal of the Washington Constitutional Convention, 1889* [Seattle: Book Publishing Company, 1962], 600).

32. This proposal was also "warmly supported" by the Democrats (*ibid.*, 602).

2

Introduction to the Recruitment Process

Judges occupy positions of consequence in American state political systems, and a heavy burden falls upon those involved in determining and operating the process used to select these judges.[1] This burden has shifted throughout the history of the recruitment of jurists to the Washington high bench, and these shifts reflect the politics of the times.

Recruitment is not only a selection process, but also an excluding process. Many are eligible but few are chosen. The recruitment process filters out some candidates and allows others to pass through to be awarded positions on the Supreme Court. But as the structure of recruitment varies, the results correspondingly vary. For example, the demands of election campaigns may attract certain candidates who do not possess the requisite qualities for serious consideration as gubernatorial appointees. Conversely, those seriously considered for appointment may lack the attributes necessary for electoral success. To understand both aspects of the recruitment process (elections and appointments) is to understand why certain

1. For a review of the history of judicial selection see Evan Haynes, *The Selection and Tenure of Judges* (Newark: National Conference of Judicial Councils, 1944), and Kermit L. Hall, "Progressive Reform and the Decline of Democratic Accountability: The Popular Election of State Supreme Court Judges, 1850–1920," *American Bar Foundation Research Journal* (Spring 1984), 345. For other discussions of judicial elections consult Bradley C. Canon, "The Impact of Formal Selection Processes on the Characteristics of Judges—Reconsidered," *Law and Society Review* 6 (1972): 579; Herbert Jacob, "The Effects of Institutional Differences in the Recruitment Process: The Case of State Judges," *Journal of Public Law* 13 (1964): 104; Patrick W. Dunn, "Judicial Selection in the States: A Critical Study with Proposals for Reform," *Hofstra Law Review* 4 (1976): 267; Jack Ladinski and A. Silver, "Popular Democracy and Judicial Independence: Electorate and Elite Reactions to Two Wisconsin Supreme Court Elections," *Wisconsin Law Review* (Winter 1967), 128; and Philip Dubois, *From Ballot to Bench* (Austin: University of Texas Press, 1980).

people with particular characteristics, backgrounds, and attitudes make it to the Supreme Court while others do not.

Once judges assume their seats on the Supreme Court, many constraints are placed upon them. The robes of office are tangible reminders of a multitude of norms historically impressed upon them in their new role. Judges are passive participants in the affairs of the state; that is, they must wait for disputes to be brought to them. Once a dispute is presented, it is not the judiciary but members of an independent legal profession who are charged with presenting the facts, issues, and arguments. In the adversarial process, it is the lawyers who are the litigant managers; the judges often function merely as referees. Also, the Supreme Court is made up of individual jurists, and the views of at least a majority of these individuals must be reconciled in order to reach a final decision. Further, the judges answer to the electorate either directly in elections or indirectly through the pressures of public opinion.

Although the constraints are substantial, within these bounds the jurists can and do exercise considerable discretion. A ruling in a close case often can be best explained by reference to the preferences and attitudes of the judges. To understand why persons with certain attitudes have survived a particular version of the recruitment process is to understand to a significant degree why this person, after becoming a judge, chose one of several viable decisional alternatives in resolving a legal dispute.

As suggested in the introductory chapter, the recruitment process of judges reflects a basic dilemma of American democracy. Judicial selection in Washington relies upon majoritarian choices on the one hand, and makes a strong commitment to judicial independence on the other. Judges at all levels have, since statehood, been elected by registered voters during the regularly scheduled elections. Even those jurists who are appointed by the governor to fill vacancies created by resignations or deaths must face the judgment of the electorate at the next general election in order to continue on the bench, and are then politically accountable to the electorate. Nonetheless, when judicial recruits don the robes of office as committed and competent jurists, they are expected to remain above the fickle stresses of public opinion and the strains of politics. In order to administer evenhanded justice, judicial independence is expected. This is a basic dilemma inherent in American state judiciaries.

This tension, though, was not always generally perceived by those involved in the Washington State judicial system. Partisan accountability and political mandates were not seen as inimical to the rule of law in the early days of Washington statehood. The voter perceived partisan accountability as part of his or her contribution to the electoral process, and, correspondingly, the judge viewed his electoral mandate as a vindication of his political party loyalties. It took many years, many changes in procedures, and, ultimately, changes in judicial and electoral thinking before the dilemma was clearly perceived. Then, the stresses and strains of politics struck a new balance between majority rule and judicial objectivity. The pressures of the tension eased for the moment, but often manifested themselves in the next round of recruitment. It is not an exaggeration to suggest that the very essence of judicial recruitment politics was and is the tension between these two antagonistic forces—the thesis of public accountability and the antithesis of judicial independence. The judicial recruitment system strives for, but as yet has not found, the synthesis.[2]

The Structure of Judicial Recruitment

Judicial recruitment in Washington has attracted a variety of participants, who at one time or another were intimately involved in the process that brought judges to all levels of the state benches. The candidates, various groups (especially the lawyers' professional organizations and political parties), the voters, the governors, and special commissions or committees have all at various times assumed and sometimes shared responsibilities for recruiting judges. The evolution of their activities over the years has provided a framework for, or given structure to, the selection of judges by which the process can be understood.

The *candidates*, either through self-motivation or through the urgings of others, place their names before convention delegates, file for available judicial seats, or urge their names upon appointing authorities. The *bar associations* or committees of lawyers recommend judicial aspirants to the governor or to the electorate through endorsements, selection committees, bar polls, or informal contacts.[3] *Political parties*, as for other public offices, nominate judicial

2. For a discussion of judicial accountability, see C. Sheldon and N. Lovrich, "Judicial Accountability vs. Responsibility: Balancing the Views of the Voters and the Judges," *Judicature* 65 (May 1982): 470; N. Lovrich and C. Sheldon, "Voters in Contested, Nonpartisan Elections: A Responsible Electorate or a Problematic Public?" *Western Political Quarterly* 36 (June 1983): 241; and S. Wasby, "Accountability of Courts," in Scott Greer et al., eds., *Accountability in Urban Society* (Beverly Hills: Sage, 1978).

3. Dorothy Maddi, *Judicial Performance Polls* (Chicago: American Bar Foundation, 1977); C. Sheldon, "Influencing the Selection of Judges: The Variety and Effectiveness of State Bar Activities," *Western Political Quarterly* 30 (September 1977): 397; and

candidates, organize their election contests under partisan labels, or provide readily available lists of supporters, funding sources, and campaign workers. Additional groups, such as labor, civic, business, or other (often *ad hoc*) organizations may endorse and formally support judicial aspirants. The *electorate* commonly confirms incumbents (whether previously elected or appointed) or occasionally will choose newcomers who present favorable images.[4] The state's *chief executives*, when vacancies occur, appoint those whom they perceive as warranting a seat on the bench.

These major recruitment actors have made their contributions to the task of judicial selection at some time during a three-step sequence. The *initiation* step refers to the stage when lawyers become judicial aspirants. Some were pushed forward, others leap when opportunities occur. Several factors could account for why some attorneys are persuaded or others are self-impelled to seek a seat on the bench. For example, who or what persuaded Robert C. Finley to attempt to unseat Judge John S. Robinson in 1948? *Screening* is the step in which the qualifications of the various candidates are measured against each other on the basis of standards set by the screening actors. In the initiation phase, the aspirants, whether reluctant or eager, are scarcely, if ever, compared one with another, but during screening, the selection process becomes competitive and comparisons are all-important. The election campaign itself is the usual screening device, although sometimes a highly intense campaign is conducted prior to the formal filing for office or the submitting of a name to the governor for appointment. This "preprimary" campaigning is designed to discourage others from becoming candidates. *Affirmation* constitutes the final step on the road to the bench.[5] But more is involved in this final step than simply the designation of the victor. The recruitment procedure educates the new judge as to what he should expect when he assumes office, and, correspondingly, those responsible for affirmation have developed their own expectations about how the judge will respond to particular disputes. In most cases the mutual expectations are satisfied. As a

---

C. Sheldon, "Bar Endorsement of Judicial Candidates," *Washington State Bar News* 28 (1974): 8.

4. Philip Dubois, "The Significance of Voting Cues in State Supreme Court Elections," *Law and Society Review* 13 (1979): 757; David Adamany and P. Dubois, "Electing State Judges," *Wisconsin Law Review* (1976): 734; and H. Jacob, "Judicial Insulation—Elections, Direct Participation and Public Attention to Courts in Wisconsin," *Wisconsin Law Review* (1966): 1.

5. Richard Richardson and Kenneth Vines, *The Politics of Federal Courts* (Boston: Little, Brown, 1970).

consequence of the three-step recruitment sequence, the selection of judges can be viewed as an ever-narrowing process where the many are winnowed down to one survivor who dons the prestigious robes of judicial office.

The nature of the contribution made to this sequence by each of the various recruitment participants separately or in unison, can vary significantly. That is, different recruitment phases develop depending upon how the participants relate to one another throughout the process.

The history of judicial selection in Washington suggests that recruitment processes have indeed undergone a gradual and coherent change. An unstructured style of recruitment characterized early experiences with judicial selection. At that time, only a few participants were formally in control of access to judicial office. Over a number of years, the early style was gradually replaced by a more structured version, involving the persistent participation of a number of recruiters sharing in (or competing for) recruitment responsibilities.

A division of labor involving a clear separation of functions characterized the relations among the participants in the early style—as depicted in the example set forth in table 2.1.

In the early years, responsibility for one of the three stages quite typically was held exclusively in the hands of one of the recruitment participants. The candidates, for example, tended to be coopted by political parties which then informed those involved in the screening and affirming stages of the candidates' availability and qualifications. Also, the political party commonly assumed sole responsibility for screening the candidates through nominating conventions. The voters, then, selected from among the party candidates and

Table 2.1
Recruitment Responsibility in the Inaugural Period

	Recruitment Stages		
Participants	*Initiation*	*Screening*	*Affirmation*
Candidates	X*		
Bar associations			
Political parties	X	X	X
Governors		X*	
Electorate			X
Other groups			

*Appointments

affirmed by casting ballots for their favorite. However, straight party voting took most of the discretion away from the electorate. In the appointment process, the governor generally assumed full responsibility for screening. The electorate either affirmed or rejected the governor's appointee at the next election. Of course, different combinations of active recruiters could be hypothesized, but single responsibility for one stage or another remained the key to understanding the inaugural model of judicial recruitment.

The contemporary version involves a scheme of shared responsibilities. Rather than performing a single role, participants cooperate (or compete) with each other as each acts to some degree to initiate, screen, and affirm—as depicted in the example set forth in table 2.2.

In the structured model of recruitment evident today, the candidates share the initiation stage with others. For example, some attorneys present themselves as candidates while others are urged to seek judicial office by the bar, labor unions, or political parties. The governors share the screening function with the bar and the electorate (through primary elections) as prospective candidates for appointment and election are considered. The candidates may also make their contributions to the screening process through campaigning in the primary and general elections. The voters share affirmation with the bar and others when they designate the victors, and they maintain certain expectations about how the victors should conduct themselves on the bench. The newly elected judges also have gained a feeling for what is expected of them with the clues coming from the voters, governors, and members of the legal profession.

The Development of Judicial Recruitment

Judicial recruitment evolves—sometimes gradually and imperceptibly, and at other times abruptly—from the unstructured isolated-

Table 2.2
Recruitment Responsibility in the Contemporary Phase

	Recruitment Stages		
Participants	*Initiation*	*Screening*	*Affirmation*
Candidates	X	X	
Bar associations	X	X	X
Political parties	X	X	
Governors	X	X	X
Electorate		X	X
Other groups	X	X	X

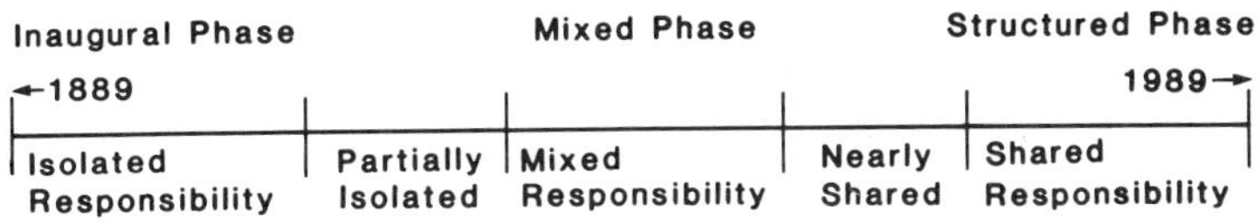

Fig. 2.1. The recruitment system as a development continuum

function phase to the structured shared-function phase. At any given time Washington's system could be located somewhere along an evolutionary recruitment continuum. (See figure 2.1.)

As the major recruiters begin to compete, consult, or anticipate the concerns of the others, and to some degree share the tasks at each stage of the selection process (as a result of cooperation or compromise), the system is evolving. The transitional phase involves mixed responsibility where, for example, the bar and candidates intermittently initiate candidacies, but the electorate alone screens during primary elections, narrowing the candidates to two.

The particular mix among the several participants throughout the three stages of the selection process varies, as suggested, over time. Nonetheless, the mix, however momentary, is both a product of and has an impact on the balance between majoritarian rule and the rule of law. For example, screening judicial candidates through partisan elections leads to a disproportionate accountability to the political parties and party loyalists. Replacing partisan elections with nonpartisan electoral processes brings about a redress of the previous imbalance between democratic accountability and judicial independence, but without the helpful cue of party affiliation, the voters are unable to enforce a significant degree of accountability, and a new imbalance is created, pressing for resolution. From this perspective, the evolution of recruitment becomes a dialectical process energized by the conflict between what the majority apparently wants and what adherence to the independence of the judiciary can tolerate.

This evolution from the early recruitment method to one more structured has had an impact on whether judges lean toward extremes or accept the inherent tension between the two values. In the beginning, the few participants involved tended to opt for a strong commitment to either independence or accountability, hence producing much or little consensus on appropriate bench behavior. Those involved in the structured contemporary recruitment phase tend to accept the inherent conflict between the two.[6] The judges

6. Nicholas P. Lovrich, Jr., and C. Sheldon, "Assessing Judicial Elections: The Effects of High and Low Articulation Systems in Washington and Oregon," *Western Political Quarterly* (June 1985).

who are products of structured recruitment will express attitudes and behavior reflecting the recognition that a viable judiciary requires a balance between both principles.[7] The history of judicial selection in the State of Washington, then, is the history of the tension between these two antithetical forces.

The following chapter traces the selection of Washington State Supreme Court judges during the inaugural years. From statehood to 1912 Washington was struggling to free itself from the tight grip of partisanship which was during that period the ultimate determinant of those chosen to become judges.

7. It is not inevitable that recruitment proceed in the progressive direction suggested by the evolutionary view expressed here. For example, political forces in the state could have amended (or still can amend) the constitution to allow gubernatorial appointment with long tenure, shifting the balance toward independence. However, if balance is what the judicial system demands, then the structured and involved recruitment now at play in Washington seems appropriate (see *ibid.*).

3

Recruitment in the Inaugural Years, 1889–1912

Article IV, Section 3, of the Washington Constitution reads in part:

> The judges of the supreme court shall be elected by the qualified electors of the state at large at the general state election. . . . If a vacancy occurs in the office of a judge of the supreme court the governor shall appoint a person to hold the office until the election and qualification of a judge to fill the vacancy, which election shall take place at the next succeeding general election. . . .

The wording clearly established elections as the primary mode of selecting supreme court judges, supported by a back-up system of gubernatorial appointments. This article was in the original 1889 constitution, and, although several attempts have been mounted to change it, the formal method for choosing judges remains basically the same.

The language of Article IV does not specify the details of the election process, and this flexibility has led to a variety of forms. Most variations involved experiments with the nominating process by which candidates won the right to have their names placed on the final November ballot and experiments with the manner in which those names were placed on the official ballot form.

Eighty-nine elections (primaries and general elections) have been held between 1889 and 1985. There have been 287 positions contested by 496 aspirants (an average of 1.7 challengers for each available position). There have been 70 contested positions in the primaries out of 131 opportunities (54%), and 60 contested campaigns at the general elections out of 161 opportunities (37%).

Incumbents have been challenged 89 times, but only 11 of these sitting jurists have been rejected by the electorate.[1]

Although the appointment process was initially intended to complement elections by providing a quick means of filling interim vacancies, it has taken on a significance not intended by the founders. Consequently, appointments warrant separate review in any study of the evolution of recruitment to the supreme court.

The *legal* link between elections and appointments has been provided by Article IV. The *political* link has been forged by a coalition between the governor, his or her political party, the legal profession, and the electorate. Virtually all of the judges appointed by the governor have been retained on the bench by the voters. There have been eighty positions subject to recruitment filled by seventy-seven judges since 1889. Fifty-two of these were appointed (68%).[2] Of these fifty-two, only four have suffered defeat at the hands of the voters in their first constitutionally mandated contest.[3] The appointment and the electoral process become inextricably interwoven, since appointment virtually assures success at the polls and some of the same forces that determine who gets elected also enter into who is appointed.

If the hypothesized recruitment systems prove to reflect the actual process, it is anticipated that during the early period of judicial selection little sharing of responsibility was evident among the several actors in the drama of recruitment. Likely, then, elections and appointments were not closely linked. It is best, then, to analyze these two aspects separately in order to better understand if and when they began to converge.

Elections during the Inaugural Years: Partisanship Prevails

On August 27, 1889, in compliance with the congressional "Enabling Act" of February 22, and in anticipation of Article XXVII, Sec. 7, of the new constitution, Territorial Governor Miles Moore issued a proclamation calling for October 1 elections for state offices

1. J. P. Hoyt (term ending in 1897), James B. Reavis (1903), Mack F. Gose (1915), O. R. Holcomb (1927), Chester R. Hovey (1923), William H. Pemberton (1925), William J. Millard (1949), Henry E. T. Herman (1932), George B. Simpson (1951), Edward M. Connelly (1947), and Morell E. Sharp (1971).

2. Six of the forty-nine were elevated to the bench by the governor simply because they were successful in the election and would have been eventually affirmed. Justices Chadwick (1908), Webster (1916), Mallery (1942), Schwellenbach (1946), Dore (1981), and Callow (1984). Judge Main's dominant showing in the 1912 superior court primary race was important to his appointment.

3. Judges Hovey (1922), Herman (1932), Connelly (1946), and Sharp (1972).

and for ratification of the fundamental law.[4] Among those officials to be elected were five supreme court judges.[5]

State political party conventions were held after delegates were selected in primary caucus elections and county conventions. Republican delegates met in Walla Walla during the first week in September and nominated Ralph O. Dunbar, John P. Hoyt, Theodore L. Stiles, T. J. Anders, and Elmon Scott for the five judicial seats. Dunbar, after taking himself out of consideration for a U.S. Senate seat, was unanimously selected by the convention.[6] On the first ballot for the remaining four seats, the delegates cast their choices among eight aspirants: J. P. Hoyt (249 votes), T. L. Stiles (236), T. J. Anders (196), E. Scott (161), Mark Fullerton (147), Col. J. Z. Moore (128), B. F. Dennison (64), and Elwood Evans (28).

Dunbar, Hoyt, and Stiles all played significant roles in the Republican convention. Dunbar and Hoyt had been touted as leading candidates for either the U.S. House or the Senate.[7] Stiles, one of the founding fathers of the State Constitution (along with Hoyt and Dunbar), was elected permanent chairman of the convention.

The next week the Democrats met in Ellensburg and nominated their slate for the October 1 balloting. There was no dearth of candidates for the state's high bench. William H. White, B. L. Sharpstein, John P. Hudson, John [James] B. Reavis, and Frank Ganahl were nominated from a pool of prominent attorneys at the convention.

Reports on the month-long campaign gave little attention to the judicial aspirants, although they participated in the mass rallies, speeches, and platform appearances characteristic of the partisan politics of the period. *The Morning Journal* supported the Democrats

4. Article IX, Sec. 3, of the state constitution reads: "The first election of the judges of the supreme court shall be at the election which shall be held upon the adoption of this Constitution and the judges elected thereat shall be classified by lot, so that two shall hold their office for the term of three years, two for the term of five years, and one for the term of seven years."

5. Chapter 8, Session Laws, 1889, p. 415. The nomination of political candidates was either through conventions or "certification." Those "representing a political party or principle" would gather together and hold a primary "election" to nominate candidates for public office. Those nominated other than by convention would have their names placed on the general election ballots through certificates, signed by not less than one hundred electors throughout the state and filed with the secretary of state. If the signatures were valid, the candidate's name was placed on the November general election ballot.

6. Dunbar was defeated in a three-man race for the congressional nomination after three ballots.

7. *The Seattle Daily Times*, September 6, 1889, wrote that "The nomination of J. P. Hoyt removes that gentleman from the senatorial contest and leaves the field clear for Squires. This was mutually agreed between Hoyt and Squires."

and *The Seattle Post-Intelligencer* and *The Seattle Daily Times*, the state's leading newspapers, backed the Republicans.

The leading contenders for the Supreme Court displayed different styles of campaigning if we are to believe the partisan press. Upon returning from the Republican convention and before a partisan rally, John Hoyt excused himself from making a speech, and Theodore Stiles states that being a candidate for judge required that "he should refrain from making a rampant partisan speech." However, his speech was "witty and clear cut" and he suggested that because the constitution was written and supported by the Republicans, they should be responsible for instituting the new government.[8] On the other hand, Democrat William White's partisanship apparently failed to befit one aspiring to a judgeship, at least according to *The Seattle Daily Times*, which reported:

> [White] . . . made one of his "abusive" speeches (Mr. White makes no other kind). Mr. White, as candidate for the most sacred office . . . does not seem to have been affected with that delicacy of respect for the high office to which he aspires, as characterizes other candidates for judgeships.[9]

Considering the overwhelming support given Republicans and their expectation of victory in October, the Republican judges could afford to refrain from highly partisan campaigning.

Some excitement was created when *The Morning Journal* published a news account from Arizona which reported that six indictments had been issued for Theodore Stiles accusing him of "dishonest practice" while an attorney in Arizona. He was "accused of speculating with the funds of Hudson and Co., bankers, from which he accumulated a considerable fortune with which he went to Washington." Stiles' explanation of the Hudson affair satisfied most and seemed complete. The Arizona account and *The Morning Journal* release appeared to be a "put up job" and distracted little from the Republican ticket.[10] Stiles, however, garnered the least number of votes among the successful Supreme Court judges on the October ballot.

John Hoyt came under some partisan suspicion when he was accused of favoring the Northern Pacific Railroad while a territorial judge. He also allegedly denied the anti-Chinese rioters of 1886 the

8. *Ibid.*

9. *Ibid.*, September 12, 1889.

10. *The Seattle Daily Times* called the accusations "A Malignant Slander" in its September 15, 1889, issue. A stockholder of *The Morning Journal* denied the story. On September 16, 1889, *The Times* published a telegram from Tucson signed by a number of prominent citizens of that Arizona city pledging support for Stiles.

right of appeal. *The Post-Intelligencer* discounted the accusations and, with some delight, pointed out that every attorney in Judge Hoyt's twelve-county district had signed a petition for his reappointment as territorial judge. The allegations failed to make any significant inroads into voter support.

In light of the journalistic style then prevailing, as well as the freewheeling politics of the time and the strong partisanship displayed in all races, it is not surprising that these "slings and arrows" aimed at the judicial candidates proved harmless.

In addition to the partisan and highly political nature of nominations and elections for judges of the Supreme Court, this inaugural period was characterized by straight-ticket voting. Not only were voters encouraged to vote the straight party ticket, but also the ballot form was designed to simplify such partisanship. The general election laws allowed the voters merely to mark the top of their political party's ballot to register their approval of all candidates on the party list from presidential electors to Supreme Court judges.[11] In 1895 the party-list ballot form was changed to the office-group ballot, but each voter still could mark his ballot once and record a vote for all candidates of a single party.

Candidates for the state's highest bench had an added advantage over many of their partisan colleagues in November. The names of supreme court aspirants preceded all other state officials on the ballot. In many elections, judges were either second or third in order of offices on the ballot preceded only by congressional and presidential electoral college candidates. Thus voter ballot "fatigue" would rarely set in this soon for those voters who chose not to vote a straight party ticket.

The fortunes of the first judicial candidates were tied to the fate of their respective political parties. No meaningful distinctions were made between aspirants for the Supreme Court and candidates for what are now regarded as highly partisan offices such as those for Congress or the State House. Initially, judicial aspirants shared speaking platforms with the other prominent politicians, although some Republican jurists displayed modest reluctance to give full attention to partisan activity. Because of the Republican dominance of politics during these earlier years, the G.O.P. judicial nominees had little to worry about in any case.

Partisanship dominated the initiation, screening, and affirmation

11. The law read: "*Provided, however,* That any elector who desires to vote for an entire group may mark a cross as above described against the political designation of such group, and shall then be deemed to have voted for all the persons named in such a group whose names shall not have been erased." Chapter 13, Session Laws, 1889–90, p. 410.

of judges to the Supreme Court until the first decade of the twentieth century when the advocates of reform, backed by the formidable forces of the Progressive Movement and assisted by some members of the legal profession, pushed for the exclusion of partisanship from judicial selection.[12] One observer described the progressives as aiming at "democratizing" state government:

> [The] progressives advocated a wide range of political reforms including the direct primary, Australian (secret) ballot, presidential preference primary . . . cross filing, . . . non-partisan local and state elections, women's suffrage, civil service . . . , popular election of senators, short ballot, corrupt practices act, . . . recall, referendum, and the initiative. [U]ltimate power [should be] in the hands of the people.[13]

The Progressives, who played prominent roles in the State Grange organization, advocated direct primaries and nonpartisanship for all judges in the state. Judges had to be removed from the corrupting influences of political parties. The difficulties Judges Root and Gordon experienced in 1908, leading to the resignation of the former and ultimately the trial of the latter, were cited by the Progressives as examples of the vulnerability of supreme court judges. The movement for reform, however, was gradual and experienced several setbacks before achieving success.

Two solutions to the problems of the political nature of judicial recruitment and excessive partisan accountability were advocated. On the one hand, Progressives pushed for a direct primary election method to replace the conventions for the nomination of judges, as well as all other public officials. On the other hand, nonpartisan judicial elections were also urged upon the state, notably by moderates in the State Bar Association.[14] Although nonpartisanship and the direct primary appear to be companion reforms, not all of those concerned with improving the judiciary advocated both proposals.

The Democrats, too, sought a nonpartisan judiciary. Reform was not necessarily foremost in the minds of the minority party, how-

12. A. Ekirch, *Progressivism in America: A Study of the Era from Theodore Roosevelt to Woodrow Wilson* (New York: New Viewpoints, 1974); L. Gould, ed., *The Progressive Era* (Syracuse, N.Y.: Syracuse University Press, 1974); and C. O. Johnson, "The Initiative and Referendum in Washington," *Pacific Northwest Quarterly* 36 (1945): 29.

13. Charles M. Price, "Initiative: A Comparative State Analysis and Reassessment of a Western Phenomenon," *Western Political Quarterly* 28 (1975): 243.

14. The Washington Bar Association held its charter meeting in 1888. A few years later the organization called itself the Washington State Bar Association. In 1933 the Washington legal profession was unified by statute (Chapter 94, Session Laws, 1933, p. 397). The law required that attorneys be members of the State Bar in order to practice law.

ever. Except for Judge Reavis and the temporary appointment[15] and short-term uncontested election in 1901 of William "War Horse" White, the Democrats had been resoundingly and consistently defeated, in spite of the fact that they presented highly qualified and respected candidates to the electorate. Candidates like B. L. Sharpstein, Alfred Battle, Richard Winsor, and John P. Judson were recognized as highly qualified for the bench. Further, the Populists and Socialists lured away from the Democrats some of the working class voters during this early period. Therefore, a nonpartisan judiciary could only enhance the chances for electing Democratic judges.

The major strategy of the Democrats was to "sacrifice" partisan opportunities, setting an example by supporting a Republican now and then, and by nominating fewer candidates than the positions available, hoping the Republicans would reciprocate. In 1902, Hiram C. Hadley was nominated by the Republicans but also received the endorsement of the Whatcom County Democrats. The King County Democrats nominated only one candidate for justice of the peace that year, although two positions were available, hoping that either the voters would split their ballots or that the Republicans would follow suit and nominate only one. Nonetheless, the voters were not yet prepared to seize the opportunity to forge a bipartisan judiciary. Hadley had no difficulty in defeating incumbent James Reavis, who had broken through the Republican monopoly in the election of 1896 with a Fusionist coalition of Democrats, Free Silver Republicans, and Populists, and the Republicans rejected the suggestion to share the judiciary with their opposition.

In 1904, the Democrats again urged a nonpartisan bench by nominating only one candidate, Alfred Battle, for the two available seats on the high bench.[16] The Republicans, confident that they held the advantage, refused to cooperate and won election for Frank H. Rudkin and reelection for Mark Fullerton.

15. See *State Ex Rel. Murphy* v. *McBride* (29 Wash. 335, 1902) for a ruling on these temporary appointments. Hadley and White had been appointed by Fusionist Governor Rodgers to fill two temporary positions created by the legislature. An aspirant for the high bench, superior court judge John E. Humphries of Seattle, brought suit to ascertain if the positions were truly temporary. The court majority, including Hadley and White, decided in favor of the temporary nature of the appointments, and the membership of the court reverted to five judges.

16. *The Seattle Daily Times,* November 4, 1904, explained the motivations of the Democrats in 1904: "For judge of the supreme court the Democratic ticket contains but one name—that of Judge Alfred Battle. This is in line with the demands for a non-partisan judiciary, it being understood that the Democrats will also vote for the re-election of Judge Fullerton. Mr. Battle is one of the leading lawyers of the King County bar, and will make an upright and impartial judge of the highest court of the state."

Table 3.1
Election Results, 1889–1904

	General		General
1889	*(Oct. 1)*	*1898*	*(Nov. 8)*
Ralph O. Dunbar (R)	34,042	**T. J. Anders (R)*	40,452
Theodore L. Stiles (R)	32,686	*Mark Fullerton (R)*	40,452
John P. Hoyt (R)	33,578	Benjamin F. Heuston (Peoples)	32,793
Thomas J. Anders (R)	34,302	Melvin M. Godman (Peoples)	32,185
Elmon Scott (R)	33,800	Thomas Young (Soc. Labor)	1,323
William H. White (D)	24,556	Thomas Lawrey (Soc. Labor)	1,066
John P. Judson (D)	24,466		
B. L. Sharpstein (D)	25,503	*1900*	*(Nov. 6)*
James B. Reavis (D)	24,539	*Wallace Mount (R)*	56,122
Frank Ganahl (D)	24,025	**R. O. Dunbar (R)*	56,092
		E. C. Million (D)	44,039
1892	*(Nov. 8)*	Richard Winson (D)	43,671
**Thomas J. Anders (R)*	35,871	Everett Smith (Prohibition)	2,606
**Elmon Scott (R)*	34,658	Thomas Young (Soc. Labor)	1,018
Eugene K. Hanna (D)	28,027	Frank Martin (Soc. Labor)	945
William H. Brinker (D)	27,399	D. M. Angus (Soc. Dem)	1,959
G. W. Gardiner (Peoples)	20,632	J. H. May (Soc. Dem)	1,972
Frank T. Reid (Peoples)	20,372	Short term:	
1894	*(Nov. 6)*	**W. H. White (D)*	48,696
**R. O. Dunbar (R)*	36,119	*1902*	*(Nov. 8)*
M. J. Gordon (R)	35,186	*Hiram E. Hadley (R)*	62,385
T. N. Allen (D)	15,570	*James Bradley Reavis (D)	33,512
John L. Sharpstein (D)	16,016	William J. Hoag (Soc. Labor)	967
H. L. Forrest (Peoples)	25,901	Thomas Neill (Soc.)	5,800
J. M. Ready (Peoples)	25,572		
H. L. Forrest (Straight Peoples Party)	224	*1904*	*(Nov. 8)*
J. M. Ready (Straight Peoples Party)	209	*Frank H. Rudkin (R)*	86,670
		**Mark A. Fullerton (R)*	94,224
John W. Peters (Prohibition)	184	Alfred Battle (D)	39,308
A. A. Byers (Prohibition)	175	A. Brarcliff (Soc. Labor)	1,330
Miscellaneous	69	J. W. Monett (Soc. Labor)	1,403
		Wm. McDevitt (Soc.)	8,924
1896	*(Nov. 3)*	D. W. Phipps (Soc.)	8,959
*J. P. Hoyt (R)	38,837		
James B. Reavis (Fusionist)	50,982		
E. N. Livermore (Prohibition)	1,205		

*Incumbent
Italicized names designate winners
Full six-year term unless otherwise indicated

The state's leading newspapers were gradually joining the cry for a nonpartisan judiciary. For example, *The Seattle Daily Times* condemned the infusion of partisanship in the selection of judges in this 1902 editorial although considering Hadley's easy defeat of Reavis, the *Times'* view appeared unrealistic:

> There is an abiding excitement in the minds of the honest voters that there should be no politics in the selection of judges, and on this account Judge Reavis [Democrat] will secure a large Republican vote, as the holdover members of the court are all Republicans.[17]

The movement to adopt direct primary elections for nominating all public officials was gaining momentum at the same time as support for a nonpartisan judiciary became commonplace. By 1907 this reform, as part of the progressive movement, had gained sufficient state-wide support to compel the legislature to replace the convention method with the direct closed primary technique. All aspirants for national and state-wide offices would be nominated by the members of the respective parties at a September balloting.

This 1907 statute brought together the nonpartisan judiciary and the direct primary, along with some degree of separateness advocated by the bar. Senate Bill 322 (which became Chapter 209 of the 1907 Session Laws) provided that "Hereafter, all candidates for elective office in this State . . . shall be nominated at a direct primary election held in pursuance of this act: . . ." The intent of the legislature was to limit the voting for any given party list to registered party members, but the Supreme Court soon struck down this "closed primary" feature, necessitating a change in the law.[18] However, "no person who desires to become a candidate for the office of supreme or superior court judge shall certify his party affiliations." And the "names of all candidates for the offices of supreme and superior court judge shall be published and posted in a separate list without party designation."

The separate ballot was attached to the bottom of all the party tickets under the designation of *Nonpartisan Judiciary Ticket* with these instructions: "To vote for a person make a cross (X) in the square at the RIGHT of the name of the person for whom you desire to vote." The names were then listed with instructions to vote for a certain number of the candidates.

17. *Ibid.*, September 12, 1902.

18. Because the legislature had failed to require the recording of a registrant's political party affiliation in a separate and earlier registration law, the Supreme Court struck down the closed primary provisions in *Arnold* v. *Mitchell* (55 WASH. 513, 1909), but the 1909 legislature corrected the error. See Chapter 82, Session Laws, 1909, p. 174.

The primary election was the crucial election for judges since section 38 of the law read:

> The number of candidates equalling the number of judicial positions to be filled, who receive the highest number of votes at the primary election, shall be candidates for such respective offices.

The election of 1908 was the first under the new primary law. Although two of the judges who had formerly been on the Republican ticket swept to victory in 1908, the top vote getter was Democrat Stephen J. Chadwick.

Of course, the philosophy behind the law was to give the nominating process to the rank-and-file members of the political parties and thereby to remove the selection of public officials from the "smoke-filled rooms" of the conventions and from the political horsetrading often found necessary by the bosses of the respective parties. The purpose of the nonpartisan judiciary ticket was to remove the judges from any partisan considerations. Unfortunately, this removal of partisanship, at least for the supreme court jurists, was short-lived.

When the 1909 legislature met in January, proposed amendments to the 1907 direct primary law were reformist and designed to strengthen the original. For example, two names for each supreme court position would be listed on the general election ballot, correcting the finality of the primary results as prescribed in the previous law. Nonpartisanship would be further emphasized by separating the judicial ballot completely from the political party tickets, allowing voters to call for the judicial ballot alone.

In February, however, the Republican legislature passed several judges' bills creating new judicial positions at the superior court level and adding two new positions to the high bench for a total of nine.[19] (In 1901 the legislature had authorized a temporary—for eighteen months—expansion of the court's membership to seven. The expansion was made permanent in 1905.)[20] So the 1910 election gained in importance because five of the nine supreme court bench positions were to be filled. Judge Root had refused to take his seat on the bench after his 1908 electoral victory, and Republican Mack F. Gose was appointed to fill the new vacancy.[21] Gose would have to face the

19. Chapter 24, Session Laws, 1909, Sec. 1.

20. Chapter 148, Session Laws, 1901, Sec. 1; and Chapter 5, Session Laws, 1905, Sec. 1.

21. Actually Root resigned at the beginning of an investigation into his dealings with former Judge Gordon. Root had been investigated by the state bar group for filing an opinion denying a rehearing of a Great Northern Railway Company case (*Harris* v. *Great Northern Railway Co.* [48 WASH. 437, 1908]) which, apparently, had

Table 3.2
Election Results, 1906–12

	General
1906	*(Nov. 6)*
*Wallace Mount (R)	71,071
*Ralph Dunbar (R)	70,828
C. W. Hodgdon (D)	31,332
E. C. Million (D)	31,268
H. L. Hughes (Soc.)	8,717
E. E. Martin (Soc.)	8,664
Two-year term:	
*Herman D. Crow (R)	69,825
*Milo A. Root (R)	69,964
Warren W. Tolman (D)	32,367
Bo Sweeney (D)	31,562
H. W. Mangold (Soc.)	8,575
W. E. Tibbits (Soc.)	8,551
1910	*(Nov. 8)*
Four-year term:	
*Mack F. Gose (R)	77,625
Horace G. Cupples (Soc.)	14,599
Warren W. Tolman (Ind.)	24,843
*George E. Morris (R)	80,706
*Frank H. Rudkin (R)	79,442
*Emmett N. Parker (R)	80,115
*Mark A. Fullerton (R)	80,248
W. E. Richardson (Soc.)	15,994
E. J. Brown (Soc.)	15,287
Samuel Sadler (Soc.)	14,938
A. H. Barth (Soc.)	14,862
Charles E. Shepard (Ind.)	25,763
Hans Bugge (Ind.)	24,988
Wm. Hickman Moore (Ind.)	26,463
Preston M. Troy (Ind.)	25,435

	Primary	*General*
1908	*(Sept. 8)*	*(Nov. 3)*
*Herman D. Crow	45,948	154,769
*Milo Root	44,965	154,341
Stephen Chadwick	56,918	155,810
Lucius B. Nash	25,951	
Oliver V. Linn	26,475	
John E. Humphries	42,079	
E. M. Carr	18,200	
Emmett Parker	34,176	
Edwin J. Brown (Soc.)		3,024
Lee Ganson (Soc.)		3,017
Theodore Weinrick (Soc.)		3,005
1912	*(Sept. 10)*	*(Nov. 5)*
*Ralph O. Dunbar	87,744	
*Overton G. Ellis	86,440	134,218
*Wallace Mount	85,610	132,710
John F. Main		63,720
W. W. Black		51,686
B. M. Wright		2,046

(Dunbar died Sept. 29 and Main won a write-in contest for the vacancy.)

*Incumbent
Italicized names designate winners
Full six-year term unless otherwise indicated

electorate in November, however, along with two new Republican appointees, George E. Morris and Emmett N. Parker. Incumbent Republicans Frank Rudkin and Mark Fullerton were seeking reelection. Thus, the G.O.P. majority in the 1909 legislature felt too much was at stake in 1910 to allow the unpredictable nonpartisan primary to decide who would serve on the Supreme Court at least for the next four if not six years.

A coalition of corporate lawyers, Republicans, and sitting supreme court judges successfully lobbied the legislature and the governor (in order to fend off a veto) to return the responsibility for nominating supreme court jurists to the party conventions.[22] On March 12, the nonpartisan judiciary law was amended to exempt the supreme court candidates from the direct primary.[23]

Concerned members of the State Bar Association, consistent with their earlier concern for nonpartisanship, but without supporting the direct primary, delivered a committee report to its annual convention in late summer 1909 in which attention was drawn to the last clause in the new law which allowed joint conventions to name a slate of candidates. The bar's standing committee on the judiciary urged:

> That in some manner a committee of three members of this association be appointed . . . for the purpose, at the proper time, of waiting

---

been reviewed and possibly edited by a railroad attorney (former supreme court justice M. J. Gordon) before the opinion was officially filed. Further, Root had accepted a free railroad pass for himself and his family, a clear violation of state law. The bar report read in part: "We are constrained to conclude that the conduct of Judge Root was a gross breach of judicial and professional propriety. . . . [His conduct] shows such a want of appreciation of the duties of a judge of the supreme court as to unfit him from occupying that position." Immediately following the public disclosure of the bar association's report on the incident, Judge Root wrote Governor Mead again on January 12, 1909. (Although he had resigned from his previous judicial post, he had been reelected in the November election to a new term beginning in January, 1909.) "[I]n light of the severe criticisms contained in the report . . . I feel that for me to qualify would be to embarrass the court and to create in the minds of the people not knowing me a suspicion entirely unjust, but which would nevertheless be highly undesirable in regard to the court and the administration of justice in the state." Although the Great Northern lost the case involving but a few thousand dollars, it narrowed the opportunities for further suits against the railroad.

22. See the letter from Rufus R. Wilson, Chairman of the Non-Partisan Judiciary League of Washington, to Governor M. E. Hay dated October 25, 1910, in *Marion E. Hay Papers*, Washington State Archives, Olympia, Washington, "Judiciary" file 26.

23. Chapter 32, Session Laws, 1909, Sec. 11. In the House, a last minute attempt to delete the convention method was turned back by an 88-22 vote. One of the arguments for a return to the convention was that it would clothe the selection of respected judicial personnel with the "dignity of the convention," rather than the crassness of public advertising used in campaigning (*The Seattle Daily Times*, March 11 and 12, 1909). The legislators complained that the primary was "forced . . . upon them the last session" by the press (*The Seattle Post-Intelligencer*, March 12, 1909). The final version passed the House on a 71 to 19 vote.

> upon the managing agents of the two leading political parties and requesting them to join in the issuance of a call for a joint state judicial convention for the nomination of judges of the Supreme Court, and that they represent to such managing agents that it is the sense of this association that such nominations be made in joint convention rather than by conventions of each party separately.[24]

The report was quickly ignored ("placed on file" without debate), thereby ending for the moment any organized efforts by the bar to influence the inner circles of the reigning Republican Party.

Actually, for the predominately Republican bar, reforms that changed the prevailing recruitment would threaten their party's control of the court. In contrast, for the minority Democrats any reforms could only enhance their opportunities. Thus, the factions in the legal profession did not break down neatly into the professionally oriented attorneys concerned with judicial independence and the more political lawyers attempting to maintain or increase party control and partisan accountability.[25]

On August 3, 1910, the Republicans met in convention in Tacoma and made known their full intention to take advantage of the restored political nomination of supreme court judges. They showed no desire to share power with any others in a joint convention. An opportunity to return to the nonpartisan primary was promptly rejected by the delegates in a 623½ to 263½ division. Some new names were mentioned for the high bench, but all the incumbents were renominated. Judge Gose had token opposition for the four-year term, and Judges Morris, Rudkin, Parker, and Fullerton were unanimously endorsed for the six-year terms.

Some dissident Republicans and most Democrats resented the reversion to a partisan convention for the nomination of supreme court judges. They had philosophical and practical reasons for their resentment—judges ought not to be products of partisan activities, and Democratic judicial candidates could entertain small hope for defeating the G.O.P. standard bearers.

24. *Proceedings* of the Washington State Bar Association (hereafter referred to as *Proceedings*) (1909), 136. The first special committee appointed by the State Bar leadership to deal specifically with judicial selection was in 1894. A motion was passed to have a committee appointed to "formulate and report . . . a constitutional amendment for the election of Judges at some time other than during a political campaign." At the same 1894 state convention the delegates tabled a motion to appoint a committee to confer with the leadership of both major parties to secure "non-partisan nominations, either through the parties themselves or by means of an independent convention" (*Proceedings* (1894), 41).

25. Such a split in the bar was experienced in other states. See Kermit L. Hall, "The Judiciary on Trial: State Constitutional Reform and the Rise of an Elected Judiciary, 1846–1860" (*The Historian* 44 [May 1983]: 353–54).

The Democrats were slated to meet in convention on Tuesday, September 7, 1910, but a group of predominantly west-side delegates and insurgent Republicans calling themselves the "Non-Partisan Judiciary League of Washington" met the day before to nominate a nonpartisan slate for the five court positions.[26] To show the convention's bipartisan conviction, two incumbent Republicans were among those suggested for support, and Republicans were invited to attend and support the meeting. The G.O.P. leadership forbade attendance. Although incumbent Republicans Fullerton and Rudkin were acceptable to the insurgents, the preconvention recommended to the regular Democratic convention a slate including two other Republicans and three Democrats.

The difficulty was to get the Democratic convention formally to nominate this bipartisan slate (it was already referred to as nonpartisan). An observer of the convention summed up the not altogether unanimous results:

> After ten hours of convention wrangling, interspersed with caucuses, during which bitter recriminations were hurled in both the Pierce and King County delegations, the new Democratic convention completed a roll call at 11 o'clock last night that gave endorsement to the judiciary slate adopted the preceding day by the insurgent Republican convention.[27]

The insurgent group had pledged that its nominees would resign two years hence and resubmit their names to the electorate if, in the meantime, the legislature reenacted the direct-primary, nonpartisan process for supreme court judges. But the general convention made no mention of such a promise should their candidates succeed in November.[28]

Although deeply divided on the endorsement of the insurgent slate, the Democratic delegates enthusiastically adopted a platform that insisted upon a nonpartisan judiciary:

26. The pledge of the Non-Partisan Judiciary League which organized the preconvention was clearly progressive: "The surest safeguards of republican institutions are courts composed of judges who derive their authority from the people, who are unswayed by party prejudices, and who, free from the influence of privilege, do not subordinate the rights of many to the exactions of the few" (*The Seattle Post-Intelligencer*, September 27, 1910). The Non-Partisan Judiciary League was led by attorney J. W. Robinson (Chairman), Rufus R. Wilson (Secretary), and William T. Beeks (Treasurer).

27. *The Seattle Daily Times*, September 28, 1910.

28. The platform did recognize the nonpartisan nature of their endorsement. "We neither ask nor expect these judges to be Democratic" (*The Seattle Post-Intelligencer*, September 28, 1910).

> The day of reckoning is at hand. The Democratic party believes in a non-partisan judiciary. It has advocated in the past and demands now the enactment of an open, truly Democratic people's primary for the nomination of all officials. It stands today for the restoration in full force of the people's right to nominate their supreme court judges, by direct vote, believing the people as well qualified to select their judges of the court of last resort as to name their constables.[29]

The preconvention had designated itself as the "Independent Non-Partisan Judiciary Party" and filed its slate with the Secretary of State. This independent designation, which would be on the ballot, placed the candidates at a disadvantage. In order to separate themselves from the Democratic Party ticket, consistent with their nonpartisan commitment, they could not appeal to those voters who normally voted a straight Democratic party ticket.[30] The appeal for bipartisan support went unheeded, and the regular Republicans prevailed in the general election. The advocates of a nonpartisan judiciary were again compelled to turn to the legislature for a rectification of the situation. The 1911 legislature complied with their wishes.

Now secure in their control of the political make-up of the Supreme Court for some time, the Republican majority of the 1911 legislature was more susceptible to the arguments for the reestablishment of judicial nonpartisanship. Part of a large, progressive legislative package approved that year (including, most notably, a constitutional amendment instituting the initiative and referendum processes) was a statute returning the nomination of supreme court judges to the voters. The solons enacted the following version:

> There shall be a separate ballot for the candidates for nomination for such judicial offices [supreme and superior court judges], which shall be the general election ballot hereinbefore referred to, and shall be printed, delivered, voted and counted as hereinbefore provided for the general election ballot: *Provided*, That any voter shall have the privilege of voting this ticket alone.[31]

29. The platform further promised "A Democratic Legislature of 1911 will effectively undo the iniquitous deed which disgraced the Republican Legislature of 1909, so that we may never again be confronted with the emergency which now compels this convention" (*The Seattle Daily Times*, September 28, 1910).

30. Candidate Shepard, in behalf of the others on the Independent ticket, brought suit before the Supreme Court to order the listing of their names under both the Democratic and separate Non-Partisan ballots. The court opined that although the Independent Non-Partisan Judiciary Party was likely not a true political party, their candidates could not have their names placed on both ballots. The judges cited a law that required candidates to choose between one party label or another for the ballot when nominated by more than one (*State Ex Rel. Shepard* v. *Superior Court*, 60 WASH. 370, 1910).

31. Chapter 101, WASH. LAWS, 1911, p. 489.

The ballot was to be entirely detached from all partisan ballots.[32]

A fairly complicated process, which at first appeared quite simple, was used to determine whose names would be advanced to the general election ballot. The intent was to nominate two candidates for each contested position, unless one aspirant garnered more than half the votes. In that case he would be placed on the general election ballot unopposed. However, voters cast *one* ballot but on that ballot they could cast *three* votes for three judges. A problem arose because some voted for candidates for only one or two of the positions. If, for instance, 10,000 ballots were cast but a position received only 5,000 votes, should a majority be determined on the basis of votes (2,501) or ballots (5,001)? The issue was resolved by an attorney general's opinion and by a supreme court decision in 1916 in favor of counting ballots.[33] Despite the initial confusion, the 1911 legislature had restored the election of supreme court judges to the nonpartisan system permanently.

Between 1889 and 1908 political party partisanship held a tight grip on all elections. The fate of each Republican, whether a candidate for secretary of state, governor, or the Supreme Court, was bound to the others (as was each under the Democratic label). Not

32. *Ibid.* The separate ballot was designed as follows:

NON-PARTISAN JUDICIARY TICKET

To vote for a person make a cross (X) in the square at the RIGHT of the name of the person for whom you desire to vote.

Judges of Supreme Court Vote for ______		Judges of Superior Court Vote for ______	
John Doe	☐	John Doe	☐
John Doe	☐	John Doe	☐
John Doe	☐	John Doe	☐

33. Opinion by Attorney General W. V. Tanner, dated October 16, 1916. Printed in Secretary of State, *Second Biennial Report, Election Division 1916*, 77–78. The supreme court case which substantially upheld the attorney general was *Mills* v. *Howell* (93 WASH. 257, 1916).

The provision of the law that created the confusion read: "The number of candidates equalling the number of judicial positions to be filled who receive the highest number of votes at the primary election, and an equal number of candidates for such positions, providing there are such candidates, who receive the next highest number of votes, shall be candidates for such respective offices and their names shall appear on the general election ballot . . . : *Provided, however,* That where any candidate for any such office shall receive a majority of all votes cast at such primary election shall be printed separately on the general election ballot . . . and the name or names of no opposing candidate or candidates shall be printed on such ballot in opposition" (Chapter 101, Session Laws, 1911).

only were aspirants from one party destined to either win or lose across the board, but as the electoral support of one party increased, or decreased, so also did it for those candidates of that party for the high bench. But beginning in 1908 the Republican monopoly on court positions was broken. Judge Chadwick, an active Democrat, led the entire nonpartisan ballot in 1908. In 1914, O. R. Holcomb joined his Democratic colleague on the court, as did Warren Tolman in 1918 and William Pemberton in 1920.

Voter turnout depends upon a variety of factors. The ballot form, the influence of national politics, the intensity of the campaigning, local issues, incumbency, and the number of candidates affect voter interest in judicial elections. But the absence of the party label also has its impact.[34] Figure 3.1 portrays the degree of voter "roll-off" in judicial elections from statehood to 1912. Roll-off simply means the percentage of voters who cast votes for the candidates for the leading offices on the ballot (e.g., presidential or gubernatorial) but fail to vote for judicial candidates. For example, in 1904, 144,669 persons voted for the gubernatorial candidates and only 140,063 voted for supreme court judges. In 1904, therefore, the "roll-off" was a mere 3.2%.

Figure 3.1 strikingly illustrates the abrupt change in voter responses after 1908 and suggests again the importance of the 1908 and 1912 change. The average roll-off vote from 1889 to that point was but 2.7%. Also during this period, with one exception, only Republicans were elected to the bench. From 1889 to 1908 only Fusionist James Bradley Reavis broke through the Republican domination in the election of 1896.[35] However, partisanship waned and voter interest in judicial elections dropped significantly in the 1910 and 1912 elections, trends which have continued to the present day. These trends are explained quite simply by the adoption in 1907 of the direct primary and the separate, nonpartisan ballot for judges. Initiation, screening, and affirmation of justices is no longer a monopoly of the political parties, or more exactly, of the Republican party and its loyalists.

Voter participation in supreme court elections remained high before 1908, but, as we have seen, beginning with the direct primary and the nonpartisan ballot, the voters' interest in the judicial elections waned considerably. No longer did they have the party label as a guide to the "identity" of the judges. No longer did the straight

34. Philip Dubois, *From Ballot to Bench* (Austin: University of Texas Press, 1980).

35. The Fusionists proved to be a temporary coalition formed around one issue having an impact only in 1896 elections. See E. Meany, *History of the State of Washington* (New York: Macmillan, 1924), 292–93.

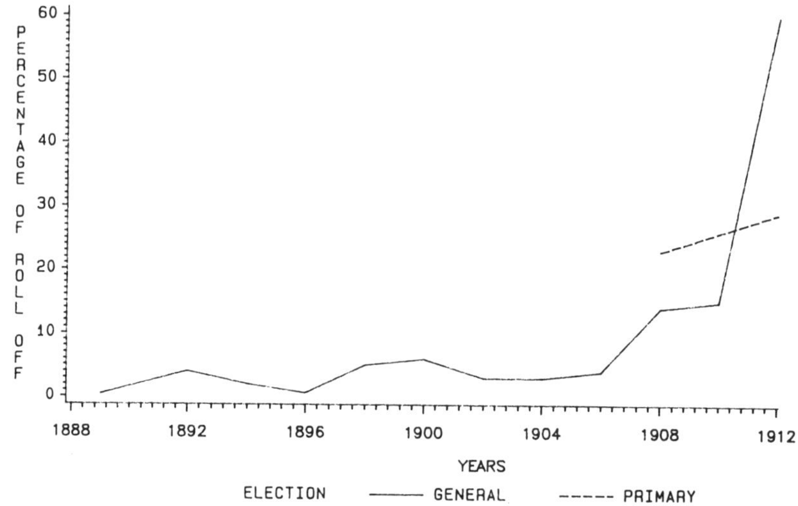

Fig. 3.1. Judicial vote roll-off, 1889–1912

party ticket voting benefit the jurists. No longer were the judges among the familiar positions on the regular long ballot. No longer were the judicial candidates the political notables who were rewarded judicial nominations after unsuccessful drives for higher public offices. No longer were judicial positions always challenged. Little wonder, then, that the voter simply ignored the judicial ticket.

The problem facing judicial candidates was further complicated. Traditional means of campaigning were no longer available. The regular party speaking platforms, rallies, engagements, and other political activities were off-limits to the judicial candidates. Fund raising responsibilities also were shifted. No longer were the party coffers open to the judiciary. The selection of judges to the Supreme Court had been changed profoundly and permanently and a new judicial independence from at least partisan accountability was evolving.

Appointments: The Governor's Passive Role

The role of the governor between 1889 and 1912 in shaping judicial recruitment was relatively passive, mostly limited to the selection of persons to fill temporary or new positions authorized by the legislature. But after the demise of party conventions for nominating judicial candidates the governor became increasingly a dominant actor in recruitment. More weight came to be given to gubernatorial appointments because these appointees were (and are) almost always affirmed by the voters. During the inaugural years the governor screened the recruits whose candidacies had been initiated elsewhere, and following the reforms of 1907, the state's chief executive began to recruit a few of his own candidates. Soon the governor assumed responsibility for both initiative and screening, and the electorate passively affirmed those he had selected. Nonetheless, several years passed before appointments became so crucial. From 1889 to 1912 gubernatorial participation remained largely passive.

Eleven of the twenty-two positions available in this early period were filled by executive appointments. But six of these eleven were temporary or new positions authorized by the legislature. The appointment of William "War Horse" White highlighted the imperfect mesh between appointments and elections in these early years. Judge Gordon had resigned in June 1900 with only six months remaining (until January 14, 1901) in his six-year term. Democrat governor Rogers quickly appointed Democrat White to fill the vacancy. However, if anyone filed for and won the position in the November elections, he would take office immediately, replacing White for the short time left in the term. Upon the urgings of fellow Democrats and in order to discourage prospective challengers, White filed for the short term, ran unopposed as it turned out, and was sworn in immediately after the general election for the remaining weeks of the unexpired term (December 6–January 14). Thus, he became the first judge to win a spot on the court under the Democrat party label, even if it was by default. Ironically, he was elected to the post that he would have continued to hold as an appointee simply because, as it turned out, no one ran against him in the general election.[36] (Wallace Mount, in the meantime, had won election to the new full six-year term of Gordon's position.)

36. Chapter 5, Session Laws, 1893, Sec. 2, pp. 8–9, which permitted the short term election for White, read in part: "If a vacancy occurs . . . , the governor shall appoint a person to hold the office until the election and qualification of a judge to fill the vacancy, . . . the judge so elected may qualify at any time within thirty days after his election, and shall hold office for the unexpired term." However, if the unexpired term ran into the next year, Chapter 119, Session Laws, 1911, Sec. 2, p. 614, dictated that "a person elected . . . to fill a vacancy for an unexpired term shall not qualify for office until the second Monday in January succeeding his election," when judges elected to regular terms would also be assuming office.

In 1956 a similar circumstance with appointment and election arose. An appointment for a short term was given to Judge Foster. However, rather than run for the remaining few weeks in the appointed term (as White had done), Foster successfully contested the new six-year term (as Judge Wallace had in 1900). See Chapter Six, *infra.* The 1893 law had been changed in 1955 to read simply that the appointee

After White finished his short term in January, 1901, Governor Rogers returned him to the bench in March when the legislature authorized two temporary positions on the Supreme Court in order to deal with the pressing backlog of cases. The appointment of White was clearly symbolic and a reward for political party services in the past. White had been one of the original Democratic party contenders for election to the first court in 1889. Also, his short-term appointment in 1900 qualified him for at least a temporary position. In addition, the people had shown support for White at the polls the previous year.[37]

According to the legislative authorization, however, Democrat Rogers had to appoint a Republican to the other temporary post, and he selected Hiram E. Hadley, superior court judge of Whatcom County. Hadley's election to the superior court bench provided an example for those who were pushing for a nonpartisan judiciary. His reelection to the Whatcom County trial bench in 1900 had been endorsed by all parties and, in a singular display of nonpartisanship, no other candidates were nominated to oppose him.[38] Thus, Democrat Rogers found in Republican Hadley an acceptable candidate from the opposition party. Hadley had the added attribute of being from the west side of the state, helping to redress an imbalance of eastern Washington judges on the high bench.

Milo A. Root and Herman D. Crow, both Republicans, were appointed in 1905 by Republican Governor Albert E. Mead, himself a leading member of the legal profession, who practiced law in

---

remained in office "until the election and qualification of a judge to fill the vacancy" (Chapter 38, Session Laws, 1955, Sec. 2, p. 321).

When the Secretary of State officially certifies the election results within thirty days after the election (RCW 29.62.130), those elected to the short terms are qualified to take their oath of office.

In 1975, however, the legislature abolished the short term election. In Chapter 120, 2nd Ex. Session Laws, 1975–76, Sec. 4, pp. 438–39, the legislature stipulated that "when both a short term and a full term for the same position are scheduled to be voted upon, a single declaration of candidacy . . . shall be construed as filing for both the short term and the full term. . . . The candidate elected to both such terms shall be sworn into and assume office for the short term as soon as the election returns have been certified."

37. William Henry "War Horse" White had been a member of the territorial legislative council, U.S. attorney for the Territory of Washington, city attorney of Seattle, Chairman of the Democratic state delegation to the 1896 National Convention, and a member of the Democratic National Committee. He was regarded as the Democrats' leading orator and could always be counted on to fire up any political gathering.

38. "A committee of three lawyers, a Democrat, a Populist and a Republican, went before each of the three party conventions in Whatcom County [Bellingham] and asked that no one be nominated to succeed Judge Hadley" (Washington State Biography File, Northwest Collection, University of Washington Library).

Bellingham both before and after his stint in the governor's chair. He was familiar with most of his professional colleagues, including Root and Crow. Geography also played an important role in his making these two appointments. Root, who previously practiced law in Olympia with John R. Mitchell, later to be appointed to the high court (1918), had moved to Seattle where he was a member of the law firm of Root, Palmer, and Brown. Root was a fine west side addition, and Crow, from Spokane, added geographical balance to the court.[39] Although a Republican, Crow had the endorsement of the Democratic State Chairman, the chairman of the Chelan County Democratic Central Committee, and the Ephrata, Chelan, and Spokane County bars. Perhaps most important was the support of Frank Reeves, a leading legislator and prominent attorney from Wenatchee.[40] With such impressive bipartisan support and with both sides of the state represented, Mead's initial appointments were well received.

However, these two appointments were not without political motives. In a 1902 progressive decision (*Green* v. *Western America Co.*)[41] the court had imposed greater liabilities onto employers in workmen's injury cases. Crow and Root, "some people alleged, were selected at the behest of insurance companies and corporation attorneys wanting to strike down the *Green* decision.[42] The two judges did assume an antilabor stance on the bench.[43]

39. A sufficient amount of reluctance and yet eagerness is coyly expressed in Milo Root's letter to the governor offering himself as a candidate for the new position: "I am informed that there is a likelihood of a law being enacted increasing the membership of the Supreme Court. The prospect of this has for some months been a matter of consideration among the lawyers of the state and the matter of my being a candidate for one of the appointment has been kindly suggested. But until about ten days ago, I did not decide to ask for one of the appointments. Thus I told Mr. Palmer and Mr. Brown, my partners, that I would like the appointment to one of the positions if it could be had without a scramble or unseemly effort on my part. So I now repeat the same statement to you. As you have been an active practitioner in this state yourself for many years and know the character, ability, and standing of the lawyers likely to be considered in this connection, I do not feel that you would care for any endorsements. However, I would be glad to furnish such if you should desire applicants for such positions to furnish endorsements." The letter, dated January 9, 1905, was followed on January 18 with a number of endorsements from superior court judges, prosecuting attorneys from both parties, Young Men's Republican Club of King County, and other prominent citizens and members of the legal profession (*Mead Papers,* Washington State Archives, "Judiciary" file).

40. *Lister Papers*, Washington State Archives, "Judiciary" file.

41. 30 WASH. 87, 1902.

42. J. F. Tripp, "Progressive Jurisprudence in the West: The Washington Supreme Court, Labor Law, and the Problem of Industrial Accidents," *Labor History* 24 (1983): 354.

43. "Both Root and Crow had been representing prominent insurance casualty companies" (*ibid.*). See Root's dissent in *Hall* v. *West & Slade Mill Co.* (39 WASH. 447, 1905).

Table 3.3
Supreme Court Appointments, 1889–1912

Justice	*Governor*	*Date*
William H. White (D)	Rogers (D)	June 1, 1900
*William H. White (D)	Rogers	March 20, 1901
*Hiram E. Hadley (R)	Rogers	March 20, 1901
*Milo A. Root (R)	Mead (R)	January 19, 1905
*Herman D. Crow (R)	Mead	January 19, 1905
Stephen J. Chadwick (D)	Mead	December 3, 1908
Mack F. Gose (R)	Mead	January 11, 1909
*George E. Morris (R)	Hay (R)	February 26, 1909
*Emmett Parker (R)	Hay	February 26, 1909
Overton G. Ellis (D)	Hay	May 10, 1911
John F. Main (R)	Hay	September 27, 1912

*New or temporary positions

Republican Mead's appointment of Democrat Stephen J. Chadwick was surrounded by special circumstances not likely to be replicated. Milo Root resigned his position on the bench under a cloud of suspicion concerning his close relationship with former Judge Merrit J. Gordon, who became an attorney for the Great Northern Railroad.[44] In the meantime, Stephen J. Chadwick's election was assured, having achieved over 50% of the total balloting in the September primary. Governor Mead appointed Chadwick to the remaining few weeks of Root's term. When Chadwick was certified by the official count of the November ballot, he then assumed his own elected position. Judge Root's name had remained on the general election ballot as a candidate for a six-year term, but he refused qualification, thereby providing another vacancy to be filled by appointment.

Republican governor-elect Samuel Cosgrove was too ill to assume executive responsibilities after his hard-fought primary campaign. At his swearing-in ceremony on January 27, 1909, he requested and was granted an immediate leave of absence by the legislature to regain his health. (He died of Bright's disease in March 1909.) Cosgrove had instructed outgoing Governor Mead to appoint an old friend, neighbor (from Pomeroy, Washington), and fellow attorney, Mack F. Gose, to the Root vacancy.[45] Although not obligated to do so (Mead was rumored to have desired the appointment for himself),

44. See footnote 21, *supra*.

45. "The appointment was made out of deference to the wishes of Governor-elect Cosgrove who is at Paso Robles, California. M. F. Gose is an old-time friend and neighbor of . . . Cosgrove. At Pomeroy for nearly a quarter of a century, Gose and

he followed Cosgrove's suggestion and offered the post to Gose on January 11, 1909.

Acting Governor Marion E. Hay, assuming control of the executive branch upon Cosgrove's leave of absence (on January 27th), had the opportunity to fill two newly created positions on the Supreme Court in February 1909. Geography was perhaps the overriding concern for Hay. Because only Judge Rudkin from Seattle represented the west side of the state on the court, Hay acted with political wisdom by drawing from west of the Cascades for his appointments. Judge Emmett Parker was a Pierce County superior court judge from Tacoma. Judge George E. Morris was a prominent lawyer and superior court judge from Seattle. Both were known aspirants for the high bench. They had been heavily endorsed for the earlier 1905 appointments, and Parker had also made a fair showing in the 1908 supreme court elections, garnering nearly 35,000 votes in a losing effort. Both always had attracted considerable support in their trial court races. Thus the two were likely appointees. Acting Governor Hay wired Judges Parker and Morris on February 26, 1909:

> Enclosed please find commission appointing you a Judge of the Supreme Court. On account of there being no appropriation for salary, I would be pleased if you would not qualify or take office until April First.[46]

Hay's appointment of Democrat Overton G. Ellis, Tacoma City Attorney, was somewhat unusual. The governor had decided early on to appoint Republican Harold Preston to the vacancy created when Judge Rudkin was elevated to the Federal Circuit Court in December, 1910. He wired Preston, who was on vacation in California:

> Judge Rudkin resigns from Supreme Court. You are hereby tendered and personally requested to accept this position to take effect May First. Letter with endorsements from prominent men throughout the state requesting me to offer you the position follows.

Fifteen days later Preston responded: "I regret exceedingly that I find myself unable to accede to you[r] request so kindly expressed."[47]

Cosgrove have been leading lawyers, sometimes engaged in trying to defeat each other in court and at others, working side by side" (*The Seattle Daily Times*, January 13, 1908).

46. *Hay Papers*, Washington State Archives, "Judiciary" files.

47. Harold Preston was President of the Washington State Bar Association in 1897 (*ibid.*).

Extensive files had been accumulated on a fair number of other serious candidates as Rudkin's elevation to the federal bench had been anticipated for months. Approximately a dozen serious aspirants were considered by the governor. Future Federal District Judge Jerry Neterer, George B. Cole, D. H. Carey, Judges W. O. Chapman, John F. Main, and Mitchell Gilliam were prominent among them. West side candidates dominated Hay's considerations. On February 28 Hay sent the following telegram to Democrat Ellis: "Recognizing your eminent ability and fitness for the position you are hereby tendered and requested to accept place on Supreme Court. . . ."[48] When congratulated for his choice, Hay admitted he had "never had the pleasure of meeting the gentleman, and his appointment was made wholly upon recommendations from attorneys in whom I have absolute confidence, not from one but from many parts of the state."[49] Republican Hay's choice of Democrat Ellis was the first time (except for the short-term appointment of Chadwick) that a governor had crossed party lines to fill a vacancy unless mandated to do so by statute.

Another set of compelling concerns faced Republican Governor Hay in the Ellis appointment which made the selection of a Democrat attractive. The Progressives had succeeded in discrediting the partisan election of judges after the 1910 election, and the appointment of Ellis would set well with them.

Hay's last appointment, John F. Main, again represents a fairly singular case. In the September 1912 primary, Ralph Dunbar, Overton Ellis, and Wallace Mount were unopposed. Dunbar led the balloting with nearly 88,000 votes but, without any previous signs of ill-health, he suddenly died on September 29, leaving actually two vacancies on the bench: the final few weeks of Dunbar's unfinished term and all of his new term, beginning in January. If someone were to be appointed before January, the new full term would still remain unfilled, necessitating another appointment. However, state law provided a resolution to the problem.

The opportunity for write-in candidates had existed since 1889. Yet, except for a few random "sticker" ballots, no serious, organized write-in campaign had ever been mounted. In the September primaries, Judge John F. Main, former University of Washington law professor, had been overwhelmingly endorsed by the voters for another term on the King County Superior Court bench. Hay's consideration of Main resulted in large part from his popularity

48. Telegram dated February 28, 1911 (*ibid.*).
49. Letter to H. A. McLean dated March 2, 1911 (*ibid.*).

with the King County voters, and he was appointed in September 1912. Immediately an extensive "sticker" campaign was launched by the attorneys in King County and by his former University of Washington law students throughout the state, with the support of the governor. A package deal was developed. With Main's appointment and his "sticker" election, former King County prosecutor and prominent Republican attorney Kenneth Mackintosh could be appointed to Main's superior court vacancy. Main's appointment depended to some extent upon his success in previous elections, and his election depended to a great extent on the fact of his appointment.

In this inaugural period between 1900 and 1912, a pattern developed in the appointment process. The politics of gubernatorial selection was the politics of *ad hoc* "endorsement." The endorsements came from a cross section of the political and legal elite and the attentive public, but rarely from established interest groups. A typical endorsement campaign in 1905, for example, added a great number of letters and petitions to the candidates' files in the governor's office. Judge Emmett Parker had letters in his file from then Tacoma city attorney Overton G. Ellis, members of the Tacoma bar, the superintendent of schools, the county surveyor, several superior court judges, the controller's office, a police court judge, the sheriff's office, the county auditor, the county treasurer, city councilmen, and the assistant city attorney.[50] Letters from leading legislators, merchants, railroad officials' fraternal lodge officers (Elks, Masons, etc.), political party officials, and newspaper editors were not uncommon. The endorsement campaigns were well coordinated. Not only were the total number of endorsements important but also the sources: the most effective represented a broad spectrum of prominent citizens and important agencies.

Formal petitions with lists of signatures were also common as evidence of support. A typical petition would announce that "We, whose names are hereunto subscribed, being members of the King County Bar, . . ." or "being registered voters in . . . County." John F. Main's campaign, for example, was highlighted by this petition to the governor:

> A committee of attorneys who are desirous of presenting your Excellency testimonials of the high esteem in which Judge Main is held by the bar of this city, have circulated petitions in various office buildings of this city, and it has been my pleasure to interview the attorneys in

50. *Mead Papers*, "Judiciary" file.

> the Empire Building and to transmit to you the endorsement of practically every attorney who has offices in this building.[51]

The governor's office staff kept count of the endorsements. A running list of candidates with the number of endorsements and from whom, with notes scribbled in the margins identifying the petitioners, served as a guide to the appointing official. Not always was the aspirant with the most endorsements chosen, but never did the governor go far down the list.[52]

This initial period of endorsement politics resulted in few actual appointments to the five original positions. Elections handled the turnover. The appointments were for the newly created positions (six total, counting the two temporary seats in 1901). Only White, Ellis, Gose, and Main were appointed to the court as Article IV of the constitution dictated. The remainder were added as a result of legislative enactments.

When appointments were pending or vacancies anticipated, the governor's office was immediatey barraged with letters of endorsement and petitions of support. The initiation phase of recruitment was dominated by coordinated efforts to gain individual endorsements from prominent citizens and to collect signatures of notables in support of one candidate or another. By 1912 all serious aspirants were compelled to initiate their own candidacy by means of petition drives and letters of support. Except for Mack Gose, appointed because of a close friendship with the governor-elect, and William White, rewarded for his hard work in party causes, these petitions and endorsements played a leading role in the screening considerations of the chief executive. None of the appointees (except Gose) appeared to have been close associates of the governor.

Geography was also a factor in the screening phase. The governor had to satisfy many diverse segments of the entire state and appointments provided the means. Both Governors Mead and Hay were urged to give considerable weight to the fact that the bench was then dominated by eastern Washington jurists and that this imbalance should be redressed.

Partisanship also played its inevitable role in the screening. Unless forced by the legislature or by special circumstances, the chief executive chose candidates from the ranks of his own political party. Of the eleven appointees, all but three were of the same political party as the governor who appointed them. One governor (Rogers)

51. Letter to Hay from Seattle attorney Donald A. McDonald, dated January 24, 1911 (*Hay Papers*, "Appointments" file).
52. *Lister Papers*, "Judiciary" file.

crossed party lines because of a mandate from the legislature. Another (Mead) appointed a rival party member (Chadwick) simply because the latter had already won election to the bench and could conveniently fill a short vacancy. Governor Hay's appointment of Overton Ellis in 1911 remained the single exception to the political party rule. Actually, this tradition still characterizes appointments today, long after partisan labels have been removed from the elections process.

The Organized Bar: Ineffective Stirrings

The organized bar adopted three approaches in its efforts to influence judicial recruitment during the inaugural years. Initially, the profession worked toward removing judicial candidates from nominating conventions and elections dominated by the political parties. Nonpartisanship was the attorneys' goal. Once achieved in 1907, the profession turned to the elimination of the direct primary as the means of nominating judges. Finally, after a reluctant acceptance of the direct primary, the organized profession devised means to influence both the governor when he filled vacancies and the electorate as they retained or replaced judges on the bench.

From 1889 to 1907 the major goal of many of the lawyers in the state was to remove the judicial candidates from the pressures of partisan campaigning and the implied political accountability associated with elections under political party labels. In a paper read to the sixth annual meeting of the Washington Bar Association (1894), Frank H. Graves isolated numerous evils attributable to judicial selection controlled by the parties:

> When . . . the courts begin to adjudicate upon questions of real or supposed party interest purely as such; questions in which is involved no great political principle, but only party or factional exigency; a party judiciary becomes an evil intolerable to be borne. . . .
>
> The second great evil of the partisan selection of our judges to which I would call attention is corporate influence in the courts. . . . I consider this the greatest of the evils resulting from a partisanly selected judiciary. Day by day, year after year, here a little and there a little, these soulless and breathless creations of the genius of modern enterprise are extending their influence, their demands and their greed. They never die; they never tire; they never sleep. . . .
>
> [Finally], the manner in which a political nominating convention . . . is organized makes it impossible to secure decent judicial nominations. . . . The convention meets and the contest over other offices goes on; the last and least thought of places to fill are the judicial nomina-

> tions. Some of us . . . have seen judicial nominations made . . . upon the principle of giving every defeated candidate a place upon the ticket, and if perchance everyone were not eligible to the bench, to dictate who should take his place.[53]

To remedy these evils, the 1894 gathering of state lawyers approved the appointment of a committee to write a constitutional amendment "for the election of judges at some time other than during the political campaign." Further, the assembled attorneys were urged to select a committee to confer with both major parties with "the object in view of securing . . . nonpartisan nominations," either as agreed by the Republicans and Democrats or by means of a separate "independent" convention.[54] Although the members tabled the motion to appoint a committee to confer with the leaders of the major party conventions, the motion represented some of the profession's thinking on a remedy for the evils of partisanship.

Not only was the bar concerned with those evils isolated by Frank Graves, but, more directly, the populist movement had struck considerable fear into the hearts of the legal establishment. The People's Party had, at its 1894 convention in Yakima, nominated two "unacceptable" candidates for the Supreme Court. (In the November general election the vote for the People's Party supreme court candidates exceeded that of the Democrats by nearly 10,000 votes, but fell short of the Republicans by another 10,000 votes.)

After 1894, rapidly accelerating political events led to the demise of the radical People's Party and the birth of the Progressive Movement which captured some of the thunder of the radicals. The organized bar remained silent until 1908, when the attorneys awoke to the possibilities of the new reforms. But they were confronted by a serious dilemma. If the profession attacked the direct primary method of nomination, the principle of nonpartisanship might by put in jeopardy. The report of the State Bar's Judiciary Committee of 1908, chaired by Corwin S. Shank, recognized the dilemma:

53. Frank H. Graves, "Non-Partisan Selection of the Judiciary," an address to the 1894 annual convention of the Washington State Bar Association published in the *Proceedings* (1894), 86–94. "Uncle Frank Graves was a forceful and delightful man. He was senior partner in Graves, Kiser and Graves, Spokane. I met him first at the annual Spokane County Bar Association dinner in the Fall of 1928. The young lawyers gathered around him, many sitting on the floor, and he regaled us with stories of his long and colorful career at the Bar. I remember him saying he had committed every crime in the book except murder and manslaughter" (Recollections of Justice Frank P. Weaver in a letter to the author). Graves successfully defended M. J. Gordon in his embezzlement trial in March 1910.

54. *Proceedings* (1894), 41.

> There would seem to be no remedy for this condition [direct primary] . . . by any change in the law, without the sacrifice of the principle of non-partisan nominations which all lawyers desire to preserve.
>
> We are therefore convinced that this association should, in some proper manner, stand sponsor for candidates for the Supreme Bench. We do not recommend any particular method. Candidates might be endorsed, or members of the Bar might be solicited to enter the contest. If the members of the association were to support their candidates actively, it is probable that such support would lead to the success of those whom they so honored.[55]

The committee recommended that a group of fifteen State Bar members be appointed by the president to investigate the question of whether and how the bar should support candidates. The sense of the motion and the discussion of it, which was not extended, was that the "Committee of Fifteen" should study the issue and recommend future courses of action. In the meantime, the judiciary committee advised that "a letter be prepared to members of this association and such others" admonishing them "to urge their clients and friends to vote upon candidates for judge."[56] The recommendation did not include any reference as to whom the bar should support.

The following year the state organization abruptly turned back a resolution that would have obligated the organization to urge both political parties to nominate supreme court judges in a joint convention. But, again, another *ad hoc* committee ("Committee on Method of Selecting Judges") of three members was formed to work separately from the "Committee of Fifteen" and to compile statistics on how judges were selected in the other states. These data would be of use to the bar in its future deliberations. The Committee of Fifteen, apparently yet unprepared, failed to report to the 1909 meeting of the state's attorneys.

The resolutions and debate of the 1910 convention of state attorneys displayed an agreement on the nonpartisan aspects of judicial selection but substantial disagreement about the direct primary method of nominating judges. The special committee of three appointed the previous year made its report, indicating that Washington's convention method was not out of line with other states, although an impressive number of states had adopted the direct primary.[57] The chairman of special committee, Arthur Remington concluded:

55. "Report of Committee on the Judiciary," *ibid.* (1908), 36.

56. *Ibid.*

57. See the state by state compilation in "Report of the Committee on Method of Selecting the Judiciary," *ibid.*, 73–77.

> With the scales so evenly balanced, the public mind so undecided, and the opinions of the ablest statesman so conflicting, it is not for any one to criticise our last legislature in its adoption in part, of both these systems [convention nominations and popular election], following as it did the practice in at least three of the older states. . . .
>
> The advantages and disadvantages of the direct primary are as applicable to the judiciary as to the other branches of government, and involve a discussion entirely beyond the province of this committee. We therefore recommend that this committee be permanently discharged.[58]

The membership agreed, and the report was "placed on file" for future reference.

The bar, however, was not yet willing to take a direct role in the selection of judges as suggested in 1908. Instead, it rejected a return to the direct primary and passed (by a 53 to 36 vote) a resolution expressing only the general consensus:

> We favor an absolute non-partisan judiciary and, to that end, recommend that the statutes be so amended as to provide for the nomination of all Judges by judicial conventions, composed of delegates elected by the whole people for that purpose only, and that no other business shall be transacted by such convention than to nominate Judges, the Judges so nominated to be elected at the general election.[59]

The difficulty with the various resolutions discussed and passed thus far by the profession was that they were mere expressions of opinion. The membership did not demand that such legislation be drafted by the bar and submitted directly to the legislature. Furthermore, the bar was not yet willing to intervene directly in the electoral process through official endorsements or advisory ballots.

The bar association presidential address, delivered by C. W. Howard in 1911, condemned the legislature for returning supreme court nominations to the direct primary and urged that the law be changed consistent with the resolution passed by the association the previous year.[60] His successor as president in 1912, W. T. Dovell, also condemned the lawmakers for not giving due consideration to a nonpartisan judicial convention for nominating judges. It was obvious, at least to the lawyers, that "the people cannot properly determine" judicial qualifications, and that to leave the selection of

58. *Ibid.*, 73–78, 82–83.
59. *Ibid.*, 86.
60. "Presidential Address," *ibid.*, 89–90.

judges to the "impulses of the voter" was as "perilous as it is illogical."[61]

But action directed at the legislature to change the law or directed at the electorate to provide advice on balloting was still not advocated. This pattern of concern from the organized bar, unaccompanied by direct intervention, prevailed for another dozen years.

The organized bar's efforts during the inaugural years were limited to encouraging a nonpartisan system of electing judges, to condemning the direct primary method of nominating candidates for the Supreme Court, and to urging a special convention technique for initiating and screening judicial candidates. They did not like most of what they saw but were yet unwilling either to go to the legislature and urge adoption of their plans or to the voters in support of various candidates.[62] The profession remained only a potential force in the recruitment of supreme court judges. The political parties still dominated all the stages of the recruitment process.

The lawyers' failures were largely due to the lack of a consensus among them. The Washington Bar Association, prior to 1933, was a voluntary organization which attracted the professionally oriented attorneys most supportive of changes that would enhance judicial independence. But, the official voices of the Bar Association did not necessarily represent the entire legal profession. Also partisanship remained behind much of the bar's efforts. The Republican attorneys, representing a majority of the profession, were often reluctant to sacrifice partisan advantage to reform. In turn, the Democrats wished only to enhance their opportunities by advocating nonpartisan elections. They stood a better chance of breaking the Republican monopoly at the polls if party labels were absent from the ballots. It is not surprising, then, that the urgings of the bar failed to attract the necessary attention for change.

61. *Ibid.* (1912), 117.

62. From its inception the Seattle Bar Association had been active in the initiation and screening of candidates for the King County Superior Court benches. The S.B.A.'s Articles of Incorporation (1906), By-Law IX, Section 2, reads: "There shall be a standing Judiciary Committee; who shall be charged with the duty of observing the practical working of our judicial system, of entertaining and examining projects for change or reform in the system, and it shall be their further duty to consider the fitness of candidates for judicial office, with power to recommend to the Association, . . . such action as they deem expedient" (SBA Articles of Incorporation, Constitution and By-Laws of the Seattle Bar Association, Seattle, WA [1906]). By 1908 the Seattle Bar was conducting its own "bar primary" among its members and publicizing the results, a technique decades away for the state group.

Summary: Traditional Form of Recruitment

The review of supreme court recruitment from statehood until 1912 verifies the hypothesized model of judicial selection with which this section began. Actually, the dominant actor in the recruitment process was the political party, namely, the Republican Party. The governor exercised some discretion, but partisanship and legislative intent limited the choices of the chief executive. Although a number of appointments were made, they were to new or temporary positions created by the legislature. The politics of endorsement also dictated to a noticeable extent whom the governor selected. The State Bar Association, still a voluntary organization and dominated by Republicans, tended to pass resolutions of protest but without political follow-up. The electorate tended to vote straight party tickets that maintained the party nominees on the bench. Little serious interaction between the candidates and voters was necessary; the party label determined the outcome.

Thus, supreme court selection from 1889 to 1912 remained simple with political parties dominating virtually the entire sequence from initiation through screening to affirmation. Only rarely did the governor intervene. Partisan accountability prevailed over judicial independence in the recruitment process. With the establishment of the direct primary and the nonpartisan balloting for judges, however, changes were in the offing.

4

From Party Lists to Separate Nonpartisan Ballots, 1912–32

After 1910, the Washington electorate was no longer provided with the familiar and meaningful labels of party affiliation as guides to voting for supreme court judges. Adherence to certain principles and policies were at least implied by the party labels. Actually, rather than freeing judicial candidates from the burdens of campaigning, the removal of judges from partisanship forced them to conduct their own campaigns. Attorney Frank Truman Post, a supporter of gubernatorial appointments as the sole method of selection, was highly critical of the demeaning solicitation of votes involved in the nonpartisan electoral system. In an address before the Oregon State Bar Association, he gave a fairly accurate portrayal of the campaigning practices in Washington:

> To see candidates for judicial honor traveling around their district, whether it be the county or the state, attending meetings and gatherings of a political or semipolitical character, having their pictures published in the newspapers, having their cards handed to the voters, having sketches published and generally circulated, in which the statement is made that they will or have gone contrary to the law in respect to certain classes of cases, as for instance that they have not and will not grant non-suits in personal injury cases, is a sight disgusting to all right-thinking men.[1]

Newspapers remained, as before, active in endorsing supreme court candidates. Earlier, *The Seattle Post-Intelligencer* had tended to support Republicans, and *The Seattle Daily Times* now and then had

1. F. T. Post, "Effect of the Direct Primary Law upon the Character, Ability and Independence of the Judiciary," *Oregon Bar Association Proceedings* (1908–10), 90. It was said that Post was instrumental in changing the direct primary law back to the convention method in the 1909 legislative session.

approved a Democrat. After 1912 the press was still active in urging the electorate to vote for certain court aspirants, but newspapers were not alone in their endorsements. Special groups developed an interest in supporting certain candidates for the high court. For example, in 1918 Walter French's paid newspaper advertisement prominently announced that he was endorsed by the Seattle Central Labor Council, Bremerton Labor Council, Committee on the Grand Army, and the Spanish War Veterans and their auxiliaries. In the same year, labor published its "advisory ballot" which urged support for Pemberton, Chapman, Mitchell, Mackintosh, and French. Edgar G. Mills also received the support of the Seattle Central Labor Council.[2]

Leaders in bar associations (state and county) were sometimes consulted by governors on appointments and occasionally the organizations appealed to the public in elections at the superior court level.[3] However, until 1924 the major professional groups—the Seattle and State Bar Associations—remained aloof from the supreme court electoral process even though attorneys became the core of judicial campaign organizations. Political studies suggest that as political party influence wanes in judicial selection, that of bar associations increases.[4] From an historical perspective this certainly has been the case in Washington. These years of transition witnessed this waning influence of political parties in the selection of judges and the growing impact of the bar associations.

2. An example of the activities of labor was reported in a 1926 newspaper account: "Members of Local Union #46, International Brotherhood of Electrical Workers, last night ratified the action of the Seattle Labor Council endorsing and recommending candidates for legislative, county and non-partisan judiciary offices, and instructed their secretary to notify all members of the organization of the stand taken . . . letters will be sent to members" (*The Seattle Daily Times*, September 3, 1926).

3. For example, in 1916 the Seattle Bar Association emphatically rejected the candidacy of former supreme court judge Milo Root who was running for a seat on the King County Superior Court bench. The State Bar's 1908 report concerning Root's actions in a rehearing in *Harris* v. *Great Northern Railway Company* (48 WASH. 437) was brought up again. The bar urged the voters to reject Judge Root at the polls (*The Seattle Daily Times*, November 2, 1916).

Governor-elect Cosgrove, although never able to assume the responsibilities of office because of illness in 1909, wrote Lt. Governor Hay that "about those two [superior court] judgeships—leave the one to the Spokane Bar Association. The appointee is to be whomever it picks" (*The Seattle Post-Intelligencer*, January 10, 1909).

4. H. Jacob & K. Vines, *Politics in the American States: A Comparative Analysis* (Boston: Little, Brown and Company, 1976), 251. A recent study brings into question the direct converse relationship between partisanship and bar influence, although this study is limited to the 1970s and is not the result of an historical analysis. See C. Sheldon, "Influencing the Selection of Judges: The Variety and Effectiveness of State Bar Activities," *Western Political Quarterly* 30 (September 1977): 400.

The Organized Bar Awakens

The experiences of the legal profession in other states provided the Washington Bar with several alternatives for influencing the outcome of judicial recruitment. First, it was common for such organizations to consult directly with governors in order to influence appointments. However, such consultations depended upon the whims of the governors who often did not feel compelled to seek the advice of the bar. Second, the practice of using advisory ballots or publicly announced endorsements, used by other groups such as labor, also was common in other states and could be used by the bar for advising the Washington electorate. Third, the bar in other states was often instrumental in circulating petitions to have the judicial candidates of their choice placed on the ballots, or the bar simply allowed favored candidates to publicize their bar support in order to impress the voter. Of course, individual members of the bar, the leadership, or even factions within the organization informally urged selected attorneys to run for judicial office, provided campaign support for them, formed their electoral organizations, raised funds, and generally endorsed favorite candidates. Actually the organized bar in Washington showed little consistency in such efforts until the events of 1924 drew them not so reluctantly into the political fray. The attorneys viewed the actions of one of their own colleagues as a direct threat to their integrity. The lawyers forthwith entered election politics with a vengeance.

A few days prior to the 1924 September primary, Attorney George F. Vanderveer, head of the Legal Bureau of the Seattle Central Labor Council and noted defense attorney, sent a circular letter to members of the letter carriers' union urging them to support court candidates Bruce Blake, W. D. Lane, and William H. Pemberton.[5] The letter did not speak well of Mr. Vanderveer's own profession, stating:

5. It was prominently pointed out by his critics that Vanderveer had been the attorney for I.W.W. insurgents and had been chief counsel in the defense of "Wobblie" leader Bill Haywood at his 1924 trial in Chicago. Vanderveer had allegedly bragged about being the "reddest of the red." See Lowell S. Hawley and Ralph Bushnell Potts, *Counsel for the Damned* (New York: Lippincott, 1953). The legal establishment had anticipated Pemberton's candidacy and found disfavor with his decisions during his two years on the Supreme Court. They sought a respected and formidable opponent for Judge Pemberton in order to turn back the threat he represented. Although he was assured of reelection as Pierce County Superior Court judge, William D. Askren was persuaded to file for the Supreme Court. He apparently did not aspire to the high bench. Within three years after his defeat of Pemberton, Askren resigned from the court and returned to private practice in Seattle.

> On one side stand progressives of this type [Blake, Lane, and Pemberton] contending for clean government in the interests of the common people. On the other stand reactionaries defending a record of corruption in office and the sacred rights of vested privilege.
>
> The average citizen does not often come into personal contact with the courts and therefore does not realize how important a part they play in the affairs of everyday life. As a result his interest has not been aroused and he has permitted the lawyers and bar associations to select his judges. Generally speaking, these are controlled by money interests.[6]

Vanderveer contended further (and correctly) that the September primary was the crucial election. He urged the letter carriers to work among those to whom they delivered mail to vote for these three judges "friendly to the cause."

Vanderveer's action prompted an emergency meeting of the Seattle Bar Association to "consider false propaganda now being spread against the State Supreme Court, and the organized attempt now being made to excite class prejudice." Mr. Vanderveer was invited by the bar to explain his circular. He attended the emergency gathering but failed to satisfy his fellow lawyers. At the close of the meeting the Seattle Bar formally and unanimously condemned the letter "and all that it implied."[7]

An organized reaction against the Vanderveer letter soon became evident. Other county bar groups condemned the circular and defended the supreme court incumbents.[8] Following the bar's lead, the state's two leading newspapers endorsed Judges John Main, William Mitchell, and William Askren.

Paid advertisements began to appear in the newspapers signed by notable attorneys and urging the repudiation of the "radical" elements involved in the attempt to defeat honest and competent judges. The ads displayed banner headlines: "ARE YOU FOR THE VANDERVEER SUPREME COURT TICKET?"[9] The final advertisement placed in the evening and morning papers immediately prior to the primary election listed the names of nearly four hundred Seattle attorneys who condemned the attempt to discredit the high court and to bring class conflict into the election. Again, they urged the election of Main, Mitchell, and Askren.[10]

6. *The Seattle Daily Times*, August 29, 1924.
7. *Ibid.*
8. For example, the Spokane Bar Association (*The Seattle Post-Intelligencer*, September 3, 1924); the Cowlitz Bar (*ibid.*, September 4, 1924); Skagit and Clallam Bars (*ibid.*, September 5, 1924).
9. *Ibid.* September 7, 1924.
10. *Ibid.*, September 8, 1924.

The electorate apparently heeded those warnings and gave Main and Mitchell the absolute majority needed to place their names on the November ballot without opposition. Askren and Pemberton would face each other in the general election for the third position on the court. Labor again issued an "advisory ballot" and urged the election of Judges Main, Mitchell, and Pemberton in November. The first two judges immediately repudiated this attempt to link their names with Pemberton.

The Washington Bar Association, for the first time as an organization, urged the defeat of an incumbent and, also for the first time, endorsed a candidate. Again, ads appeared shouting, "FINISH THE VANDERVEER SUPREME COURT TICKET BY DEFEATING PEMBERTON. ELECT JUDGE ASKREN." The text explained that "At the primaries . . . Vanderveer and other radical leaders conducted an active campaign of misrepresentation. We [the undersigned] represent no class and we do not want Supreme Court Judges who represent a class. We want a Court that is fair to all classes."[11]

The campaign against Judge Pemberton was not limited to these ads which marked the beginning of a later practice—the bar poll. The attorneys made use not only of their status within the community but also of their clientele in order to influence the outcome of the 1924 election. The efforts of the Yakima County Bar Association were illustrative of the tactics of the profession. The Yakima attorneys followed their unanimous endorsement of Askren with a mailing campaign:

> More than 5,000 general letters will be sent out to clients and acquaintances in the county, advising them of the bar's endorsement. Besides these each member agreed to send twenty to twenty-five personal letters to friends advising the election of Justice Askren. Ralph B. Williamson and Thomas E. Grady [later to sit on the high bench] were appointed a committee to prepare suitable resolutions in accordance with the bar's action.[12]

William Askren defeated incumbent Pemberton by over 70,000 votes. His victory was in no small way due to the organized efforts of the county and state bar associations. In a letter of gratitude to *The Seattle Daily Times*, State Bar president Ralph B. Williamson wrote:

> When this year the lawyers of the state deemed it for the best interests of the state to recommend to the public the election of Judge William

11. *The Seattle Daily Times.* November 2, 1924.
12. *Ibid.*, October 14, 1924.

> D. Askren to the bench in place of the incumbent Judge Pemberton, it has been extremely gratifying that you . . . have recognized that the lawyers of the state are acting with the highest of motives.[13]

Again, in 1926, Pemberton sought to return to the Supreme Court. The bar, as before, played a leading role in the campaign. First, the Seattle Bar Association passed a resolution outlining their position on Pemberton's latest campaign:

> Two years ago this association after due investigation and upon careful consideration, opposed the candidacy of William H. Pemberton for State Supreme Court judgeship for reasons then publicly stated, the chief of which was unfitness, demonstrated by his previous service in that capacity. The same reasons exist today. Therefore, be it resolved that this association again announce its opposition to his candidacy.[14]

The county-wide organization followed suit. Two hundred members of the King County Bar placed an ad in both major newspapers with a banner headline:

> KING COUNTY BAR OPPOSES PEMBERTON FOR SUPREME COURT:
> The undersigned lawyers include men of all political parties and all shades of opinion, both progressive and conservative. . . . We represent no class. We want a Court that is fair to all classes. For that reason, we severally endorse the [Seattle Bar's] resolution.[15]

The professional organizations succeeded again in helping to defeat Pemberton.[16]

13. *Ibid.*, November 2, 1924. *The Seattle Post-Intelligencer*, September 8, 1924, editorialized: "It is set forth that to ascertain the true character of a man, ask his neighbors. These know him best. Character rests upon a record, not upon a prospectus. The lawyers can properly be considered as bearing the same relation to the judges of the courts as the average man does to his neighbor. As a profession they represent no class. Every voter should give his attention to this question involving our highest state tribunal."

14. *Ibid.*, September 4, 1926.

15. *Ibid.*, September 21, 1926.

16. Actually, the active role of the bar associations in the Pemberton campaigns of 1924 and 1926 likely accounts for the increase in the number of voters taking part in the judicial elections. The roll-off in both the general and primary elections is less than usual. But, as we might expect, highly spirited campaigns attract voters. For example, 1914 and 1916 saw a considerable participation rate in the primaries because of highly contested campaigns. The 1914 November balloting remained high because of the sharp contest between Stephen Chadwick, William Pemberton, and Edgar Mills. The participation rate in the 1916 general election, in contrast, dropped considerably simply because the outcome had been decided at the primary.

The legal fraternity was still concerned with the general question of the selection of supreme court judges quite apart from the "emergency" created by Judge Pemberton's campaigns. In 1921 the State Bar adopted the American Bar Association's Canons of Professional Ethics. By endorsing Canon II, the bar formally committed itself to an active role in the recruitment of judges.[17] Bar president Chester R. Hovey, who within a few months would himself be appointed to the Supreme Court, and acting within the spirit of Canon II, successfully urged his fellow lawyers to appoint a special committee to "recommend to the next meeting of the bar association some plan lawyers can agree upon for the purpose of selecting judges."[18]

Heretofore the bar had been engaged in debates over the relative merits of gubernatorial appointment, partisan and nonpartisan election, and nomination by convention or direct primary.[19] Although effective consensus on courses of action was lacking, by 1924 the profession was able to agree on an organizational change: it made the heretofore ad hoc committee on the selection of judges a permanent standing committee of the State Bar and thus a part of the profession's formal structure.

Further, the initial success at going public with their endorsements in the 1924 defeat of Pemberton led bar president Williamson in his 1925 presidential address to urge his colleagues to continue their efforts in advising the electorate:

> We are fortunate in this state. . . . [T]he people of the State of Washington are looking to lawyers to so advise them . . . and are willing to act upon that advice. . . . I think we should as lawyers shoulder this responsibility and be responsible to the people of this state for the maintenance of our courts on the highest standard of

17. *Proceedings of the Washington State Bar Association* (1921), 13–14. Article X of the constitution of the Washington State Bar Association adopts the A.B.A.'s Code of Ethics, Chapter 126, Session Laws, 1921, Sec. 15, p. 415: "Canon II, The Selection of Judges. It is the duty of the bar to endeavor to prevent political considerations from out-weighing judicial fitness in the selection of judges. It should protest earnestly and actively against the appointment or election of those who are unsuitable for the Bench; and it should strive to have elevated thereto only those willing to forego other employments . . . which may embarrass their free and fair consideration of questions before them for decision. The aspiration of lawyers for judicial position should be governed by an impartial estimate of the ability to add honor to the office and not by a desire for the distinction the position may bring to themselves."

18. *Proceedings* (1921), 51.

19. Some interest was shown toward the Merit Plan of the American Judicature Society as a possible compromise among the various alternatives. However, in 1925 the society's project, later to be called the Missouri Plan, was still a novelty (Charles W. Hall, "The Choosing of Public Officials," *Proceedings* [1925], 44–45).

learning, integrity and industry that the personnel of our bar affords.[20]

The bar did shoulder this responsibility by again successfully urging the defeat of Pemberton in 1926.

By the 1920s most of the campaigns of the serious court aspirants were organized and conducted by committees of lawyers. For example, O. R. Holcomb's reelection campaign in 1926 was conducted by his attorney "friends": an executive committee of fifty-six lawyers. Such groups commonly formed subcommittees along functional lines: for fund raising, scheduling speaking engagements, canvassing (fellow lawyers and clients), direct mailings, and handout literature. By 1928 short radio announcements were often made during the campaigns. But by far the most common campaign material involved endorsements by lawyers.

Petitions signed by members of the profession, published in the newspapers, and displayed in handout materials gave prominence to professional support for the candidates and constituted a primitive form of a bar poll. Attorney Louis B. Schwellenbach headed Walter French's successful effort to unseat incumbent Holcomb in 1926, and public endorsements by fellow lawyers provided professional visibility to the campaign. Justice Holcomb was not without his following among the members of the bar. His newspaper ads were signed by over 300 members of the King County Bar and acknowledged that "His candidacy [was] endorsed by a great majority of the lawyers in the state and by the following named and many other lawyers in King County. . . ."[21] The legal profession was clearly becoming an independent but not a unified force in the selection of judges.[22]

20. Ralph B. Williamson, "Presidential Address," *Proceedings* (1925), 22–23.

21. *The Seattle Daily Times*, November 4, 1928. In like manner, W. G. McLaren, a candidate for King County Superior Court, introduced his advertisements with: "85% of ALL KING COUNTY LAWYERS are supporting him. Below is a partial list of lawyers who endorse his candidacy. Among them you will find the leaders of their profession, men held in high esteem by this community, lawyers who represent clients in every walk of life" (*ibid.*).

22. In 1929 the lawyers considered a "bar primary" similar to that which had been used by the Seattle Bar as early as 1908. But apparently no consensus formed around such a departure from the profession's heretofore ad hoc activities. Nonetheless, individual members of the profession and the county bars increased their "endorsement" activities in order to sway the voting public. For example, Justice Tolman was publicly endorsed by virtually all of the organized county bars in his 1932 reelection bid. Additionally, lawyers would send out letters to their clients urging support. Typical was the letter from E. L. Skeel of Seattle to five hundred clients of the Roberts, Skeel and Holman law firm: "I urge that you take special care to express your preference for the candidates for judicial offices. . . . I stated in my letter before the

The dilemma that had confronted the partisans among the attorneys in previous years had been resolved. Nonpartisan elections for judges were (albeit reluctantly) accepted. Now the efforts of the profession were directed toward replacing the previous accountability to political parties with more accountability to the legal profession. However, judicial independence was actually thereby enhanced, because the general electorate tended to by-pass the judicial ballots or, if voting for judges, tended to follow the advice of lawyers. Except for the Pemberton candidacy, the bar had not reached a consensus, leaving the judges largely unafraid of reprisals from the legal profession.

Between 1912 and 1932 the recruitment of judges to the state's court of last resort evolved into a fairly complex process within which a number of participants cooperated and competed. No longer did the political party dominate the process as the single most important recruitment actor. Initiation, screening, and affirmation of judicial candidates were now shared among several participants. But the participation was rather unpredictable.

The Role of the Voters during the Transition Period

In the previous chapter we already noted a sudden drop-off in voter participation in both the general and primary elections for judicial offices. This trend continued. Figure 4.1 indicates, first, an overall increase in the rate of voter "roll-off." More and more voters seemingly suffered ballot fatigue and failed to cast their votes for candidates for the Supreme Court. Second, a considerable disparity existed between the roll-off in the primary and the general elections. The average roll-off in the general elections was approximately 50% (one out of two voters did not bother to cast a judicial ballot), whereas in the primary the average was around 28% (nearly one of three failing to vote for judges). The gap closed between primary and general election turnouts only slightly during the end of this period of transition.

Several explanations are possible for the variations displayed in figure 4.1. As we have seen, explanations for the increasing roll-off

---

primaries that it was the duty of attorneys to inform their friends and clients as to the qualifications of those who are candidates for election for judicial positions. This is for the reason that attorneys actively practicing at the bar are in a position to secure information not ordinarily available to the layman. With this thought in mind I again take the liberty to indicate my preference for the contested positions" (Letter from Skeel to Tolman dated November 4, 1932. *Tolman Papers*, Washington State University Archives). The McMaster, Hall and Schaefer firm of Vancouver, Washington, also sent out about five hundred of Judge Tolman's circulars to their clients.

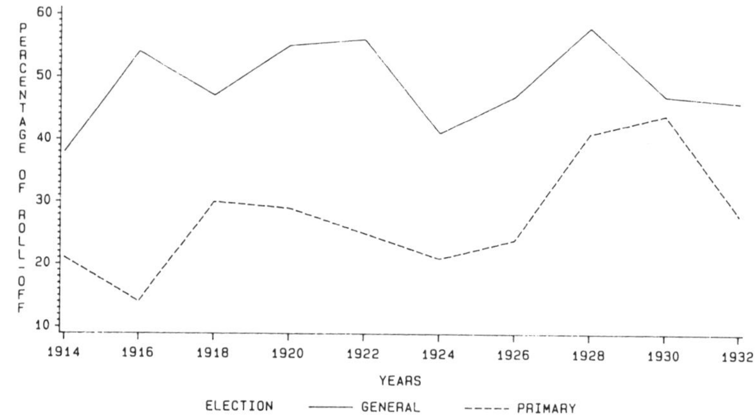

Fig. 4.1. Judicial vote roll-off, 1914–32

lie largely with the nonpartisan direct primary electoral system. But during this period of transition new factors intervened to influence the voting turnout. The granting of the vote to women, the finality of most primary election results, the form of the ballots, and the large influx of voters during highly visible presidential election years all contributed to the variations in voter participation.

Although the original constitution as proposed in 1889 contained a provision for women's suffrage, it was placed on the ratification ballot as a separate measure and was rejected. The 1909 legislative session approved a proposed women's suffrage constitutional amendment which was placed on the 1910 ballot and ratified by the electorate. Amendment 5 read: "There shall be no denial of the elective franchise at any election on account of sex." The 1912 primary and general elections were, then, the first in the state giving full participation to women. It was not the voting behavior of *women* in 1912 and subsequent elections which caused a decline in judicial voting, but simply because the great influx of *new* voters presented an increasing opportunity for a greatly expanded electorate to ignore judicial candidates.

In the previous year (1911) the legislature had approved a separate ballot for judges, removing their names from the bottom of all party tickets.[23] Although voters were given a judicial ballot, its very separateness was a deterrence, and so it is not altogether surprising that a considerable number of voters neglected the judicial ballot.

In 1916, King County, containing approximately 44% of the state's voters, used voting machines for the first time in many of their

23. Chapter 101, Session Laws, 1911, sec. 1, p. 489.

urban precincts. By 1918 approximately half the voting places in the state's largest urban area had voting machines. But because of the relatively complicated manner in which the primary results were interpreted in order to certify candidates for the general election, the judicial ballot was separated entirely from the voting machines.[24] The voters in the most populous county were thereby disadvantaged in those areas using voting machines in that it was a bit awkward to pull levers for all partisan candidates and then, on a separate paper ballot, mark X's for supreme court judges. This undoubtedly contributed to some of the roll-off in the elections of 1916 and 1918. Space on the machine was later provided for judicial candidates.

Part of the revamping of supreme court elections in 1911 was to assure that every two years, three of the nine judges would present themselves to the electorate for retention.[25] The exception, of course, would be those elections involving appointees who, as before, had to be elected at the next general election after their appointment. As before, all aspirants (incumbents as well) would run against each other (except those appointed to finish out the shorter term of those they replaced). Those who received the highest number of votes moved on to the final November ballot. If they received more than half the votes cast for *all* judges in the primary they ran unopposed in the final balloting. If only a plurality of votes was attained, then the name of the next highest candidate was advanced to battle it out with the leading candidates in the general election. Hence, the primaries remained fairly competitive and obviously attracted more voter interest than the often uncontested general election races.

Figure 4.1 indicates a substantial roll-off in comparison to earlier years and also shows an increasing lack of voter interest over these years of transition. From 1889 to 1914, twenty-nine of the thirty-four positions (85%) listed on the supreme court ballots were contested, and many of these involved close races. However, during the period of transition twenty-six of the thirty-five positions (74%) were contested in the primaries and only twelve of thirty-six (33%) were contested in the general balloting. After the 1926 statutory requirement that candidates file for specific positions, the number of contested races dropped even farther.[26] These uncontested races

24. *The Seattle Post-Intelligencer*, September 7, 1918.

25. Chapter 119, Session Laws, 1911, sec. 1, p. 614.

26. Chapter 68, Session Laws, 1925, sec. 1, p. 66. Between 1914 and 1926, 95% of the positions in the primaries and 38% in the general elections were contested. Subsequently (1928–32) only 43% in the primaries and 27% in the general balloting experienced competitive races.

Table 4.1
Election Results, 1914–26

	Primary	*General*
1914	*(Sept. 8)*	*(Nov. 3)*
**Herman D. Crow*	53,016	119,575
*Mack F. Gose	43,032	
**Stephen J. Chadwick*	72,200	159,287
William H. Pemberton	45,904	94,474
Edgar G. Mills	52,365	105,445
O. R. Holcomb	48,700	131,277
John E. Humphries	46,098	69,055
E. B. Preble	26,494	
1916	*(Sept. 12)*	*(Nov. 7)*
**Emmett N. Parker*	124,218	178,670
**Mark A. Fullerton*	124,103	178,136
**George E. Morris*	119,897	175,086
Charles E. Claypool	87,186	
Edgar G. Mills	109,699	1,055
Peter Husby	188	44
Four-year term:		
J. Stanley Webster	117,580	170,653
Elihu F. Barker	70,365	54
1918	*(Sept. 10)*	*(Nov. 5)*
**John F. Main*	49,167	88,058
**John R. Mitchell*	58,308	111,387
W. O. Chapman	40,924	58,359
Charles E. Claypool	31,981	
William H. Pemberton	39,226	48,648
Edgar G. Mills	37,874	34,658
Frank Pierce	25,061	
Kazis Krauczunas	7,202	
F. W. Girand	13,661	
Four-year term:		
**Kenneth Mackintosh*	97,021	98,339
Two-year term:		
**Warren W. Tolman*	55,199	86,563
Walter M. French	50,211	
1920	*(Sept. 14)*	*(Nov. 2)*
**Warren W. Tolman*	133,572	182,397
**O. R. Holcomb*	128,958	177,815
**J. B. Bridges*	125,421	178,818
Walter B. Beals	96,505	
1922	*(Sept. 12)*	*(Nov. 7)*
**Mark A. Fullerton*	101,088	137,587
**Kenneth Mackintosh*	108,624	138,476
**Emmett N. Parker*	95,860	134,208
W. D. Lane	91,338	
Bruce Blake	93,420	
Two-year term:		
*Chester N. Hovey	69,050	
William H. Pemberton	95,612	125,399
1924	*(Sept. 9)*	*(Nov. 4)*
**John F. Main*	108,860	203,820
**John R. Mitchell*	117,383	212,446
*William H. Pemberton	92,754	102,258
W. D. Lane	77,503	
William Askren	97,806	173,616
R. H. Back	40,017	
Bruce Blake	91,719	
1926	*(Sept. 14)*	*(Nov. 2)*
(Pos. 1)		
*O. R. Holcomb	85,166	
Walter M. French	103,180	164,704
(Pos. 2)		
**Warren W. Tolman*	150,563	149,676
(Pos. 3)		
**J. B. Bridges*	74,578	121,998
C. D. Cunningham	43,730	
William H. Pemberton	63,017	72,233

*Incumbent
Italicized names designate winners
Full six-year term unless otherwise indicated

Table 4.2
Election Results, 1928–32

	Primary	*General*
1928	*(Sept. 11)*	*(Nov. 6)*
(Pos. 1)		
**Mark A. Fullerton*	186,302	204,815
(Pos. 2)		
**Emmett N. Parker*	153,976	191,218
Burton D. Onstine	35,347	
(Pos. 3)		
**Walter B. Beals*	169,019	197,530
(Pos. 4)		
Bruce Blake	79,845	111,608
Preston M. Troy	40,546	
**O. R. Holcomb*	93,912	145,251
1930	*(Sept. 9)*	*(Nov. 4)*
(Special election because of Walter French's death in September)		
**Adam Beeler*		78,178
Ralph Bell		68,438
Russell H. Fluent		2,466
Austin E. Griffiths		3,801
P. C. Shine		3,817
(Others)		2,998
(Pos. 1)		
**John F. Main*	146,026	144,163
(Pos. 2)		
**John R. Mitchell*	157,356	146,345
(Pos. 3)		
**William J. Millard*	135,980	133,507

	Primary	*General*
1932	*(Sept. 13)*	*(Nov. 8)*
(Pos. 1)		
**Warren W. Tolman*	138,055	197,631
Will Beardslee	45,008	
Austin E. Griffiths	109,457	139,409
(Pos. 2)		
**O. R. Holcomb*	153,581	230,035
Charles A. Reynolds	115,584	
(Pos. 3)		
**William J. Steinert*	211,536	228,134
(Pos. 4)		
*Henry E. T. Herman	102,819	
Bruce Blake	155,958	229,415

*Incumbent
Italicized names designate winners
Full six-year term unless otherwise indicated

failed either to excite or perhaps even to have much meaning for the voters. The increase in election roll-off seems not surprising under these circumstances.

What the evolution of recruitment meant to the electorate during these years of transition was that their role in affirmation became largely symbolic. Public accountability was waning. Voters cast their ballots for judges most of whom were incumbents and who ran unopposed on the final November ballot. The crucial races, most often in the primaries, attracted fewer voters than the general elections. Therefore, even though voter roll-off was less in the primaries, if a choice was to be made between two or more aspirants, fewer participated in that choice. Also the voters were now sharing their role of affirmation (which previously was shared with political parties) with the governor.

The Appointment Process: Toward an Independent Role

From statehood until the progressive reforms of 1907 and 1910, the political parties had dominated the recruitment of judges to the state's high bench. Gubernatorial appointments tended not to complicate recruitment in these earlier years. Beginning but gradually, the governor exerted an independent force through his appointments to fill vacancies. The bar associations (state and county) also assumed a more forceful role in the process. By the time nonpartisanship was fully instituted, interactions among the major actors in the recruitment process were common, but regular and close relationships had not yet evolved.

This period immediately following the nonpartisan and direct primary electoral changes saw a gradual replacement of the general endorsement politics with a system of initiation and screening by attorneys, bar associations, and special groups. The attorneys of the state assumed a supporting and sometimes, when unified, a starring role in the drama of judicial selection.

Democratic governor Ernest Lister soon experienced the voracity of endorsement politics which proved to be the dying gasp of old-style recruitment. In 1913 Justice Chadwick was a leading candidate for a presidential appointment to the federal bench. He was even called to Washington, D.C., to talk personally with President Wilson. As rumors of the possible vacancy spread, Governor Lister's office was flooded with inquiries and endorsements. In a letter to C. H. Neal, the governor wrote:

> I already have applications from possibly between 40 and 50 attorneys who desire the appointment. In all cases this is not a direct application from the parties but recommendations from friends. The longer I occupy this position the more I realize that the matter of appointments is the hardest proposition to handle.[27]

Chadwick's promotion to the security of the federal bench did not materialize, however, and Lister's first appointment came only after he was halfway into his first term. Indeed, the circumstances which had led to Lister's electoral victory in 1912 bore directly on his first appointment.

According to Section 15 of Article IV of the state constitution, "judges of the supreme court and the judges of the superior court shall be ineligible to any other office" during their elected term. The intent was to remove judges from the temptations of higher office while serving on the bench. The Honorable W. W. Black of the King County Superior Court ran on the Democratic ticket against Lister and others for the party's gubernatorial nomination and garnered a plurality of the votes in the 1912 September primary.[28] Lister conceded defeat and returned to Tacoma with thoughts of residency at the governor's mansion purged from his mind. However, attorneys Charles A. Reynolds and Frederick Bausman succeeded in having the Supreme Court disqualify Black on the basis of Section 15, allowing runner-up Lister to carry the Democratic colors to victory in the November general election.[29]

27. Letter dated May 14, 1913, *Lister Papers*, "Judiciary" file. Governor Lister acknowledged receipt of an endorsement from a superior court judge and further described his misgivings about the endorsement process: "During the short term that elapsed between the death of Judge Crow and the announcement of the appointment the friends of fifty or sixty Attorneys and Jurists expressed their endorsement. There were two reasons for making the appointment promptly; the first being, of course, the fact that the Supreme Court is somewhat behind in its work now and I felt that there should be no delay in placing the ninth member on the Bench; the second reason was that everything indicated that if there was a delay I would have before me the names of four or five hundred which you can readily see would have made more difficult the decision" (Letter to E. P. March dated October 29, 1915. *Lister Papers*, "Judiciary" file).

28. The vote in the 1912 Democrat Primary for governor was:

Black, 8,166	Godman, 5,517
Lister, 7,629	Dunphy, 5,357
Million, 5,739	Chester, 3,980

The totals were votes for first and second choices, a voting method used in the primary only.

29. *State Ex Rel. Reynolds* v. *Howell* (70 Wash 467, 1912). *The Seattle Town Crier*, October 30, 1915, p. 6, gave credit to Bausman for "clearing the legal underbrush out of Mr. Lister's pathway to the executive office."

When Justice Crow died in October 1915, the governor already had two prospective appointees in mind: Richard Saxe Jones, and his successful counsel in the *Black* case, Frederick Bausman. Neither seemed to be anxious for the appointment, although both came highly recommended by their colleagues. Jones refused the offer, and the governor turned immediately to "staunch Democrat" Bausman, who accepted.[30]

Table 4.3
Supreme Court Appointments, 1915–21

Justice	*Governor*	*Date*
Frederick Bausman (D)	Lister (D)	October 26, 1915
J. Stanley Webster (R)	Lister	November 20, 1916
Kenneth Mackintosh (R)	Lister	March 30, 1918
Warren W. Tolman (D)	Lister	May 11, 1918
John R. Mitchell (D)	Lister	May 11, 1918
Jessie B. Bridges (R)	Hart (R)	June 1, 1919
Chester R. Hovey (R)	Hart	September 14, 1921

Lister's choice was lauded by the profession. Bausman was one of the state's leading experts in the field of criminal law, an area in which the Supreme Court appeared to lack expertise.[31] Apparently both Lister and Bausman viewed his appointment as temporary, however. The judge soon displayed signs of restlessness and let it be known that he would not be a candidate for the remainder of Crow's term. There was not "enough action" for his quick mind, and Olympia, in his view, lacked "swiftness."[32]

On January 26, 1916, Republican Judge J. Stanley Webster of the Spokane Superior Court announced his candidacy for the antici-

30. Jones responded in writing to the supreme court offer after Lister had turned to Bausman as his alternative: "I desire to thank you for the kindness which you have shown me in the matter of a Judgeship in the Supreme Court. As I stated to you, it would be impossible for me to accept the position. I am sure that no more efficient lawyer could have been selected by you than Mr. Frederick Bausman of this city, he being eminently qualified for the position, and it has been a great surprise to his friends to know that he would accept the position at all." The low salary then received by the high court jurists was apparently one major reason for Jones's refusal (Letter dated October 30, 1915, *Lister Papers*, "Judiciary" file).

31. *The Seattle Legal News*, May 8, 1915, observed that Bausman "possesses enough brain and legal ability to supply three or four ordinary lawyers." Bausman had also been "one of the most earnest and energetic workers" in Lister's campaigns (Letter to T. H. Bowden dated October 29, 1915, *Lister Papers*, "Judiciary" file).

32. *The Seattle Legal News*, February 12, 1916. The *News* reported that it was "generally understood" that Bausman would not be a candidate for the remainder of Crow's term.

pated Bausman vacancy. Webster had been the Spokane County deputy prosecutor who helped gather evidence in the grand jury indictments and trial of former supreme court judge J. M. Gordon eight years earlier.

In July of 1916 Bausman publicly announced that he would resign after the September primary. This timing would allow "the governor to appoint the high man [in the primary vote] as [my] successor, taking it for granted, of course, that the high man would . . . be perfectly agreeable to the governor. . . ."[33] Webster swamped his opposition (Elihu F. Barker) in the September balloting by 117,580 to 70,365 votes and would be unopposed in the November election. Bausman felt that he could now resign effective on October 19. He urged Democrat Governor Lister to appoint Republican Webster "for the two months between now and the beginning of his term [because] the Supreme Court needs the additional man now."

Of course, Lister was not legally bound to appoint Webster to the remaining weeks of the Bausman vacancy. In 1911 the legislature had enacted a statute requiring that an elected supreme court justice "shall not qualify for office until the second Monday in January succeeding his election."[34] If the law was a valid addition to the constitutional provision (Article 4, section 3), which simply states that the governor shall appoint "a person to hold office until the election and qualification of a judge to fill the vacancy . . . ," then the governor could appoint someone from his own political party rather than Webster to the remaining two and a half months of the term (from October 19, when Bausman planned to resign, to early January) or perhaps Bausman could be persuaded to stay on. If the law was invalid, Webster could assume his seat immediately upon the official canvassing of the November election. Even though only a short term was at stake, the question was important enough to compel Lister to ask his attorney general for an opinion on the validity of the 1911 statute.

Attorney General Tanner advised Lister of the likely unconstitutionality of the law and that Webster could take the seat for which he was elected as early as the first week in December when the results of the final November balloting would be officially certified.[35] Faced with this earlier date, the governor proceeded to appoint Webster to the remaining few weeks of the Bausman vacancy. (However, Bausman remained on the bench until November 20.) In a letter to attorney Frank Reeves, Lister explained that "under these circum-

33. *Ibid.*, July 22, 1916.
34. 9043-1, Remington and Ballinger Code.
35. *Lister Papers*, "Judiciary" file.

stances I am sure you will agree with me that it would be unwise to appoint anyone other than the man elected to the position for the short period of about three weeks."[36]

Lister's first two appointments, then, were not altogether what he had anticipated. His initial choice felt ill at ease in the position and begged out, and his second was foisted on him by the untimely resignation of his first appointee and the election results. His third appointment appeared, again, somehow to be thrust upon him. Kenneth Mackintosh, member of a prominent Seattle pioneer family, King County Superior Court judge, and former King County prosecutor, had been active in Republican politics. His superior court position was through an appointment by Republican governor Hay. If partisan politics is an important factor in the appointment of judges, and it is, why did Democrat Lister select Republican Mackintosh? Actually, the vacancy left by Justice George E. Morris's death on March 6, 1918, allowed Lister to extricate himself from a potentially embarrassing partisan situation.

Clay Allen, U.S. Attorney for the Western District of Washington, had been extremely active in Governor Lister's previous campaign, was a close personal friend, and had been singularly successful in persuading federal officials in the state, the so-called "federal brigade," either to support the governor or at least to remain neutral in the 1916 campaign.[37] Under threat of dismissal, Allen had continued to back the chief executive in an unsuccessful attempt to reorganize the state's Democratic party, further antagonizing entrenched party leaders. Thus, when Allen's reappointment for another term as U.S. Attorney was due, his commission was held up at the urging of the anti-Lister faction of the party. Allen continued as U.S. Attorney only because of the impasse between the two factions of the Democratic party. If Allen's commission was not forthcoming, Governor Lister would suffer political embarassment. But if the reappointment materialized, the anti-Lister faction would be further antagonized, splitting the party even more deeply.[38]

The solution was provided by the Morris vacancy. Lister needed only to appoint a King County judge to the Supreme Court and then fill the superior court vacancy with his loyal friend.[39] As many as

36. *Ibid.*

37. *The Seattle Sunday Times*, March 31, 1918.

38. "To Lister and his friends the idea of appointing Allen to a place on the King County Bench, besides recognizing Allen's ability, also afforded an opportunity to escape from all entanglements within the Wallace-Fogarty [anti-Lister] faction" (*ibid.*).

39. "In selecting Mr. Allen for a county judgeship Governor Lister has availed himself of the opportunity to kill two birds with one stone. First, he has been able to

twenty names were under consideration for the supreme court vacancy. Judge Walter French of Kitsap County (elected to the high bench in 1927), Judge John R. Mitchell of Thurston County (appointed by Lister in May, 1918), and Attorney General Tanner were among them. However, only Judge Mackintosh's promotion would create the desired King County vacancy for Allen. Further, Lister expressed some concern that a vacancy caused by Republican Justice Morris' death should be filled by another Republican.[40] Another factor which did not escape the governor was that Mackintosh had already made known his intention to run for the Supreme Court in the fall elections.[41] Likely, with the popular support given him in previous King County court contests, he would be a serious challenger to any of Lister's appointees.

Mackintosh, as was commonly the practice then and is still today, had been serving as "visiting" judge throughout the state, helping those jurisdictions with full dockets and those in need of an outsider to hear certain cases.[42] He thus had developed a reputation in all corners of the state which was indispensable to a successful statewide supreme court campaign.[43]

More advantages than disadvantages accrued to the governor in choosing Mackintosh. Although it appeared as if the chief executive was again circumscribed in his appointment, the selection of the popular King County jurist represented good politics. Perhaps his

---

give practical demonstration of appreciation for the political loyalty of Allen during the last campaign, when the federal group of office holders were divided in their allegiance, most of them holding aloof from the governor, and second, he has solved an embarrassing situation resulting from the failure of Mr. Allen to obtain a reappointment at the hands of the president" (*The Seattle Post-Intelligencer*, March 31, 1918). Allen preferred the trial bench and the Seattle area where he resided.

40. ". . . but probably the governor figured it out that inasmuch as Judge Morris was a Republican, in politics, a Republican should succeed him, and that he could with good grace name a Democrat to the vacancy resulting from the elevation of a county judge to the higher bench" (*ibid.*).

41. According to one weekly magazine, even before the death of Judge Morris, "it was generally understood that Judge Mackintosh would offer himself as a candidate for supreme court judge . . . next fall. His appointment anticipates the election" (*The Town Crier*, April 6, 1918). See also *The Seattle Sunday Times*, March 31, 1918.

42. *Ibid.*

43. Visiting judges had to be commissioned by the state's chief executive (Article IV, Sec. 7 of state constitution). To promote certain high court possibilities, the chief executive was occasionally persuaded to bestow certain aspiring judges with "visiting credentials." For example, Frank C. Paine had written Governor Lister on November 17, 1915: "Personally, I am still anxious that Judge [Bruce] Blake's acquaintance throughout the state be extended as far as possible and sincerely hope that through your good offices he may have an opportunity of holding court in many of the counties outside of Spokane during the coming months" (*Lister Papers*, "Judiciary" file).

next appointments would allow the full exercise of gubernatorial prerogatives.

Justice Overton Ellis, after seven years on the Supreme Court, and Justice J. Stanley Webster, after only two years, both resigned from the bench on May 11, 1918. Ellis was anxious to return to Tacoma and private practice, while Webster aspired to the U.S. Congress and was organizing a campaign for the Republican nomination. Governor Lister was ready with the replacements. He appointed John R. Mitchell of Thurston County and Warren W. Tolman of Spokane on the same day in May.

Democratic Judge John R. Mitchell was not a newcomer to appointment politics. He had been a serious contender for virtually all of the supreme court vacancies during Lister's term of office. Mitchell's Thurston County court had also developed a state-wide reputation because cases involving the state as litigant were heard in Thurston County (Olympia). One of the problems faced earlier by Lister was whom to appoint to fill Mitchell's vacancy once he was elevated to the Supreme Court. The Thurston County Superior Court position was perhaps as important to the governor as the vacancy on the state's court of last resort. By May 1918, an acceptable superior court candidate, John M. Wilson, was available, and Mitchell could be moved upstairs.[44]

Warren Winfield Tolman of Spokane had been a serious candidate for earlier appointments but was not well known on the west side of the state. As a former Chairman of the Spokane County Democratic Central Committe, member of the state senate (1901–5), candidate for Congress (1902), and a "Lister Democrat" (involved, like Clay Allen, in the struggles of the governor to gain control of the Democratic Party organization),[45] Tolman was known to the governor, and his party credentials were impeccable.

Tolman's endorsements were impressive. The Spokane Bar Association, a number of prominent attorneys, a former Senator, several judges, some Republicans, an official of a title and trust company, *The Spokane Spokesman Review* (eastern Washington's leading newspaper), dignitaries of the Washington Water Power Company, and a number of real estate officials all wrote in support of Tolman. There was some conjecture that Judge Blake would be appointed to the Webster vacancy and that Tolman would be appointed to Judge Bruce Blake's superior court position. However, Tolman had made it clear to Governor Lister that he would accept the lower court offer

44. *Spokane Spokesman Review*, May 12, 1918.
45. *Ibid.*

only if it would eventually lead to a supreme court position. The state's high bench was what he wanted: "My ambitions have been directed toward the Supreme Court and the salary there, though less than I am now making . . . [is adequate]."[46]

Blake actually led all others in the tally of endorsements, gathering at least seventy-four signatures. Tolman's name on Lister's tally sheet was supported by forty-six and Walter French by fifteen. Blake had written the governor in April 1918: "It has been my one ambition in life since I began to study law to at some time be on the Supreme Bench of the State of Washington." But Tolman had the better partisan credentials.[47] (Blake had to wait until the election of 1932 to achieve his lifelong ambition.)

The dictates of geography also came to Tolman's assistance. Judge Webster had been a Spokanite and it was generally felt that his replacement also ought to represent the state's second largest city. Tolman's appointment allowed him to join the court on May 11, 1918, the same day Judge Mitchell began his appointed term.

Republican Lieutenant Governor Louis F. Hart became governor upon Ernest Lister's death in June 1919. He had assumed responsibility for the executive branch several months earlier when Lister's health prevented his continuing the strenuous task of governing. As acting chief executive, Hart was able to make his first appointment to the supreme bench.

Chief Justice Stephen J. Chadwick tendered his resignation in May 1919, in order to join the prestigious Seattle law firm of Hughes, McMicken, Ramsey, and Rupp. Always a popular state figure, Democrat Chadwick was actually preparing to run for the U.S. Senate. Written in pencil on the bottom of the governor's letter to Chadwick, acknowledging receipt of the letter of resignation, was the name "Bridges."[48]

Jessie B. Bridges had been prominent in legal circles but was a political neophyte. In his only run for public office he had been elected prosecuting attorney for Grays Harbor in 1895. However, he was the "best known lawyer in southwest Washington," had served on many state bar association committees, wrote the probate

46. *Lister Papers*, "Judiciary" file.

47. On November 14, 1916, Governor Lister had written Tolman thanking him for his support in the November balloting. The governor hinted at his indebtedness to Tolman: "My great hope now is that the administration of the State's affairs, during the coming four years, will be such that those who supported me so loyally during the campaign will never have cause to regret their action." At the bottom of the letter was a handwritten sentence: "I want to thank you for the good work you did in my behalf," signed "Lister" (*ibid.*).

48. *Hart Papers*. State Archives, File RGII-8, Box 36, May 26, 1919.

code which the legislature adopted in 1917, built a reputation as a corporate attorney, and had been president of the Washington State Bar Association (1908). Although a nominal Republican, Bridges had not been active in partisan politics.[49] Bridges' appointment appeared to have had nothing to do with political activities. He was chosen primarily if not exclusively for his legal talents and leadership of the bar, the first to be chosen for these characteristics alone. Perhaps Hart's status as "acting" governor constrained him from making a purely political appointment.

Justice Wallace Mount had been seriously ill for a considerable period of time in 1921. An ailing heart curtailed his court work in February and forced him from all court duties in March.[50] Governor Hart appointed Republican Chester R. Hovey of Ellensburg to fill the vacancy. Hovey was forty-five years old, had not been active in politics, and, like Bridges, had not held any political office except that of prosecuting attorney for Kittitas County from 1889 to 1901 and again from 1910 to 1912. Judge Mount's long illness had allowed for a considerable number of supreme court aspirants to contact the governor's office, and Hart had a long list from which to choose.[51] Hovey had universal support from the legal profession. A few months before he accepted the high court appointment he had been elected president of the Washington State Bar Association.

With the possible exception of the fact that he was from eastern Washington (Mount had been from Spokane), no political factors appeared to be associated with Hovey's appointment.[52] Like Hart's appointment of Bridges in 1919, merit and wide support from the bar accounted for Hovey's selection. Certainly Governor Hart had no dearth of worthy political figures on the list to fill Mount's vacancy.

Hovey had gained a reputation in water and irrigation law. His unpopular but able defense of a few landowners who were fighting an irrigation project in Ellensburg had won him the praise of his legal colleagues but the condemnation of some of his clients and neighbors. "It was the knowledge of his courageous action on Judge Hovey's part which in large part led Governor Hart to tender Hovey an appointment to this Court."[53]

49. *The Seattle Daily Times*, May 27, 1919.

50. Wallace Mount died on September 5, 1921.

51. *The Seattle Post-Intelligencer*, September 8, 1921.

52. Governor Hart wrote G. W. Nash (President of Washington State Normal School) that "I felt in fairness to all of the state that Judge Mount's successor should come from East of the Mountains" (Letter dated September 9, 1921, *Hart Papers*, "Supreme Court" files).

53. Address by Otto B. Rupp at Memorial Services in honor of Judge Hovey in Olympia at the Temple of Justice, May 2, 1955.

Republican governor Roland H. Hartley (1925–33) was the first chief executive to serve a full two terms and to run for a third. He also had the distinction of appointing more supreme court judges than any previous governor. (Since then, both Langlie and Evans have made eight appointments.) Although a volatile and partisan executive, Hartley's appointments to the high bench often disregarded partisan considerations.

Justice Oscar Raymond Holcomb, a Democrat defeated at the polls in September 1926, after twelve years of service on the Supreme Court, was promptly returned to the high bench in April 1927 by Hartley to fill the vacancy created by the death of J. B. Bridges. Although the appointment raised a few eyebrows among members of the governor's own party, the considerations that went into the selection were not unique. Holcomb was from eastern Washington (Ritzville) and had been practicing law in Seattle only since his defeat in September. His appointment would redress the geographical imbalance favoring the west side of the state. Justices Fullerton and Tolman were at that moment the only representatives of eastern Washington.[54]

Democrats had assisted Hartley in turning back a serious recall effort mounted by dissidents in his own party the previous year. Appointing a Democrat would give some recognition to that assistance. Also, Justice Bridges had been intermittently absent from the court over the months before his death. By promptly appointing the experienced and hard-working Holcomb, the court could begin immediately to attack its docket.[55] Governor Hartley was purging his own administration of disloyal department heads and cabinet members exactly when the court vacancy occurred, and he likely did not welcome an extended screening of a great number of judicial aspirants.[56] Additionally, Holcomb had had the support of the bar in his September bid for reelection. Clearly, he was available, competent, and above controversy. The appointment seemed not all that out of the ordinary under the circumstances.

Hartley's next appointee, William J. Millard, had been a leader in the Washington State Bar Association (Secretary-Treasurer 1920–28), secretary-clerk for the Supreme Court (1917–19), and, finally, librarian for the Supreme Court since 1919. In this latter capacity he was known to all those who served on and practiced before the state's

54. *The Seattle Post-Intelligencer*, April 16, 1927.

55. Because of the crowded docket "members [of the court] . . . expressed the hope that the governor would not delay action beyond a reasonable time" (*The Seattle Daily Times*, April 17, 1927).

56. The appointment was to become official on April 19. But because the governor couldn't remember O. R. Holcomb's initials, the commission had to be corrected and the appointment delayed until April 22 (*ibid.*, April 20, 1927).

Table 4.4
Supreme Court Appointments, 1927–32

Justice	*Governor*	*Date*
Oscar R. Holcomb (D)	Hartley (R)	April 22, 1927
William J. Millard (R)	Hartley	December 1, 1928
Walter B. Beals (R)	Hartley	April 16, 1928
Adam Beeler (R)	Hartley	September 30, 1930
Henry E. T. Herman (R)	Hartley	September 23, 1931
William J. Steinert (R)	Hartley	May 23, 1932

highest bench, having assisted in researching many of the legal matters before the Supreme Court. Although a Republican, Millard had not been involved in partisan politics and had not been implicated in the pro- and anti-Hartley split in the Republican ranks. His appointment in January 1928 to fill the vacancy left by Justice Askren's resignation, again seemed based more upon experience and competency than upon politics. As with the selection of Holcomb, Millard could be counted on to help the court move forward on its docket immediately without the need for a period of transition.

Governor Hartley's appointment of Judge Walter Beals in April 1928 seemed also to be of a nonpartisan and nonpolitical nature. Beals was a highly popular King County Superior Court judge of Republican leanings, although far from being an activist in the G.O.P. The political advantage of the Beals appointment, however, was important to the governor. He could gain praise for remaining above petty politics by elevating the respected Beals to the high bench and at the same time create a vacancy at the less conspicuous superior court level which he could then fill with a political appointee. As with Governor Lister's appointment of Mackintosh in 1918, the spot vacated by Beals allowed Hartley to reward one of his consistent supporters. On the same day in April, Hartley announced the selection of Judge Beals to the Supreme Court and of Adam Beeler to the King County Superior Court bench.

Adam Beeler was extremely active in Republican politics. He had served in the state legislature for three terms, had been "identified with the Hartley organization in the House," had sought the lieutenant governorship nomination in 1924, and was a serious candidate for that position again in 1928.[57] However, another Hartley supporter, state Senator Paul Houser, was interested in the second

57. *Ibid.*, March 7, 1928.

spot on the Republican ticket in 1928. If Beeler pursued his candidacy for lieutenant governor, the King County vote would be split, thereby permitting a possible anti-Hartley candidate on the ticket. The Beals and Beeler appointments would clear the way for Houser. The possibility was not lost on the governor.[58]

A year and a half later, on September 16, 1930, Judge Adam Beeler was promoted to the Supreme Court to succeed Walter French who had died of a heart ailment but three days earlier.[59] Because of the timing of the appointment, a question arose concerning the need for a special election in November. The Supreme Court ruled that Beeler would have to stand for election in November to finish out the remaining two years of French's unexpired term.[60] A "sticker" or write-in campaign was quickly organized, and Beeler handily defeated four other aspirants.

Geography and politics played equal roles in Hartley's appointment of Henry E. T. Herman, a prominent member of the Spo-

58. *Ibid.* "Clearing the field for State Senator Paul W. Houser as administration candidate for lieutenant governor, Governor Hartley, yesterday announced the advancement of Judge Walter B. Beals . . . to the vacancy of the Supreme Court bench and Beeler to Beal's opening on the Superior Court Bench. Four years ago Beeler and Charles H. Heighton both of Seattle split the West Side votes for lieutenant governor sufficiently to allow W. Lon Johnson of Colville to win. A fight between Beeler and Houser threatened a similar situation this year" (*The Seattle Post-Intelligencer*, March 8, 1928).

59. Governor Hartley was again provided with a double opportunity. With the promotion of Beeler to the high bench, an opening was created for another appointment at the superior court level. "Attorney John B. Van Dyke is reported to be seriously considered by Governor Hartley for appointment to the King County bench succeeding Justice Beeler. For some time it has been known in political circles that the governor has been anxious to place Van Dyke upon the State Court bench and the elevation of Justice Beeler affords this opportunity" (*The Seattle Daily Times*, September 19, 1930).

60. *State Ex Rel. Rummens* v. *Superior Court* (160 Wash. 520, 1932). The "sticker" campaign referred to the use of gummed slips of papers with the candidates names already printed on them simply to be pasted on the appropriate space on the ballots. The appointment by Governor Hartley was announced on September 16, and Beeler resigned as King County Superior Court judge on September 30. Thus the appointment was made after the September primary but barely within the thirty-day statutory requirements before the final November balloting. After failing to get the governor to call a special election in which all candidates could be listed, and losing at the state supreme court level in an effort to postpone the election until two years hence, Beeler and his supporters mounted a write-in campaign. Bruce Blake and Judge A. W. Hawkins withdrew their names and threw their support to Beeler. Beeler was endorsed by several county bars, the Washington State Federation of Labor, and "various organizations of women, veterans and business men." Six of the most populous counties used voting machines in 1930, creating difficulties for Beeler's campaign. "The arrangement of the paper rolls [in the write-in spaces of the machine] is such that a few stickers will prevent them from operating. Election inspectors have been notified to allow no stickers to be taken into the machines. But any voter needing assistance can call upon election officials for help" (*The Seattle Post-Intelligencer*, November 4, 1930).

kane bar, to replace Mark Fullerton. Fullerton was from eastern Washington (Colfax), and the only east-siders remaining on the bench were Holcomb and Tolman.[61] Additionally, Herman had been active in Republican political circles and "[f]or a number of years, since before the first election of Hartley [had] been an outstanding supporter of the executive."[62] Herman had also ingratiated himself with the governor by providing the leadership in support of gubernatorial policies at several Republican conventions.

William Joseph Steinert, popular King County Superior Court judge, was the last Hartley appointment closing out the era of transition. Adam Beeler's political aspirations were apparently frustrated by his tenure on the state's high bench, and he resigned in May 1932 to make (as it turned out) an unsuccessful run for the United State Senate. Steinert had been active in Republican political circles but appeared not to aspire to higher elective office.[63] The appointment of Beeler's replacement that late in the year permitted only a few months preparation for the September primaries, and Steinert initially refused the offer. After an unsuccessful attempt to persuade at least one other superior court judge to accept the promotion, Hartley turned again to Steinert and, with heavy pressure from the sitting members of the Supreme Court, Steinert reluctantly accepted.[64] Political considerations were not entirely absent from the Steinert appointment, however. Hartley needed King County support in his reelection bid. He hoped that choosing the popular judge from Seattle would enhance his chances for remaining in the governor's chair.

Hartley's six appointments to the Supreme Court exemplified this era of the cleansing of the selection process of obvious and primary partisan concerns and the gradual acceptance of nonpartisanship. The governor's appointments showed a balance between political and nonpartisan concerns. Political motivations prompted the appointments of Beals, Beeler, and Herman. On the other hand, the appointments of Holcomb, Millard, and Steinert represented nonpolitical motivations where competency, judicial reputation, profes-

61. *The Seattle Daily Times*, September 21, 1931.

62. *Ibid.*, September 23, 1931, and *The Seattle Post-Intelligencer*, September 23, 1931.

63. Steinert had been "prominent in Republican Politics" (*The Seattle Daily Times*, May 22, 1932).

64. "[H]e is said to have rejected the appointment at least once. Following Steinert's original rejection of the offer, the place was held vacant and he was again approached, finally assenting a few days ago after persistent pressure from other members of the supreme court" (*The Seattle Post-Intelligencer*, May 21, 1932).

sional concerns, and the needs of the court dominated. Beals, a nonpolitical appointee, who nevertheless was named for political purposes, reflected a composite of Hartley's appointments. Beals's reputation as a competent, popular, and hard-working judge received serious consideration, but in addition his promotion to the high bench allowed the political appointment of Beeler to the lower court bench.

An independent gubernatorial role in the recruitment process was evolving. The governor no longer acted merely as an agent for legislative authorizations filling new or temporary positions on the Supreme Court. The governor invited his own counsel and mixed partisan motivations. Governors Lister and Hartley used appointments as rewards for loyal supporters. Governor Hartley chose from the leadership of the bar. These mixed and yet unpredictable motivations characterized recruitment during the transitional years.

Summary

The bar associations at all levels became a factor in the appointments of high court judges. Previously, individual attorneys had written in support of one candidate or another, and those finally selected at least had some support from segments of the bar. Evidence of organized bar influence now was found in Hart's two appointments of former presidents of the State Bar. Previously, endorsements had been crucial in the governor's final appointments. Now, although those selected by the governor had received a number of general endorsements, these petitions and letters had to share influence with another consideration as partisan politics gained in impact. Bausman, Mackintosh, Beals, Beeler, Tolman, and Herman ascended to the high bench primarily for political reasons. Political motivations were somewhat indirect in the cases of Mackintosh and Beals who were chosen in order to provide vacancies on the trial bench for close allies of the governor, while the others clearly were directly rewarded for political service and loyalty to the governor. Such obvious use of political rewards and maneuvers had been largely missing from the earlier appointments.

More groups with diverse interests were active in recruitment during this period of transition. More participants were making their voices heard in the governor's deliberations. The bar, gubernatorial politics, and partisanship interacted to elevate a number of the newer members of the Supreme Court. Although those appointed for purely partisan reasons were far from incompetent, it is likewise clear that competence and professionalism were also recognized in such appointments as those of Holcomb, Millard, and Steinert.

This era of transition saw also a rise in the influence of the bar in the electoral process. The beginnings of a bar poll and of formal bar endorsements were evident. However, those attorneys who individually endorsed judicial candidates, and those members of the bar associations who did so collectively, were still not the only interested parties using their names and positions in an attempt to influence the selection process. In a sense the bar was simply another pressure group striving for access both to the governor and to the electorate through the vehicle of endorsements. Still unsure of itself, the legal profession was beginning to awaken to the opportunities for influencing election results provided by the nonpartisan direct primary system. The electorate assumed more of a symbolic role in the primary and general elections. Fewer voters participated in primary judicial elections and fewer yet in the general elections, because most of the real contests were settled in the primaries, leaving little incentive for voter participation in the November balloting. Incumbents, whether initially appointed or elected, dominated the winner's list.

By the end of 1932 the interactions in initiating, screening, and affirming supreme court aspirants had become fairly complex with more participants making contributions throughout the process, although such participation was often still tentative. Supreme court recruitment was in a transitional phase.

5

The Supreme Court in Times of Stress, 1933–49

Worldwide events shaped the course of the state's highest bench for the next two decades as they shaped the course of virtually all of American politics. The year 1932 saw the voters of the state cast aside the Republicans and commission the Democrats to deal with the dislocations of the Great Depression. As politicians and the public struggled to meet the demands of the economic crisis, the Second World War was thrust upon them with all its dangers and unpredictabilities. These indeed were times of stress.

Gubernatorial Appointments

Clarence D. Martin assumed the reins of state government in 1933 as part of the Democratic tide that swept the country. In his inaugural address Governor Martin set the tone for the new era:

> [The purpose of my administration will be to] change the spirit that rules Olympia so that the people may know that the state government of Washington no longer is purely political, but primarily economic.[1]

Martin's first and most important cabinet appointment as director of the Department of Efficiency was former Spokane Corporate Counsel James M. Geraghty. Geraghty had "long been an important factor in Democratic state affairs," had been "an old friend of the Governor," and was his "chief political adviser."[2]

1. Division of Archives and Records Management, *Washington State Archives Guide to the Governor's papers 1853–1976* (1977), 51.

2. *The Seattle Daily Times*, August 15, 1933. The three leading figures around Governor Martin were: Geraghty, who had known the governor for years, had been instrumental in persuading the governor to run for office, and had managed his campaign; Donald A. McDonald, majority leader of the House of Representatives in

In dire need of additional revenues to fund public education—there was fear that in September of the next year schools would not be able to open—the people had approved an income tax measure (Initiative 69) the previous November, and in 1933 the Democrat-dominated legislature passed a business and occupation tax which had been a crucial part of the administration's revenue program.[3] Both measures were immediately challenged in the courts. With the ailing Emmett Parker absent, the Supreme Court had split 4-4 on the constitutionality of both measures. Rehearings were scheduled for the next term.[4] On August 8, 1933, Justice Parker submitted his letter of resignation, and six days later Governor Martin announced the appointment of his loyal director of efficiency, James M. Geraghty, to the vacancy.[5]

Despite the political motivations of the appointment, at the swearing-in ceremony on August 15, Governor Martin urged his close friend to "call them as you see them" and promised that his commission was "without any strings attached." Martin concluded appropriately: "Jim, I want you to know that you are free as the air. I know you will use your own judgment at all times." Predictably, Geraghty responded: "I am glad you said that. If I didn't know you felt that way I wouldn't have accepted this appointment."[6] Perhaps both were sincere, but nonetheless both knew that on "Geraghty's shoulders [rested] the responsibility of breaking a deadlock over the case instituted to test the validity of the two laws."[7]

Olympia and old fraternity brother and classmate; and George F. Yantis, Speaker of the House of Representatives.

3. The B & O tax provided $6 million for public education and the income tax measure earmarked $1 million for schools.

4. On June 15, 1933, Chief Justice Beals announced that the Supreme Court was deadlocked over the income tax measure and the case was held under advisement or until all nine justices could hear the case. Judges Mitchell, Millard, and Steinert dissented from the decision. They maintained that since the court could not agree, the lower court's decision stood. This meant that, as decided by the lower court, the income tax would be in violation of the Fourteenth Amendment to the state constitution that required all direct taxes to be uniform on all categories of property (*Culliton v. Chase* [173 Wash. 309, 1933]).

5. Donald A. McDonald of Seattle was the only other person seriously considered for the appointment.

6. *The Seattle Post-Intelligencer*, August 16, 1933. No formal agreement had been negotiated yet between the Washington Bar Association and the governor to collaborate on appointments where initiation and screening were shared by the two. But during the same week that Governor Martin was considering the two serious contenders for the Parker vacancy (McDonald and Geraghty), the State Bar was holding its annual convention in Spokane. Their support was clearly for James Geraghty: "His name was discussed at the meeting of the Washington State Bar Association here last week and the judgment of the lawyers was that Mr. Geraghty is well fitted for the job" (*The Spokane Spokesman Review*, August 15, 1933).

7. *The Spokane Spokesman Review*, August 15, 1933. Geraghty apparently welcomed

Chief Justice Walter Beals rescheduled an earlier rehearing on the two cases, and the fate of the governor's revenue program was again up to the judges. Martin's appointment of Geraghty was vindicated when, three weeks after his appointment, Geraghty broke the deadlock and the business and occupation tax was validated. However, the court struck down the income tax initiative with Geraghty dissenting.[8]

Apparently Governor Martin's uneasiness over the purely political aspects of his initial appointment led him to reconsider the methods and criteria for filling subsequent vacancies on the benches of the state. Previous governors had granted some deference to the legal profession through its county bar associations by seeking advice on superior court appointments. And now and then leaders of the state's professional group were asked for assistance on supreme court appointees, but no formal arrangements had been negotiated prior to any appointments. Subsequent to the Geraghty appointment, the heretofore separate activities of the legal profession and the governor's office converged to create a cooperative appointment process whereby mutually acceptable persons were elevated to the Supreme Court. The legal profession continued to pursue independent projects designed to influence or change the election of judges, but the attorneys succeeded in institutionalizing their relationship with the chief executive in the recruitment of persons to fill vacancies on the state's high bench. Attorney Elias A. Wright, chairman of the bar's Committee on the Selection of Judges and Bar Activities Related Thereto, recognized the arrangement forged with the governor at the 1936 State Bar Convention:

> There have been no judicial vacancies in our State in the last year, and, of course, it has not been necessary to collaborate with the Governor in a decision for the appointment of a successor in any instance. The

---

the opportunity provided by the supreme court appointment. He discovered that the political advising, decision making, and style in Olympia were considerably different from those back at city hall in Spokane. Certainly he could continue to advise his old friend Governor Martin from his office in the Temple of Justice. A close friend in the legal profession, Frank Truman Post, wrote the judge shortly after his appointment: "I felt that the political job [Director of Efficiency] you were going to take would not be satisfactory to you and that you would not be entirely happy therein. I am glad that you have had the opportunity to get out of the job and take an office which I believe you will enjoy" (Letter dated August 31, 1933, Geraghty family letter file).

8. In *Culliton* v. *Chase* (174 WASH. 363, 1933), the majority of Holcomb, Main, Mitchell, Millard, and Steinert invalidated the income tax with Geraghty voting with the minority. In *State Ex Rel. Stiner* v. *Yelle* (174 WASH. 402, 1933), Geraghty joined the majority composed of Tolman, Beals, Holcomb, and Blake to uphold the B & O measure. Holcomb appears to have switched his vote on the income tax measure between the original deadlocked decision of June 15 and this September 8 ruling.

Chairman has talked with Governor Martin a number of times, and the intercourse has been very pleasant, harmonious and cooperating.[9]

The George B. Simpson appointment the next year inaugurated the new arrangement for appointments to the court of last resort. On August 16, 1937, Justice Warren W. Tolman announced his intention to retire effective September 20, giving Governor Martin over a month to recruit a replacement. On prior arrangement with the Washington State Bar Association, the governor asked for the advice of the bar's standing Committee on the Selection of Judges. The committee either suggested or, at the very least, approved the appointment of Clark County Superior Court Judge George B. Simpson. Simpson had been a well-respected member of both the profession and the bench and was active in the bar associations (he had been president of the Clark-Skamania County Bar for three terms). Although a Democrat, he had not been active in partisan politics nor was he tied closely with the governor or his policies. In contrast with Martin's first appointment, in his appointment of Simpson partisan and political motivations were secondary with much credit due to the intervention of the bar's selection committee. Governor Martin did, however, reward a loyal supporter, Charles W. Hall, former state senator and counsel who argued for the business and occupation tax in 1933, with appointment to the Simpson vacancy on the trial bench.

In response to the Simpson appointment, the chairman of the Committee on the Selection of Judges reported to the lawyers assembled at the 1938 annual convention that "We had a very agreeable consultation with the Governor in collaboration, having to do with the appointment to fill a vacancy on the Supreme Court,"[10] and that the committee members were pleased with Simpson's promotion to the state's court of last resort.

The practice previously common for the appointment of superior court judges was now adopted by the State Bar and the governor for the recruitment of justices to the Supreme Court. To this day the practice persists.[11]

9. Report of the Committee on Selection of Judges and Bar Activities, *State Bar Review* 2 (1936): 85.

10. Report of the Committee on Selection of Judges, *Washington Law Review & State Bar Journal* 13 (1938): 286.

11. From the Simpson appointment until and including that of Justice Durham in 1985, twenty-nine judges were elevated to the state's high bench by governors. Of these, six failed to receive the bar's approval but largely because the governors neglected to ask the lawyers for their approval or because the appointees had already won election to the court. With the appointments they could begin their terms a few weeks sooner.

Table 5.1
Supreme Court Appointments, 1933–46

Justice	*Governor*	*Date*
James M. Geraghty (D)	Martin (D)	August 15, 1933
George B. Simpson (D)	Martin	September 20, 1937
Samuel M. Driver (D)	Martin	May 9, 1940
Joseph A. Mallery (R)	Langlie (R)	November 9, 1942
*Thomas E. Grady (R)	Langlie	November 25, 1942
Edward M. Connelly (D)	Wallgren (D)	April 22, 1946
E. W. Schwellenbach (D)	Wallgren	September 3, 1946
*Don G. Abel (D)	Wallgren	November 7, 1946

*Temporary appointments

Governor Martin's last appointment to the Supreme Court was to replace his first appointee. James Geraghty died suddenly on April 29, 1940, and in less than two weeks the governor elevated Samuel M. Driver to the Supreme Court. Driver had long experience in Democratic politics as secretary to Congressman Sam B. Hill, as Deputy Prosecutor of Spokane County, and, after several years of private practice, as U.S. Attorney for the Eastern District of Washington. Again, as with Simpson appointment, the bar played an important role in initiating and screening candidates. In their 1940 annual report to the bar convention, members of the Committee on the Selection of Judges reported that their recommendations were given "fair and considerate treatment by Governor Martin at all times." They added: ". . . however, other governors will be elected and it is quite possible . . . that in future times we will not have so happy a situation as we have had in the past."[12]

But with the election of Republican and fellow attorney Arthur B. Langlie in 1941, the "happy situation" continued. The State Bar found a sympathetic response to their appeals for a share in the recruitment of judges to fill vacancies at all levels of the state bench. Recognition of the close cooperation was given in the report of the State Bar's Committee on Selection of Judges to the 1941 annual gathering of the State Bar. Following closely the script of the previous year, J. P. Dillard reported for the committee:

> The State of Washington is fortunate in having Governor Langlie, who is a lawyer, as head of our state and who appreciates the service

12. Report of the Committee on Selection of Judges, *Washington Law Review & State Bar Journal* 15 (1940): 199–200.

> that the Washington State Bar Association can render him in assisting in the selection of capable lawyers as judges of the Supreme Court.[13]

However, Langlie's first opportunity to fill a vacancy on the high court provided him and the bar with little choice. Pierce County Superior Court judge Joseph A. Mallery ran a close second to incumbent John F. Main in the 1942 primary balloting. Ill health prompted Main to refuse nomination, moving Mallery to the November ballot without opposition and thus assured of victory. On October 13, Justice Main passed away, and Langlie appointed Mallery to finish out the few weeks remaining in Main's term since the seat would be Mallery's anyway in January by virtue of his electoral victory.

Governor Langlie's second appointment was to fill a temporary position vacated by Samuel Driver, who was granted a leave of absence to enter the armed services in World War II. His appointee, Thomas E. Grady, had served as president of the Yakima Bar and in 1940 as the President of the Washington State Bar. By prior arrangement, Governor Langlie solicited the assistance of the Washington State Bar to initiate and screen candidates for the temporary vacancy. "Upon recommendation of the . . . State Bar Association's committee for the selection of judges, Grady was appointed." Grady's recommendation from the bar was "based . . . on [his] years experience as a trial lawyer and trial judge, and on his familiarity with the legal problems arising in a diversified agricultural community."[14] The fact that he was a Republican simplified the appointment.

In 1945 Monrad C. Wallgren became the first U.S. Senator and also the first U.S. Congressman to be elected governor. Democrat Wallgren appointed three members of the state's high bench during his short tenure, and all were selected within a five-month period in 1946. Samuel Driver, a few months after his return from military service, was appointed to the federal bench by President Truman. Governor Wallgren promptly selected Democrat Edward M. Connelly to fill the vacancy. Connelly was regarded as a brilliant trial lawyer and had served as prosecuting attorney for Pacific County and deputy prosecutor for Spokane County before being appointed U.S. Attorney for the Eastern District of Washington. "He always had a great interest in politics, where he took a foremost part. . . ."[15] Although few challenged Connelly's credentials, the organized bar

13. *Ibid.*, 16 (1941).
14. *The Seattle Times*, August 1, 1948.
15. *Washington Reports.*

was highly critical of the governor for failing to consult them. Henry Elliott, chairman of the bar's selection committee, reported to his fellow attorneys in 1946:

> Since [Wallgren] has assumed office he has received the suggestions and approved lists tendered by the committee, but he has been either unwilling or unable to promise or give the same cooperation which his predecessors gave. As a result the committee has received no pledge of policy and the appointments made have generally disregarded the recommendations and endorsements of the committee.[16]

Connelly's tenure on the high bench, however, was short-lived. Seven months later he was defeated in his first attempt to gain electoral approval.

Judge Blake announced his retirement effective September 1, 1946, prompting a heated primary campaign for his seat between Tom Grady and Edgar E. Schwellenbach, superior court judge of Grant-Douglas counties and member of a prominent eastern Washington political family. Schwellenbach was "an active and aggressive Democrat and took a prominent part in local, state and national party affairs."[17] He swamped Grady by over 80,000 votes in the July 9 primary, and rather than appointing someone else to the short vacancy between September and January (or leaving it unfilled), Governor Wallgren immediately selected Schwellenbach to finish out the few weeks left in Blake's term. This permitted Wallgren to be credited with appointing a fellow Democrat and allowed Schwellenbach to get started in his new post sooner than if he waited until January when he assumed his elected position on the bench. Again, the State Bar was not consulted, although little furor resulted simply because of the short tenure of the appointment and the fact that Schwellenbach would in any case soon assume the responsibilities of the office.

Partisanship played a role in Wallgren's last appointment, although the selection was only temporary. Walter Beals accepted a commission with the U.S. military authorities to serve as presiding judge of United States Military Tribunal No. 1 at Nuremberg, Germany, and assumed responsibility for overseeing the trial of twenty-three Nazi doctors charged with war crimes. Under the same statutory provision that authorized Judge Grady to temporarily occupy the spot vacated by Samuel Driver four years earlier, Gov-

16. Report of Committee on Selection of Judges, *Washington Law Review & State Bar Journal* 21 (1946): 250.
17. Memorial Services, 52 Wn 2d xviii (1958).

ernor Wallgren appointed Don G. Abel to fill in for Beals. Abel had been active in Democratic politics for several decades. In 1932 he had been a candidate for Congress and had served as Governor Martin's director of the Department of Public Service. In 1936, President Roosevelt had appointed him head of the Works Progress Administration for the State of Washington. In 1942 Abel showed his interest in the Supreme Court by attempting to unseat Judge John S. Robinson in the primary election. The selection of Abel may have pleased the Democrats but found little favor with the State Bar.[18]

In summary, Wallgren was able to select three judges to the state's high bench. One was picked simply because he was elected to the position and would soon assume its responsibilities; another was defeated in the November elections only seven months after his appointment; and the third was appointed to a temporary position that likely would not extend beyond a year. The bar association was not consulted on any of these appointments. According to Henry Elliott, chair of the State Bar's Committee on the Selection of Judges, initially the committee had been charged with "the task of securing more cooperation" between the governor and the bar. Hopefully, "the governor would appoint no persons . . . who did not have the approval of the bar." But the experience with Wallgren indicated the weakness of the arrangement. It had "no official standing" and "rested" solely upon the whole-hearted and voluntary cooperation . . . of the bar and the executive." The lawyers were urged to remain alert to alternative methods for selecting judges.[19]

The most striking aspect of the appointment process during these times of stress was the arrangement between the governor and the State Bar to consult closely on appointments. The agreement was simply that the governor promised not to appoint anyone who did not have the approval of the bar as determined by the profession's judicial selection committee. The function of the lawyers' committee was two-fold. The members would initiate and screen for the governor or, if the governor had an appointee in mind, the members would determine if he or she met the standards the bar felt necessary. The bar came to view their role as more of a right than a

18. Governor Wallgren was not altogether convinced that he was authorized to appoint a temporary replacement for Beals under the "Protection of Persons in Military and Naval Service" law of 1941 (Chapter 201, Session Laws, 1941, p. 592). It was unclear whether Beals' appointment to preside at Nuremberg constituted being "ordered into active service." However, the appointment of Abel remained unchallenged.

19. Report of the Committee on Selection of Judges, *Washington Law Review & State Bar Journal* 21 (1946): 249.

privilege granted them by the state's chief executive, but it required years to develop mutual trust before such a "right" was recognized by the governor.

The Bar: Efforts toward an Expanded Role

The legal profession, through its state organization and through its largest local affiliate—the Seattle Bar Association—expanded its activities beyond the roles of advising the governor on appointments and of providing the nucleus for election campaign organizations. For many attorneys the need was for a change in the formal means by which judges were selected: they thought the state constitution should be amended to replace nonpartisan primary elections and the gubernatorial appointment system. For others the task was to work within the present system to gain a larger voice in appointments and elections.

Two national movements in the profession spurred the bar's efforts. In 1933 the Washington State Bar Association became one of the earlier state organizations to join the national movement toward unified or integrated bars.[20] Under an integrated bar every attorney in the state must be a member of the bar in order to practice law. Compulsory membership (or the closed shop) provided the profession with considerable clout with the public and the legislature. One of the areas of enhanced influence would be in the selection of judges. Now the Washington State Bar could speak for all the attorneys in the state. Additionally, the American Judicature Society conducted a nationwide campaign in 1934 on behalf of its commission plan for the selection of judges, subsequently known as the American Bar Association Plan, the Merit Plan, or the Missouri Plan.[21] The Washington attorneys had some familiarity with the American Judicature Society's plan as early as 1925, but until 1934 had not formally pushed for a constitutional amendment that would institute the plan.[22]

One of the major standing committees in the newly unified bar was the Committee for the Selection of Judges and Bar Activities

20. An act to create an association to be known as the "Washington State Bar Association"; to provide for its organization, government, membership and powers; to regulate the practice of law and to provide penalties for the violation of said act (Chapter 94, Session Laws, 1933, p. 397). For an analysis of the development of the unified bar movement see D. McKean, *The Integrated Bar* (Boston: Houghton Mifflin, 1963).

21. G. R. Winters, "The Merit Plan for Judicial Selection and Tenure—Its Historical Development," G. Winters, *Judicial Selection and Tenure: Selected Readings* (Chicago: American Judicature Society, 1973), 29.

22. *Proceedings of the Washington State Bar Association* (1925), 44.

Related Thereto. Although previous judicial committees had been appointed at the urging of the membership to investigate problems relating to the selection of judges, now, with continuing membership and the backing of what appeared to be a unified profession, the committee took over permanently the responsibility of overseeing the recruitment of judges.

The first task of the new standing committee was to ascertain the degree of dissatisfaction with judicial recruitment among the general membership. What were their attitudes toward judicial selection? In October 1934 the results of a bar referendum indicated that the attorneys of the state were willing to move ahead on judicial selection reform. Of those responding, 66% (1,120) favored a change in how judges were selected. A commission plan won slight approval over gubernatorial appointment as the preferred change.[23] The committee had its mandate, however slight, to draft and urge upon the state legislature and the people a constitutional amendment that would effectively remove the voting public from the screening and affirming phases of the recruitment process by eliminating the direct primary and relieving the governor of sole responsibility for appointments. The committee's initial proposal brought judicial selection under the control of an independent commission composed of the governor, the board of governors of the bar association, and three voters appointed by the governor.[24]

The bar conducted its campaign for the judical commission on two fronts. In August 1934, Governor Martin created an Advisory Constitutional Revision Commission consisting of "nine public spirited citizens" who were to "outline the amendments [to the constitution] necessary to open the way for the reorganization, consolidation and modernization of . . . government."[25] The bar's selection committee consulted with and testified before the governor's group, urging members to adopt the bar's commission plan. Although the constitutional commission accepted a version of the bar's proposal, the legislature showed no interest. Additionally, the bar moved on its own toward gaining legislative approval of a constitutional amendment. Although the reception of the joint judiciary committee in the legislature was cordial, no proposal emerged.[26]

23. *The State Bar Review* 1 (1934): 11. The Commission plan description in the bar questionnaire was: "Do you favor [changes] to provide for the appointment of Supreme and Superior Judges by a commission consisting of the Governor . . . the governors of the state bar association, and three electors to be appointed by the governor?"

24. *The State Bar Review* 1 (1935): 23.

25. P. Beckett, *From Wilderness to Enabling Act: The Evolution of the State of Washington* (Pullman: Washington State University Press, 1968).

26. *The State Bar Review* 2 (1935): 7.

Undaunted by these failures, the Committee on Selection of Judges and Bar Activities Related Thereto again submitted the same commission plan to the next legislature. Some urgency was expressed by the chairman of the committee as he anticipated some of the unacceptable antics likely to be used in the September and November 1936 elections. Violations of Canon 28 of the American Bar Association were likely, and candidates advocating the Townsend Plan, the Old Age Pension, and other political policies would undoubtedly threaten incumbent judges and other worthy judicial aspirants. As a result of these "crass" forms of politics, "the members of the Bar will be more thoroughly disgusted with our present system."[27] But again, the proposal never was reported out of the legislative committees even though the bar had laid some groundwork and had rewritten the proposal "to meet all questions."[28]

An appraisal of the chances of the constitutional proposal achieving approval in the 1939 legislature led the committee to withhold it from consideration, as "there will not be sufficient support for that bill." Modifications were made and approved by the board of governors of the bar, which provided not only for broader participation in the selection process than under the earlier commission plan, but also for less drastic revision of the present system.[29] However, the modified plan (H.J.R. 11) failed to be approved and was never reported out of committee largely, the bar leaders felt, because it was submitted to the legislature too late in the session.[30] However, the successful working relationship with Governors Martin and Langlie on appointments gave the attorneys some hope.

By 1946 the reluctance of Governor Wallgren to collaborate with the selection committee stimulated renewed efforts to change the constitution. In a long and thorough report to the annual meeting of the State Bar in 1946, longtime chairman of the selection committee Henry Elliott reviewed the history of the bar's activities. He generally concluded that what had been accomplished depended too much on the whims of the governor in appointments, and on the political biases of the voters in elections. Therefore, he urged the bar to adopt the American Judicature Society's and the American Bar Association's version of the merit plan and to work toward its approval in the legislature. The plan, briefly, provided for (1) nomination of judges by a special commission composed of three lawyers, three laypersons, and the state's chief justice; (2) appointment by the governor from a list of three nominees submitted by the commis-

27. *Ibid.*, 2 (1936): 85.
28. *Washington Law Review & State Bar Journal* 11 (1937): 225.
29. *Ibid.*, 14 (1939): 262.
30. *Ibid.*, 263.

sion; and (3) final approval or disapproval by the voters, the appointee running on his record only. If the electors voted adversely, the process began again when the commission submitted new names to the governor.[31]

The board of governors of the bar unanimously approved the committee's recommendation, and the State Bar Association adopted the recommendation at its annual meeting without dissent. The State Bar was now committed to conduct a program of education "to the end that responsible groups of citizens may be led to consider the merits of the proposed plan and to support" the bar in its efforts before the legislature.[32]

Despite the unanimous support expressed by the bar in 1946, reactions were not as clear as might have been anticipated. The pros and cons of the American Bar Association plan were thoroughly debated at the 1947 convention. No recommendation came out of the deliberations, but it was clear that the unanimity of the previous year had broken down. The opportunity for constitutional change had come and gone.

The activities of the organized legal profession were not limited to effectuating formal constitutional revisions. A logical division of labor was evolving in the 1930s and 1940s between the State Bar and its county and city affiliates. While the unified State Bar worked with governmental officials to change the constitution or to reach an agreement with the governor on appointments, county bar groups led by the Seattle (King County) bar acted independently of the state leadership to devise methods to influence the voting public. Although the Seattle attorneys had previously conducted polls on an *ad hoc* basis, in 1928 they gave serious consideration to a permanent "bar primary" whereby the membership would be polled on their preferences for King County judicial candidates, with the results released to the media.[33] On June 29, 1932, the Seattle Bar finally adopted the bar primary concept, and under the auspices of its "Plebiscite Committee," the results of an August 23, 1932, poll were released. The poll was limited to superior court positions in King County, but clearly established this technique as an effective means of advising the voting public.

The Seattle Bar publicized its poll by radio and newspapers. Its ads in the *Seattle Times* and *Seattle Post-Intelligencer* read:

31. A history of the Missouri Plan and its political impact is found in R. Watson and R. Downing, *The Politics of the Bench and Bar* (New York: Wiley, 1969).
32. *Washington Law Review & State Bar Journal* 21 (1946): 255.

> JUDGING THE JUDGES
> The lawyers in their own primary held August 23, 1932, expressed their composite conviction by a very definite vote that the following named judicial candidates are best qualified:

The ad then provided the list of approved candidates and also stated:

> This information is offered in response to innumerable requests for the opinion of lawyers as to the qualifications of judicial candidates. The business of the lawyers is to do your law business well. This cannot be done without good judges.[34]

Similarly, the 1934 press release reported the results of its plebiscite and argued that voters should take the advice of attorneys as seriously as they would if doctors were advising on which surgeon to choose to perform an operation.

> Doctors know about the work and capabilities of their fellow doctors; just so with engineers and flyers and bankers and lawyers. The collective judgment of over 800 attorneys is the best guide to the voters.[35]

Although the Seattle Bar's poll failed to rate the candidates for the Supreme Court, other county bar organizations were not reluctant to express their collective preferences. Three methods characterized their efforts, some of which were also used by the Seattle Bar. First, unlike the Seattle organization's formalized poll, many of the other county bars held straw votes or informal plebiscites at regular or specially called meetings, resulting in some vague numbers which nonetheless became part of the supreme court campaigns. For example, the 1932 campaign of Warren Tolman depended to a great extent upon these endorsements. Typical quotes from news releases were: "endorsed by practically every member of the local bar," "virtually unanimous," "accorded general support," "endorsed by a large majority of the members."[36]

Second, members of the profession would mail cards urging their

33. From notes taken from the files of the Seattle Bar Association office. The late Helen Geisness, longtime executive secretary of the Seattle Bar, graciously assisted in tracing the involvement of the Seattle Bar in polling.
34. *The Seattle Times*, September 12, 1932.
35. Seattle Bar Association judicial primary files.
36. From Warren W. Tolman Scrapbook, Washington State University Library Manuscripts & Archives Division, Pullman, Washington.

clients to vote for particular candidates.[37] Members also sent out letters to their clients and friends under their law firm letterheads urging support for those candidates receiving bar endorsements.[38]

Finally, members of the profession readily consented to endorse candidates and have these endorsements published in paid advertisements in local newspapers. For example, the 1936 candidacy of John S. Robinson was enhanced by a full-length and three-column-wide newspaper ad which stated: "The following is a partial list of the lawyers of King County endorsing Mr. Robinson as possessing outstanding ability, character and fitness for the bench." A list of over 600 names was attached.[39] The next logical step by the State Bar Association would be to consolidate these separate activities (the Seattle Bar Poll, county bar straw votes, attorney recommendations, and endorsement lists) with a statewide bar primary. As we shall shortly see, events of 1947 and 1948 forced this logic upon the profession.

The concerted efforts of the State Bar to effectuate constitutional change to bring the selection of judges under the control of a form of the American Bar Association Plan reached its zenith in the mid-1940s. Subsequently, the plan had its strong advocates and was repeatedly urged upon the bar, the legislators, and the public, but it failed to gain effective support during this period. Several reasons can be suggested for the waning enthusiasm. First, the concerns of observers of the Supreme Court were diverted for the next few years toward the internal politics of the court and toward the election process as a means of rectifying the situation. Second, Arthur Langlie was returned to the governor's mansion, and a level of cooperation was reached between him and the bar which up to that time had not been matched, and, some would argue, has not since been achieved. Finally, under the leadership of the Seattle Bar, the profession turned its attention toward swaying the voters in judicial elections by means of a highly publicized "bar primary." In sum, the organized bar's enthusiasm for constitutional change was replaced

37. E. L. Skeel of the law firm of Roberts, Skeel & Holman sent the following letter to over five hundred clients: "I urge that you take special care to express your preference for the candidates for judicial office. . . . I stated in my letter before the primaries that it was the duty of attorneys to inform their friends and clients as to the qualifications of those who are candidates for election for judicial positions. This is for the reason that attorneys actively practicing at the bar are in a position to secure information not ordinarily available to the layman. With this thought in mind, I again take the liberty to indicate my preference for the contested position" (*ibid.*).

38. For example, the firm of Palmer, Askren & Brethorst sent cards worded: "We would appreciate your vote for the following judicial candidates: Warren W. Tolman, O. R. Holcomb, William J. Steinert, Henry E. T. Herman (*ibid.*).

39. *The Seattle Times*, November 1, 1936.

with a disposition toward easier and perhaps more effective means of influencing judicial recruitment.

Elections: A Return to Partisanship?

As in earlier times, the roll-off rate for both primary and general elections was substantial but, unlike before, the rate increased during these times of stress. Between 1912 and 1932 voter "fatigue" resulted in just over half the voters (51.5%) failing to mark their judicial ballots in the November elections as compared with 55.4% between 1934 and 1946. The roll-off for primaries from 1912 to 1932 was 31.4%, but in the subsequent period increased to 36.5%. Since the establishment of the nonpartisan ballot in general elections, the trend had been toward fewer of the voters participating in the affirmation of judicial aspirants. Thus, some of the earlier explanations account for the continued roll-off; however, some special factors add to the trend after 1932.

Part of the fluctuations illustrated in figure 5.1 are explained by the more visible and attractive presidential and gubernatorial races every four years that brought out a considerable number of voters who did not bother to vote for supreme court candidates. In the presidential years of 1932, 1936, 1940, 1944, and 1948, the roll-off increased in both primaries and general elections. Additionally, fewer voters were attracted to the supreme court contests than previously because there were fewer contested elections. Out of a possible twenty-five races, only five were contested in the general election (20%) as compared with 33% in the earlier period. Slightly

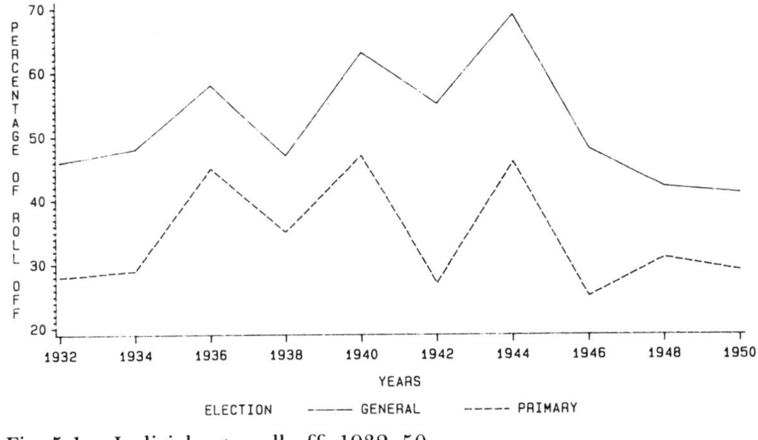

Fig. 5.1. Judicial vote roll-off, 1932–50

over half (52%) of the positions were challenged in the primaries as contrasted with nearly three-fourths (74%) previously. Such a decrease in meaningful competition accounted for part of the lack of voter interest. Also, the voter had to ask for the judicial ballot specifically since it was separate from the party ballots at the primaries. Many voters simply forgot. On the general election ballot, the judicial candidates were separated from the party candidates (although on the same ballot), and while a single mark could be made to vote for all candidates of one party, the voter had to vote specifically for each judicial candidate.

The State Grange, through the initiative process, successfully forced the legislature to institute a blanket primary for all political offices beginning with the 1936 election.[40] Rather than requiring voters to call for the ballot of one party or the other at the polling place, the new method allowed the voter to cast a nominating vote for candidates of any party. Crossing party lines became a common practice. The new blanket primary law also resulted in a new form for the nominating ballot. The form was changed from party lists to office groups (requiring the voter to cast ballots for each office separately). Additionally, the list of candidates for the nonpartisan Supreme Court was the first of the state offices to be voted on in the primary after the candidates for national office. However, on the general election ballot, the party list form remained (permitting straight-ticket voting) with the nonpartisan supreme court candidates listed at the end of the long ballot.

Because of the new blanket primary, record numbers of voters participated which, ironically, only tended to increase the roll-off vote for judges.[41] But because supreme court candidates were listed near the front of the September primary ballot, the fall-off was probably less than if these candidates had been listed last, as they were in the November general election ballot.

But statistics fail to give a feeling for the spirit of some of the campaigns between 1932 and 1946. For example, incumbent James Geraghty barely survived a challenge in the 1934 primary, winning nomination by only 111 votes, but then soundly defeated his challenger, Ralph G. Bell, by nearly 44,000 votes in November. Partisanship as well as religion played crucial roles in the Geraghty

40. Chapter 26, Session Laws, 1935, p. 60.

41. In 1932, prior to the establishment of the blanket primary, 403,231 voters cast their ballots for governor. In 1934, 333,795 voted for senator. In 1936, the first year under the blanket system, 504,197 voted for governor and in 1938, 440,558 cast ballots for senator. The average roll-off for 1932 and 1934 was 33.2% and for the two years after the blanket primary, 40.3%.

campaign. Geraghty was known as a Democrat and as a Catholic, facts that his opponents attempted to emphasize. The Democrats continued their sweep of elective offices in the 1934 state balloting, carrying Geraghty with them. Geraghty described the spirited campaign to an old party friend in Spokane:

> The final campaign of newspaper advertising was very effective. Possibly I could have gotten through without it, but in view of what Judge Bell was doing the advertising had psychological value. Bell had large billboards along the highways, and in many other respects carried on a campaign such as was never before known in a judicial election. He had looked forward to this race for a long time and was untiring in his efforts. He toured the state several times, and appeared to have been present at nearly every meeting. I have no doubt he has the mental qualifications for a judge, but he had in addition to that the physical qualities of a race horse, because he was everywhere under all conditions. . . .
>
> The larger newspapers with few exceptions were generally friendly. What I lacked was publicity in the smaller papers, and that was supplied by the later advertising. Of course, I was helped by the general swing, and had the endorsement of various groups, like the Federation of Labor, which must have been effective. Being the first name on the ballot, too, was a help.[42]

As the judge pointed out, an advantage was gained by winning the plurality in the primary, which placed his name first on the general election ballot.

When John Mitchell announced his intent to retire in 1937, a total of six candidates filed for his position, with superior court judge John S. Robinson eventually defeating his rival by over 78,000 votes in November. Support from the legal profession accounted for much of Robinson's success. Clyde Jeffers survived a five-man race in the 1938 primary in which "extremism" and partisanship played leading roles. Joe Mallery nearly defeated incumbent John Main in 1942, losing by only 685 votes. But when Main later withdrew, Mallery, with the assistance of an opinion from the Supreme Court, became the victor.[43]

42. Letter to R. L. Rutter of Spokane, November 10, 1934 (Geraghty Family Letter File).

43. In the 1942 primary Main had the "greatest" number of votes, Mallery the "next greatest," and Ewing the "next greatest" after Mallery. Section 5212 of the Remington Revised Statutes read, "The name of the person who receives the greatest number of votes and of the person who receives the next greatest number of votes for each position, shall appear on the general election ballot. . . ." According to the Attorney General, Section 5212 meant that only Mallery's name would appear on the

Finally, in 1946 two experienced supreme court judges were defeated by challengers who possessed political savvy, recognizable names, and partisan credentials. Superior court judge Matt Hill, Republican aspirant for the state senate in 1932 and his party's nominee for Congress in 1938, replaced incumbent Edward Connelly in a highly partisan race. Edgar Schwellenbach, brother of Louis B. Schwellenbach, Secretary of Labor in the Truman administration, defeated Tom Grady, who had just completed three years on the high court in a temporary position. Thus, although there were fewer contests and less voter interest in supreme court elections, spirited campaigns were conducted and close contests experienced. Mere incumbency was no longer enough to ensure election.

Radio advertisements had played a role in political campaigns before 1932, but the airwaves became a strong force in judicial campaigns during this period. Although newspapers certainly continued to play an important part in the campaigns, the radio seemed to be developing into a more popular means of direct communication between judicial aspirants and the electorate. Backgrounds, relevant experiences, integrity, honesty, and courage (with an occasional reference to the area of the state with which the candidates wished to be associated), characterized the radio "spots."

The newspapers displayed three forms of campaign materials besides an all too rare "news" piece about campaign organizers or an announcement of endorsement by some group. First, small ads with a picture of the candidate above a catchy phrase like "Honesty and Integrity" or "Experienced" were dispersed among the pages of the leading newspapers. Second, a primitive form of the bar poll, conducted by the candidate himself, and a long list of names of the supporters were printed in large newspaper ads. For example, in Judge Robinson's 1942 and Judge Hill's 1946 campaigns, large, nearly full-page documents were used listing the names of between 500 and 1,000 attorneys endorsing the candidates.[44] Most often, at

final ballot following Main's withdrawal. Ewing challenged the opinion, and the Supreme Court accepted the view of the Attorney General. Since Ewing never had the highest nor the next highest number of votes, his name could not appear on the November ballot. The court split on whether Main's name should appear on the final ballot, even though he had withdrawn. See *State Ex Rel. Ewing* v. *Reeves*, 15 Wn. 2d 75 (1942).

44. In a box in the middle of the list of names, the ad announced: "Former U. S. District Judge George Donworth says: 'Judge Robinson is an able lawyer and an upright judge. It will be unfortunate if the people of the state should lose his service on our highest court'" (*The Seattle Times*, September 6, 1942). In 1938 Jeffers had a similar ad with over five hundred names and a "boxed" endorsement from the retiring incumbent, O. R. Holcomb. See *The Seattle Post-Intelligencer*, November 6,

the end of the long list of names was attached the phrase: "and many others!"[45] Finally, the leading newspapers would give editorial endorsement to one candidate or another, usually the incumbents.

Partisanship, which in the years just preceding this time was minimal, seeped into a few of the judicial races. Perhaps because of the blanket primary, the New Deal sweep and subsequent Republican resurgence, or the political backgrounds of the candidates, some challengers and incumbents felt that identity with a particular political party would be helpful.[46] In most cases it was. In 1938 it was a conflict between the Commonwealth Federation of Washington (a highly partisan, loosely knit group of New Deal and Roosevelt supporters)[47] and the Pro-America Ticket (a Republican women's organization). Clyde Jeffers was supported by the Pro-America group which announced in its ads: "Republicans! This is the latest edition of the Pro-America ballot with voting suggestions for all those interested in eliminating the Commonwealth Federation from the political picture." The issue to them was conservation vs. radicalism. Voters were urged to take advantage of the blanket primary and "raid" the other party in order to nominate the weakest Democrats. The Commonwealth Federation's candidate was Bruce Little. The intensity of the partisanship of the 1938 judicial campaign was apparent from a report in *The Seattle Times*:

> King County precinct committeemen [are attempting] to get votes for a candidate for the Supreme Court . . . on the ground that he is a Democrat and an extreme "liberal." The . . . committeemen say the opposition to their candidate is headed by a "man of the most reactionary stripe . . . a critic of the New Deal . . . who speaks and breathes hatred of Franklin D. Roosevelt."[48]

Name familiarity and partisanship played roles in the 1946 campaigns. Matt Hill had made an impressive, although unsuccessful, campaign for Congress in 1938. He then was an announced op-

---

1938. To counteract the impressive listing, Jeffers' opponent, Ernst Card, ran a newspaper ad announcing that Guy Kelly, "State Chairman of Attorneys and Majority of Attorneys of this state too numerous to list" had endorsed him (*The Seattle Times*, November 6, 1938).

45. *The Seattle Times*, November 3, 1946.

46. The Washington State Bar Association had anticipated the resurgence of politics and partisanship, which partially explained their desire for reforms.

47. The Commonwealth Federation was composed of "Labor, Democrats, liberals, old age pension unions, Workers' Alliance," and Democratic precinct committeemen (*Seattle Times*, November 4, 1938).

48. *Ibid.*, September 2, 1938.

Table 5.2
Election Results, 1934–38

	Primary	General
_1934_	_(Sept. 11)_	_(Nov. 6)_
(Pos. 1)		
*Walter B. Beals	186,699	245,413
Bryce Little	65,314	
(Pos. 2)		
*Bruce Blake	197,528	226,618
(Pos. 3)		
Ralph C. Bell	101,320	132,224
*James M. Geraghty	101,431	176,153
Ernest M. Card	54,085	
_1936_	_(Sept. 8)_	_(Nov. 3)_
(Pos. 1)		
*John F. Main	252,198	259,587
(Pos. 2)		
*William J. Millard	239,369	255,638
(Pos. 3)		
John E. Belcher	37,082	
John S. Robinson	99,414	222,292
Will G. Beardslee	55,104	
Roscoe R. Fullerton	36,803	
H. I. Kyle	39,609	
William R. Bell	65,311	144,028

	Primary	General
_1938_	_(Sept. 13)_	_(Nov. 8)_
(Pos. 1)		
*William J. Steinert	264,370	291,386
(Pos. 2)		
*George B. Simpson	247,375	278,334
(Pos. 3)		
C. G. Jeffers	96,943	215,946
Ernest M. Card	78,704	156,373
Bryce Little	67,426	
C. L. Holcomb	60,877	
George F. McAulay	39,904	

*Incumbent
Italicized names designate winners
Full six-year term unless otherwise indicated

Table 5.3
Election Results, 1940–48

	Primary	*General*
1940	*(Sept. 10)*	*(Nov. 5)*
(Pos. 1)		
**Walter B. Beals*	298,647	308,083
(Pos. 2)		
**Bruce Blake*	281,311	291,766
(Pos. 3)		
**Sam M. Driver*	266,827	277,610
1942	*(Sept. 8)*	*(Nov. 3)*
(Pos. 1)		
*John F. Main	67,437	
Joseph A. Mallery	66,752	200,921
Edwin C. Ewing	39,036	
Eret Lafayette Casey	26,275	
(Pos. 2)		
**William J. Millard*	150,539	188,667
Ray G. Gruhlke	25,345	
(Pos. 3)		
**John S. Robinson*	114,802	189,393
Don G. Abel	80,867	
1944	*(July 11)*	*(Nov. 7)*
(Pos. 1)		
**William J. Steinert*	196,856	266,163
(Pos. 2)		
**George B. Simpson*	189,320	260,804
(Pos. 3)		
**Clyde G. Jeffers*	188,472	258,099
1946	*(July 9)*	*(Nov. 5)*
(Pos. 1)		
**Walter B. Beals*	237,994	299,911
(Pos. 2)		
Thomas E. Grady	106,187	
E. W. Schwellenbach	188,296	328,972
(Pos. 3)		
Matthew W. Hill	125,814	236,620
R. W. Clifford	48,174	
*Edward M. Connelly	106,281	163,492
1948	*(Sept. 14)*	*(Nov. 2)*
(Pos. 1)		
*William J. Millard	125,843	268,501
Thomas A. Grady	125,762	293,985
Roy DeGrief	72,854	
Simon Wampold	71,437	
(Pos. 2)		
**John S. Robinson*	166,125	328,077
Robert C. Finley	108,964	207,307
L. C. Brodbeck	50,816	
Ray C. Gruhlke	26,615	
(Pos. 3)		
**Joseph A. Mallery*	209,476	441,472
Raymond W. Clifford	153,570	

*Incumbent
Italicized names designate winners
Full six-year term unless otherwise indicated

ponent of the Commonwealth Federation and endorsed by the Pro-America organization. Although losing to the highly popular Congressman Warren Magnuson, Hill's name and Republican affiliation were known to many. His opponent, incumbent Ed Connelly, had been appointed by Democrat Wallgren and had been active in Democratic political circles. He relied upon the Democratic organization in an attempt to fend off Hill's challenge. In Everett, for example, at a Democratic rally a speaker identified as an assistant attorney general "called for party support of Judge Connelly." He was reported to have also said that while the court is "supposed to be non-partisan it is useless to have the governor propose and the legislature enact good legislation, unless there is a Supreme Court which will delegate it constitutional."[49] On his part Hill emphasized the nonpartisan nature of the judiciary.

Prominently displayed in his literature was the observation that this was "a non-partisan judicial ballot" and he was "the non-partisan Judge" running for the Supreme Court.[50] Hints of religion entered the fray when it was observed that Hill was a leading layman in the Baptist Church and a high degree Mason, and that Connelly was a Catholic.

Certainly interest groups were still active in high court races and played an important if not equal role with the bar association at this point in time. For example, challenger Ernest M. Card in his 1938 campaign was endorsed by the Tacoma Life Underwriters, King County Club of the United Veterans of Washington, Masters of Pierce County Grange, Mayor of Tacoma, a "group of merchants," and a number of "lumber executives." The Municipal League, a reform organization in Seattle composed predominantly of Republican and business-oriented members, often endorsed judicial candidates. For example, Jeffers picked up their support in 1938.

What characterized elections during the period was, on the one hand, an increasing lack of voter participation in primaries and especially in general elections, and, on the other hand, a more decisive affirmation role assumed by those who did cast their ballots. During the period from 1932 to 1946 eight justices were appointed. However, two of these were to temporary positions (Grady and Abel), and two were appointed to complete unexpired terms because they had already won elections (Mallery and Schwellenbach). In all, five judges were promoted to the Supreme Court because of electoral victories, and only four were appointed by the governor

49. *Ibid.*, November 1, 1946.
50. *Ibid.*, November 3, 1946.

to permanent positions. More judges, then, were elected than appointed. Also, two appointees were defeated in their initial attempt to receive affirmation from the voters (Connelly and Grady). Indeed, the electorate insisted upon more than incumbency and experience.

Another trend during this period of stress was a growing concern by, and an increasing role for, the attorneys of the state either as organized in the State Bar or as *ad hoc* groups in support of one candidate or another. Finally, the intensity of the times was reflected in the partisanship which was infused into several of the races, especially in 1934, 1938, and 1946.

Events of 1947 and 1948 are treated separately here simply because they were unique, not part of any discernible pattern. Nonetheless, these events had a profound impact on judicial recruitment. Two major forces in the selection of supreme court personnel coalesce, forging a permanent partnership.

1947–48: The Forging of a Coalition between the Profession and the Electorate

Perhaps the prevailing political issue of the 1940s and 1950s was the conflict between public and private electric power advocates. The rivers of the Pacific Northwest are deep, wide, and fast-rushing. These rivers could provide, it was thought, an unlimited source of energy. But which would be more efficient in taming these rivers and supplying industry and homes with inexpensive power—privately or publicly owned power systems? It was this issue which provided the back-drop for the most traumatic legal, political, and personal episodes in the history of the Supreme Court.

In 1946 the Public Utility District of Skagit County proposed to buy all assets of the Puget Sound Power and Light Company, a large private company, for the price of approximately $135,000,000. If the purchase was approved by the courts, the sale would involve the largest single issue of revenue power bonds in the nation. The Washington State Grange, a powerful and progressive force in state politics, advocated public power and had pressed for the purchase of Puget Sound Power and Light. Weyerhauser Timber Company attempted to block the sale and acted as a "friend of the court" in the litigation. A Skagit County Superior Court judge ruled in favor of the sale and the case was appealed to the Washington Supreme Court.[51]

51. Decided by superior court judge Brickey on May 10, 1946.

On September 4, 1946, oral arguments were heard, and in early January 1947, Chief Justice William Millard called for a rehearing because of a 4-4 split vote and of a change in court personnel. (Since the original arguments had been made, Beals had left for his assignment at the war crimes trials in Nuremberg, and Connelly had been defeated at the polls by Hill.) Upon assuming the responsibilities of the office of chief justice on January 13, 1947, Joe Mallery vacated the rehearing decision, intending to file the decision as a 4-4 split which would allow the lower court's ruling to stand. However, the next day, upon the insistence of his brethren, the full court met and reversed the chief's decision. The rehearing on the Puget Power sale was again scheduled for January 30.

By March all the judges except Millard had signed either Mallery's draft approving the sale (written as the majority opinion) or Hill's which was intended as a dissent, but the vote remained on a 4-4 deadlock. Three months later Millard still had not affixed his signature to an opinion. A run on Puget Power stock on the New York Stock Exchange resulted because of rumors of pending approval of the sale (the stock was then $11.00 a share, but if the sale was approved the guaranteed return was to be $18.00 per share). The State Grange at its annual convention held in June at Port Angeles passed a resolution critical of the delay in the litigation. With the pressure on, five of the justices took an unprecedented step and made public a letter they had sent to the Grange convention explaining why no decision had been reached in the P.U.D. case.[52] The judges held Millard solely responsible. Millard's colleagues disclosed the wording of an internal memo sent to the errant judge urging him to act:

> The standing of this court will be affected if it should be established that the stock-market manipulations can be directly attributable to the manner in which this court functions or fails to function.
>
> You have in your power to stop the further spread of rumors that are detrimental to this court simply by functioning on this case.
>
> Do you think you can justify the continuance of this situation on the theory that you cannot yet make up your mind on a matter fully submitted to you on September 4, 1946?
>
> You owe it to this court to do your duty and function on this case immediately.[53]

52. Judges Simpson and Schwellenbach were "out of the city" and did not sign the letter to the Grange. Initial reports had Judge Hill signing, but subsequent accounts excluded him from the signatories. Judge Hill's recollections were that he had not signed.

53. *The Seattle Times*, June 5, 1947.

Millard voted to void the sale on the very day he received the memo.[54] However, he bitterly lashed out at his colleagues:

> The action of Judge Mallery and his four associates in making an issue out of the manner in which the members of this court conscientiously attempted to perform their duty is without precedent in the history of the court. I do not see how anyone can arrive at any other conclusion other than that it is the opening gun in Chief Justice Mallery's campaign for re-election.[55]

Subsequently it was learned that Millard was heavily in debt, had borrowed from persons who indirectly were involved in litigation before the high court, and had written several checks that were returned because of insufficient funds.[56] Rumors of bribes also circulated. The head of the State Grange disclosed that he had been contacted by an unknown person who had assured him that for $5,000 he could gain the court's approval of the sale.[57]

Three investigations were launched in sequence.[58] First, the Thurston County prosecutor conducted a preliminary inquiry (with assistance from a *Seattle Post-Intelligencer* reporter), isolating three yet unsubstantiated charges against Millard:

1) That Judge Millard issued checks under conditions which constituted a crime.
2) That Judge Millard borrowed money from parties beneficiary to litigation during the pending of a relevant supreme court case.

54. The question involved in the case as posed by the majority was, "Where does the Skagit district get power and authority to purchase 'this whole vast system extending over eighteen counties?'" According to the relevant statute (known as the Grange Power Law because it resulted from an initiative drive spearheaded by the Grange and labor in 1930), a public utility district was allowed to purchase power "within or without" its boundaries. To purchase a power system like Puget, which extended over virtually all of Western Washington, went far beyond the intent of the 1950 statute. "Without" was narrowly construed by the majority. Additionally, the state constitution forbade municipal corporations (and public utilities) from owning stock or bonds. The court majority, per Judge Hill, concluded: "The evidence clearly demonstrates that the facilities here sought to be acquired are unreasonably large and entirely inappropriate for the accomplishment of the primary purpose of the Skagit district." Although the case was resolved and the issue of relations between Millard and the other members of the court, especially with Mallery, seemed at an end, Millard's troubles were just beginning. *State Ex Rel. P.U.D. District of Skagit* v. *Wylie* (28 Wn. 2d 133 [1947] at 152).

55. *The Seattle Post-Intelligencer*, June 17, 1947.

56. See the *Wenatchee Daily World* for a series beginning August 28, 1947, on Millard's financial problems.

57. *The Seattle Post-Intelligencer*, September 9, 1947.

58. Chief Justice Mallery had previously asked Van Hinkle to bring criminal charges against Millard in order to clarify the many issues. Hinkle refused. The personal conflict between the two justices continued even after they left the bench.

3) That Judge Millard permitted himself to be improperly influenced in arriving at a judicial decision.[59]

With these unproven charges in hand, Prosecutor Van Hinkle turned to state Attorney General Smith Troy for assistance in conducting a more thorough investigation. At the end of January 1948, A. G. Troy sent his report to Van Hinkle in which he concluded that at least one bad check had been written by the judge, and that he had "borrowed money from pinball operators and a club official during the pendency of a decision [*State* v. *Brumm*, 27 Wn. 2d 960 (1947)] in which they had a pecuniary interest," but no evidence existed suggesting that he had given them any judicial consideration. Troy finally concluded that there was no "evidence that [Millard] permitted himself to be improperly influenced in arriving at a judicial opinion in the Skagit County P.U.D. litigation." Nonetheless this

> does not . . . relieve Judge Millard from all public accountability for his actions nor does it foreclose all the public processes which may be brought to bear on this situation.
>
> [The] high honors and privileges [of judicial office] carry with them the compensating elements of high moral character, rigid self-discipline, and absolute integrity in private as well as public life. It is not sufficient within the code of judicial ethics for a judge to avoid evil; he must avoid even the appearance of evil. . . .
>
> In our opinion it is within the authority and the discretion of the legislature . . . to review this matter in relation to the ethical question raised. . . .
>
> Any further cognizance of the issue must be left to the people and to the legislative processes they initiate.[60]

The attorney general isolated two courses of action remaining: removal of Millard either by impeachment (Article V, Sections 1 and 2) or by a joint resolution of the legislature (Article VI, Section 9). A constitutional amendment could be initiated by the legislature and approved by the people to create less drastic and cumbersome means of rectifying similar situations, but it could not be used retroactively. Troy's report made no mention of Mallery's actions in making public the internal memo and the court's vote in the P.U.D. case before the final decision.

Finally, the Seattle Bar Association succeeded in having the State

59. Letter from Smith Troy, attorney general, to Van R. Hinkle, Thurston County prosecutor, dated January 31, 1948.

60. *Ibid.* See also *The Seattle Post-Intelligencer*, February 1, 1948, for a published copy of the letter (report).

Bar consider conducting its own investigation of the situation, using the attorney general's report as a beginning.[61] After considerable deliberation, the board of governors of the Washington State Bar Association made the following report to the members in April condemning both Millard and Mallery:

> [The] Board . . . believes: (1) that it is the duty of the Bar to vigorously disapprove personal conduct of a member of the Court which casts discredit upon that member of the Court; (2) that it is the duty of the Bar to vigorously disapprove release of information as to judicial deliberations by judges in any case pending before the Court; (3) that it is the duty of individual members of the Bar to inform themselves fully with respect to all such matters; and (4) that the final disposition of such matters must rest, with the electorate, acting either at the polls or through the legislature.[62]

At the annual convention of the State Bar in 1948 a resolution was introduced that read in part:

> WHEREAS, The said conduct of Judge Millard disqualifies him from holding a position on the Supreme Court of this state, now, therefore, *Be it Resolved* by the Washington State Bar Association, in convention duly assembled, That we condemn said conduct by Judge Millard and urge his defeat at the coming election.

The convention's resolutions committee reported that they had given considerable study to the resolution and concluded that "This Committee does not undertake to say this Association should participate as an Association to defeat any such judge." The problem was not the uniqueness of such action but rather "the limited call for and attendance upon this convention" and the "short time for discussion."[63] After an attempt to amend the resolution to reflect the

61. The State Bar's resolution said, in part: "NOW, THEREFORE, BE IT RESOLVED, that the Board of Governors request the Attorney General and the Prosecuting Attorney of Thurston County to submit to the Board of Governors as soon as completed a full report of their investigation, and BE IT FURTHER RESOLVED, that upon receipt of such a report the Board of Governors will duly consider the same and convey to the members of the Washington State Bar Association its conclusions and recommendations upon all matters encompassed by the resolution of the Board of Trustees of the Seattle Bar Association" (*Washington State Bar News* 1 [19 October 1947], 31). Animosities between Millard and the Seattle Bar and his brethren had been developing over many years. For example, in 1936 Millard took to task those of his colleagues who had voted to uphold the income tax. See his concurring opinion in *Jensen* v. *Henneford* (185 WASH. 209, 1936), at 225, and *The Seattle Times*, January 30, 1936.

62. *Washington State Bar News* 2 (April 1948): 13.

63. *Washington Law Review & State Bar Journal* 23 (1948): 310–11.

concerns of the committee, it was tabled, leaving the board of governor's resolution in force. These actions at least suggested that now was the time for the organized profession to intervene in the electoral process as they had done in 1924 and 1926. This challenge was accepted by the Seattle Bar Association.

As early as 1908 and 1909 the Seattle Bar had conducted "bar primaries" for superior court contests and had reinstated the practice in 1932. However, at no times had they submitted the candidates for the high court to this process. For the 1948 elections they were prepared for the first time ever to include supreme court candidates in their preference poll. The results of the poll prior to the September primary were clearly unfavorable to Millard and Mallery. For Position 1 Grady led with 440 votes, Millard had 195, DeGrief 105, and Wampold 99. Clifford outpolled Mallery for Position 3, 555 to 271. Incumbent John Robinson had a substantial margin over his nearest rival Robert C. Finley (634 to 152) for Position No. 2. The Tacoma Bar Association followed the lead of the Seattle attorneys and endorsed Grady, Clifford, and Robinson. The Republican women's Pro-America organization also supplied its recommendations, urging support for Robinson, Grady, and Clifford. They commented that Millard "brought notoriety upon the supreme court through his personal financial dealings" and that Mallery was only a temporary chief justice and should be replaced.[64]

Despite the efforts of the bars and the Pro-America group, Millard survived the initial screening and faced Tom Grady in the November election (only 81 votes separated them). In another bar poll prior to the November elections 1,054 Seattle attorneys voted and, again, overwhelmingly endorsed Tom Grady over Millard (761 to 198). The State Grange joined the attorneys and, in an unprecedented declaration, urged the defeat of Millard. Henry P. Carstensen, State Master of the Grange warned that:

> If the voters return Judge Millard to office it might well be interpreted as a carte blanche for any judge to engage in such activities as have been attributed to Judge Millard.
>
> Such an outcome is unthinkable to the State Grange leadership, for it would seem to indicate a breakdown in the judicial branch of our government.[65]

The voters heeded the bar, the Grange, and others by giving Grady a strong majority.

64. Joseph A. Mallery Papers, on file with the author, hereafter referred to as *Mallery Papers*.
65. *Ibid.*

Mallery, however, turned back the challenge of Clifford by nearly 50,000 votes in the primary. Mallery's victory could be attributed to support from labor, the Grange, name familiarity, and his own efforts.[66] He spent nearly $3,700 in his campaign, a fairly large sum for a court race in those days.[67] Also, Mallery's opponent did not have the credentials and familiarity as did Millard's rival, Tom Grady. Judge Robinson again picked up the bar endorsement over Finley in the November race for Position 2 (825–139) and the voters followed suit returning him to the court for another full term.

Summary

The lessons of the times of stress, and especially of 1947 and 1948, are many. First, the bars in 1948 assumed a permanent and public role in elections, unlike the short-lived reaction of the legal profession to Pemberton's campaigns in 1924 and 1926. Henceforth, the Seattle Bar initially and the State Bar eventually would conduct candidate preference polls of their members before each contested election. Rarely has the electorate ignored the advice of the lawyers.

Second, although partisanship had played a role in campaigns prior to 1949 and would occasionally provide some support for a candidate now and then, by 1950 it was clear that the bar associations and other interest groups had supplanted the political parties as a force in judicial elections. It now remained largely to the governor, through appointments, to weigh partisan factors.

Third, the "unification" of the State Bar in 1933, which brought together all of the attorneys in the state, explained to a great extent the renewed interest in judicial reform displayed by the attorneys. The integration or unification movement was designed to further the professional interest of the bar, one of which was to temper public accountability with a stronger role for lawyers in the selection of judges. Henceforth, the split between the more politically oriented attorneys and those moderates concerned with professional interest was less pronounced. (The efforts of the political lawyers moved to the legislative arena.) Professional encourage-

66. *The Seattle Times*, October 23, 1948.

67. Mallery had been a Granger for over thirty-six years and had been a hard worker for the progressive reforms (initiative, referendum, and recall) in the 1912 Grange efforts. The Grange newspaper viewed the P.U.D. issue and Mallery's actions as follows: "'Joe' Mallery's greatest achievement in the way of public service did not occur until June of last year. . . . Then, with a fighting courage which refused to countenance an intolerable situation that had developed in the court, he boldly led five other justices in a public statement criticising the conduct of a member of the court, Judge Millard" (*Mallery Papers*, June 12, 1948).

ment also came from national organizations such as the American Bar Association, American Law Institute, Judicial Council Movement, and the American Judicature Society. However, by the 1950s the legal profession largely abandoned its efforts to bring about constitutional changes in the methods of recruitment to the Supreme Court. Some enthusiasm was generated in the 1970s but without success. The appointments process and elections now provided the attorneys with sufficient influence over the recruitment of justices to the high court. Perhaps, also, as the profession grew and the legal problems of the state diversified, the attorneys were unable to reach a sufficient consensus on constitutional amendments to successfully convince the legislators and the electorate.

Finally, as a result of the clash of personalities and the airing of personal problems, the justices needed time to improve their images with the public and the profession.

In sum, recruitment to the Supreme Court prior to the 1930s and 1940s involved largely spontaneous efforts among electorate, candidates, the bar, interested parties, and the governor. However, now, judicial recruitment in Washington was witnessing some structured coordination between the bar and governor and the lawyers and the electorate. Public accountability was expanding but in the sense that the judges were simply becoming accountable to more "publics." It remains to be seen whether these early efforts at some coordination will be strengthened and possibly institutionalized.

6

Transition to a Structured Recruitment System, 1949–69

In the 1948 elections, after a four-year hiatus, Arthur B. Langlie was returned to the governor's chair to begin an unprecedented second and third terms as the state's chief executive (1949–57). The governor honored the agreement he had made in his first term to work with the State Bar Association in initiating and screening aspirants for vacancies on the state's benches. Additionally, the success of the Seattle Bar Association's poll in the 1948 defeat of Judge Millard encouraged members of the legal profession to continue their efforts to influence the electorate. Further, as before, about one-third of those who cast their ballots for the more visible political candidates ignored the judicial ballot, although this roll-off tended thereafter to stabilize.

What the judicial recruitment system was experiencing was a consolidation of previous practices into a structured form. It became common for the major participants in recruitment—the governor, the bar, the electorate, and the candidates—to share in an often cooperative effort the responsibilities for initiating, screening, and affirming aspirants to the Supreme Court.

Appointments in the Era of Transition

Governor Langlie had some constraints placed on his choices during his first term (1941–45). Justice Mallery had already won the primary and was appointed to fill in until his election became official, and Grady's appointment was to a temporary position. However, at the beginning of his second term, Langlie was able to exercise more freedom in his selections.

Clyde Jeffers announced his retirement quite unexpectedly on August 6, 1949, to become effective a month later. This was two days

Table 6.1
Supreme Court Appointments, 1949–68

Justice	*Governor*	*Date*
Fred G. Hamley (R)	Langlie (R)	September 6, 1949
Charles T. Donworth (R)	Langlie	September 12, 1949
Frank P. Weaver (R)	Langlie	May 21, 1951
Ralph O. Olson (R)	Langlie	September 10, 1951
Richard B. Ott (R)	Langlie	January 24, 1955
Harry E. Foster (R)	Langlie	July 8, 1956
Robert T. Hunter (D)	Rosellini (D)	October 11, 1957
Orris L. Hamilton (D)	Rosellini	January 22, 1962
Frank Hale (D)	Rosellini	January 14, 1963
Marshall A. Neill (R)	Evans (R)	April 24, 1967
Walter T. McGovern (R)	Evans	January 8, 1968

after Judge Steinert had made known his intention to leave the bench by September 12. Both jurists had been suffering from heart ailments, and Steinert had been having problems with his eyesight. Pursuant to his previous agreement with the chairman of the State Bar's selection committee, Governor Langlie was "expected to delay his appointment of a successor until the bar submitted its list of qualified candidates." Actually, the bar's certified list had been filed with the Governor's office prior to the announced retirements, but the committee was asked to do some further checking. The committee "would not be able to meet until August 19,"[1] delaying the appointment. The brief impasse was of Langlie's making, however.

The governor's first choice for the Jeffers' vacancy was an old political ally and personal friend of many years, Frederick G. Hamley. Hamley had served with Langlie on the Seattle City Council in 1935 when the former had been a candidate of the Order of Cincinnatus, a reform group, and the latter had been endorsed by the order. When Langlie was elected mayor, Hamley was appointed head of the City Water Department. When Langlie moved to Olympia in 1941 to begin his first term, Hamley accompanied him, first working in the attorney general's office as special assistant to the governor and then shortly thereafter as Langlie's appointee to head the Department of Public Service. At the end of the governor's first term, Hamley left for an assignment in Washington, D.C., as assistant general solicitor for the National Association of Railroads and Utilities Commission. He returned only briefly to advise the

1. *Seattle Times,* August 7, 1949.

governor on legislative matters in 1949 while on leave from his Washington, D. C., office.

The appointment took more time than anticipated because the original list from the selection committee did not contain Hamley's name. "After . . . Langlie indicated his desire to appoint Hamley,"[2] the list was returned to the committee and Hamley's name added. Thus, Langlie remained true to his promise not to appoint anyone to the state benches who did not have the approval of the bar.

Actually Hamley had been absent from the state for nearly six years and was not well known to the profession. Even his brief tenure as adviser in 1949 failed to provide wide circulation with the profession. Consequently, many members of the bar expressed some concern over the appointment, although he was found qualified by the bar's selection committee. Political obligation played no role in the selection. As one close observer of the appointment recalled: "Close personal acquaintance and association throughout the years and confidence in the ability of Hamley were the considerations of the Governor." Despite the absence of Hamley's name from the committee's initial list, the chair was able to report later that "There has been the finest cooperation between the Governor and this committee."[3] The incident prompted the committee to expand its initiation function by requesting each county bar to submit names of potential candidates so that an up-dated and comprehensive list "would offer ample opportunity to this committee and to the governor for full consideration of the person best qualified for appointment to the Supreme Court."[4]

Charles T. Donworth was Langlie's choice to fill the Steinert vacancy. Although Donworth's name had been on the bar's recommended list, his selection "came as a surprise in legal circles as Langlie had been expected to appoint an Eastern Washington man after naming Hamley." Only Grady and Schwellenbach represented

2. Anonymous response to a questionnaire mailed in 1978 by the author to all members of selection committees involved in the earlier appointments. Hereafter cited as *Selection Committee Survey*.

3. *Washington State Bar News* 4 (July 1950): 26. One member of the selection committee during this period recalled: "Rather, generally, the appointments by the Governors have been from the recommended list of the bar association. The only particular case I can think of off-hand where the bar association received almost a directive appointment from the Governor was when I was a member of the judicial committee. A list had been submitted to Governor Langlie and he countered with an inquiry as to whether we would be interested in accepting Frederick Hamley. Since we were all aware Hamley was a close friend of Governor Langlie, there was some question in our mind whether the Governor was breaking the previous policy on appointments. As it turned out, Judge Hamley was one of the most brilliant appellate judges that was ever a member of the supreme court" (*Selection Committee Survey*).

4. *Washington State Bar News* 4 (July 1950): 26.

the eastern part of the state on the Supreme Court. Donworth was a life-long Republican but had not been active in politics. His father had been one of the state's pioneer lawyers and served on the federal bench for a time before forming a law firm with his son. The younger Donworth had served for two years as Seattle assistant corporate counsel (city attorney) in the 1920s and was president of the Seattle Bar Association in 1934. Other than his party affiliation, Donworth had no political attributes that would make his appointment attractive to the governor. The family name, his ties with Seattle, activities in the bar, and obvious competency more than made up for the lack of political ties or close friendship with the chief executive.[5]

Frank P. Weaver, Langlie's next appointee to the court, was the first law professor appointed to come directly from the classroom. (John F. Main had taught law at the University of Washington but served thereafter on the Superior Court for four years.) Weaver had been Dean of Gonzaga Law School (1944–48), taught real property at the school since 1928, and carried on an active practice in Spokane.

He recalled the circumstances of his appointment several years later:

> Spokane County, the second most populous, was not represented on the Court. Spokane Bar Association thought it should be represented. I was their "fair haired boy."
>
> What the politics involved were, I do not know nor do I care. I had carried "some water to the elephant." I was a delegate to the Republican National convention in 1944. I was a personal friend of Thomas E. Dewey, the nominee. He was also a friend of Governor Langlie. Whether this had anything to do with my original appointment, I do not know.[6]

Although Weaver had been Dewey's eastern Washington campaign manager during both of his presidential campaigns, he had not been active in any of Langlie's races. He had the respect of his profession and served as president of the Spokane Bar Association in 1946. As

5. Frank P. Weaver, a close friend and colleague of Donworth recalled: "Carl's appointment was political—but not by reason of the donee but the donor. I never heard Carl say he had done *anything* in politics except give money. Langlie had to pick himself off the floor to placate the King County Bar because of his Hamley appointment. . . . Thus, Langlie tried to remedy a situation. . . . There was another consideration never put in writing but still discussed. Carl was a Catholic. There was none on the court. Carl's standing was so great, that even the Masons couldn't stop his appointment" (undated letter to the author).

6. Undated letter to the author circa 1974.

with other Langlie appointees, Weaver had the approval of the State Bar's selection committee.

In August 1951, Justice Beals announced his intention to retire the next month after twenty-three years on the supreme court bench. A few days after the announcement, Governor Langlie appointed superior court judge Ralph Olson of Bellingham to the vacancy. Olson, in contrast with Langlie's previous three appointments, had extensive judicial experience. He had served as police judge for ten years and fifteen years as Whatcom County Superior Court judge. Olson was the "judges' candidate" and his name had been on previous lists of the bar. He had been elected president of the Superior Court Judges Association in 1947 and was highly regarded by all those who practiced before him. Two factors favored the selection of Olson. First, none of Langlie's recent appointees had had judicial experience, and some criticism had been generated by this oversight. Further, if geographical balance was heeded, the governor should appoint someone from outside Seattle and Spokane. Olson satisfied both of these considerations. One member of the selection committee recalled the Olson appointment with these words:

> I do not think there was any political consideration as such given to his appointment and feel it probably was more a geographical recommendation of a highly considered person as at the time of the appointment, there was no member of the supreme court from the Second Congressional District. Personally, I do not feel that the Governor fulfilled any political obligation to Judge Olson. I do not know what Judge Olson's political preferences were, although I got to know him quite well while he was in the supreme court.[7]

On January 15, 1955, Justice Olson suffered a fatal brain aneurism after having served a little over three years on the high court. Within the week Governor Langlie named his replacement: Judge Richard B. Ott of Adams County. Langlie had previously appointed Ott to the trial bench in 1949. The new justice was not unfamiliar with Republican politics. He had been city attorney and mayor of Ritzville, was elected Adams County prosecutor, and had served two sessions in the state legislature. He continued thereafter as legislative lobbyist for the State Bar Association. He had acted as "visiting" judge throughout the state, serving on a temporary basis to help clear the crowded dockets of other jurisdictions while there was a dearth of Adams County cases. Thus, he became known to the

7. *Selection Committee Survey.*

profession and the judiciary. He had been "a strong supporter" and "good friend" of the governor. Finally, his name was on the bar's qualified list. There was no doubt that he wanted the position, having unsuccessfully contested Hugh Rosellini for a spot on the court in 1954. Ott was a logical choice for the governor.[8]

Langlie's final appointment to the high court did not progress as smoothly as earlier selections. Too many alternatives confused an ordinarily simple process. Justice Hamley had been nominated by President Eisenhower, upon the recommendation of Langlie as head of the Republican Party in the state, to the Ninth Circuit Court of Appeals in May 1956. He was confirmed on June 29 and sworn in July 6. On that day he resigned from the Supreme Court with five more months remaining in his term (July 6–January 14). This relatively simple act of resignation by one person actually created three vacancies. The circumstances were not altogether different from those in 1900 when Judge White was appointed and then elected to a short term.[9] First, to complete the remaining weeks in the unexpired term (until January 14), a candidate was required to survive the September primary and November general elections. In the meantime, an appointee would fill in until the survivor of the elections was qualified (thirty days after the election or December 6). Finally, on January 14, a new full six-year term would be filled by another victor of the primary and general election balloting.

Actually, three separate persons could have been involved; one appointed, one elected to the short term replacing the appointee, and one elected to the full term. Six candidates filed for the full term, including Harry Ellsworth Foster, and three filed for the short term, including William J. Millard. Governor Langlie quickly appointed Foster to the vacancy, giving him a distinct advantage in his race for the full term since incumbency is so often vital to a campaign. Although not active in Republican politics, Foster had developed a respected image in the legal profession. He had served as assistant attorney general for several years, was on the Judicial Council, and twice had been President of the Thurston-Mason Counties Bar Association.

8. In a letter to a Judge Wilkins of the Superior Court in Seattle, Langlie wrote the following: "Your recent letter recommending that Richard B. Ott be appointed to fill the vacancy . . . has been received. The committee for the selection of judges of the State Bar Association submitted a list to me of those who they felt were qualified to render this public service, and after careful consideration I am today appointing Judge Ott to that position" (Letter to Judge W. J. Wilkins from Langlie dated January 21, 1955. *Langlie Papers,* "Judicial file," Washington State Archives).

9. See p. 53, *supra.*

Some critics of Langlie's appointment felt that since the court would not meet between July and September, the short interim appointment was really not important. The vacancy could have remained unfilled. Others thought that he had broken a promise not to appoint any of the contending lawyers in the race for the full term.[10] The voters, it was felt, should be allowed to make their choice unencumbered by the symbols of incumbency. Paul Coughlin, one of Foster's opponents was, of course, critical of the appointment:

> Langlie gave Foster a campaign contribution from public funds [his paycheck] and the opportunity of having his picture taken wearing judge's robes. The only time he has worn them was when he had his picture taken.[11]

Langlie said that he appointed Foster without

> giving any consideration to political considerations. All I can say is that when a court vacancy occurs I proceed to fill it. I delayed the appointment and understood when I filled the vacancy the court had considerable business to transact.[12]

Certainly the appointment made some sense. By picking one of the several candidates on the ballot in November an easy transition in January would be possible should that appointee prevail in the balloting.

An era of unprecedented cooperation between the bar and the administration characterized the tenure of Governor Langlie. He voiced his pleasure with the relationship in a 1952 address to the State Bar Association's annual meeting:

> I am glad to be here today to express my thanks to the Bar Association of this State for the excellent cooperation I have had, while serving as your Governor, in the matter of filling vacancies in our judicial posi-

10. One of Foster's opponents gave the following account of the campaign: "Governor Langlie had breached his word to the Bar and appointed Ellsworth Foster to the bench during the campaign. This, of course, did me under" (Letter to the author, n.d., 1978). Foster's campaign materials took advantage of incumbency in a unique way by wedding it to the bar's selection committee recommendation: "I was appointed to the Supreme Court last summer to succeed Chief Justice Frederick Hamley and am now a judge of the Supreme Court. . . . The Governor appoints only from a panel certified by a committee of the State Bar Association as competent to serve in that capacity. I was so certified, my opponent was not" (*The Seattle Times,* November 2, 1956).

11. *Ibid.*, September 6, 1956, micro.

12. *Ibid.*

> tions. . . . [T]he people have expressed extreme confidence in your recommendations and there has been little opposition to the many posts that have been filled.[13]

Of course the bar association was also pleased:

> The Committee wishes to state that it had the usual fine relationship with Governor Langlie with respect to this appointment which our State Bar has enjoyed throughout his incumbency. The policy of the Governor in requesting a certified list of qualified lawyers from the State Bar Association from which to make an early appointment has proven to be a satisfactory method of handling judicial appointments.[14]

It was hoped that this close relationship between the governor and the profession would continue under Governor Rosellini, an attorney who assumed the responsibilities of state government in 1957.[15]

Democrat Albert D. Rosellini promised to continue the cooperation with the bar association. Like fellow attorney Langlie, he was fairly familiar with the leading lawyers throughout the state. His first appointment went to his friend, Robert Hunter, who had been active in Democratic politics most of his adult life. North central Washington and the activity associated with the Grand Coulee hydroelectric project were his legal and political bailiwick. He headed the Grand Coulee and Grant County Democrats, was active in nearly all of Mon Wallgren's campaigns for Congress, the Senate, and the governorship, and won some important legal battles in personal injury cases associated with the Grand Coulee project. When Judge E. W. Schwellenbach moved up from the Superior Court to the Supreme Court in 1946, Governor Wallgren had appointed Hunter to that vacancy on the trial bench.

Schwellenbach died on September 22, 1957, and Hunter was asked by members of the bar for permission to submit his name for the vacancy. Hunter was acquainted with many members of the

13. *State Bar Journal* (November 1952): 240.

14. *Washington State Bar News* 8 (July 1954): 28.

15. C. D. Cunningham, Chairman of the Committee on Judicial Selection, wrote governor Rosellini shortly after the latter had assumed the responsibilities of office that the bar was ever ready to assist in initiating and screening appointments: "In the event of a vacancy . . . this Committee obtains information from the local Bar Associations as to those who would accept the appointment and those who are best qualified to fill the vacancy. The Committee then submits to your office a list. . . . From the list submitted the appointment is made. This practice has been followed by your predecessors . . . and we are very solicitous that your office follow a like practice" (Letter dated February 12, 1957. *Rosellini Papers*, Washington State Archives).

selection committee, and he and Rosellini had been classmates at the University of Washington School of law in the 1930s. Since Hunter had succeeded to Schwellenbach's position on the Superior Court, his Grant and Douglas County colleagues thought he should again succeed to Schwellenbach's high court seat in 1957. Hunter had served as president of the Superior Court Judges' Association, was on the Judicial Council, and like Richard Ott before him, had served throughout the state as "visiting judge," helping other jurisdictions clear their crowded calendars. (Hunter attributed his selection to the fact that he had remained visible statewide through the visiting judge system, although his court was in remote Douglas-Grant counties.)[16] The bar committee fashioned a list of "12 or 14 names," one of which was Robert Hunter. On October 9, Governor Rosellini announced Hunter as his choice for the vacancy.

Orris Hamilton, whose name was also on the certified list, had always been interested in Democratic politics. His father had been elected for two terms as Washington's attorney general in the 1930s, and he had "cut his teeth" on politics by working for his father and for several federal agencies in Washington, D.C., while studying law at night at American University. Hamilton returned from World War II, resumed activity in partisan politics, and was elected prosecuting attorney for Benton County. Governor Wallgren appointed him to the Superior Court in 1948.

When Schwellenbach died in 1957, Hamilton actively sought the appointment which went to Hunter.[17] Again in 1962, upon the retirement of Justice Mallery, Hamilton desired the appointment but anticipated that the selection would go to someone on the west side of the state. Hamilton wrote a personal letter to the governor, checked with the bar to be assured his name was still on the list, and casually went about his business, expecting not to hear from Rosellini. The governor acted as expected and offered the appointment to Judge Frank Hale of the Pierce County Superior Court. But Hale, worried about having to organize a state-wide campaign on such short notice, and also concerned about being short of the minimum number of years for judicial pension eligibility, refused the offer.[18] Rosellini then called Hamilton, who quickly accepted the appointment.

In December of the same year Justice Foster died of a heart

16. Interview with Justice Hunter, April 2, 1977.
17. Interview with Justice Hamilton, April 5, 1977.
18. Kerry Radcliffe, "Cases, Courtroom and Conviction: A Judicial Biography of Justice Frank Hale" (unpublished research paper, Department of Political Science, Washington State University, 1975); and interview with Hale, December 29, 1976.

ailment after a prolonged illness. Six weeks later Rosellini announced the appointment of Frank Hale, who now felt secure enough to accept the offer. Hale had been a long-time New Deal Democrat. Before World War II he had been appointed deputy prosecutor for Pierce County and then as assistant U.S. attorney. Upon return from the military, he rejoined the U.S. Attorney's office. In his only partisan run for public office, he was defeated for the Democratic nomination for county prosecutor by his future close friend and fellow jurist, Hugh Rosellini. However, despite the loss, he was awarded an appointment as Tacoma justice of the peace and police judge where he served until his election to the superior court bench in 1953.

Although Hale's name had been on the bar's certified list the year before, it had not been among those submitted to the governor for the Foster vacancy. Undeterred, Rosellini simply made reference to the earlier list.[19] The absence of Hale's name from the current list was simply an oversight. Knowing that he had turned down the offer earlier, the committee apparently decided not to consider him for subsequent openings. Attorney Carl H. Skoog, a member of the bar's board of governors, had been told by a member of the committee that they had not considered Hale for the Foster vacancy. Skoog's view of the incident appears correct:

> I believe that it was purely a matter of oversight. I felt that perhaps that I was at fault in that Hale, being a resident of my district, I should have asked the committee to consider him as a candidate. Frankly, I thought that since he had been on the prior list not too long before it would not be necessary.[20]

Apparently the governor thought similarly.

During the eight years of Governor Rosellini's administration three supreme court jurists were appointed to vacancies. Following a long-established tradition, each of these appointees was affiliated with the political party of the governor. Each also had been somewhat active in partisan politics prior to selection to the bench and each had been a superior court judge. Although some confusion surrounded the timing of the bar's certification of Hale, each of the

19. Governor Rosellini remembered the appointment with these words: "[H]is name had appeared on *a* Washington State Bar Association list. I knew him personally as a good lawyer, a good judge and a man of high integrity, common sense and good judgment. These factors coupled with recommendations from many members of the Bar who had observed his judicial behavior were quite significant in my selection" (emphasis added; *ibid.*, letter to Kerry Radcliffe dated April 1, 1975).

20. *Ibid.*, letter to Kerry Radcliffe dated March 11, 1975.

three were approved by the profession's selection committee. Finally, with only token opposition (or none, in the case of Hale), all won approval from the voters at the next general election. One actively sought the appointment, one remained relatively passive but welcomed the offer, and one at first refused and then was persuaded to accept the appointment the second time. As in the Langlie era, judicial recruitment involved considerable coordination between candidates, the bar, and the governor.

Republican Daniel J. Evans began in 1965 what turned out to be an unprecedented three consecutive terms as governor. By the end of his administration in 1977, he had appointed eight justices to the Supreme Court. The cooperation with the bar association continued and the recruitment procedure previously established was maintained. At the very beginning of his administration, Evans outlined his ideas on selecting judges, pressing for a standardized process:

> I would hope that some real work could be done along this line. With the leadership of an association like the King County Bar and the Washington State Bar Association, giving me some guidance, giving me some opportunity, to do the best job possible in selecting members of the judiciary. I am personally interested in, perhaps, even a voluntary commission and would certainly consider the possibility of agreeing beforehand to accept from such a list the appointment of members of the judiciary.[21]

Soon thereafter he questioned "whether it is wise to fill judicial vacancies at election time solely from among attorneys who are willing to campaign for public office?" Perhaps it would be better to fill "such vacancies only by appointment?"[22] The governor's enthusiasm for a form of the Missouri plan or a special commission for nominating judges soon waned, however, but his concern for the judiciary remained, and the attention his administration paid to judicial recruitment was substantial.[23]

Evans characterized his style of recruitment as "collective screen-

21. *Washington State Bar News* 20 (May 1966): 21. George McCush, president of the State Bar Association, responded to Evans' suggestions: "We are very pleased with your desire to make the best possible judicial appointments and with your willingness to commit yourself to selection of judges from a list submitted by the Bar Association as a result of a careful standardized screening process of potential appointees. This is very commendable and desirable procedure and the State Bar Association is anxious and willing to assume its responsibility in this connection and to cooperate fully with you" (Letter dated May 3, 1966, *Evans Papers*, Washington State Archives).

22. *Washington State Bar News* 20 (December 1966): 71.

23. Interview with Governor Evans (March 27, 1979). Later Evans became concerned with the lack of a challenger in the Missouri Plan's retention election. He saw it leading to a "Judge-for-Life" tenure system.

ing." Walt Howe, the governor's special counsel, along with Richard Hemstad and James Dolliver, administrative assistants (all attorneys), consulted regularly and closely with the governor on judicial appointments (Skip Li replaced Howe during Evans' second and third terms). Occasionally Attorney General Slade Gorton was consulted. They advised the governor to work closely with the bar:

> If you are aware of someone with ideal qualifications, you may wish to consider contacting the local Bar Association to insure that he is on the list submitted. Otherwise, your selection should be from that list, unless it is a patently inappropriate list.[24]

Only after consideration of professional qualifications would "political background be of interest" to them.

Halfway into his first term, Evans had his initial opportunity to fill a vacancy on the Supreme Court. Justice Ott announced his plans to retire by April 1, 1967. Marshall Neill, Senate Republican Caucus leader and long-time legislator, recalled that he was apparently in the "right place at the right time" for the appointment. His version of the appointment indicates that, indeed, time and place meshed well for him:

> [I was] upstairs in the Senate as [Evans'] Senate leader and carrying the ball for his program. [I would go] down daily [to his office] and pound the table, disagreeing a lot of the time. But I followed him, he was my [party] leader. So when the word came that Judge Ott was going to retire I knew there was going to be an opening. I just went downstairs and said that is what I want.[25]

Others were interested in the appointment, but Neill was the obvious choice. The close working relationship described by Neill, the friendship and confidence that had developed between the two over the years, the fact that Neill was from eastern Washington (as was Ott), and a favorable rating from the bar combined to assure Neill's selection.

Neill had served in the state House of Representatives from 1949 to 1957 when he moved to the Senate. He was House Minority Leader when freshman Representative Evans began his political career in the lower house. Ultimately, Evans became the House floor leader, while Neill was in a leadership position in the Senate. Long before Evans moved to the executive branch, these two had worked

24. Memo dated January 11, 1966. *Evans Papers*, State Archives.
25. Interview with Judge Marshall Neill, December 3, 1976.

closely together on legislative and policy matters. Neill had developed considerable respect on both sides of the aisle and with the many lobbyists in Olympia. He was an experienced campaigner and, with the backing of a large segment of the King County Bar, had an excellent chance for subsequent election. Thus, the appointment had all the necessary elements of success. On April 24 Neill took his oath of office as a justice of the Supreme Court.

Judge Walter T. McGovern was Evans' second appointment to the Supreme Court. McGovern had been involved in Republican politics, having been an active member of the King County Republicans and of the Evergreen Republican Club before becoming a judge. He had made Evans' acquaintance through the Young Republicans and was a resident of the forty-third legislative district, which Evans had represented. At an early point in his career he had seriously considered running for mayor of Seattle.

McGovern made a name for himself as a reform judge. He successfully challenged a thirteen-year incumbent in 1958 for a municipal court post. Again, in 1964 he defeated an eight-year veteran of the Superior Court in King County and won by a substantial majority. These two victories gave McGovern considerable publicity and "substantial lawyer support." He was not a close friend of the governor and had "never been really active in [Evans'] campaigns." However, "he was strongly supportive of him." When Justice Donworth announced his intention to retire, friends of McGovern "talked with people close to the Governor."[26] His name was placed on the "qualified" list of the bar association, and on December 5, 1967, McGovern's appointment was announced. It met with approval, especially with residents of King County.

Evans' first two appointments were not unlike Langlie's second term selections. Neill, like Hamley, was a close friend of the governor and had worked with him on a variety of political matters. McGovern, similar to Donworth, was a product of King County and was highly respected among legal and political circles. All four were Republicans, and three of them went on to distinguished careers on the federal benches. (Neill and McGovern as federal district judges and Hamley as 9th Circuit Court of Appeals judge.)

Elections: 1950–68

The behavior of the judicial electorate was becoming fairly predictable. Although participation in primary elections remained approx-

26. Interview with Judge Walter McGovern, October 4, 1976.

imately at the same level as in the previous period (an average fall-off of 35.5% as compared with 36.4% from 1934 to 1950), increased interest was shown during the general elections. Between 1934 and 1950 over half of those who cast their ballots in the general election failed to vote for judges. However, between 1950 and 1970 those who ignored the judicial ballot dropped slightly (47.2%). The voter participation increased even though fewer positions on the court were being contested.[27]

In those contested races in the final November balloting, the modern era experienced more intensely contested races than before. Between 1934 and 1950 the six contested final races resulted in an average of 39.6% roll-off, while between 1950 and 1970 the five contests were ignored by only 32% of the electorate. What these statistics suggest is that the electorate was making a clearer contribution to the final affirmation of judges than previously. Likely reasons are the more visible role played by the legal profession, the greater coverage provided by the media and the general impact of television, the increase in spending for campaigns, and the general recognition of the importance of the judiciary.

Both Langlie and Rosellini actively supported the electoral contests of their appointees. This was especially the case with Hamley's and Hamilton's first elections, although it was not entirely absent in other races. Both the support from popular governors and the use of the governor's party organization brought heretofore missing elements into the recruitment formula.

The Seattle and Washington State Bar Associations contributed to the interest in the general elections by their preferential polls which were released to the media prior to each contested election. As we have seen, this had not been customary in previous eras. Finally, the Supreme Court attracted high-caliber contestants. Of course, highly competent recruits were involved earlier, but now the races seemed more consistently to attract better qualified aspirants. Pay had been increased, and prestige was higher.[28] All in all, a seat on the Supreme

27. In contemporary times 15.8% of the positions were contested in the general elections and 37.1% were opposed in the primaries. Previously, from 1934 to 1950, 25% of the general election positions and 50% of those in the primaries were contested. Thus, contrary to what might be expected, the decrease in contested races did not cause a decrease in voter interest.

28. The salaries for supreme court justices were established in the constitution (Article IV, Sec. 14) at $4,000. However, the constitution permitted the legislature to increase salaries from time to time. The following table lists the salaries throughout the years:

1889–1907	$4,000	1965–1972	$27,500
1907–1919	6,000	1972–1974	33,000

Court became more desirable. Perhaps, also, as with Hamley, Neill, and McGovern it could lead to an appointment to the federal bench—the epitome of one's professional career. A review of some of the leading campaigns will illustrate the higher level of interest developed among the electorate.

Justice George B. Simpson was opposed by Robert C. Finley in the 1950 September primary. Whoever won would be voted on the November ballot unopposed. Simpson was clearly the front runner, having served with distinction on the high court since 1937, while his opponent had already suffered defeat in trying to unseat Judge Robinson in 1948. To gain support from the profession and to have an impact on the Seattle Bar Association's preference poll, Simpson sent out an appeal for support to all the members of the bar:

> I am seeking re-election to the Supreme Court . . . and desire and request your support of my candidacy. For your information regarding my qualifications for the position, I present the following brief sketch of my record: . . .
>
> . . . . During my thirty years' service as a judge on the bench of the Superior and Supreme Courts of this state, I have endeavored, to the best of my ability, to decide all cases and questions with fairness and impartiality and in strict accord with the constitution and the laws. . . .
>
> I submit my record for your consideration and request your favorable support on my candidacy.[29]

Simpson was successful in gaining the bar's endorsement. He received 643 votes in the poll to 209 for Finley. Simpson's newspaper ads interestingly reflected the politics of the period. According to Simpson, the greatest threat to American Democracy came from the "bureaucrats, pinks and communists" at home and abroad. However, he argued, the Supreme Court was the bulwark of the defense against such threats:

1919–1943	7,000	1974–1975	34,825
1943–1947	8,500	1975–1977	39,412
1947–1949	10,000	1977–1979	45,000
1949–1953	12,000	1979–1980	48,200
1953–1957	15,000	1980–1984	52,500
1957–1965	20,000	1984–	66,000

Until 1968 Article IV, Sec. 14, prevented increases in salaries during the term for which the judges were elected. Section 14 read that judges would receive salaries for services "which shall not be increased after their election, nor during the term for which they shall have been elected." Amendment 54 became Article XXX in 1968, allowing increases during the terms for which they had been elected. Thus, when the legislature increased the judges' pay, all received that increase.

29. Letter dated August 1, 1950 (author's Supreme Court file).

Table 6.2
Election Results, 1950–68

	Primary	General
_1950_	_(Sept. 12)_	_(Nov. 7)_
(Pos. 1)		
*George B. Simpson	159,189	
Robert C. Finley	189,082	399,882
(Pos. 2)		
*_Fred G. Hamley_	100,592	290,030
Hugh Rosellini	129,636	280,200
Lyle L. Iverson	48,604	
William J. Millard	88,593	
(Pos. 3)		
*_Charles T. Donworth_		355,559
_1952_	_(Sept. 9)_	_(Nov. 4)_
(Pos. 1)		
*_E. W. Schwellenbach_	451,630	577,733
(Pos. 2)		
*_Matthew Hill_	413,964	530,130
(Pos. 3)		
*_Ralph Olson_	405,692	525,355
(Pos. 4)		
*_Frank P. Weaver_	395,226	505,784
_1954_	_(Sept. 14)_	_(Nov. 2)_
(Pos. 1)		
Hugh J. Rosellini	217,660	511,597
Richard B. Ott	185,607	
(Pos. 2)		
*_Joseph Mallery_	282,773	449,877
(Pos. 3)		
*_Frank Weaver_	274,291	436,898
_1956_	_(Sept. 11)_	_(Nov. 6)_
(Pos. 3, short term)		
William J. Millard	241,210	548,901
H. Doane Brodie	140,779	
Herbert H. Seiler	94,464	
(Pos. 3, full term)		
*_Harry E. Foster_	144,625	413,097
John F. Dore	114,698	354,529
William J. Millard, Jr.	107,872	
Paul Coughlin	74,845	
Cadwell F. Corrigan	68,690	
George E. Smith	51,393	
(Pos. 1)		
*_Charles T. Donworth_	**	457,998
Lyle Higgins		254,403
(Pos. 2)		
*_Robert C. Finley_		553,040
(Pos. 4)		
*_Richard B. Ott_	**	364,558
Jerry T. Haggarty		349,564
_1958_	_(Sept. 9)_	_(Nov. 4)_
(Pos. 2)		
*_Richard B. Ott_	191,146	369,190
William J. Millard, Jr.	126,857	277,062
Henry C. Perkins	51,641	
Lyle Higgins	48,077	
(Pos. 3)		
*_Robert T. Hunter_	214,738	465,523
Jerry T. Haggarty	127,110	
Fred T. Smart	48,049	
(Pos. 1)		
*_Matthew Hill_	**	483,682

Table 6.2 (*continued*)

	Primary	*General*		*Primary*	*General*
1960	*(Sept. 13)*	*(Nov. 8)*	*1966*	*(Sept. 20)*	*(Nov. 8)*
(Pos. 1)			(Pos. 1)		
**Frank P. Weaver*	429,634	595,071	**Hugh Rosellini*	314,277	568,704
			Vaughn E. Evans	196,937	
(Pos. 3)			(Pos. 2)		
**Hugh Rosellini*	481,850	547,018	**Frank P. Weaver*	315,334	523,755
(Pos. 2)			(Pos. 3)		
**Joseph Mallery*	291,165	587,309	**Orris Hamilton*	304,431	511,129
Jerry T. Haggarty	203,084				
1962	*(Sept. 11)*	*(Nov. 6)*	*1968*	*(Sept. 17)*	*(Nov. 5)*
(Pos. 1)			(Pos. 1)		
**Robert C. Finley*	213,365	516,862	**Robert C. Finley*	335,344	610,538
			Vaughn E. Evans	172,814	
(Pos. 3)			(Pos. 2)		
**Harry E. Foster*	286,309	492,869	**Frank Hale*	398,040	591,680
(Pos. 2)			(Pos. 3)		
**Charles Donworth*	217,165	494,552	**Walter McGovern*	427,150	622,039
Robert T. Kennedy	153,522				
(Pos. 4)			(Pos. 4)		
**Orris Hamilton*	191,616	497,086	**Marshall Neill*	389,167	578,642
William C. Goodloe	176,697				
1964	*(Sept. 15)*	*(Nov. 3)*			
(Pos. 1)					
**Richard B. Ott*	358,765	637,515			
Vaughn E. Evans	259,287				
(Pos. 2)					
**Matthew Hill*	481,082	621,592			
(Pos. 3)					
**Robert T. Hunter*	470,772	614,897			
(Pos. 4)					
**Frank Hale*	468,733	608,957			

*Incumbent
**No primary contest as only two filed.
Italicized names designate winners
Full six-year term unless otherwise indicated

> You want your kind of man like Judge Simpson with *experience* and *devotion* to duty to uphold your rights and to continue to serve you. A vote for Judge Simpson . . . is a vote for an AMERICAN defender of your rights and freedom [emphasis in original].[30]

The judge gained further support by publishing endorsements from former supreme court judges Jeffers and Steinert. Again, names of members of the legal fraternity were prominent in published ads.

Finley countered with an emphasis upon his own broad and impressive experiences as attorney for the Federal Alcohol Control Administration, probation officer and attorney with the Justice Department, and counsel for the Office of Price Administration. Also, geography played an important role since Finley stressed his Seattle and Renton legal practice, while his opponent was still identified with less populous Vancouver and Clark County even though he had been in Olympia for the last thirteen years.

Despite the fact that both contestants were or had been Democrats, partisanship permeated their campaigns. Finley had the endorsement of the Americans for Democratic Action predominately composed of Democrats, and the conservative Simpson was recommended by Pro-America, the National Organization of Republican Women. Finley was able to overcome the incumbency advantage and the bar's endorsement by defeating Simpson by 30,000 votes in September. His name appeared on the November ballot unopposed.

Although the organized bar had supported Simpson, the lawyers failed to anticipate the fine showing by Finley. Simpson later attributed his defeat to the complacency of the legal fraternity. But he had been relatively isolated from the public's consciousness while serving on the bench and had never had to mount a statewide campaign, since in his two previous elections he had been unopposed. In contrast, Finley had faced incumbent John Robinson in both the primaries and the November balloting in 1948. Although defeated by 120,000 votes, Finley gained experience from the earlier encounter, had a state-wide organization, and had developed name familiarity among the voters.

The most interesting campaign from the perspective of the electorate in 1950 was that between Justice Hamley and superior court judge Hugh Rosellini. They differed in their politics (Republican vs. Democrat), in their backgrounds (city councilman and state execu-

30. *The Seattle Post-Intelligencer*, September 8, 1950.

tive vs. legislator and trial judge), and in their styles (aggressive vs. reactive). The endorsements for Hamley were impressive. He was supported by the Seattle Bar Association's polls (614 to 107), by the Pro-America organization, by five former supreme court justices, by the immediate past president of the State Bar Association, by the past president of the American Bar Association, and by the governor. However, labor and Americans for Democratic Action endorsed Rosellini.

Hamley's ads identified him as *The Non-partisan Candidate* for the supreme court. The voters were urged to contact one of the over four hundred attorneys listed in the ad who "lives near you. He will be happy to tell you why it is important for you to go to the polls . . . and vote for Justice Frederick G. Hamley."[31]

Rosellini, who lacked the active support of the bar establishment, countered with ads that stated:

> In some campaigns for Judgeships, a small list of attorney's names will appear advocating the election of a particular candidate. I want the public to know that in my race . . . I have not solicited attorneys to sign for me. I do not want any attorney to feel under obligation to me, nor I to him. A Judge's conduct should be above reproach in this matter. He should be just and fair in the trial of every case, for our Courts must ever remain the bulwark of our Republic.[32]

The strong showing by Rosellini in the primaries had not been anticipated by Hamley supporters. The incumbent was saved from defeat only by the fact that two other candidates gained enough votes to prevent Rosellini from achieving an absolute majority in the September balloting. Hamley and Rosellini moved on to the general election campaign and the contest heated considerably.

A few days before the November 7 balloting, Hamley delivered a hardhitting attack suggesting a variety of factors that he felt voters should consider. He asserted that he was "no longer primarily concerned about this election in my capacity as a judge" but rather he was "now primarily concerned, as a citizen, in preserving the integrity of our courts."

> I ask you then to carefully consider whether this is merely a contest between two personalities. Or is the issue far greater? Is this really my personal election battle? Or is it the fight of all citizens who see in this campaign a bold attempt, by undisclosed interests laden with money and ingenuity, to pack the highest court of the state?

31. *Ibid.*
32. *Ibid.*, September 10, 1950.

> [Our Democracy means] our courts must never fall under the control or dominance of any group or special interest.
> You can't buy integrity but you can vote for it.[33]

Hamley's supporters leveled three charges at Rosellini: first, his ads implied he was the incumbent supreme court judge; second, he was attempting to buy the election; and third, special interests were running his campaign. If successful, his supporters would "pack" the court in favor of special interests.

Rosellini had used the word "retain" on some of his campaign materials, implying he was an incumbent. However, his materials also (sometimes in small print) announced that "presently" he was a superior court judge.

Rosellini's records were opened to the media in order to refute the charge of excessive influence by special interests. He announced that most of his campaign expenses were paid for from his savings and a second mortgage on his home. Finally, "with nine Judges sitting on our Supreme Court . . . , is it fair to claim that ONE JUDGE ELECTED BY THE PEOPLE . . . WILL PACK IT? Is it fair to the other eight Judges?" Rosellini continued:

> In some campaigns malicious rumors are spread to discredit one candidate and thus ensure the election of another. . . . A Judge should be above such conduct. He should be just and fair even in the heat of a political race with his future at stake. It is my considered belief that a Judge should remain courteous in the face of political clamor and indifferent to partisan influences. . . . 'With Malice toward None' I seek your vote.[34]

In response, Hamley claimed he had "conducted his campaign completely free from misrepresentation of any sort," and that he had "*never* attempted to use his association with Christian organizations as a means of obtaining votes." He said that he was beholden to no one.[35]

The incumbent turned the vote around and edged Rosellini in the final balloting by a mere 9,800 votes.[36] The intensity of the campaign

33. *Ibid.*, November 2, 1950.
34. *Ibid.*
35. *Ibid.*, November 3, 1950. The issue of religion surfaced near the end of the campaign. Rosellini's Catholic background was downplayed by his supporters and many of the fundamentalist Protestant churches gave active support to Hamley.
36. After the election, some of Rosellini's supporters talked of voting machine problems in King County which may have deprived their candidate of votes. No investigation was conducted, however, and any suggestion of fraud was soon dropped.

encouraged more than three-fourths of the voters going to the polls in November 1950 to cast their ballot for supreme court judge. Hamley soon was elevated to the Federal Court of Appeals where he served with distinction and earned a national reputation for appellate reform. Rosellini earned his spot on the Supreme Court by defeating Richard Ott in 1954.

The attraction of the 1956 election campaign was due more to the uniqueness of the positions and persons competing than to any strident campaigning or partisan issues. William J. Millard was running again, this time for the thirty-eight days left in Hamley's six-year term. If Millard succeeded he would not hear any cases, review any opinions, or even move into the Temple of Justice. However, if he served even this brief period his state pension would increase, according to a complicated formula, from $291.66 to $500 a month. His campaign, such as it was, was actually based on his desire to increase his retirement pay.[37] William J. Millard, Jr., the justice's son, was running against appointee Harry Ellsworth Foster for the full six-year term, as was also John F. Dore, a noted legal and political figure in Seattle. Incumbents Donworth and Ott (the latter, whom Rosellini had defeated in 1954, was appointed by Langlie in 1955) were also being challenged. Justice Finley had no opposition.

The Seattle Bar Association recommended Brodie, Foster, Donworth, and Ott. The Associated Republican Women and *The Seattle Post-Intelligencer* endorsed the same candidates. For the first time in several decades the State Bar held a preferential plebiscite for the November election and recommended the election of Foster, Donworth, and Ott. In both the primary and general elections, good behavior and judicial dignity prevailed among the various candidates and their supporters. For example, candidate Haggarty admitted that his "opponent [Ott], appointed by Governor Langlie, is a gentleman." *The Seattle Post-Intelligencer* accurately portrayed the 1956 campaigns: "The races were within the dignity of the courts and could be termed 'popularity contests' with the candidates pointing out their own qualifications."[38] Despite the blandness of the campaigns, approximately two-thirds of those going to the polls

37. In July, Millard wrote potential supporters making the following appeal: "I filed for the Supreme Court short term of 38 days to secure my pension and to enable me to pay my debts. . . . I have not the funds with which to finance an extensive campaign, therefore I am writing you and to other friends requesting that they pass the word in my behalf to their friends and acquaintance, especially to those who subscribe to the same principles to which you and the undersigned are committed" (Letter undated but received in the governor's office July 30, 1966. *Evans Papers*, State Archives).

38. *The Seattle Post-Intelligencer*, November 7, 1950.

completed their ballots and cast their votes in the Foster-Dore race, giving Foster the victory.

The 1958 elections involved incumbent Richard Ott (in his third supreme court race in four years) running for a six-year term, Justice Hunter, and Justice Hill, who was unopposed. The 1958 campaigns had some unique features. First, there were no long lists of lawyer endorsements in newspapers and in handouts. Second, there was the clear presence of labor as a campaign force. The first phenomenon was due to a ruling of the board of governors of the Washington State Bar Association. The governors thought that when a lawyer lent his name to a campaign by means of an endorsement list, he might be in violation of Canon 30 of the Canons of Judicial Ethics. A request for endorsement "subjects a practicing attorney to undue pressure . . . since . . . no lawyer desires to offend the man before whom he must practice."[39]

The infusion of labor politics was due to two factors. Endorsements by labor and other interest groups moved in to fill the gap left by the absence of attorney endorsements. Also, on the November ballot in 1958 was a highly political antilabor "right to work" measure (Initiative 202). Labor mobilized effectively to defeat the measure and, as a result, made an impact on candidates and other issues on the ballot. Justice Ott was particularly concerned over accusations that he was antilabor. He attributed this view to the fact that he was from an eastern Washington farming community, and that labor simply assumed he would be unsympathetic to their cause.[40] In response, his ads cited several prolabor cases in which he had written the court's opinions. He also accumulated a number of labor endorsements, largely from local and eastern Washington unions.

The Seattle Bar Association's plebiscite gave Ott and Hunter substantial majorities over their opponents in the primary, and the November poll of the state bar overwhelmingly supported Ott. As the single expression of the preferences of the legal fraternity, the bar polls helped Hunter and Ott to roll up safe majorities in the elections. Ott's majority was substantially better than that gained two years earlier.

None of the judicial contests in the next fifteen years went beyond the primaries. Not until 1973, and then by a particular change in the election laws, was there a contested race on the general election ballot.

Name familiarity plays an important and sometimes confusing

39. *Washington State Bar News* 13 (June-July 1959):26.
40. Interview with Judge Richard Ott, October 6, 1976.

role in elections. Perhaps the impact is greater in nonissue elections such as the nonpartisan contests for judicial positions which already suffer from considerable voter fatigue. For example, in 1964 incumbent Governor Dan Evans defeated former Governor Albert Rosellini. Two years later Justice Hugh Rosellini, not a close relative of the recently defeated former governor, was challenged by attorney Vaughn Evans. Fearing that the voters might mistakenly view the race as a rerun of the previous Evans-Rosellini contest, Hugh Rosellini worked extra hard to turn back the challenge. In the next election Vaughn Evans again filed against incumbent Chief Justice Robert Finley. The threat of name confusion compelled Finley to write Governor Evans for assistance:

> As you well know, the perennial Mr. Vaughn Evans—no relation to you, and I daresay not even a speaking acquaintance—filed the last minute and will be opposing me for re-election in the September 17 Primary. Apparently, he is again hoping to ride piggy-back on your name familiarity and standing with the electorate of Washington. . . .
>
> The foregoing is prefatory to expressing the hope that you can in an appropriate manner take some action to clarify or straighten out any existing name confusion in the minds of the . . . voters.

On September 11 the governor's office issued the following "news brief":

> In response to a reporter asking the Governor today if Vaughn Evans, perennial candidate for Chief Justice of the State Supreme Court (and now running against Chief Justice Finley), were related to him, Governor Evans said: I hope that no one associates Vaughn Evans' candidacy in any respect with the Governor's race four years ago. Vaughn Evans is certainly no relative of mine. I have a great deal of respect for Chief Justice Finley—of his capabilities and his background—although I do not take public position on races of a nonpartisan character.[41]

In subsequent campaigns, however, the governor was to forget his promise to remain aloof from nonpartisan contests.

Elections during this period of transition often involved a number of participants vying for the attention of the electorate. The Grange, bar, labor, and quasipartisan groups awarded their endorsements, and the governor lent his support. On occasion, however, name

41. Letter from Finley to Evans dated August 26, 1968. The news brief was dated September 11, 1968. *Evans Papers*, State Archives.

familiarity tended to intervene, adding to the unpredictability of the outcome. The nature of the elections still remained tentative, with each contest still setting its own style. However, the organized bar had asserted itself into the appointments and elections of the jurists and was now institutionalizing its role in the recruitment sequence.

The Increasing Role of the Bar in Elections

The most distinctive trend during this period had been the strengthening role of the organized profession in judicial elections. Since 1948 the Seattle Bar Association, and soon thereafter the State Bar, regularly conducted preferential polls of their memberships in contested judicial elections and released the results to the news media. Their goal, of course, was to influence the outcome of elections by advising the voter and by providing campaign materials for those candidates favored in the polls. Nonetheless, the voter became confused by the sometimes conflicting results of the preferential polls and of endorsements by members of the legal profession. A candidate could be overwhelmingly supported in the polls, but his opponent could still accumulate a fairly impressive list of attorneys endorsing his candidacy. Thus, either the polls were misleading, the endorsements meaningless, or both practices questionable.

As previously stated, other difficulties with endorsements arose. Canon 30 of the Canons of Judicial Ethics cautioned that a judicial candidate "should refrain from all conduct which might tend to arouse reasonable suspicion that he is using the power or prestige of his judicial position to promote his candidacy," and others should not "do anything in behalf of his candidacy which would reasonably lead to such suspicion." There was fear that the common campaign practice of attorney endorsements could possibly violate Canon 30. The practice of candidates polling the bar by means of post cards not only to solicit endorsements but also to request permission to use the attorney's name in advertisements had caused some complaints.

To deal with the threat of unchecked endorsements and the soliciting of funds, the Washington board of governors of the State Bar in 1958 adopted a rule forbidding "any use of the names of lawyers wherein lawyers are designated by their names and their profession in public and advertisements in support" of judicial candidates. Thus, the elections of 1958 were conducted without benefit of long lists of endorsements published in the media and handed out to prospective voters. Interestingly, the level of voter fall-off remained stable.

The criticisms of the 1958 restrictions on endorsements were

The Temple of Justice, the oldest public building on the capitol grounds. Construction was begun in 1910 and the exterior was completed in the 1920s. In 1987 extensive work was begun to fortify the building against earthquake damage.

Elmon Scott, 1889–99.

Ralph O. Dunbar, 1889–1912.

Theodore L. Stiles, 1889–95.

John P. Hoyt, 1889–97.

Mark Fullerton, 1898–1931.

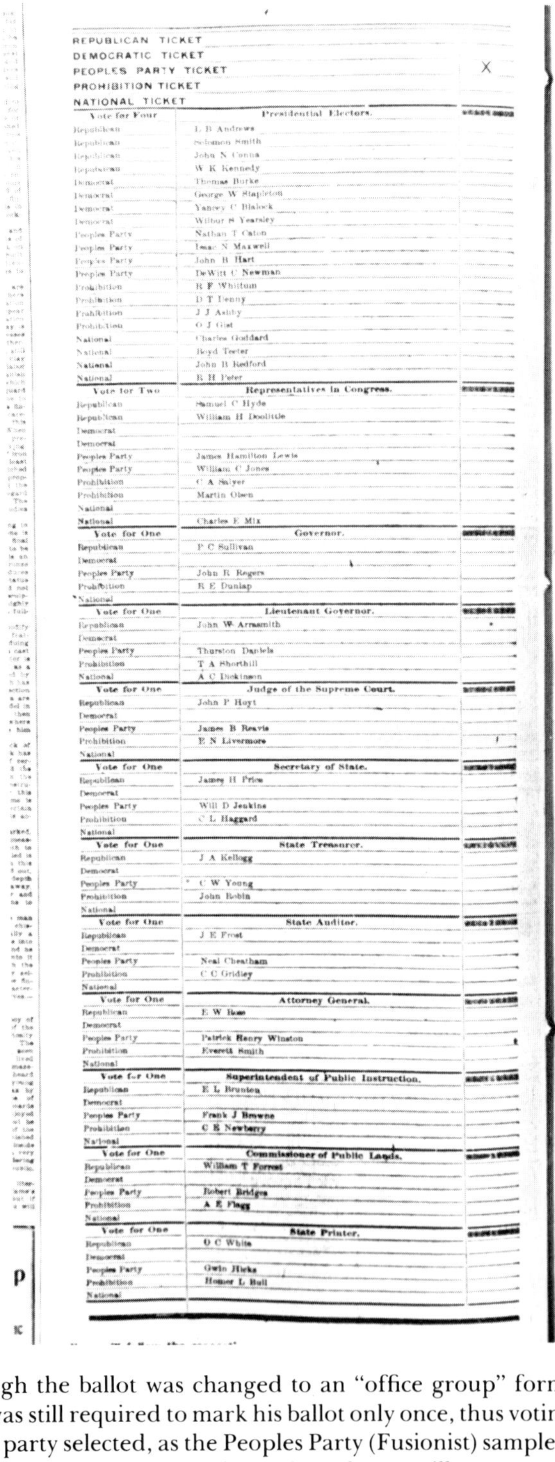

REPUBLICAN TICKET		
DEMOCRATIC TICKET		
PEOPLES PARTY TICKET		X
PROHIBITION TICKET		
NATIONAL TICKET		
Vote for Four	Presidential Electors.	
Republican	L B Andrews	
Republican	Solomon Smith	
Republican	John N Conna	
Republican	W K Kennedy	
Democrat	Thomas Burke	
Democrat	George W Stapleton	
Democrat	Yancey C Blalock	
Democrat	Wilbur S Yearsley	
Peoples Party	Nathan T Caton	
Peoples Party	Isaac N Maxwell	
Peoples Party	John B Hart	
Peoples Party	DeWitt C Newman	
Prohibition	R F Whitlum	
Prohibition	D T Denny	
Prohibition	J J Ashby	
Prohibition	O J Gist	
National	Charles Goddard	
National	Boyd Teeter	
National	John B Redford	
National	R H Peter	
Vote for Two	Representatives in Congress.	
Republican	Samuel C Hyde	
Republican	William H Doolittle	
Democrat		
Democrat		
Peoples Party	James Hamilton Lewis	
Peoples Party	William C Jones	
Prohibition	C A Salyer	
Prohibition	Martin Olsen	
National		
National	Charles E Mix	
Vote for One	Governor.	
Republican	P C Sullivan	
Democrat		
Peoples Party	John R Rogers	
Prohibition	R E Dunlap	
National		
Vote for One	Lieutenant Governor.	
Republican	John W Arrasmith	
Democrat		
Peoples Party	Thurston Daniels	
Prohibition	T A Shorthill	
National	A C Dickinson	
Vote for One	Judge of the Supreme Court.	
Republican	John P Hoyt	
Democrat		
Peoples Party	James B Reavis	
Prohibition	E N Livermore	
National		
Vote for One	Secretary of State.	
Republican	James H Price	
Democrat		
Peoples Party	Will D Jenkins	
Prohibition	C L Haggard	
National		
Vote for One	State Treasurer.	
Republican	J A Kellogg	
Democrat		
Peoples Party	C W Young	
Prohibition	John Robin	
National		
Vote for One	State Auditor.	
Republican	J E Frost	
Democrat		
Peoples Party	Neal Cheatham	
Prohibition	C C Gridley	
National		
Vote for One	Attorney General.	
Republican	E W Ross	
Democrat		
Peoples Party	Patrick Henry Winston	
Prohibition	Everett Smith	
National		
Vote for One	Superintendent of Public Instruction.	
Republican	E L Brunton	
Democrat		
Peoples Party	Frank J Browne	
Prohibition	C E Newberry	
National		
Vote for One	Commissioner of Public Lands.	
Republican	William T Forrest	
Democrat		
Peoples Party	Robert Bridges	
Prohibition	A E Flagg	
National		
Vote for One	State Printer.	
Republican	O C White	
Democrat		
Peoples Party	Gwin Hicks	
Prohibition	Homer L Bull	
National		

Although the ballot was changed to an "office group" form in 1895, the voter was still required to mark his ballot only once, thus voting a solid ticket for the party selected, as the Peoples Party (Fusionist) sample ballot appearing in the October 29, 1896, *Seattle Daily Times* illustrates.

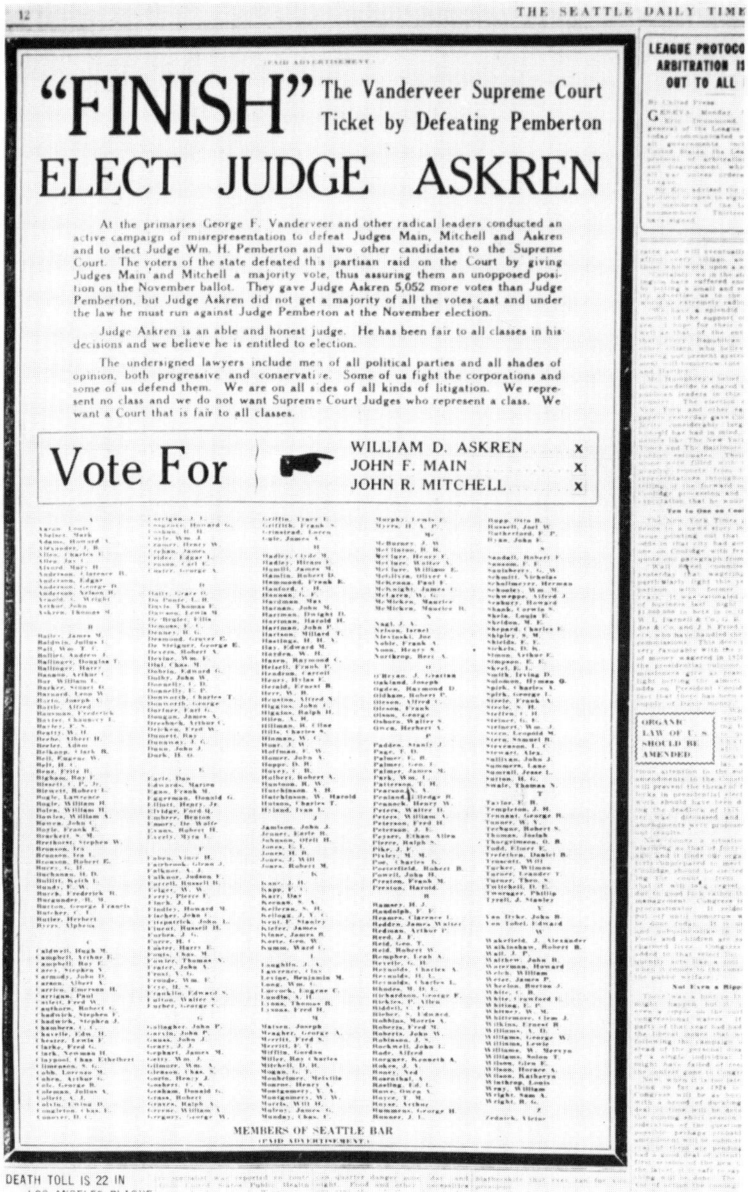

12 THE SEATTLE DAILY TIMES

(PAID ADVERTISEMENT)

"FINISH" The Vanderveer Supreme Court Ticket by Defeating Pemberton

ELECT JUDGE ASKREN

At the primaries George F. Vanderveer and other radical leaders conducted an active campaign of misrepresentation to defeat Judges Main, Mitchell and Askren and to elect Judge Wm. H. Pemberton and two other candidates to the Supreme Court. The voters of the state defeated this partisan raid on the Court by giving Judges Main and Mitchell a majority vote, thus assuring them an unopposed position on the November ballot. They gave Judge Askren 5,052 more votes than Judge Pemberton, but Judge Askren did not get a majority of all the votes cast and under the law he must run against Judge Pemberton at the November election.

Judge Askren is an able and honest judge. He has been fair to all classes in his decisions and we believe he is entitled to election.

The undersigned lawyers include men of all political parties and all shades of opinion, both progressive and conservative. Some of us fight the corporations and some of us defend them. We are on all sides of all kinds of litigation. We represent no class and we do not want Supreme Court Judges who represent a class. We want a Court that is fair to all classes.

Vote For

WILLIAM D. ASKREN X
JOHN F. MAIN X
JOHN R. MITCHELL X

MEMBERS OF SEATTLE BAR

(PAID ADVERTISEMENT)

LEAGUE PROTOCOL ARBITRATION IS OUT TO ALL

DEATH TOLL IS 22 IN

This and similar ads were prominently displayed in the state's leading newspapers in 1924, illustrating the awakening of the legal profession to the importance of nonpartisan elections. *The Seattle Daily Times*, November 2, 1924.

AGAINST Township Organization

Republican Ticket

Democratic Ticket

Socialist Ticket

Socialist Labor Ticket

Prohibition Ticket

Progressive Ticket

Non-Partisan Judiciary Ticket

Beginning with the 1912 ballot, supreme court candidates were listed separately on a "Non-partisan Judiciary Ticket." Note on the sample ballot appearing here from the October 26, 1912, *Seattle Daily Times*, that only two names are listed. Ralph Dunbar, winner of the September primary, who would have been listed, died. John F. Main, who was appointed to replace him, conducted the first successful write-in campaign to retain his seat.

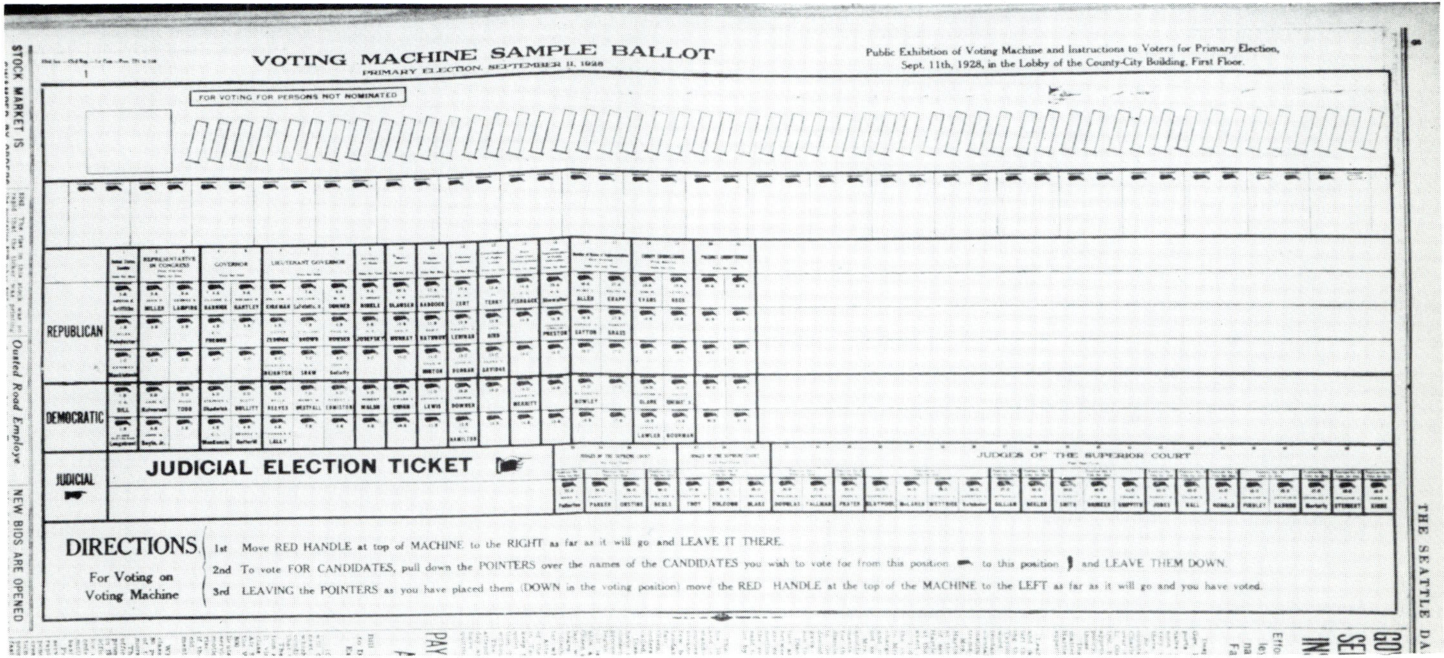

By 1928 the voting machine was used in nearly all urban areas. The nonpartisan judicial candidates were placed separately from the political party aspirants on the ballot. *The Seattle Daily Times*, September 7, 1928.

Vote for Judge

MATTHEW W. HILL

The Non-Partisan Judge Endorsed By These More Than 1000 Lawyers FOR THE

SUPREME COURT

POSITION NO. 3

Non-Partisan Judicial Ballot, Tuesday, November 5

and many others!

Lawyer endorsement played a leading role in judicial campaigns almost from the beginning. Judge Hill's ads in 1946 included over 1,000 names of attorneys from James Abbott to James Zylstra "and many others!" *The Seattle Daily Times*, November 3, 1946.

A selection of campaign ads from the modern court.

Frank Parks Weaver, 1951–70.

Robert C. Finley, 1951–76.

Carolyn R. Dimmick, 1981–85.

William J. Steinert, 1932–49.

Court 5, 1979–80. Back row: Hicks, Horowitz, Dolliver, Williams. Front row: Hamilton, Rosellini, Utter, Stafford, Brachtenbach.

Hugh J. Rosellini, 1955–84.

sharp. Fund raising could be hampered. The bar's poll, sometimes viewed as only a popularity contest, would be the only expression of the preferences of the legal fraternity. Other pressure groups could move in to fill the void with their own endorsements. Heretofore, pressure group endorsements were used primarily to influence the vote of the group's membership, but now they could be used to sway the electorate at large. Finally, candidates could find it difficult to gather those financial and moral commitments at the early stages of initiation needed to test their chances and to discourage potential opponents.

As a result of a vote at the 1958 Annual Convention and a 1959 recommendation of the Ethics Committee, the board of governors softened its rules on endorsement. Soliciting funds and names for endorsements was again possible but it could not be done directly by the candidate himself.[42]

The use of bar polls or plebiscites indicating the preferences of the legal fraternity was a regular feature of elections after 1948. Even prior to that year, the Seattle bar had been prominent in influencing the outcome of elections in King County by means of its plebiscites. By 1950 a division of labor obtained between the Seattle and State Bar Associations. The Seattle attorneys assumed full responsibility for polling which they began to share with the state association in 1956 (and relinquished completely in 1974). For its part the State Bar had sole control over advising the governor on appointments. With most of the attorneys in Seattle and King County, and with nearly half the voters in the Seattle metropolitan area, the Seattle bar's preferential polls became an important part of the recruitment of supreme court judges.

A special Judicial Plebiscite Committee was established by the board of trustees of the Seattle bar in 1950. But their concern was limited to primaries since most judicial elections were decided in the September balloting. In 1956 the State Bar took over the neglected responsibility for advising the public in the general elections. This division of labor continued until 1962 when both the Seattle and State Bars conducted polls for the primaries. Finally, in 1974 the Seattle group dropped supreme court candidates from their polls and left both primary and general election recommendations entirely to the State Bar. Of the nineteen contested races (counting both primary and general elections) between 1950 and 1969 the voters ignored the advice of the Seattle and State Bar plebiscite only three times (the Finley, Rosellini, and Millard victories in 1950, 1954 and 1956). (See table 6.3.)

42. *Washington State Bar News*, 14 (August 1960): 43.

Table 6.3
Bar Polls for Supreme Court Candidates, 1950–68

		Primary		*General*
Year	*Candidate*	*Seattle Bar*	*State Bar*	*State Bar*
1950	*Simpson	643		
	Finley	209		
	**Hamley*	614		
	Rosellini	107		
	Iverson	78		
	Millard	65		
1952	All Unopposed			
1954	*Rosellini*	302		
	Ott	735		
1956	*Millard*	134		
	Brodie	450		
	Sieler	127		
	**Foster*	526		1,677
	Dore	188		618
	Millard, Jr.	43		
	Coughlin	223		
	Corrigan	8		
	Smith	117		
	**Donworth*	1,021		2,144
	Higgins	61		129
	**Ott*	906		1,970
	Haggarty	179		313

Despite general satisfaction with the results of their "cooperation" with the electorate through their preference polls and their success in advising the governor on appointments, the State Bar turned its attention toward improving the system by which judges were selected, although not with the full enthusiasm of most of the membership. In 1966 the Committee on Methods of Selecting Judges recommended to the State Bar that they work closely with the Superior Court Judges Association and with members of the Supreme Court to gain an agreement on how to select judges in the state. Although the committee was not unanimous, they did favor a modified A.B.A. or Missouri Plan similar to that used in the state of Nebraska. A committee of attorneys, judges and lay persons would compile a list from which the governor would appoint. After one year the appointee would stand for election. Rather than running

Table 6.3 (*continued*)

		Primary		*General*
Year	*Candidate*	*Seattle Bar*	*State Bar*	*State Bar*
1958	**Ott*	829		1,851
	Millard, Jr.	134		298
	Perkins	17		
	Higgins	30		
	**Hunter*	813		
	Haggarty	122		
	Smart	78		
1960	**Mallery*	841		
	Haggarty	233		
1962	**Donworth*		1,748	
	Kennedy		138	
	**Hamilton*		1,350	
	Goodloe		574	
1964	**Ott*	1,068		
	Evans	258		
1966	**Rosellini*	800	1,708	
	Evans	95	199	
1968	**Finley*	1,265	1,866	
	Evans	148	231	

*Incumbent
Italicized names designate election winners

on his record alone, others could file against the incumbent.[43] In 1970 the bar's proposal was introduced in the legislature. But enthusiasm for a new system of selecting judges was lacking and the plan died in committee.

The participation of the bar in judicial recruitment between 1950 and 1969 was largely confined to consolidating its position in both appointments and elections. Since the beginnings of the arrangement with the governor to advise on filling vacancies, all of the appointees had been approved by the bar's selection committee. But this record was not easily achieved as the attorneys had to renegotiate the agreement with each incoming administration and to make adjustments in the arrangement from time to time. The relationship

43. *Ibid.*, 20 (Sept.–Oct. 1966): 54.

between governor and bar had not involved to the stage where both could assume the cooperation of the other.

The record of advising the voters appeared excellent. However, the bar poll tended to support incumbents who traditionally had also been supported by the electorate. Also in two of the three campaigns where the advice of the lawyers was ignored, the insurgents had been heavily supported by labor. (The Millard victory in 1956 was a special case. Nearly a nonelection, the winner would serve only a few weeks in the short term under contention.) What this suggests is that in crucial contests the organized bar was not monopolizing the process. Finally, the voting statistics indicated that the electorate in both primary and general elections was beginning, however slightly, to pay more attention to the separate judicial ballots. What was developing was the slight tipping of the scales toward public accountability although the "public" was to be broadly defined. Actually several "publics" were vying for the attention of the judiciary.

7

Institutionalized Recruitment in the Modern Period, 1969–86

The recruitment sequence of the modern period is an institutionalized process throughout which a number of active participants compete or cooperate to gain the attention of the voters and each other in order to promote or to block candidacies to the Supreme Court. Because of the structured participation of a number of groups in the recruitment process, an uneasy balance between the needs of judicial independence and the demands of public accountability has been struck.

The Role of the Bar Appointments in a Structured System

Since 1933 governors have usually consulted with the State Bar Association's judicial selection committees regarding the appointments to fill vacancies. At various times the relationships between the committee and the governor have been strained, but to a significant degree the advice of the organized bar is now heeded, and in turn, the desires of the governor are a major consideration in the committee's deliberations. Because of its role in the recruitment process, it would be instructive to view in some detail the activities of the State Bar's selection committee.

The standing committee has had various titles through the years—for example, "Judicial Selection and Bar Activities Related Thereto," "Judicial Selection, Tenure and Compensation," "Courts and Judicial Selection," "Judicial Selection, Tenure and Qualifications," and "Judicial Recommendation"—but its primary purpose has been to recommend to the board of governors of the State Bar those candidates the committee members feel are best qualified for the Supreme Court. In turn, the board submitted those recommendations to the governor.[1] Certainly, no legal requirement mandated that the governor follow the bar's advice.

The members of the selection committee were appointed by the board of governors (as were all the standing committees), and although the criteria for appointment to the committee were unwritten, the informal requirements were: (1) extensive courtroom and appellate experience, (2) no judicial aspirations, (3) little activity in partisan politics, (4) recognition in the legal profession, and (5) residence in a specific area of the state. The members had not been limited to a particular term on the committee, but three years was most common. The committee had varied in size over the years from five to twenty-four. In recent years the board had expanded the committee in order to make it more representative of the legal profession by appointing more women and younger members.

The procedure of the standing committee depended somewhat upon the wishes of the chairpersons and members. Generally, however, the committee acted as a clearing house for initiating candidacies[2] and, in addition to those supplied by members of the selection committee itself,[3] received names for consideration from attorneys who contacted the committee on behalf of themselves or their friends, from the governor's office,[4] and from lists formed by

1. Initially the committee did not submit its certified list of names to the board of governors but sent it directly to the chief executive. In 1972 the board insisted that it first certify the committee's work. See *Washington State Bar News* 22 (July 1972): 33.

2. By 1950 the state committee had centralized all initiation and screening for potential appointees to the Supreme Court. *Ibid.*, 4 (July 19, 1950): 26.

3. According to a former committee member: "Each member of the Committee would make an independent investigation of potential candidates in his area by consulting his local bar association officers, its members, and those who might be interested in appointment, including interviewing the judges of our local Superior Courts" (1975 survey of former members of bar's board of governors and judicial selection committee. Questionnaires were sent to all available judicial selection committee members and bar presidents who held office between 1949 and 1975. Members of the board of governors between 1962 and 1975 were surveyed. Hereafter referred to as *1975 Survey*).

4. One former member of the committee wrote that during his tenure "the Governor usually submitted a list of names to the committee and asked the committee to indicate the names of those on the list regarded as qualified for appointment—to fulfill his agreement not to appoint anyone the Bar felt was not qualified. Other names were not, as a rule, solicited."

A former high court judge also has pointed out the fact that the governor can take the initiative: "I am aware of instances where a governor, desiring to appoint a particular lawyer to the bench, has requested the Bar to consider that individual and advise the governor whether or not the individual is fully qualified. If the Bar does not consider the person to be qualified, he is not added to the list of those recommended." Also from a selection committee member: "Governors have been known to send lists back with the request that a specific person be added to the list so that when he appoints that person, he can say he did so on the recommendation of the Bar Association" (*1975 Survey*).

previous committees. The availability of those on past lists and of new candidates was determined through personal contact.[5]

Personal data on new candidates were gathered not only from committee members who likely knew the potential nominees, but also from questionnaires sent to the candidates requesting background information, data on community service activities, professional experiences, and expressions of views on judging and so forth.

In most cases this was enough information to allow the committee to decide, but sometimes a member from the home jurisdiction of the aspirant was asked to review the questionnaire, contact knowledgeable lawyers and judges, and perhaps interview the candidate. More recently the practice was for the whole committee to interview each candidate. The information carried over from previous lists was updated in much the same manner.

The committee met two or three times a year and reviewed all the data, discussing, debating, and deciding whether to place a particular candidate's name on the recommended ("well-qualified")[6] list. Special meetings may have been called when a vacancy suddenly occurred and additional considerations were warranted, but the committee tried to keep the list current for all appellate appointments.

The data collected were numerous but the sources few. First, to maintain the anonymity necessary for a frank exchange, the number of people contacted by the committee remained manageable.[7] Second, since most of the candidates were personally known to the membership, there was little need to go outside the confines of the committee for information. Third, the initiating and screening processes had to remain relatively obscure from the public to be effective. Disclosure of names accepted or rejected or the release of incomplete information could destroy the confidence peculiar to the bar's relations with the governor. The constraints on the committee

5. For descriptions of how the earlier committees worked see *Washington State Bar News* 3 (September 1949): 82; 3 (July 1949): 73; 4 (July 1950): 26; and 5 (August 1951): 50.

6. In 1983 the board of governors debated the issue of ranking the names on the list sent to the governor. Two classifications—"qualified" and "well qualified"—were considered as a means of separating names on a list already taken from a pool of "excellent" candidates. The board voted unanimously to use the single standard of "well qualified" for all those who were designated as competent by the selection committee. *Ibid.*, 37 (June 1983): 42–44.

7. A former committee member confirmed the need for a closed screening process: "[I]ndividual members may be contacted by [non-committee members] but it is unlikely or an exceptional case. . . . In fact, the investigation . . . has to be undertaken with a great deal of discretion" (*1975 Survey*).

were not altogether different from those on the Standing Committee of the Federal Judiciary of the American Bar Association.[8]

After the committee's deliberations, a list containing from three to ten names was submitted to the board of governors of the bar association. The governor may have informed the committee as to the number of names he or she preferred to have on the list. (The number of names submitted to the board had on occasion exceeded twenty.) Earlier, if the committee was under pressure of time, the list might have been sent directly to the governor. The names on the list were not ranked. On rare occasions the board deleted from or added a name to the list before submitting it to the governor for consideration.

What sorts of qualifications did the members of the committee and of the board of governors of the bar look for when they initiated and screened candidates for appointments? Table 7.1 lists those qualifications former members regarded as important and unimportant. The leaders in the bar tended to look for those kinds of qualifications that pertained to the practice of the law and those which attorneys might best appraise.[9]

It was during Governor Evans' administration that the bar began systematically to insist on these qualifications before approving

8. Joel Grossman, *Lawyers and Judges: The ABA and the Politics of Judicial Selection* (New York: John Wiley, 1965).

9. Although geography, electability, and political party affiliation were regarded as inappropriate criteria for consideration by the profession, a great number of respondents to the *1975 Survey* commented that these considerations actually enter into their deliberations. They assumed that the governor would appoint a candidate of his own party persuasion, and that geographical balance on the bench would be maintained. Also, the ability of the appointee to retain his seat in a statewide election would be of some concern. The attorneys on the selection committee fashioned their recommendations to be consistent with the geographical and political party preferences of the governor. For example, one committee member recalled: "The Committee usually made an effort to make recommendations which would include members of the same political party as the Governor so that the Governor would have an opportunity to make an appointment of a judge having his same political affiliation" (*1975 Survey*). Electability is also important according to another committee member: "A matter of great importance to the individual candidate and therefore to the public as it affects who is willing to become a candidate is the probability of survival in elections. The person who has great ability and good temperament often is not a realistic candidate because to survive in a state-wide election he must have name familiarity and financing. Thus, these factors are as likely to control who will be a candidate as are the probabilities one would be a good appellate judge" (*1975 Survey*). Chairman Philip D. MacBride of the selection committee gave recognition to the role of geography in his report to the association: "Having in mind that the geographic distribution of membership in the Court is frequently a factor in determining a Governor's selection, the list should be fairly representative of different parts of the state and should be sufficiently large to afford the Governor assistance as well as choice in the exercise of his prerogative to name who he pleases" (*Washington State Bar News* 5 [August 1951]: 50).

Table 7.1
Most Important and Least Important Judicial Qualifications

Important	*Unimportant*
Legal competency of candidate	Religion
Judicial personality (temperament)	Friendship
Standing or prestige in the legal community	Political experience
Age and health	Political party affiliation
Standing or prestige in community or state	Geography
Prior judicial experience	Degree of public service
Political and legal philosophy	Electability

SOURCE: 1975 survey.

names for its list. However, after working closely with the bar in his first term, Evans began to assert more independence. He tended to hold the organized bar at arm's length, relying more heavily upon his own legal advisers. He, however, still asked for and largely followed the advice of the selection committees. The factors which entered into the appointments of Neill and McGovern had not been altogether different from previous appointments. The concerns of politics, friendship, and competency played equal roles. However, after 1969 a new and significant factor in both appointments and elections entered into the recruitment process. The addition of the Court of Appeals to the judicial system not only changed the number and kinds of cases heard by the Supreme Court and the manner in which the justices conducted their deliberations, it also established an apprenticeship on the intermediate court as an important requisite for selection to the Supreme Court.

Certainly, the recruitment of supreme court justices did not suddenly "mature" with the beginnings of the Court of Appeals, but a number of subsequent effects can be traced back to the establishment of the court. The new court had a special meaning for Governor Evans, as he was given the authority by the legislature to appoint all the new judges to the bench. An informal agreement was struck with the legislature to appoint representatives from both political parties (the split was seven Republicans and five Democrats). Again, the screening involved in the initial appointments provided the governor and his advisers with more experience in screening and with a pool of potential appointees. The bar's selection committee also recognized the importance of the Court of Appeals by first forming only one list of approved candidates from which the governor could select persons to either the Court of Appeals or the Supreme Court. However, now, separate lists (which may contain the same names) are kept for each division of the appeals bench and for the Supreme Court.

As during his first term the bar continued to send Governor Evans its approved list upon his request. Although the bar insisted upon a rank ordering of names or presenting a preferred list, Evans convinced the attorneys that they should only screen to determine whether or not those on the list were qualified. The bar leaders relented when reminded that the governor had the constitutional power to appoint without them. Later the governor began sending names of those he thought might be interested in the position to the bar to supplement their listing. The initiation phase, then, also was performed by the governor's office. Subsequent Governors Ray and Spellman relied heavily on the form and content of the relationship between bar and governor established by Evans.

The Role of Governors in Contemporary Recruitment

The governor had sole constitutional obligation to fill a supreme court vacancy by appointment. But at the next general election following appointment, each selectee had to stand for election in order to retain the seat. A prospective vacancy was most often anticipated by the legal community itself. The governor and his or her administrative assistant would then start receiving numerous inquiries from prospective candidates and their friends. Generally, the candidates submitted resumes and some were interviewed by the governor or by his or her legal counsel. Background information was collected even though the candidates were known to the chief executive. The governor's close assistants assumed most of the responsibilities for the screening and accumulation of data.[10] Upon the request of the governor at the time the vacancy was officially announced, the selection committee of the State Bar was asked to submit its recommendations with, perhaps, some relevant data on the candidates. (Often an approved list of aspirants was already on file in the governor's office.) If some difficulties with the committee's recommendations were anticipated, the governor could have made the appointment without the bar being contacted. Rarely, however, was such a drastic move necessary.

10. A former governor stated that he "used administrative assistants to gather information. [They] always checked with area legislators, and in some instances local governmental officials. They also did routine checks for personal habits, etc., that might militate against a successful career on the bench." Another also used his assistants to "check the background of the candidate." Or, those finally appointed have been "'known personally to the Governor' or to one of [his] assistants. Thus, [he] had at [his] disposal a good deal of first hand information" (undated letters to author).

The governor's influence over the deliberations of the bar's selection committee was substantial. All he or she needed was a "qualified" rating from the bar so that the favored aspirant could be placed on the list. By requesting that the committee investigate a favored candidate, by returning the list to the committee for reconsideration, by suggesting the number of names to be placed on the list, or by informally checking with the committee to determine how a certain candidate might be rated, the governor retained the initiative. The committee, of course, found it expedient to be receptive to gubernatorial wishes. Without a receptive governor the committee would be without a purpose. However, a clearly unacceptable aspirant did not receive the bar's approval. By the time the recommended list was formed, informal negotiations had probably averted a confrontation.

The governor's office could have checked with various government agencies and with the bar office to assure that none of the candidates had had embarrassing problems with traffic offenses, tax problems, conflicts of interest, moral problems, or professional improprieties. Before the final selection was made, the governor consulted with his or her immediate staff plus a few respected lawyers, bar leaders, and judges. (Members of the Supreme Court previously appointed by the governor could also have been consulted on the "needs" of the court as well as on the competency of candidates who may have argued cases before the high bench.)

A recent governor described the process the chief executive went through:

> In making my selections to fill vacancies on the Supreme Court, I would first ask the . . . [state bar] to submit a list of the people they had approved for appointment to the bench. Then I would have my Executive Assistant check the background of the candidates most of whom I would know personally, . . . Then I would consult with other attorneys that I had faith in, sometimes would consult with some of the members of the bench, and then make my decision.[11]

Another chief executive followed a similar process:

> In case of a vacancy on the supreme court I will first get in touch with the . . . bar and request their recommendation. . . . Each of the judges appointed by me to the supreme court has been known personally to me or to one of my assistants. Thus, I had at my disposal a good deal of first hand information, the recommendation of the . . . bar as well as the advice of persons whose judgment I trusted.

11. Unattributed quotes are from letters, questionnaires, or interviews where the person being questioned was promised anonymity.

Factors which influenced the executive's appointments probably were not altogether different from those factors which the bar also regarded as important. However, the governor also consulted with sources outside the profession and weighed some elements which were not typically regarded as relevant by the lawyers.

Electability was an important consideration. Could the appointee mount a successful campaign at the next general election following the appointment? Political party affiliation and political experience were recognized by the governor as broad general requirements within which more detailed professional criteria were weighed. Virtually all of the appointees had been of the same political party as the appointing governor, but only a few had led active political lives. These political factors were acknowledged by a recent high court appointee. For the governor, the crucial qualification was "the popularity of the applicant with the people and the probability of the appointee's ability to be elected at the next general election." The judge recognized that, of course, the applicant must have "the same political affiliation as that of the Governor." The bar's selection committee purposely placed qualified candidates on the list from the chief executive's political party, thereby making political choices easier. But, according to one governor, political alternatives were examined only as part of many other considerations. His "primary concern was whether the person would make a good judge, . . . his status among his peers, . . . his electability and finally the question of his political affiliation and political activity."

One attorney familiar with the concerns of a governor emphasized geographical considerations. "He did attempt to give some allowance for geographical representation on the Supreme Court, realizing that the Court involved the entire State . . . and not just the most [populous] counties."

Although the gubernatorial sources and criteria for selection of high court jurists coincided significantly with the bar's, the political base of the chief executive was much broader and his or her political concerns were separate.

Clearly, the bar has had an input in all recent administrations. But that input was limited: first, to what the profession could add to the process by its appraisal of candidates' legal acumen and judicial potential; and, second, to the degree the bar could assist in legitimating an appointment.

The governor performed the "political" role complemented by the "expert" role of the profession. It was, however, the linkage of these two roles which contributed to the web of forces providing impetus to the appointment of high court judges in Washington. The relationship between governor and bar is one of reciprocity. The state's chief executive needed the expert advice of the profession as well as its legitimation of his or her choice. The bar obviously needed the governor's good will in order to influence the appointment. Each listened to the other and each added different dimensions to the recruitment process.

The Appointments of Governors Evans, Ray, and Spellman

Charles F. Stafford had been considered for the two previous vacancies filled by Evans. He had been a superior court judge for Skagit County since 1952 and was one of the first twelve judges appointed to the Court of Appeals. Stafford was somewhat active in Republican politics prior to his selection to the bench, but that had been more than eighteen years earlier (he had served as Secretary-Treasurer of the Skagit County Republican Central Committee and as Skagit County prosecutor). He knew the governor only through formal occasions, such as the inauguration of the new Court of Appeals. Stafford was not unfamiliar with the Supreme Court, having acted several times as *pro tempore* justice under a 1962 constitutional amendment designed to help the high court with its overloaded docket.[12] Also, he was from northwestern Washington, a region which had not been represented on the court since Justice Olson. Stafford was also approved by the bar's selection committee.

Stafford had "seriously gone out for both" of the previous vacancies. He had talked with Don Eldridge, Speaker of the House in Olympia, one or two "prominent Republicans in Skagit County," and with Jim Dolliver who handled judicial recruitment for the governor. However, on hearing about the retirement of Matt Hill, he "did nothing." He thought that the governor "knows who I am. . . . If he wants me I'm here. He knows I will accept. . . . Strangely enough, I got the appointment."[13] Stafford attributed his selection largely to the efforts of his longtime friend, Republican legislator Don Eldridge. Eldridge had served with Evans in the legislature and, like Marshall Neill, had been responsible for the governor's legislative program in the late 1960s. Evans heeded the urgings of

12. H.J.R. 6 became Article IV, Sec. 2(a). See C. Sheldon and F. Weaver, *Politicians, Judges and the People* (Westport, Ct.: Greenwood, 1980), 52–57, for a discussion of H.J.R. 6.
13. Interview with Justice Charles Stafford, May 2, 1977.

Table 7.2
Supreme Court Appointments, 1970–82

Justice	*Governor*	*Date*
Charles E. Stafford (R)	Evans (R)	January 1, 1970
Morell E. Sharp (R)	Evans	May 28, 1970
Morell E. Sharp (R)	Evans	May 13, 1970
Robert F. Utter (R)	Evans	December 20, 1971
Robert F. Brachtenbach (R)	Evans	November 20, 1972
James M. Dolliver (R)	Evans	May 6, 1976
Fred H. Dore (D)	Ray (D)	January 2, 1981
Carolyn R. Dimmick (R)	Ray	January 2, 1981
Vernon R. Pearson (R)	Spellman (R)	January 18, 1982
James A. Andersen (R)	Spellman	July 25, 1984
Keith M. Callow (R)	Spellman	January 2, 1985
Barbara Durham (R)	Spellman	January 14, 1985

his former legislative colleague and appointed Stafford to the high court in January 1970.[14]

In April 1970, Frank Weaver announced his intention to retire on May 21, the exact day he had taken his oath of office nineteen years earlier. This vacancy created several problems for the governor, the bar, and the candidates. Superior court judges Morell Sharp, Robert Utter, and Al Bradford were leading candidates, but Evans made it clear that his first choice was his administrative assistant, James Dolliver. Dolliver had a background of partisan political activity as assistant to United States Representative Jack Westland and then as a close supporter and adviser to the governor since 1963. Dolliver wanted the appointment, his name was approved by the bar's selection committee, and it appeared that his promotion was assured.

In an unprecedented action, the Washington State Bar's board of governors removed Dolliver's name from the approved list, apparently for two reasons. Dolliver had practiced law full time for only a little more than a year in 1954 and then between 1962 and 1964. For the leaders of the bar, this was not long enough. Also, a few board members thought that the appointment represented a form of cronyism and political favoritism in which the profession ought not to be involved.

14. Eldridge had written Evans on January 27, 1967, about his friend: "Judge Stafford has gained a fine reputation in our area as being a most fair and impartial jurist, and is well recognized across the state for his integrity and judgment in judicial matters. He would be a great addition to the State's highest court" (Letter dated January 17, 1967, *Evans Papers*, State Archives).

Governor Evans was inclined to ignore the bar and move ahead with his appointment. After hearing of the board's decision, Evans explained his ideas concerning appointments, thereby clearly indicating that Dolliver was still very much in the running.

> I think the most important thing is to have a person on the Supreme Court who is the best person I can find—the most perceptive and most understanding.
>
> I have not always picked from the list and I will retain my independence to choose whomever I please, which is the constitutional prerogative of the Governor. My inclination is that for balance on the court, we should be seeking someone who is not a judge.[15]

Three problems had to be weighed if the governor was to follow through with the Dolliver appointment. First, 1970 was a nonelection year for superior court judges, which meant that they could run for the Supreme Court without giving up their incumbencies on the lower bench. Therefore, a number of well-known and experienced judges might file against Dolliver. (Judge Charles T. Wright of the Thurston-Mason County Superior Court had already announced his intention to challenge the appointee in the September primaries.) Second, without the clear endorsement of the bar association, the appointee would face a formidable task in the elections which were only four months away. The needed funds, endorsements, and campaign organization might not be promptly forthcoming. Finally, if the governor defied the bar, or if he insisted that the board reconsider, the heretofore good relations with the legal profession (interestingly, largely due to Dolliver) would seriously suffer. Given all these difficulties, Dolliver and the governor agreed not to go ahead with the appointment. At the time the governor's aide "thought that was the end" of his hopes for a position on the bench.

The governor then turned to the other candidates on the board's approved list and came up with Judge Morell Sharp of the King County Superior Court, a long-time acquaintance. Sharp and Evans had met in the early fifties at the very outset of Evans's political career. Judge Sharp recalled their meeting quite clearly:

> I met him [while I was] President of the King County Young Republicans. The King County Republican Headquarters called me one day. They said they had this young man who had just been discharged from the Navy and he was interested in politics and they're going to

15. *The Seattle Times*, April 22, 1970.

send him over [for me] to talk with him. I remember Dan coming into the office and so obviously we put him to work immediately.[16]

Sharp had been elected councilman and mayor of the small Seattle suburb of Beaux Arts and had also served on the first Metro Council as the representative of nine eastside towns. (The council coordinated policies in such areas as pollution control and transportation for the greater Seattle metropolitan area.) In 1967 Evans had appointed Sharp to a newly created superior court judgeship in King County. The governor now felt at ease with his appointment of Sharp to the Supreme Court, not anticipating the curious twists of events that would evolve from his actions.[17]

Following his appointment, Judge Sharp had only one month to file for election to the remainder of Weaver's term and only four months to organize a state-wide campaign. Judge Charles T. Wright carried through with his previously announced intention to run for a seat on the court and defeated Sharp in the September primaries. Wright won by over 12,000 votes, although Sharp had public support from Evans, the backing of the bar association, endorsement by a large number of superior court judges, and the campaign clout of the Republican organization. He became only the fourth appointed justice since statehood to be defeated in his first try at election.[18]

In May of the next year, Justice Walter McGovern resigned to accept an appointment to the Federal District Court. Governor Evans promptly reappointed Sharp to the Supreme Court. The justice did not feel he had actually been rejected by the voters and, therefore, accepted the new appointment without hesitation, because he said, "I wanted to get back on the bench."[19] Sharp felt that his defeat had been due to special factors unrelated to an electoral rejection: name familiarity, the lack of labor support, and the short period of time to organize his campaign, none of which dealt with his competency or qualifications. Evans "had no problems" with the reappointment.[20] He did wait for the bar's list, but made it known

16. Interview with Judge Morell Sharp, October 4, 1976.

17. In response to the appointment of Sharp, John Huneke, President of the State Bar Association, wrote Governor Evans: "The Bar Association believes he is eminently qualified and we compliment you on this selection. We fully appreciate that you have no obligation to anyone in making such appointments, but we are pleased when such coincides with our views, and we wish to express our appreciation for any consideration which might have been given the Bar recommendation. We will endeavor to keep an up-to-date list available for any assistance it may be in the future" (Letter dated May 1, 1970, *Evans Papers*, State Archives).

18. The others defeated in their first try after appointment were Chester Hovey (1923), Henry Herman (1932), and Edward Connelly (1946).

19. Interview with Judge Morell Sharp, October 4, 1976.

20. Interview with Governor Evans, March 27, 1979.

that he was going to appoint Sharp anyhow. Evans felt he was qualified earlier and nothing had happened to change that appraisal.

Within a short time, a federal bench opening became available, and Governor Evans recommended Justice Sharp. On December 17, 1971, only a year after having been defeated at the polls and a few months after returning to the high court, Sharp resigned to take his oath as a new Federal District judge for Western Washington.

The real and potential issues that arose out of the Dolliver affair in the spring of 1970 prompted the State Bar Association to adopt new rules for their judicial selection committee. Previously, the names of all the certified candidates had most commonly gone directly to the governor from the selection committee. Now the board of governors would be given the committee's list in order to conduct its own screening. The board, then, would submit a list of not less than five names to the governor. Names could be deleted or added to the committee's list by board members. They also agreed not to hold any emergency meetings beyond the committee's twice yearly sessions. Finally, the process of initiation was broadened; any person interested in an appointment could apply to the committee.

The governor objected strongly.[21] What disturbed Evans was the narrowing of the list by the board which, earlier, had prevented the appointment of Dolliver. He would rather have had a list made up by the selection committee that included the names of all of those who had applied and were qualified. Also, he felt that emergency meetings might be necessary. Governor Evans responded to the board's new rules with his own counter-proposals. He urged the bar to keep an updated list of all qualified candidates. The bar would, upon request, submit the full list to the governor. On his part, the chief executive could submit a name or names, "which may or may not be on the bar list, to the Board of Governors for investigation and comment." Finally the governor would "make his appointment, hopefully of a person who has been approved by the Board of Governors."[22]

John Huneke, president of the State Bar, recognized that the constitutional prerogative was the governor's and softened the board's stand on some points. If the governor had additional persons not on the initial list the bar "would be only too happy to consider them, check the individuals through our procedures, then

21. Scribbled in the margin of a copy of the new rules sent the governor was "Jim, Dick—Pls. see me. I think this is unsatisfactory as hell." ("Jim" and "Dick" were Evans' Administrative Assistants, James Dolliver and Richard Hemstad.) (*Evans Papers*, State Archives).

22. *Ibid.*, undated letter (probably August 3, 1970).

report back to your office promptly."[23] With one exception, the meshing of the bar's and the governor's approaches was followed in all subsequent appointments to the Supreme Court.

With Sharp's elevation to the federal bench, the governor was given his fourth opportunity within two years to fill a vacancy on the court. Judge Robert F. Utter was one of Evans' initial appointments to the newly created Court of Appeals, having been on the bar's recommended list for several years. Utter had not known the governor well and had not been active in party affairs, although a life-long Republican. Nonetheless, he had developed a reputation as an innovative and reform-minded judge. He began his judicial career as commissioner for the King County Juvenile Court in 1959. Five years later he was elected to the Superior Court. His efforts on behalf of juvenile rehabilitation and reform were widely recognized. Beyond his professional activities, Utter was involved in a number of civic affairs. He was a leader in the YMCA, was founder of the Big Brothers of Seattle and of Job Therapy, Inc., and was on the boards of Friends of Youth and the Seattle Day Nursery. The Seattle Junior Chamber of Commerce named Utter "Outstanding Young Man" for 1964. Church activities also consumed much of the judge's time.

After the difficulties experienced by the governor in filling the Weaver vacancy, the selection of Judge Utter was a pleasant experience for all concerned. Utter had judicial experience, the endorsement of the bar, and, obviously, had been a winner at the polls. Geography also was in his favor. King County, at that moment, was "represented" only by Justice Finley. At age forty-one, Justice Utter was one of the youngest appointees to the Supreme Court.

In the spring of 1972, Marshall Neill became the third Evans appointee to be nominated for a federal judgeship. Justices McGovern and Sharp had already ascended to the more secure and prestigious federal bench, and Neill's confirmation was certain. The governor's office began its search for a replacement.

While serving in his last few sessions of the legislature, Evans had been impressed by a young Republican legislator from Yakima, Robert Brachtenbach. The two became political allies and friends and had worked together on legislative programs when Brachtenbach was minority leader in the House and Evans was serving the first years of his initial gubernatorial term. Brachtenbach had been active in professional and civic affairs in Yakima and, after leaving the legislature, served on an educational study commission established by the governor.

23. *Ibid.*, letter dated August 20, 1970.

Brachtenbach recalled several years later the details of his appointment. A meeting with Evans was arranged so that Brachtenbach could promote an acquaintance for a court of appeals appointment.

> I had breakfast with [the Governor] when he happened to be in Yakima one day. I mentioned this person's name to him and he said he didn't think he could appoint him for various reasons but would [I] be interested in it. I thought for a long time and said "No." . . . Later on, three or four years later I became more frustrated in practicing law simply because of the volume and pressures and all the private practice problems that lawyers will tell you about. There was a vacancy coming up and several prominent members of the bar asked me if I would be interested. I thought about it and simply went to the Governor and said to him: "You offered me one appointment and I said no. If you offer me another one I'll take it if it's on the Supreme Court."[24]

Brachtenbach had been one of the contenders for the second Sharp vacancy, but geography dictated against his appointment.[25] When Neill, from eastern Washington, was slated to move up to the federal bench, Brachtenbach was a strong contender to fill the upcoming vacancy. He had the endorsement of the bar's selection committee (and the board of governors), and his lack of judicial experience actually was a point in his favor. Evans' theory of appointments included a desire to bring balance on the bench in terms of backgrounds and experiences. Evans felt that Brachtenbach's experience in civil law, the commercial code, education, and the legislative branch would balance out the backgrounds of the other justices. He was also electable, having the experience of legislative campaigns behind him. On September 5, 1972, Evans announced the appointment of Brachtenbach to become effective as

24. Interview with Justice Robert Brachtenbach, April 5, 1977.

25. On November 26, 1971, Governor Evans wrote Brachtenbach about their discussion and the pending vacancy: "I have examined the Court situation since our conversation, and while I have made no commitments, nor have even any favorites at the moment, I do see a couple of problems. Geography is not a prime consideration, but we are faced with the rather unique situation that no judge on the present Court can really be considered to have come from King County. Judge Finley, of course, ran about twenty years ago from the Renton area, but did so under unusual circumstances which make him more a labor representative on the Courts than a King County representative. I also have one or two very close associates who may be interested, although I have made no contacts, as yet, and have no idea whether there is an interest. . . . I can think of few people who would equal your excellence on the Court, and your electability, which is an important element in any final consideration" (Letter dated November 26, 1971, *Evans Papers*, State Archives).

soon as Neill completed some unfinished business of the court. Brachtenbach took his oath of office November 20, 1972.

For his last appointment to the Supreme Court, Governor Evans turned again to his close friend and adviser James Dolliver.[26] Justice Finley passed away suddenly on March 23, 1976. Three days later Evans announced his intention not to seek a fourth term as chief executive. He now was relatively free of political pressures and could act independently of the State Bar Association. Any criticisms that might accompany Dolliver's appointment could be ignored.

Dolliver explained the circumstances of his second effort to be appointed to the Supreme Court:

> I'm not quite sure what happened. I think everyone was sort of dancing around a bit. I think . . . the bar was a little ashamed of what they did to me in 1970. I may not be as good as I think I am but I'm not as bad as they led people to believe. I think they felt a little ashamed about that. The Governor didn't want to lay them up on the line again. . . . What ultimately happened as I understand it, is they in effect took no position. They didn't say "OK." They submitted no list of names to the Governor. He had nothing in his possession indicating who they would or would not endorse. He didn't ask for any. He simply said he was going to appoint Dolliver, period![27]

Evans had appointed some 100 judges throughout the state system. He said that he would "rank Jim Dolliver among the very highest I have appointed."[28] He predicted that Dolliver would be "a people's judge. No higher attribute can be given. He has exceptional intellect and wisdom, and the ability to make tough decisions." Evans agreed that his appointment was political. "They [appointments] are made by the Governor and in that sense they are all political, but I've made them all based on capacity and ability."[29]

26. In January 1976, Dolliver again took himself out of contention for a federal judgeship because of the lack of approval from the American Bar Association. The Washington State Trial Lawyers Association had also thought his "experience in the judicial field and in the practice of law [was] extremely limited" (*The Seattle Times*, January 30, 1976).

27. Interview with Justice James Dolliver, April 5, 1977.

28. *The Seattle Times*, April 23, 1976.

29. *Ibid.*, May 7, 1976, micro. Actually the Washington State Trial Lawyers Association announced that they did not oppose Dolliver's appointment to the Supreme Court. The Court, in their view, "functions more like a legislative body, concerned with establishing general rules of law, weighing competing interests and determining public policy" (*ibid.*, May 16, 1976). This function was substantially different from that of the trial bench, and Dolliver clearly had the necessary experience. In addition, he had been a law clerk to Justice Hamley while the judge was on the Supreme Court. In September, Dolliver also prevailed in the State Bar Association's preferential poll. His two opponents were preferred by 38% of the bar, but Dolliver received 50% of the vote (12% expressed no preference among the candidates).

Governor Evans' selections to the Supreme Court were clearly the result of a mix of political, personal, and professional concerns. Neill, Brachtenbach, Dolliver, and Sharp to some extent were partisan companions of the governor either in the legislature, the executive branch, or during the early years of his political career. All of his appointees were Republicans and some were moderately to extremely active in politics at some stage in their careers. All were declared qualified by the State Bar Association, although Dolliver's endorsement didn't come until his first campaign. All, except Sharp, were reaffirmed by the voters at their initial (and subsequent) election attempts. Some, but not all, were fairly close friends of the governor. The governor was the highest-ranking Republican in the State (Washington's two Senators were Democrats), a circumstance that helps explain why three of his appointees were elevated to the federal bench during the Nixon administration. This attests to the balanced mix of "politics" and "professionalism" that characterized Evans' appointments.

Justice Horowitz was seventy-five on January 5, 1980. According to the mandatory retirement act, he was required to retire at the end of the calendar year. Accordingly, he left the bench and returned to his old law firm in Seattle on December 31, 1980. Thus, two vacancies were created. One for the few days remaining in his term (between January 1 and January 12) and the other for the new six year term which began on January 12. Court of appeals judge Fred Dore had won election to the latter position, but the short term spot remained vacant. Governor Dixy Lee Ray appointed Dore to the vacancy, even though it would be but a few days before he would be sworn in as an elected judge. By appointing Dore, the governor was able to fill his spot on the Court of Appeals, and if that appointment came from the trial bench, she would have another vacancy to fill. Had Dore not resigned a few days early from the Court of Appeals to accept the governor's offer, all the subsequent vacancies could have been filled by incoming Governor John Spellman.[30]

King County superior court judge Carolyn R. Dimmick applied to the bar's selection committee for consideration for the Dore Court of Appeals vacancy created by his election to the high court. She wrote to Governor Ray about her interest. However, by the time the governor was considering the bar's list of twelve finalists during the last few weeks of her administration, Justice Wright had passed

30. Ray selected King County Superior Court Judge Patrick Corbett as Dore's replacement and district court judge Frank L. Sullivan was appointed to Corbett's vacancy. All of these appointments appeared to be "midnight" selections by a lame-duck administration. However, they were the result of considerable screening and consultation. For example, Ray was interviewing to fill Dore's spot in November.

away (on November 6, 1980) after a prolonged illness, and discussions had shifted toward filing the supreme court vacancy. In the interview with the governor, Judge Dimmick talked about the court of appeals spot, while the governor seemed to be talking about the high court vacancy. Dimmick recalled that had the only vacancy been on the Supreme Court, "I would not have applied. I did not plan to move to Olympia and work in the Supreme Court. So when you [ask], did I apply for it, it just was there, suddenly, when I had applied for another opening."[31] However, to everyone's surprise, except the ebullient Governor Ray, Dimmick was offered the supreme court position in December, she accepted and was sworn in on January 2, 1981.

The appointment was notable for a variety of reasons. Justice Dimmick became the first woman to sit on the Washington Supreme Court and only the fourteenth to be serving at that time on state courts of last resort in the country. Also notable, for the first time since Overton Ellis' appointment in 1911, a governor had voluntarily crossed over party lines and appointed someone from the opposition's ranks. Dimmick's partisan credentials were gained early in her career. As deputy prosecuting attorney, she had actively campaigned for her boss, Republican Charles O. Carroll. However, since her appointment as district court judge (which had been recommended by the King County Commissioners, who were predominantly Democrats) in 1965, Dimmick had withdrawn from active partisan affairs. Nonetheless, when Democrat governor Ray appointed Republican Dimmick, another tradition was broken.[32]

Although Republican governor John Spellman served only a single term (1981–84), he had the unique experience of appointing four members to the state's court of last resort. Two of his appointments were dictated by special considerations, another was a matter of convenience, and the fourth appeared more traditional.

Spellman's appointment of Vernon Pearson was an opportunity thrust upon him. Justice Floyd Hicks had served on the court for nearly five years but had found the physical demands to be onerous. He was suffering from cataracts on both eyes (one had been operated on with only limited success) and consequently the reading necessary at the appellate level was burdensome. Also, the commuting from Tacoma to Olympia each day (about sixty miles) became

31. Interview with Justice Carolyn Dimmick, April 14, 1983.

32. Dimmick remembered that during the interview with the governor, she was never asked about party activity or even affiliation, even though the talk with the governor was mostly centered on general state issues. Justice Dimmick remembered the interview as a "pleasant chat" (*ibid.*).

difficult. The justice had been involved in two accidents along the route over the years. Although he was not at fault, the experiences had weighed heavily on him. The announced retirement of Judge Robert Jacques from the Pierce County Superior Court gave Hicks the opportunity to return to the same bench from which he had launched his judicial and political career nearly twenty years earlier. He contacted the governor about his desire to return to the trial court and to Tacoma, and Spellman agreed to appoint him to the Jacques' vacancy.

When he heard of Hick's pending appointment, Judge Vernon R. Pearson of Division II of the Court of Appeals in Tacoma wrote the governor indicating his interest in the Supreme Court vacancy. He reminded Spellman: "I had something geographically in common with [Hicks]. I also pointed out to him that none of the appointments to the Supreme Court had ever come from Division II of the Court of Appeals. . . . I kind of indicated to him that [Division I in Seattle] didn't have corner on the talent. I sent a copy of my letter also to the State Bar screening committee."[33]

Pearson had been one of the original twelve members of the Court of Appeals, appointed in 1969 by Governor Evans. Although a Republican, Pearson had not been involved in partisan affairs "to any great degree." He had played a leading role in wresting the control of the Pierce County Republican organization from the conservative Goldwater wing of the party in the 1960s but that had been his "only venture" into politics.

Governor Spellman, himself an attorney, interviewed those candidates who had the approval of the bar's selection committee and after a strong endorsement from the Pierce County bar, he chose Pearson from among a half-dozen finalists (one of whom was James Andersen). Pearson assumed office on January 18, 1982, and was affirmed by the voters in the September 1982 primary election.

The appointment of James A. Andersen followed a more traditional route. Andersen had been a successful Seattle trial lawyer for twenty-three years and had served in the state legislature for several sessions (1958–72), rising to top Republican leadership positions in both the House and the Senate. Three years after his resignation from the legislature to devote full-time to his private law practice, he was appointed by Governor Evans to the State Court of Appeals in 1975. In the meantime, Justice Charles Stafford had been fighting a prolonged battle with cancer, succumbing to the disease in July 1984. Governor Spellman quickly interviewed a number of prospec-

33. Interview with Justice Vernon Pearson, April 13, 1983.

tive replacements with court of appeals judges Barbara Durham and Andersen emerging as leading candidates for the vacancy. Both had the approval of the bar's selection committee and both possessed several years of judicial experience. Andersen, however, had partisan credentials from his fourteen years in the legislature, and apparently for Spellman the interests of women were already met with the presence of Justice Dimmick on the court. Also, Andersen had been a serious contender for two federal appointments and, if not for the extensive pressure from the Pierce County Bar, he would have gained the appointment that went to Justice Pearson.[34] Spellman would pick-up much needed support from women for his reelection bid with a Durham appointment but, on the other hand, an Andersen selection would be looked on favorably from the Evans wing of the Republican Party. The deciding factor seemed to be Andersen's close finishes in previous appointments. It would be viewed by many as a breach of faith for the governor to ignore him again. Also his highly successful trial experience was impressive. Spellman offered him the position, he accepted, and was sworn in on July 25, 1984.

Court of Appeals Judge Keith Callow claimed election victory over Edward Heavey in the November 1984 balloting for retiring Justice Rosellini's position. However, Rosellini died on November 26 before he could finish the final days of his long tenure on the high bench, leaving a short and temporary vacancy.[35] Some members of the Supreme Court urged the governor to fill the spot as soon as possible in order for the bench to keep current on its growing case load. Callow was the logical choice since he had won the election to that position and would soon be serving on the bench anyhow. He had caught-up on his court of appeals assignments and was ready for the move. The appointment also would place him ahead of the other new justices on the seniority list.[36] The governor was also

34. In 1976, President Ford nominated Andersen for a vacancy on the U.S. District Court in Tacoma. Senate confirmation of Andersen and twelve other federal judicial appointees was held up by the Democratic controlled U.S. Senate, however, until the outcome of the Ford-Carter election contest. After Carter's election, all thirteen nominees were permanently pidgeonholed and Democrat Senator Henry M. Jackson's long time supporter, Jack Tanner, was appointed by President Carter and confirmed by the Senate, supplanting the Ford/Andersen appointment.

35. Hugh Rosellini was sworn in on January 10, 1955. His twenty-nine years, ten months, and sixteen days on the court had been exceeded only by Mark Fullerton's thirty-two years, eight months, and twelve days and John F. Main's thirty years and seventeen days.

36. Seniority has few tangible advantages other than making one eligible for the chief justice's post sooner. The justices' names are listed in the *Washington Reports* according to seniority and preferences for some administrative assignments are given

provided with an opportunity to fill Callow's spot on the appeals bench, although this vacancy had been anticipated since Callow's victory in November. The appointment to the appeals bench went to the governor's counsel and chief of staff, C. Kenneth Grosse.

Governor Spellman's appointment of court of appeals judge Barbara Durham was the product of a rather creative arrangement fashioned to confront a number of possibly adverse circumstances. Justice Carolyn Dimmick was being considered for a presidential appointment to the Federal District Court in Seattle. Should all proceed smoothly, her confirmation would most likely come in the spring of 1985. (She was sworn in on April 17, 1985.) When should she vacate her spot on the Supreme Court?

First, an early resignation from the court before confirmation for the federal bench from the U. S. Senate constituted a risk. Even with the whole-hearted support of Washington's senior senator, Republican Slade Gorton, and with her Republican and conservative credentials (and the Reagan administration had been under pressure to appoint more women to the federal courts), the unpredictable could happen to frustrate her federal appointment.

However, if the justice waited until her federal appointment was official before resigning, her vacancy on the state bench would be filled by an appointee of Democratic governor-elect, Booth Gardner, who would take office in January 1985. With this appointment likely coming from the state's lower courts, another vacancy would be filled by the incoming governor.

But another intervening element complicated the timing of an appointment even further. Justice Dimmick had just been reelected to a new full six-year term beginning in January 14, 1985. If she vacated her supreme court seat before then, actually two openings would be created: one for the remainder of her short term which ended in January and one for the new six-year spot to which she had just been elected and which began in January. Governor Spellman could appoint someone to the short-term vacancy but was unsure about being able to fill the vacancy for the full term. To complicate matters further, Judge Durham had also just been elected to a new full six-year term on the Court of Appeals, creating the same dilemma for appointments to her position should she be elevated to the high court early.

priority. Seniority can sometimes be used to advantage in reelection campaigns. Clearly, seniority does not play the role at the Washington court as it does at the U.S. Supreme Court. See Walter F. Murphy, *The Elements of Judicial Strategy* (Chicago: University of Chicago Press, 1964).

Senator Slade Gorton suggested a way out of the dilemma. According to the state constitution (Article IV, Sec. 3) the newly elected judges would take their oaths of office on "the second Monday in January next succeeding their election," or January 14 in this case. But the governor-elect would take office on "the Wednesday after the second Monday in January" following his election (RCW ch. 8, Sec. 43.01.090). If Dimmick took the oath of office for her new term on Monday, January 14 and resigned before governor-elect Gardner was sworn in at noon on Wednesday, January 16, Spellman would have the opportunity to appoint her successor. With assurances from Gorton that the federal appointment was a certainty, Dimmick contacted the governor and informed him of her intention to resign and of his opportunity to appoint. She also made it clearly understood that she would like to see her close friend Barbara Durham appointed to the vacancy.

Judge Dale Green, defeated in the November election by William C. Goodloe, and attorney Richard Hemstad, former aide to Dan Evans and the choice of Senator Gorton, were considered, but Durham was the leading candidate from the beginning. She had the judicial experience, bar support, the recognition of her court of appeals colleagues, and Justice Dimmick's clear endorsement. She had also nearly been appointed back in July, and Spellman then had all but promised her the next appointment. Finally, the spot being vacated by the first woman on the state's high bench ought to be filled by another woman. Spellman put it this way: "I think it is significant that we continue to have a woman on the court. Once that precedent was established, it should be maintained. It had been my hope to name not just a woman to the court, but a minority person . . . during my term as governor. I would certainly not want to fail on both counts."[37]

Judge Durham considered herself a "virtual clone philosophically" of the justice she replaced. She also was eager to begin her tenure in order to redress the liberal tendency of the court: "I think the new blood on the court will bring us back more to the middle. It's a real challenge."[38] The announcement of the governor's intention to appoint Durham to the pending vacancy was made on November 30, 1984. The promotion of Durham permitted Spellman to place his long time friend and Georgetown Law School classmate, Walter E. Webster Jr., in Durham's vacated court of appeals position. The whole process had taken several weeks to put together although it

37. *Spokane Spokesman-Review*, December 1, 1984.
38. *Ibid.*

appeared to be the result of last minute arrangements to allow Republican Spellman to name some "midnight" judges.

The process by which governors have filled vacancies on the Supreme Court in recent times has become predictable, although on occasion special circumstances dictated the appointment of a particular candidate. The relationship between governors and the legal profession is institutionalized although each governor may weigh the bar's input slightly differently. The bar is now assumed to be a legitimate participant in the recruitment process with appointment requiring the profession's approval.[39] Partisan considerations remain important as the merits of various candidates are weighed and experience on the Court of Appeals has become a very important factor. Additionally, the vacancies created at other levels of the state benches by these promotions to the Supreme Court are part of the gubernatorial deliberations.

Also, judicial appointments are now gaining much attention from the state's chief executive. All recent governors have personally interviewed a number of candidates when vacancies occur. Inquiries into specific legal issues were avoided (e.g., abortion, capital punishment) but each governor sought to make sure the candidate's judicial philosophy coincided with his or her view of the proper role of courts in state government. For example, Governors Ray and Spellman queried candidates about the proper balance between law making vs. interpreting. Judicial mingling in legislative matters was, in their view, to be avoided. Actually, those interviewed had anticipated more political questions and were impressed with the general knowledge of "judging" displayed by the chief executive.

Elections: 1970 to the Present

The overall voter participation in the modern period exceeded that of the previous years. The "roll-off" in the voting averaged 33.7% in the primaries (compared to 35.5% in the previous period) and 43.3% in the general elections (compared with the previous 47.2%).

The specific races were not strikingly unique in style, although some close challenges were mounted. Both of Governor Evans' 1970 appointees drew formidable opponents in their first bid for electoral affirmation. William C. Goodloe, former Republican state chairman

39. This nexus between the governor and the bar has so evolved that the official programs for induction ceremonies now explain that "When a vacancy occurs on the Court, a list of prospective appointees is submitted to the Governor by the State Bar Association," although it is admitted that this is a "tradition not required by statute." See Official Program for the Induction of James A. Andersen, July 24, 1984.

and state legislator, challenged Justice Stafford, and Charles Wright filed against Justice Sharp. The governor came to the assistance of both his appointees. He sent a letter to all Republican precinct committee persons and to all lawyers in the state urging support for Stafford and Sharp. The letter was printed and distributed by the office of the Republican state chairman. The letter stated in part:

> Although members of the court are non-partisan—and properly so—I am soliciting your support and assistance to the two challenged appointees. Being non-partisan, judges have no organizational support to help them in this statewide race.

Neale V. Chaney, state Democrat chairman, reacted predictably with indignation. He recognized that while "the governor has the power to make appointments," the voters should decide whether "they have the qualifications to remain on the bench." Through his blatant support of the judges the governor was acting irresponsibly.[40] Former Democrat and Rosellini appointee Robert Hunter, whose name was also on the ballot, had been omitted from the governor's letter of support but later gained Evans' election-eve endorsement.[41]

Name familiarity was also important in the Sharp and Wright race. Although Sharp was supported by 80% of the attorneys in the bar poll, by nearly all of his colleagues on the King County Superior Court bench, and by the governor and the Republican Party organization, he went down to defeat before the efforts of Judge Charles T. Wright. Judge Wright had been appointed in 1949 to the Thurston-Mason County court, a position held for many years by his father. Located in Olympia, the court heard cases involving state

40. *The Seattle Post-Intelligencer*, September 15, 1970. Justice Stafford had written Governor Evans requesting assistance in his election campaign in October: "The day you notified me of my appointment you gave your assurance that assistance would be available if I had opposition. I had no conception of either the extent or the complexity of a state-wide race. . . . Now that the election is over, I want to thank you for your invaluable support. I am sure that it could have been quite a different battle without it. A governor's support of his new appointees is not new, unusual, or questionable. Governor Langlie gave his support to Judge Hamley when it was needed in his first judicial election. Governor Rosellini gave similar assistance to Justice Hamilton in the first election after appointment. In each case the support was made directly through department directors and other members of the official family" (Letter dated October 2, 1970, *Evans Papers*, State Archives).

41. The night before the primary, Governor Evans included Hunter in his endorsements. In response to Chaney's criticism, Evans said it was "typical of the diatribes that come from that direction. I was just standing behind my appointees." Evans thought that Hunter "deserves re-election" (*The Seattle Times*, September 15, 1970).

government. Consequently, such cases (and the judge deciding them), received state-wide attention. The State Labor Council and Grange gave Wright their endorsement. Nonetheless, the voters were thought to have confused Wright with the popular former King County superior court judge, Eugene A. Wright (then on the Federal Court of Appeals) drawing important Seattle votes away from Sharp. Further, the juxtaposition of *Sharp* against *Wright* symbolically worked in favor of the latter. Both candidates played on their names. However, "Vote Wright" attracted more votes then "Vote Sharp." Decisive to the Wright victory was the support of the formidable political organization put together earlier by former legislator and gubernatorial candidate Martin Durkan and by Joe Davis, head of the State Labor Council. It provided the necessary grass-roots activities, for example, lawn signs, brochures, and door to door delivery of campaign materials.

Important also was the fact that Judge Sharp was simply not the campaigner that Judge Wright was. Sharp appeared to be ill-at-ease in his efforts at soliciting the support of the electorate. Wright, in contrast, seemed to relish the experience. Additionally, Mrs. Wright proved to be an excellent organizer and campaigner.

In 1972, court reform dominated the campaign with judicial selection of particular interest. The emphasis fit well into the developing concern of the legal profession, judges, scholars, and attentive citizens for revision of the judicial section (Article IV) of the state constitution. Understandably, those contending for a seat on the high court were either skeptical of any changes in elections or were generally noncommittal. Utter, who faced no opposition, was free to take to task those who argued that elections were the best means of recruiting judges. He suggested that the time needed to campaign could be better spent conducting the state's legal business in the temple of justice in Olympia. The money saved from not campaigning could tempt more competent attorneys to the high court who presently found it difficult to leave lucrative practices to run for the bench.

Two years later, Chief Justice Hale announced his intention to retire at the end of his term in 1975. For the first time in nearly two decades a wide-open race involving no incumbent and a full six-year term was at stake. Five candidates were attracted, all qualified, but all with different experiences and backgrounds. Judge Charles Horowitz of the Court of Appeals had been a noted legal scholar and former president of the Seattle Bar Association. Harold J. Petrie, who was also a judge of the Court of Appeals, had served as state director of Labor and Industries under Governor Evans. Francis E.

Holman, superior court judge, former legislator, and first chairman of the State Public Disclosure Commission, also filed for the vacancy, along with Lem Tuai, former Seattle city councilman and attorney for the General Services Administration, and Robert Comfort, a respected Tacoma attorney. The campaign was a contest of credentials. Horowitz led in the state bar poll and was endorsed by the Teamsters. Petrie was supported by the State Labor Council and was second in the Pierce County and state bar polls. Holman gained the endorsement of the Washington Education Association and placed third in the state bar plebiscite. Comfort led in the Pierce County poll, although receiving only a 6% "excellent" rating in the state poll. Tuai was last in the state-wide poll but had gained recognition in King County from his earlier race for mayor of Seattle. Name familiarity in King County helped Tuai to move on to the general election against Horowitz, who ultimately prevailed in the November balloting.

The most interesting aspect of the 1976 race was that Congressman Floyd Hicks defeated court of appeals judge Keith Callow without leaving his Washington, D.C., office. Of course, much effort and money went into his campaign. Although Hunter's seat was an open position, unlike two years earlier, only two contestants were attracted to the race. Court of appeals judge Vernon Pearson, who had seriously thought about the race, withdrew when Hicks announced, and no others filed for the position. (It was not uncommon for persons simply to pay the filing fee in order to gain free publicity.)[42] Given the credentials of the two announced contestants, the chances of a third candidate winning were indeed slim.

Earlier Hicks had expressed an interest in running for the Supreme Court, and on July 20, 1976, he announced, "I'm going after it" (the seat vacated by Justice Hunter). He had recently been suffering from an inner-ear ailment but felt improved enough to make the run: "The only question was whether I was recovered quickly enough, and I just have to take a chance on that."[43] Hicks had been a Pierce County Superior Court judge before serving twelve years in Congress from the sixth district. Callow led in the state bar poll, but Hicks' name familiarity and prominence led to his victory.

42. For example, one judge commented to the author that his opponent did exactly that in order to gain some advertisement: "After the election . . . [he] told me he had just come to Washington from California and was not well known. . . . [F]or the filing fee he got his name on every ballot in the state. He said he never thought he would win but the advertising he received was worth several times the cost."

43. *The Seattle Times*, July 20, 1976.

James Dolliver's initial electoral defense of his court post was challenged in 1976 by two formidable opponents: former state legislator Fred Dore and Walla Walla prosecutor Arthur Eggers. Dore's prominence west of the mountains and Eggers' support from Eastern Washington split the anti-Dolliver vote in the primary. Dore led all three contestants, Dolliver trailed by nearly 100,000 votes, and Eggers was a distant third. The campaign for the November balloting promised to be interesting. Dore continued to stress his twenty-seven years of legal and courtroom experience and noted that his opponent had been rejected in his recent bid for a federal appointment because of his lack of years in the actual practice of law.

Governor Evans intervened in the race, providing his and the Republican party's support for his appointee. Dore received the endorsement of labor and assistance from his many Democratic friends and clients. The state bar poll favored Dolliver. The race was decided in the last few days of the campaign with a blitz of thirty-second TV ads by Dolliver's supporters, bringing him victory by over forty thousand votes. The costs of the campaigning exceeded any previous contest, with Dolliver spending $91,521 and Dore $45,852. The race also introduced TV as an effective medium for judicial candidates which, of course, also accounted for the high costs of the campaigns.

Orris Hamilton's retirement in 1978 left another open position, the third in succession. As in 1974, it was a contest of credentials and endorsements. Again Callow led in the state bar poll and had the judicial experience as well as the endorsements of the Teamsters and the Seattle Police Officers Guild. William Williams had served twenty years on the Spokane County Superior Court and gained the State Labor Council's endorsement. Francis Holman entered the race with Washington State Education Association support. Attorney Rodrick Dimoff, another contender, was a respected practicing attorney.

Holman and Williams won nomination and moved on to the general election. During the campaign they had only good things to say about each other. For example, Holman admitted before a group of attorneys:

> I cannot in all honesty tell you I'd be a better judge than Bill. We each have different gifts and experiences and talents. He has more experience on the bench and I have more experience as a lawyer. We'd both do you a good job. I cannot enter into a fight with my friend Bill because I know him too well.

Table 7.3
Election Results, 1970–84

	Primary	*General*
1970	*(Sept. 15)*	*(Nov. 3)*
(Pos. 1)		
**Robert T. Hunter*	277,752	568,108
Vaughn E. Evans	186,286	
(Pos. 3)		
**Charles Stafford*	276,446	552,165
William C. Goodloe	188,219	
(Pos. 4)		
*Morell Sharp	212,325	
Charles T. Wright	224,441	551,961
(Pos. 2)		
**Marshall Neill*	336,377	539,785
1972	*(Sept. 19)*	*(Nov. 7)*
(Pos. 1)		
**Orris Hamilton*	409,484	697,277
George Faler	209,186	
(Pos. 2)		
**Hugh J. Rosellini*	402,418	739,119
Melvin Love	315,020	
(Pos. 3)		
**Charles T. Wright*	322,511	685,518
Lloyd Shorett	317,232	
(Pos. 4)		
**Robert F. Utter*	516,193	677,060
1973		*(Nov. 6)*
(Pos. 1)		
**Robert F. Brachtenbach*		441,075
Dale B. Sawyer	**	278,014
1974	*(Sept. 17)*	*(Nov. 5)*
(Pos. 1)		
Charles Horowitz	121,145	498,917
Francis E. Holman	75,832	
Harold J. Petrie	60,271	
Robert A. Comfort	38,710	
Lem Tuai	106,346	377,445
(Pos. 2)		
**Robert C. Finley*	294,112	589,196
(Pos. 3)		
**Robert F. Utter*	285,772	579,433
1976	*(Sept. 21)*	*(Nov. 2)*
(Pos. 1)		
Floyd V. Hicks	397,970	851,427
Keith M. Callow	254,317	
(Pos. 2)		
**Charles F. Stafford*	482,293	794,859
(Pos. 3)		
**Robert F. Brachtenbach*	464,286	763,416
(Pos. 4)		
**James M. Dolliver*	212,091	635,509
Arthur R. Eggers	121,086	
Fred H. Dore	310,502	594,070

Table 7.3 (*continued*)

	Primary	*General*
1978	*(Sept. 19)*	*(Nov. 7)*
(Pos. 3)		
William Williams	126,831	386,244
Keith M. Callow	101,419	
Francis E. Holman	125,230	365,721
Rodrick Dimoff	30,435	
(Pos. 2)		
**Hugh J. Rosellini*	335,193	589,999
(Pos. 1)		
**Charles T. Wright*	342,176	597,348
1980	*(Sept. 16)*	*(Nov. 4)*
(Pos. 1)		
**Robert F. Utter*	468,235	900,532
Dan Clem	244,662	
(Pos. 3)		
Fred H. Dore	409,662	925,641
Edward P. Reed	325,868	
(Pos. 2)		
**James Dolliver*	567,700	895,590
1981		*(Nov. 3)*
(Pos. 1)		
**Carolyn R. Dimmick*	**	590,164
1982	*(Sept. 14)*	*(Nov. 2)*
**Robert F. Brachtenbach*	391,920	758,111
**Charles F. Stafford*	397,383	764,912
**Vernon Pearson*	387,114	742,433
1984	*(Sept. 18)*	*(Nov. 6)*
(Pos. 1)		
William C. Goodloe	223,931	745,901
Dale M. Green	187,747	659,345
Michael J. Hemovich	104,419	
William E. Rosell	77,203	
Victor Felice	53,949	
(Pos. 3)		
Keith Callow	307,896	847,082
Edward Heavey	238,094	532,710
Eddie Yoon	80,213	
**Carolyn R. Dimmick*	470,993	1,105,375
Alan Merson	178,305	
**James A. Andersen*	529,079	1,087,344
1985		*(Nov. 5)*
**Barbara Durham*	**	552,675
1986	*(Sept. 16)*	*(Nov. 4)*
**James M. Dolliver*	398,343	794,520
**Robert F. Utter*	387,133	774,780
**Fred H. Dore*	398,417	789,756

*Incumbent
**No primary
Italicized names designate winners
Full six-year term unless otherwise indicated

Williams reciprocated: "We've been on the same side on the issues. Fran is a successful, intelligent man and he'd do you a good job."[44] Because of the overwhelming support from eastern Washington, along with some from the King County area, Williams edged Holman in the general balloting. Certainly the campaign failed to distinguish the candidates sufficiently for even the observant voter to make a considered choice.

The 1980 judicial elections featured a challenge to incumbent Chief Justice Robert Utter, who had developed a solid reputation for competence and liberalism over his nearly ten years on the high bench.[45] His reputation was such that he had been unopposed in his two previous elections. However, in 1980 a few citizens became disturbed over the Supreme Court's supposed "permissiveness" in criminal cases, and Chief Justice Utter became the center of that protest.

Kitsap County Prosecutor Dan Clem had sought the death penalty in a case involving rape, robbery, and murder. During the trial, the Supreme Court handed down a decision (*State* v. *Martin*, 94 Wn 2d 1 [1980]) allowing an accused to plead guilty to first degree murder and thereby avoid the death penalty. The accused in the case being handled by Clem promptly pleaded guilty (thereby escaping the gallows) and was sentenced to life imprisonment. In protest, local citizens urged Clem to file against Utter. The chief justice had recently been criticized by other prosecutors for being "soft on crime," and the challenge by Clem was symptomatic of that criticism.[46] Utter generally ignored the specific charges leveled at him by Clem.[47] In the only direct responses to these charges, Utter said he was prohibited from answering because of the Code of Judicial Conduct, but did say that Clem's statements and campaign materials were "false" or a "complete misrepresentation." With the endorse-

44. *Ibid.*, October 20, 1978.

45. See C. H. Sheldon, "An Interpretation of the Judicial Process: The Washington Supreme Court as a Small Group," *Gonzaga Law Review* 13 (Fall 1977):123.

46. In March it was reported that members of the Washington Association of Prosecuting Attorneys were looking for someone to run against Utter because he was "soft on crime" (*The Seattle Post-Intelligencer*, March 23, 1979). Michael Redmond, Executive Secretary for the association, attempted to correct an erroneous impression. Redmond apologized to the justice for what had been reported, and the President of the Association, Dean Bender, announced that "criticism of this kind is deplorable and seems to be no less than an attempt to undermine the . . . Judiciary." He felt that Utter had "served with honor and distinction" (*The Seattle Times*, April 8, 1979).

47. Dan Clem's ads played on the theme of *Network*, an award-winning movie of the time: "I'm mad as hell and I won't take it any more."

ment of the Seattle Police Officers Guild, the State Labor Council, and an overwhelming lead in the bar poll, Utter easily turned back the challenge.

In the other 1980 race for the Supreme Court, Court of Appeals judges Edward P. Reed and Fred H. Dore faced each other. (Dolliver was unopposed for his election to a full six-year term.) The Reed vs. Dore race was again simply a contest over respective qualifications without reference to possible issues. Dore had been a legislator and twice a candidate for attorney general. Reed's activities had been largely legal and judicial. Both were approved by the Seattle Police Officers Guild. Dore had the support of the State Labor Council, but Reed won the bar poll. Name familiarity gave Dore an insurmountable lead in King County, and he swept to victory by nearly 75,000 votes in the September primaries.

Carolyn Dimmick drew no opposition in her bid for voter confirmation in the 1981 balloting, nor did the trio of Brachtenbach, Pearson, and Stafford in 1982.

The 1984 races, however, were numerous, and some were hotly contested. Two open seats were available, and each featured experienced but thus far unsuccessful court campaigners. Chief Justice Williams announced early on that he would not seek reelection. Consequently a number of aspirants' hopes were raised. King County Superior Court judge William C. Goodloe, a seasoned campaigner who had sought a seat on the court in 1970 and 1962, filed early for the position. Partisan politics were clearly reflected in his background with eight years as a state legislator and a stint as state chairman of the Republican party. Judge Dale M. Green, a member of the Court of Appeals, Division III, in Spokane; Michael J. Hemovich, a respected trial attorney and former president of the State Bar; William E. Rosell, a Seattle banking attorney endorsed by the Republican party; and Victor Felice, an attorney from Spokane, also filed in order to contest Goodloe for the position.

Despite support from labor, Democrats, retiring Justice Williams, and the *Seattle Post-Intelligencer*, Hemovich lost out in the September primary elections along with Felice and Rosell. Goodloe's west-side support and name familiarity and Green's victory in the bar poll and endorsement by the *Seattle Times* moved them to the November general election. With the assistance of Republican party contacts, Goodloe gained ready access to local voters. He traveled throughout the state in a motor home meeting with local citizens at every opportunity. Local supporters assisted by buying space in local newspapers in order to place a standardized ad containing quotes from leading newspapers extolling the virtues of Goodloe. These quotes, however, pertained to Goodloe's early efforts in the state legislature and some were thirty-four years old.

Few issues of substance surfaced during the campaign. Both Green and Goodloe were viewed as capable of redressing the imbalance on the court caused by some of its liberal rulings in criminal law. Both emphasized their judicial experience; Green as an appellate judge and Goodloe as a trial jurist. Geography appeared to be the major factor separating them, although something was made in the media of Goodloe's partisan background. Green emphasized the need for Eastern Washington representation on the court and his ability to understand the needs and desires of rural and farming areas of the state. Although Judge Green was endorsed by the State Bar Association, he was confronted with the impossible task of overcoming his anonymity on the west side of the state. In his effort to gain an identity with the Seattle and Tacoma voters, he neglected the electorate to the east of the Cascades, which he had assumed would give him full support. Expensive television ads throughout the state in the closing days of the campaign were featured by both candidates. Goodloe edged Green with the outcome not known for several days until absentee ballots were counted.

Following his victory, Goodloe was fined the maximum allowed by the law ($500) by the Public Disclosure Commission for "flagrant and multiple violations" of the law. He had failed to file his campaign financing reports on time, his supporters had failed to include their names on the newspaper ads purchased throughout the state, and his reports neglected to include the expenses incurred by these ads (amounting to approximately $2,000). Goodloe's campaign treasurer claimed the reports didn't arrive in time because of insufficient postage. The judge, after the hearing before the commission, felt he had honored the spirit of the public disclosure law and that he had not intended to deceive the voters.[48]

Alan Merson's challenge to incumbent Dimmick was more of a crusade than a well-organized and serious campaign. Merson was out to challenge the restrictions of Canon 7 (which limit what judicial candidates can discuss in campaigns). He leveled no criticism toward his opponent, but argued that the court ought to be more activist, lobbying the legislature for reforms. The voters took little note and returned Dimmick to the court.

48. The Public Disclosure Commission unanimously refused to turn the matter over to the public prosecutor, and Goodloe's transgressions failed to impress the Judicial Qualifications Commission, which issued no reprimand.

Keith Callow, court of appeals judge in Seattle, running his third race for the Supreme Court, had the endorsement of the State Bar, had won the coveted "Brandeis Judge of the Year" award from the state Trial Lawyers Association and had carried with him the endorsement of the state's leading newspapers. His opponent, Edward Heavey, had Democratic support, Washington Education Association endorsement and labor backing.[49] Both had name familiarity; Heavey had been a legislator and on the King County Council, and Callow had been a judge since 1971 and was recognized from his earlier races for the high court. Eddie Yoon, a Korean-born 1974 graduate of the University of Washington law school with offices in Tacoma was clearly an unknown and was quickly eliminated in the primary. The final race between Heavey and Callow was a contest between contrasting liberal-activist and conservative-restraintist images. Callow accused his opponent of too much activism: "He intends to be a policy-maker and that's the legislature's job." But Heavey countered that "the court should be more involved in the functions of society and should establish some leadership to avoid the use of courts."[50] The voters apparently accepted the restraintist approach and overwhelmingly endorsed Callow. With his short-term appointment he moved up to the high bench the first week in January.

Justice Barbara Durham, appointed to Carolyn Dimmick's vacancy on January 2, 1985, ran unopposed for retention in the November balloting.

Although some apprehension on the part of the judges was evident in unguarded moments when the 1986 election approached (some of the judges took full advantage of speaking opportunities in order to remain visible, rudiments of volunteer committees were formed, and funding for campaigning tentatively solicited), no one filed against the trio of justices seeking reelection. Chief Justice Dolliver's and Justices Utter's and Dore's names appeared alone on the November ballots, assuring their retention for another six-year term. The formidable task of challenging any of these seasoned campaigners would require more funds and energy than anyone or any group was willing to risk.

One striking feature of elections (and appointments) since 1970 was the role played by the new intermediate Court of Appeals. The Court of Appeals interposed at least two new elements into the

49. The chairwoman of the state Democratic party urged support for Heavey in a statewide mailing to Democrats.

50. *Spokane Spokesman-Review*, October 22, 1984.

recruitment sequences. First, membership on the intermediate appeals bench added to the credentials of candidates.[51] They could and did argue that they had experience directly relevant to the demands of the job as a justice of the Supreme Court. They were skilled in writing opinions and reviewing appeals; experiences that the trial judges lacked. Second, the staggered six-year terms of the appeals judges freed at least two-thirds of them every two years to mount a challenge to a justice, secure in the knowledge that if they lost, they still retained their positions on the intermediate bench. In contrast, the superior court judges had to run for reelection every four years to retain their seats on the trial benches. They, thus, could safely take on a supreme court justice only every fourth year.

Elections and the Activities of the Bar

The question of attorneys lending their names to be placed in newspaper ads and handouts still plagued the profession. To some it was demeaning and to others it was misleading. In 1958 the bar had moderated its view, and endorsements again became common practices in judicial elections.

By 1970, the bar's board of governors felt compelled again to adopt stronger rules. Not only were the new rules designed to further ethical considerations but, incidently, to strengthen the impact of the bar's preferential polls. The bar leadership wanted these plebiscites to remain the single public expression of the preferences of the attorneys. Because of questions of ethics and because the "voting public require and seek the advice of the Bar," the board dictated that: (1) no names of lawyers could be used in public advertising in support of judicial candidates; (2) the results of polls of lawyers on their candidate preference should be made available to the public; and (3) lawyers were encouraged to make monetary contributions to candidates. However, these contributions must be made "anonymously in a manner that will assure . . . that the candidate" not know the source.[52] The endorsement restrictions

51. From 1970 until the present, the number of court of appeals judges whose names were on the ballot was substantial. Ten incumbent or former court of appeals judges were involved in the September primaries (Stafford, Horowitz, Petrie, Callow, Utter, Dore, Reed, Green, Andersen, and Pearson). Actually, more appeals court judges participated in contested races than superior court jurists and newcomers from other facets of the legal profession.

52. *Spokane Spokesman-Review*, October 1970, 12–21. Because of a conflict between the political campaign contribution disclosure aspects of the 1970 ruling (anonymous contributions) and the Seattle City Charter and other ordinances compelling public disclosure of all funding in political campaigns, the board of governors adopted a

were, however, short-lived. Two years later, a conflict between the newly adopted Code of Professional Responsibility and the 1970 rule forbidding the use of attorneys' names in ads caused the board to allow, again, endorsements by attorneys.[53]

Actually, the use of attorney endorsements by candidates had now come full circle. The ambivalence toward such endorsements experienced since 1958 had resulted in strengthening the impact of the bar's preferential polls. However, now, the endorsements could well work at cross purposes with the bar poll. Those candidates failing in the poll could still muster an impressive list of attorneys to suggest that the official poll was either incorrect or incomplete. Of course, the contradiction between the polls and endorsements was possible only if it was assumed that the legal profession spoke with a single voice, or that they could reach a significant consensus regarding qualifications for the Supreme Court. This was, indeed, a weighty assumption.

Starting with the 1970 contested races, the Seattle or State Bar conducted sixteen bar polls (thirteen in the primaries and three in the general elections). In six of these races, the voters ignored the recommendations of the legal profession. (See table 7.4.) In comparison to the earlier experience with bar polls, the electorate now was exercising some independence from the influence of the profession.

In addition to their efforts to influence appointments and elections, the legal profession had continually concerned itself with statutory and constitutional reforms, many of which would effect judicial recruitment. The legal profession realized that constitutional reform required broad-based support because of their failures when they went it alone in previous efforts. The bar now turned toward cooperative efforts with other groups. Between 1971 and 1973, a coalition of groups worked separately and then cooperatively to reform Article IV. The State Bar, the Judicial Council, judges' groups, the American Judicature Society, the Citizens' Committee on Washington Courts, the Senate Judiciary Committee, and

---

resolution that the sources of contributions "not be disclosed to the candidate" unless the law requires it. *Washington State Bar News* 22 (April 1972): 4. In 1973 a statewide public disclosure initiative was passed requiring candidates for virtually all public offices to file reports of contributions and expenditures. See H. Bone, "Open Government by Initiative: Notes on Washington's Experience," *Policy Studies Journal* 2 (Summer 1974): 251, and Bone and C. M. Fey, *The People's Right to Know* (Seattle: Institute of Governmental Research, University of Washington, 1978).

53. Code of Professional Responsibility, DR 101 (B) (1). *Washington State Bar News* 22 (August 1972).

Table 7.4
Bar Polls for Supreme Court Candidates, 1970–84

		Primary		*General*
Year	*Candidate*	*Seattle Bar*	*State Bar*	*State Bar*
1970	**Hunter*	1,096	2,015	
	Evans	133	280	
	**Stafford*	1,074	2,048	
	Goodloe	148	275	
	*Sharp	1,092	1,874	
	Wright	139	456	
1972	**Hamilton*	1,104	2,402	
	Faler	**	200	
	**Rosellini*	1,241	2,361	
	Love	161	217	
	**Wright*	227	594	
	Shorett	1,237	2,001	
1973	**Brachtenbach* (no primary)			2,190
	Sawyer			157
1974	**Horowitz*		58%†	
	Holman		16	
	Petrie		22	
	Comfort		6	
	Tuai		3	
1976	*Hicks*		16%‡	
	Callow		72	
	**Dolliver*		50	70%‡
	Eggers		22	
	Dore		16	24

the Governor's Committee on Constitutional Revision cooperated to produce Senate Joint Resolution (S.J.R.) 113. The proposed constitutional amendment included a commission plan system of selecting judges, much like the Missouri plan earlier backed by the bar.

S.J.R. 113 was never submitted to the voters as disagreements over the plan soon surfaced. Although all could agree on the need for judicial reform and none criticized the whole package, important groups opposed some of the details of the proposal. Labor strongly opposed the commission plan for recruitment. Under the nonpartisan election system, labor was a potent factor in the recruitment process, but under the proposed plan their influence would be negligible. The State Bar supported the commission idea, but was

Table 7.4 (*continued*)

		Primary		General
Year	Candidate	Seattle Bar	State Bar	State Bar
1978	*Williams*		24%§	52%§
	Callow		57	
	Holman		19	48
	Dimoff		1	
1980	**Utter*		86%‡	
	Clem		13	
	Reed		65	
	Dore		34	
1984	**Dimmick*		2,877	
	Merson		514	
	Green		1,411	
	Hemovich		929	
	Goodloe		928	
	Felice		63	
	Rosell		46	
	Callow		2,892	
	Heavey		460	
	Yoon		85	

Italicized names designate election winners
*Incumbent
**not rated
†"Excellent"
‡"Preferred"
§"Favorable"

concerned about who would manage the proposed unified court system. The attorneys worried that the Supreme Court could not supervise the entire state system without assistance. Other interested parties found fault with other provisions of the proposal. Without a unified front, S.J.R. 113 would assuredly be rejected by the voters. Upon the suggestion of the chairman of the Senate Judiciary Committee (Pete Francis), the proposal was withdrawn, and all parties were urged to compromise their differences before submitting an amendment to the voters.

By 1975 the bar, judges, citizen's groups, and politicians had settled their differences sufficiently to have another version of Article IV ready for introduction to the legislature. Support for the new proposal (S.J.R. 101) seemed universal. However, opposition from the Superior Court Judges Association gradually gathered strength.

The judges questioned the constitutionality of submitting a revision of an entire article of the constitution to the voters for a simple "yes" or "no" response. To gain support from some of the critics of the earlier proposal, the commission plan for recruiting judges was dropped from S.J.R. 101, leaving the present system intact. This exclusion caused some defections.

After voting in favor of the amendment, the board of governors of the State Bar reconsidered the issue and, shortly before the election, voted to oppose the proposal on the grounds that it gave "to the legislature too much control over the judiciary and infringes on the separation of powers."[54] This reversal by the board of governors, according to one participant in the reform movement, was due to a change in leadership. The new president of the State Bar was "a resident of eastern Washington, [and] had on occasion been identified as an opponent" of S.J.R. 101.[55]

The State Bar was instrumental in writing the constitutional proposal and, ironically, was also instrumental in defeating it. With the legal profession and the trial judges on record against the proposed constitutional amendment, it was not surprising that the voters rejected the proposal in November on a 408,832 to 427,631 vote. Although four years later the voters approved a constitutional amendment to set up a Judicial Qualifications Commission to deal with problems of judicial discipline, S.J.R. 101 was the last formal push toward large-scale replacement of Article IV. The absence of any reform of judicial selection in S.J.R. 101 suggested that if any change was to be implemented in the near future, it would likely come in the informal relations between the governor, the bar, the electorate, and the candidates.

The activities of the organized bar throughout the several years of the modern period were varied, changing and often effective. The State Bar's judicial preference poll remained the single most conspicuous contribution. Endorsements by the bar were important, but the few years when such endorsements were forbidden indicated that they were not essential. Of course, the activities of the Judicial Selection Committee in recommending possible appointees to the governor remained another strong influence in judicial recruitment. The bar's ventures into formal constitutional changes had repeatedly led to defeat. Nevertheless, the legal fraternity seemed to be satisfied with or to have generally accepted the present system.

54. *Washington State Bar News* 29 (November 1975): 26.

55. Phillip Winberry, "Washington State Court Reform," in Lee Powell, ed., *Court Reform in Seven States* (Chicago: American Bar Association, 1980), 148.

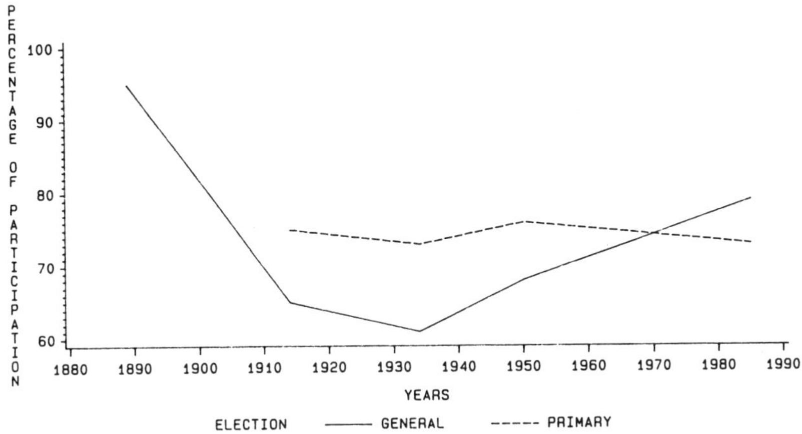

Fig. 7.1. Voter participation in contested Supreme Court elections (percentages beyond 1980 are estimated)

The Electorate in Contemporary Recruitment

The nature of the responses of the electorate to judicial campaigns in the modern period holds the key to an understanding of the effects of the recruitment process. A review of election "roll-off" since 1889 should prove useful. Since the move to direct primaries and nonpartisan balloting, the interest of the voter in judicial races has remained fairly stable. Figure 7.1 reports the average percentage of voters casting ballots for judges over the periods delineated by the recruitment analysis.

Since 1912 and until recently, nearly two-thirds of those who voted in any particular election cast their vote for a judicial aspirant in a contested general election. Three-fourths of those who went to the polls in the primary elections made a choice between contestants in a supreme court race. However, gradually the interest in judicial elections has increased in the November balloting. Considering the innumerable demands made on the attention of the average voter this increase may actually be fairly remarkable.

The increase can be attributed to a variety of factors. First, the use of the mass media, especially television, has brought the contestants to the attention of more voters. Costs of campaigning have correspondingly increased (see table 7.5).[56] Also, the state's high bench

56. The data in table 7.5 were obtained from Public Disclosure Commission Reports and S. S. Story and J. J. Robinson, "Judicial Campaigns for The Supreme Court and Court of Appeals in the State of Washington: An Analysis of Campaign Contributions and Expenditures in Contested Elections" (unpublished paper, Political Science Department, Washington State University, 1985).

Table 7.5
Campaign Expenditures, 1973–84

Year	Candidate	Primary	General	Totals
1973	Brachtenbach	*	$8,118	$8,118
	Sawyer		2,616	2,616
1974	Horowitz	$50,143	$22,710	$72,853
	Petrie	10,970		10,970
	Tuai	7,568	4,230	11,797
	Holman	7,316		7,316
	Comfort	2,147		2,147
1976	Hicks	$25,068		$25,068
	Callow	30,105		30,105
	Dolliver	63,821	$27,700	91,521
	Dore	39,624	6,228	45,852
	Eggers	24,894		24,894
1978	Williams	$23,692	$7,078	$30,770
	Holman	18,624	4,618	23,242
	Dimoff	2,418		2,418
	Callow	44,038		44,038
1980	Utter	$48,502		48,502
	Clem	13,771		13,771
	Dore	43,870		43,870
	Reed	52,885		52,885
1984	Goodloe	$13,750	$3,289	$17,039
	Green	30,804	29,660	60,464
	Hemovich	24,154		24,154
	Rosell	5,659		5,659
	Felice	5,548		5,548
	Dimmick	18,640		18,640
	Merson	20,793		20,793
	Callow	107,000	7,688	114,688
	Heavey	65,264	74,707	139,971
	Yoon	4,201		4,201

*No primary election

has been involved in more visible and contentious policy-oriented decisions (largely because of the change in its jurisdiction in 1969), raising the consciousness of the voters in the state. Finally, although the number of contested races has not significantly increased in recent times, those who make it to the general elections have been fairly evenly matched, drawing more voters to the judicial ticket.

The judicial voters today are more attentive. They want access to a considerable number of sources on judicial candidates and consult a number of them.[57] They are somewhat informed,[58] familiar with courts,[59] and responsible.[60] They clearly regard judicial elections as important matters and public accountability as necessary.

Conclusions: The Relationship between Recruitment and Judicial Independence and Public Accountability

The voters' participation in the screening and affirmation processes in contemporary elections has remained fairly stable while displaying an ever increasing interest. Gubernatorial appointees and candidates supported in bar polls have sometimes lost, indicating a somewhat independent role on the part of the electorate. On the other hand, such irrelevant factors as name familiarity also influence the voters. The effect of name familiarity is certainly not limited to nonpartisan judicial elections, but in such elections it can mean that the electorate has even less inclination to weigh the qualifications of the candidates simply because of the lack of meaningful issues. Nonetheless, the judicial voter is not without the desire or the means to cast a considered ballot in contested races for the state benches.

Today, with rare exception, candidate credentials constitute the crucial materials of the campaigns. The bar poll was established as the collective expression of the opinion of the legal profession and

57. These data are based upon a survey of a sample of Washington voters conducted immediately following the 1982 primary election in jurisdictions having at least one contested judicial race. For a summary of the results, see *Judiciary: The Quarterly for Washington's Court System* (Spring, Fall, Winter, 1983).

58. *Ibid.* Fifty-one percent of the judicial voters recognized at least two names (out of four) of judicial candidates that were on their ballots. However, they were cautious about the knowledge they possessed. Only 24% said they were informed enough to cast their judicial ballots, and 27% admitted they knew nothing about the candidates.

59. The following table reports the reactions of the judicial voters to the question: "In comparison to elections for other offices in state and local government, how would you rate the importance of judicial elections?"

Less important	6%
Just as important	64%
Most important	30%

Thus a majority regarded judicial elections as important exercises.

60. The voter respondents indicated a respectable level of familiarity with courts in the state:

Intimately familiar	2%
Broadly familiar	11%
Familiar	29%
Somewhat familiar	48%
No familiarity	11%

for a short time constituted the only indication of the preferences of the attorneys. Now, however, endorsements by individual attorneys are again common practice. Endorsements by special groups are also now common. The State Labor Council, for example, usually throws its support to one or another of the candidates. However, labor as a whole rarely agrees on a single candidate. Teamsters' support or the endorsement of the Maritime Trades Union often counter the support of the Labor Council. Such support from special groups (other than the bar) tends to be confined solely to the membership of the group, whereas attorney endorsements, bar preferential polls, and law enforcement surveys are designed to influence the public generally. Recently, both political parties have attempted to sway voters with their support despite the nonpartisan nature of the offices.

What is evident from this review of the modern elections system is that there are overlapping influences exerted by the governor, special interests, the candidates, the bar, and the electorate. The original recruitment process functioned on the basis of a more clearly defined division of labor. That is, the governor initiated through the appointment process, the bar screened through its selection committees and its bar polls, and the electorate affirmed in primary and general elections. But now, these and other participants tend to be involved in virtually all stages of the total process.

The contention suggested at the outset of this analysis of supreme court recruitment was that as the process evolves the conflict between judicial independence and public accountability would be balanced.

The major participants in the recruitment of judges today are the electorate, the candidates themselves, the legal profession, the appointing governor, and interest groups. To what degree do these recruitment actors tolerate the conflict between independence and accountability? Answers to the question can best be provided by asking the participants themselves. In 1982 a sample of the electorate, of attorneys in three jurisdictions, and all judicial candidates throughout the state were asked to respond to statements on the functions of judicial elections. Two of these statements emphasized the independence and acountability aspects of judicial recruitment, and two presented compromises between the two extremes.[61]

The public accountability statement suggests that judicial elec-

61. These data were gathered from the September 1982 survey of registered voters (see footnote 57), of a sample of attorneys in the three jurisdictions under study (Seattle, Bellevue, and Stevens County) and of all the candidates for judicial office (opposed and unopposed) throughout the state.

tions are identical to elections for other political offices. The primary function is to give to the candidates a mandate and then to hold them to that mandate. The statement reads: "Elections should tell the judges what the people want, and the judges *should follow* the people's desires." Agreement to this statement would lead to a "delegate" view of judicial recruitment in which the judges act as the public's delegate and remain accountable to the voters.

The statement emphasizing the judicial independence aspect of elections implied that those who are elected to the bench must simply be trusted that they will do their best without interference from the electorate or the public. The function of judicial elections is largely to legitimate the results and then allow the judges to go about their business, unhampered by public demands. The statement reads: "Elections should support those judges who are independent of public opinion and remain *unaffected* by the people's demands." This is the "trustee" view of elections.

Two compromise functions were presented to the respondents. A "stewardship" function represents a balance between independence and accountability. Elections should be used to keep the judges in touch with society so that when those cases arise that present public policy issues the judges are not without some sensitivity. The statement reads: "Elections should only *inform* the judges of the general feelings of the people so that judges don't become too isolated."

Finally, forms of judicial discipline must be available to the public or their representatives. In Washington only four means are present: impeachment, recall by a joint resolution of the legislature, censure or removal by the Supreme Court upon recommendation of the Judicial Qualifications Commission, and, finally, elections. As of 1983 only one recommendation for discipline has gone to the Supreme Court from the Qualifications Commission. Thus, elections remain the practical means of removing judges for cause. The statement presented to the respondents with this "recall" function read: "Elections should serve the sole purpose of *removing* lazy, corrupt, and or incompetent judges from the county or state courts."

The four alternative functions attributed to judicial elections can be placed on an accountability—independence continuum. Figure 7.2 illustrates this placement. The contention is that in the institutionalized system of recruitment, the major participants would tend to be more tolerant of the conflict between the two extremes on the continuum. The responses of the voters, attorneys, and candidates are indeed encouraging, although the views of these actors are not entirely unequivocal. (See table 7.6.)

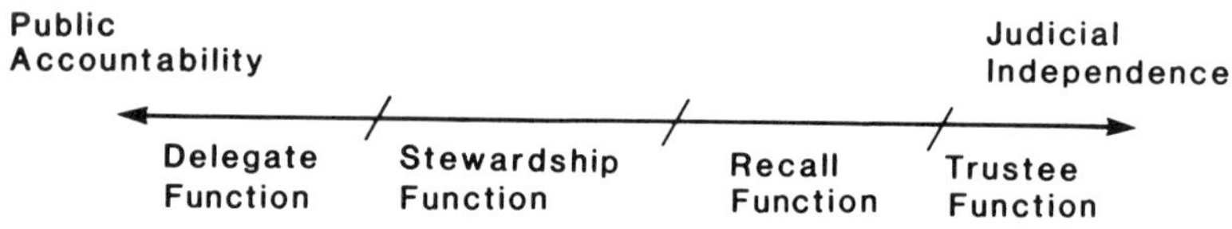

Fig. 7.2. Independence-accountability continuum

Table 7.6
Functions of Judicial Elections from the Perspectives of the Major Actors
(Percentage "strongly" agreeing)

		Actors	
Functions	*Judicial Voters*	*Attorneys*	*Opposed Candidates*
Delegate	45%	9%	20%
Stewardship	51	57	57
Recall	55	39	24
Trustee	27	45	37

Support for the stewardship function exceeds the support for the two extremes, although the recall perspective draws some supporters from among the electorate.

When institutionalized recruitment systems of today are compared to the unstructured systems similar to the earlier years, evidence shows that now (1) the citizens participate more in judicial elections (except during the inaugural years of partisan elections); (2) they consult more sources of information on candidates; (3) they are more knowledgeable about candidates and the courts; and what is more important, (4) they tend to support the compromise versions of judicial elections.

Judicial recruitment in Washington has evolved from the simple system dominated by the political party with its emphasis upon public acountability through the ad hoc and unstructured years of experimentation to the institutionalized system of today. Accompanying this movement has been a gradual balancing between the demands of judicial independence or rule of law and public accountability or majoritarian democracy. Of course, there is no guarantee that the balance will remain.

Since 1889, the recruitment sequence has produced seventy-seven judges, some of whom stayed on the bench but a few months and others of whom served over a quarter of a century. Each has made some contribution to the rich traditions of the court. Because of the prerequisites for practicing law and for judgeships, the seventy-seven judges have much in common. Nonetheless, the constraints of the recruitment system shape to some degree the character of the bench in each of the five periods isolated in the foregoing analysis. The next chapter records and analyzes the results of recruitment by looking at the backgrounds of the judges. We know how the judges got to the state's high bench. Now we want to understand who those are that have survived the often contentious recruitment process.

8

The Survivors, a Biographical Record

We may have "a government of laws, not of men," but government does not run itself. Flesh and blood provide the laws. Nonetheless, laws are, at best, unsure guides. What does the law mean? What choices should be made between contrasting laws? What if a law is wrong? A number of questions of this nature come quickly to mind, but the point has been made: there is a need for humans to assure a government of laws. One of the leading participants in the process of government of laws is, of course, the judge. He or she makes a contribution to the meaning of laws and thus to the directions taken by the state.

This chapter concerns these judges' backgrounds and experiences. It constructs a profile of the "typical" judge and reports the coincidences of backgrounds among the seventy-seven jurists who have served in eighty-five positions since 1889.[1]

What is known about the jurists who have served on the state's court of last resort has largely been gained from analyzing their opinions, which are carefully recorded in the *Washington Reports.* But who were the writers of these opinions? What provided them with the opportunities to be appointed or elected to the court? What events in their past might explain their particular views of the law?

1. Although the total number of persons selected for the Supreme Court is seventy-seven, several served in two separate positions. Between 1890 and 1912, Judges White, Hadley, and Chadwick were selected twice to the court. Judge Holcomb, first elected in 1915, was defeated in 1927, but returned immediately to the bench through gubernatorial appointment. Between 1933 and 1948 Judge Grady served in a temporary position and then was later elected. Judge Millard served a second but short term in 1956, and Judge Foster was appointed to a short term and then elected to a full term the same year. In 1970 Justice Sharp was appointed, then defeated in an election, and subsequently reappointed in 1971. The statistics in the tables account for these additional appointments or elections, bringing the total of positions filled to eighty-five. Judges Webster, Schwellenbach, Mallery, Dore, and Callow were appointed to fill short-term vacancies in the same positions to which they were elected and are not counted twice.

Although each judge has experienced unique and telling events throughout his or her busy life, and each of these events affected the person in different ways, there are certain background variables that have been shown to be important to an understanding of judges.[2] For analytical purposes, background variables fall into three major classes: ascriptive, acquired, and affiliated.[3] Ascriptive variables are those over which the subject has had no control. Race, age, gender, place of birth, parentage, and so forth, are examples. Acquired background variables are those characteristics and experiences which, in the course of a career, the subject acquired. They are largely a matter of choice, although the tendency is for a person to be attracted more to one than to another because of early socialization. Type of legal practice, public offices, religion, and education are acquired attributes. Affiliated variables are a matter of choice and involve membership in political, professional, civic, and social organizations such as political party, lodge membership, social club activities and involvement in charitable groups.

The assumption is that although each of these categories stand alone, they tend to reinforce each other and tend logically to hold together. For example, a judge may have been born into advantaged circumstances (ascribed), attended a private college and prestigious law school (acquired), joined the Republican Party (affiliated), and be appointed to the bench by a Republican governor. The judge may have also retained membership in the Seattle Golf Club, Rainier Club, or continued as a member of the Masonic Order. The behavior displayed by such a judge indicates some disdain for public accountability shaped by a conservative but restraintist view of his role. There is a "logic" among these variables, and they tend to reinforce each other.

Despite the particularistic forces impinging upon court aspirants in each of the five recruitment periods, those surviving the winnowing process have much in common. Each has been shaped by the

2. Scholars have debated the importance of backgrounds as explanatory variables. The debate still rages suggesting that, at the very least, these variables ought to be reported and analyzed. For some of the leading works primarily concerned with the U.S. Supreme Court see: Henry J. Abraham, *Justices and Presidents* (New York: Oxford University Press. 1974); Beverly B. Cook, "Sentencing Behavior of Federal Judges: Draft Cases—1972," *University of Cincinnati Law-Review* 2 (1973): 597; David J. Danelski, "Values as Variables in Judicial Decision-Making: Notes Toward a Theory," *Vanderbilt Law Review* 19 (1966): 721; Joel B. Grossman, "Social Backgrounds and Judicial Decision-Making," *Harvard Law Review* 79 (1966): 1551; John R. Schmidhauser, *The Supreme Court: Its Politics, Personalities, and Procedures* (New York: Holt, Rinehart and Winston, 1961); C. Neal Tate, "Voting Behavior of U.S. Supreme Court Justices," *American Political Science Review* 75 (1981): 355.

3. See B. B. Cook, "Sentencing Behavior."

intellectual and professional lessons coming from the study of the law. Most have had the benefit of some college education. All were residents of the state, and most were native Washingtonians. They have all experienced, although to varying degrees, the practice of law with its traditions, ethics, rules, and roles. Many have served apprenticeships in another state court, and many have led active political lives. Most had been active members of the bar. Certainly, all were vital members of their respective communities. And all had survived the politics of appointment or elections. Finally, all had to confine themselves to the roles and traditions of the Supreme Court once they donned their robes of office. What is perhaps striking is that any significant diversity in the backgrounds of the seventy-seven jurists can be detected.

There still remains to the judges a fairly wide area for the play of varying views regarding the role of judges in the political system, the role of government in the lives of the people, and the proper stance to be taken toward accountability or independence.

Court Profiles: From 1889 to 1912

The typical judge who served during the inaugural years of the court was born out-of-state in a rural setting; his father's occupation usually was farming. The judge had attended public schools and then a private college. He either studied law with an attorney (clerked) or at a recognized law school. He practiced in a small partnership and had some judicial experience before either election or appointment to the Supreme Court at the age of forty-seven. The judge was a Protestant, and had been fairly active in Republican politics and in bar association affairs. He had held at least one public office, had been a Freemason and had retained membership in a number of social clubs. He served an average of eleven years on the state's court of last resort before resigning, often to take up law practice again.

The typical judge might have served as a prosecutor (30% had) as well as in the legislature (35%). He was as likely to have lived in Eastern as in Western Washington. If he went to law school it would likely have been a prestigious institution (Michigan, Columbia, Virginia). Actually, the judges who served from 1889 until 1912 were a fairly impressive lot. They managed to get the state's legal system off to a firm start. (See table 8.1.)

Table 8.1
Backgrounds, 1889–1912

Name	Birth Place	Occupation Head of Family	College	Legal Education	Prior Legal Experience**	Age at Selection	Politics	Religion	Residence
Thomas J. Anders	Ohio	Farming	None	Michigan	Prosecutor	51	R		Walla Walla
Elmon Scott	Vt.	Farming	None	Clerk	Sole	36	R		Pomeroy
Ralph O. Dunbar	Ill.	Carpenter	Willamette	Clerk	Sole	44	R	Congregational	Goldendale
T. L. Stiles	Ohio	Merchant	Amherst	Columbia	Sole	41	R		Tacoma
John P. Hoyt	Ohio	Farming	Ohio St.	Union	Private	48	R		Seattle
Merritt J. Gordon	Canada		None	Clerk	Judicial	38	R		Olympia
James B. Reavis	Ky.	Farming	Kentucky	Clerk	Partner	49	D	Christian	Yakima
Mark Fullerton	Oreg.	Farming	Willamette	Clerk	Private	41	R		Colfax
*William H. White	W. Va.		Vermillion	Clerk	Partner	58	D		Seattle
Wallace Mount	Oreg.	Tailor	U. Oregon	Clerk	Judicial	42	R	Presbyterian	Sprague
*Hiram E. Hadley	Ind.	Farming	Earlham	Union	Judicial	47	R	Presbyterian	Bellingham
Frank H. Rudkin	Ohio		Washington & Lee	Washington & Lee	Judicial	41	R	Catholic	Ellensburg
*Milo A. Root	Ill.		None	Albany	Partner	42	R	Congregational	Seattle
*Herman D. Crow	Ohio	Lawyer	Wesleyan	Clerk	Partner	54	R	Congregational	Spokane
†Stephen J. Chadwick	Oreg.	Lawyer	Willamette	U. Oregon	Judicial	45	D	Epsicopalian	Colfax
*Mack F. Gose	Mo.	Farming	Whitman	Clerk	Partner	50	R	Episcopalian	Pomeroy
*Geo. E. Morris	N.Y.	Minister	Union	Albany	Judicial	47	R	Methodist	Seattle
*Emmett N. Parker	Pa.	Miller	Whittier	Cincinnati	Judicial	50	R	Quaker	Tacoma
*Overton G. Ellis	Mo.	Physician	U. Missouri	U. Virginia (Clerk)	Partner	51	D		Tacoma
*John F. Main	Ill.	Farming	Princeton	Michigan	Judicial	48	R	Presbyterian	Seattle

*Appointed
**Experience refers to practice immediately prior to selection
†Appointed to short term before assuming elected position

From 1913 to 1932

The representative jurist who served between 1912 and 1932 was again from out-of-state and grew up in rural circumstances. The occupation of his parents was a bit more diversified, but they likely supported their family through farming. The judge was fifty-eight years old when appointed to the high court bench and had previously served as a state trial judge.

The jurist attended public schools, matriculated at a public, out-of-state college, and received his law degree from a fairly impressive law school. He likely was in a small firm or partnership while practicing law in Western Washington and was active in Republican politics and bar association affairs. He was a member of a number of social groups and of the Masonic Order. The judge attended a Protestant church.

More of the judges during this period were appointed to their post than previously (72% as compared to 48%), were products of public education, and studied at a law school rather than clerking to learn the tools of their trade. Prosecutorial experience and practice with a small law firm was becoming common. Most of the judges had prior judicial experience before recruitment to the court. They were older when selected and served less time on the court than their predecessors. Although still active politically (and Republicans) fewer served in the legislature and in other public offices than before. Some Democrats were also finding their way to the state's court of last resort. Eastern Washington had lost representative parity to the Westside, with Seattle providing over one-fourth of the judges.

The judges who attained positions on the Supreme Court remained an impressive lot. They still were somewhat representative of attorneys in the state, although their educational backgrounds suggested that they might have been a cut above their colleagues in the profession. (See table 8.2.)

From 1933 to 1949

The typical supreme court jurist during the "times of stress" (the Great Depression and the Second World War) grew up, as before, in rural, out-of-state, farming surroundings, and attended an out-of-state public college and law school. He had considerable experience as a public prosecutor, had served on the trial bench, and was appointed to the Supreme Court from an Eastern Washington constituency.

He was active in partisan politics, somewhat attentive to state bar affairs, but had not served in the legislature or held any other public office. The jurist was a member of several social organizations (Elks, Rainier Club, golf clubs, etc.), and was a high degree Freemason. He was of the Protestant faith. The judge was older and served only nine years on the court. His political and legal philosophy tended between moderate to liberal and neutral to restraintist.[4]

What distinguishes these judges from their predecessors was their Democratic party affiliation, age when appointed, greater prosecutorial experience, and an increasing number who received an in-state college and law training (over one-third went to the University of Washington School of Law). Also they were joiners. Nearly all had belonged to some social group. All the jurists had attended law school (although Geraghty attended Georgetown after having been a member of the Washington Bar), but only one had matriculated at a prestigious law school (Robinson graduated from Columbia). Nearly half the jurists had served in the military, and most were from Eastern Washington. Spokane had been the home-base for one-fourth of the judges. (See table 8.3.)

From 1949 to 1969

The judge who served from 1949 to 1969 was born and raised in a town or city setting within the state. He attended public schools, a public college in Washington, and received his law degree from the University of Washington School of Law. His prebench practice was

4. The ideological orientations for the earlier judges are known for only a few. These classifications are based upon the views of law clerks and experienced appellate attorneys surveyed in 1977 and upon an analysis of voting behavior discussed in the following chapters.

The 1977 Survey of 166 law clerks and two hundred experienced attorneys who had, over the years, argued several times before the justices, asked each respondent to rate the justices, along the spectrums of liberal-conservative and activist-restraintist. These terms were defined as follows:

"A conservative such as Justice John M. Harlan would tend to view the law as a restraint on human behavior rather than an opportunity, to regard the free enterprise system as the best means to improve society, and to take a strong 'law and order' line toward criminals. A liberal such as Chief Justice Earl Warren would tend to take the 'opposite' view.

"A restraintist was exemplified by Justice Felix Frankfurter. He tended to believe that cases should be decided on narrow grounds, precedent should be closely followed, deference must be granted to the political branches, important economic, social and political issues should be avoided and moral judgments eschewed. An activist, exemplified by Justice William O. Douglas, generally took the 'opposite' approach."

Table 8.2
Backgrounds, 1913–32

Name	*Birth Place*	*Occupation Head of Family*	*College*	*Legal Education*	*Prior Legal Experience***	*Age at Selection*	*Politics*	*Religion*	*Residence*	*Political Philosophy*
*O. R. Holcomb	Ind.	Attorney	S.W. Indiana	Chicago-Kent	Judicial	48	D	Episcopalian	Ritzville	Mod.
*F. Bausman	Pa.		Pittsburgh	Harvard	Partner	54	D		Seattle	
†J. S. Webster	Ky.	Farming	None	Michigan	Judicial	39	R	Christian	Spokane	
*W. W. Tolman	Ill.	Farming	None	Northwestern	Partner	57	D	Baptist	Spokane	Lib./Neu.
*K. Mackintosh	Wash.	Lumber, real estate	Stanford	Columbia	Judicial	43	R	Methodist	Seattle	Con./Res.
*John Mitchell	Va.	Farming	Virginia	Clerk	Judicial	57	D	Baptist	Olympia	Con./Res.
*J. B. Bridges	Ind.	Farming	DePauw	Clerk	Partner	57	R	Universalist	Aberdeen	Mod.
*Chester Hovey	Mass.		None	Clerk	Private	48	R		Ellensburg	

W. H. Pemberton	Ohio		Earlham	Clerk	Judicial	47	D	Methodist	Bellingham	Lib./Act.
Wm. D. Askren	Iowa		None	Clerk	Judicial	40	R	Presbyterian	Tacoma	
Walter French	Mich.	Grain buyer	Hillsdale	U. Washington	Judicial	53	D	Episcopalian	Tacoma	
*Walter Beals	Minn.		None	U. Washington	Judicial	52	R		Seattle	Mod./Res.
*Wm. J. Millard	Mo.	Railroad worker	None	Georgetown	Law Library	45	R	Episcopalian	Olympia	Lib./Act.
*Adam Beeler	Ind.	Farming	Indiana	George Washington	Judicial	48	R		Seattle	
*H. E. T. Herman	Ill.		None	Washington U.	Private	40	R		Spokane	
*Wm. J. Steinert	Ky.	Seamstress	Central Kentucky U.	Michigan	Judicial	52	R	Presbyterian	Seattle	Con./Res.
Bruce Blake	Ind.	Attorney	U. Chicago	Michigan	Judicial	51	D		Spokane	Lib./Neu.

*Appointed
**Experience immediately prior to selection
†Appointed to short term before assuming elected position

Table 8.3
Backgrounds, 1933–49

Name	*Birth Place*	*Occupation Head of Family*	*College*	*Legal Education*	*Prior Legal Experience***	*Age at Selection*	*Politics*	*Religion*	*Residence*	*Political Philosophy*
*James M. Geraghty	Ireland	Farming	None	Georgetown	City Attorney	63	D	Catholic	Spokane	Lib./Act.
*George B. Simpson	Wash.		Willamette	Willamette	Judicial	56	D	Methodist	Vancouver	Con./Res.
John S. Robinson	Ohio	Farming	Michigan	Columbia	Partner	57	R	Congregational	Seattle	Con./Res.
Clyde C. Jeffers	Iowa	Farming	None	Iowa	Judicial	58	R	Presbyterian	Ephrata	Con./Res.
*Sam M. Driver	Oreg.		None	U. Washington	Prosecutor	48	D	Protestant	Spokane	Lib./Act.
†Joe A. Mallery	Wash.	Farming	Reed	U. Washington	Judicial	46	R	Methodist	Tacoma	Mod./Neu.
*Tom E. Grady	Wis.	Farming	None	Minnesota	Partner	62	R	Presbyterian	Yakima	Mod./Res.
*Ed. M. Connelly	Wash.		Gonzaga	Gonzaga	Prosecutor	54	D	Catholic	Spokane	Lib./Act.
†E. W. Schwellenbach	S. Dak.		None	Wisconsin	Judicial	59	D	Episcopalian	Ephrata	Lib./Neu.
*Don G. Abel	Kans.	Attorney	U. Washington	U. Washington	Private	52	D	Presbyterian	Chehalis	Lib./Act.
Matthew W. Hill	Mont.	Railroad worker	U. Washington	U. Washington	Judicial	53	R	Baptist	Seattle	Con./Res.

*Appointed
**Experience immediately prior to selection
†Appointed to short term before assuming elected position

with a small law firm in Western Washington. The judge was active in the Republican Party and in bar affairs. He belonged to several social organizations and was also active in veteran's groups after having served in the military during World War II. He was fifty-three years old when appointed to the court and remained on that bench for twelve years. His religion was Protestant, his residence was Seattle, and his legal-political philosophy was middle-of-the-road.

The 1949–69 jurists differed from their predecessors in that most were native Washingtonians and were trained at the University of Washington. None received Ivy League or prestigious law school education. Prosecutorial experience was no longer an important factor in their backgrounds. Most of them were recruited to the court by gubernatorial appointment. More of them were also involved in bar activities and civic affairs than before, and fewer were Freemasons. Finally, farming and rural backgrounds had nearly disappeared.

Although politically active Republicans dominated the bench, the jurists tended to reject extreme philosophical outlooks. The 1949–69 bench was a relatively middle-of-the-road group with a more parochial perspective gained from their in-state births and schooling. However, they were still a diverse lot in most of their background features. (See table 8.4.)

1970 to the Present

The contemporary justice was born in the state in an urban setting. He or she practiced law in Seattle with a small law firm and likely served as a prosecutor at some point. The father's occupation placed him or her in the professional class. The jurist attended public schools in Washington, a public in-state college, and the University of Washington Law School. Most had prior judicial experience at the superior court or court of appeals levels. The justice was active in Republican party affairs and also much involved in professional activities. Civic projects and organizations were important. He or she was fifty-four years old upon promotion to the court and had, thus far, served six years in the office. Middle-of-the-road legal and political philosophies were adopted by the justice.

The contemporary judges are not altogether distinguished from their immediate predecessors. However, their parents tended more to come from the middle to upper-middle professional classes. In-state public education prior to law school was more common to the modern jurists, while their legal education (University of Washington and top ranked schools) not only set them apart from

Table 8.4
Backgrounds, 1949–69

Name	*Birth Place*	*Occupation Head of Family*	*College*	*Legal Education*	*Prior Legal Experience***	*Age at Selection*	*Politics*	*Religion*	*Residence*	*Political Philosophy*
*Fred G. Hamley	Wash.	Farming	None	U. Washington	Private	46	R	Unitarian	Seattle	Mod./Neu.
*Charles Donworth	Wash.	Attorney	Yale	U. Washington	Partner	57	R	Catholic	Seattle	Con./Res.
Robert C. Finley	N.C.	Druggist	Duke	Duke	Sole	45	D	Methodist	Renton	Lib./Act.
*Frank P. Weaver	Pa.	Blacksmith	Michigan	U. Washington	Professor	51	R	Episcopalian	Spokane	Mod./Res.
*Ralph Olson	Minn.	Banking	Carleton	Minnesota	Judicial	49	R	Presbyterian	Bellingham	Mod./Res.
Hugh J. Rosellini	Wash.	Wholesale food distributor	Puget Sound	U. Washington	Judicial	46	D	Lutheran	Tacoma	Lib./Act.
*Richard B. Ott	Wash.	Hotel owner	Idaho	Idaho	Judicial	58	R	Episcopalian	Ritzville	Con./Res.
*Harry E. Foster	Ohio	Attorney	U. Washington	U. Washington	Partner	58	R	Quaker	Olympia	Mod./Neu.
*Robert T. Hunter	Okla.	Attorney	U. Washington	U. Washington	Judicial	50	D	Presbyterian	Ephrata	Mod./Neu.
*Orris Hamilton	Wash.	Attorney	None	American	Judicial	47	D	Presbyterian	Prosser	Mod./Neu.
*Frank Hale	Wash.	Machinist	U. Washington	Clerk	Judicial	52	D		Tacoma	Mod./Neu.
*Marshall Neill	Wash.	Florist	Washington State	Idaho	Assistant Attorney General	53	R	Episcopalian	Pullman	Mod./Neu.
*Walter McGovern	Wash.	Salmon broker	U. Washington	U. Washington	Judicial	46	R	Catholic	Seattle	Mod./Neu.

*Appointed
**Experience immediately prior to selection

their predecessors but also from their colleagues in the legal profession generally. Prosecutorial experience tended also to be more important than in the 1949–68 benches. Clearly, the lower benches were a prerequisite for a seat on the Supreme Court (88% had prior judicial positions). Western Washington also dominated the "geographical" make-up of the high bench, with the Seattle area providing three out of five of the jurists. Although the members on the bench represented middle-of-the-road ideologies, the liberals tended to outnumber the conservatives, and there were twice as many activists as restraintists. (See table 8.5.)

Summary

Although each period of the court's development represented fairly distinct groups of judges, certain commonalities can be observed. Throughout the history of the bench, Protestants with Republican political affiliation were appointed to the court by Republican governors. The judges had attended better than average colleges and law schools, and were active in the bar and social and fraternal organizations (especially Freemasonry). At no time did ideological extremists dominate the bench. Also their ages when appointed or elected suggest that the jurists had had sufficient time to prove their legal and political acumen while many years of productive judicial life still remained. They also had the benefit of several years' experience on the state's lower benches before their selection to the high court.

Some trends also are evident. First, the composition of the court reflected the changes that the whole state experienced. For example, the ascribed attributes of the judges evolved from young sons of pioneer immigrants that came west to the land of opportunity where class and fortune were largely irrelevant to a modern group of native-born, older sons of successful families. The affiliated characteristics have tended away from Freemasonry and fraternal groups to civic and professional affiliations. Although partisan political affairs remain important, the few who held other public offices recently were legislators. Most had served as nonpartisan judges at other levels and therefore had eschewed overt partisan activities. The geographical representation of the bench had generally shifted from Eastern to Western Washington and more specifically to Seattle.

Trends are also evident in the judges' achieved characteristics. Education at private schools, colleges, and law schools has been replaced by training at public institutions. Out-of-state educational

Table 8.5
Backgrounds, 1970–85

Name	*Birth Place*	*Occupation Head of Family*	*College*	*Legal Education*	*Prior Legal Experience***	*Age at Selection*	*Politics*	*Religion*	*Residence*	*Political Philosophy*
*Morell Sharp	Oreg.	Accountant	Oreg.	Northwestern	Judicial	49	R	Episcopalian	Seattle	Mod./Neu.
Charles T. Wright	Calif.	Attorney	Puget Sound	U. Washington (Clerk)	Judicial	60	I	Episcopalian	Olympia	Con./Res.
*Charles Stafford	Wash.	Business	Whitman	Yale	Judicial	52	R	Methodist	Anacortes	Mod./Neu.
*Robert Utter	Wash.	Insurance	U. Washington	U. Washington	Judicial	41	R	Baptist	Seattle	Lib./Act.
*R. Brachtenbach	Nebr.	Farming	U. Washington	U. Washington	Partner	41	R		Yakima	Lib./Neu.
*James Dolliver	Iowa	Attorney	Swarthmore	U. Washington	Adm. Assist.	51	R	Methodist	Olympia	Lib./Act.
Charles Horowitz	N.Y.	Tailor	U. Washington	U. Washington	Judicial	69	D	Jewish	Seattle	Lib./Neu.

Wm. Williams	Idaho	Powerline man	Idaho	Gonzaga	Judicial	56	D	Congregational	Spokane	Mod./Neu.
Floyd Hicks	Wash.	Farming	Central Washington	U. Washington	Congress	62	D	Protestant	Tacoma	Mod./Neu.
*Vernon Pearson	N. Dak.	Minister	Jamestown	Michigan	Judicial	58	R	Methodist	Tacoma	Lib./Neu.
†Fred Dore	Wash.	Attorney	Seattle U.	Georgetown	Judicial	55	D	Catholic	Seattle	Lib./Neu.
*Carolyn Dimmick	Wash.	Master mariner, teacher	U. Washington	U. Washington	Judicial	51	R	Protestant	Seattle	Con./Res.
*J. Andersen	Wash.	Coal miner	U. Washington	U. Washington	Judicial	59	R	Episcopalian	Bellevue	
†Keith Callow	Wash.	Coach	U. Washington	U. Washington	Judicial	59	R	Methodist	Seattle	
*Barb. Durham	Wash.	Theater manager, teacher	Gonzaga	Stanford	Judicial	42	R	Catholic	Seattle	
Wm. Goodloe	Ky.	Engineer	U. Washington	U. Washington	Judicial	64	R	Christian Scientist	Seattle	

*Appointed
**Experience immediately prior to appointment
†Appointed to short term before assuming elected position

attendance gave way to in-state matriculation. Now most of the jurists attended the University of Washington School of Law. Ideologically the trend has been away from restraint and conservatism to a middle-of-the-road perspective with regard to political and legal philosophies. However, the liberals and activists now have fairly strong representation.

Many of the trends in judicial backgrounds can be attributed to similar changes in the economic and political culture of the state. As the state grew and developed, the backgrounds of the judges changed accordingly. A judicial recruitment system that can quickly reflect those changes is a system that is appropriate. Clearly, the modern recruitment system now in effect in Washington is sensitive to the needs and demands of the society which it serves.

9

The Business of the Supreme Court

The preceding chapters have explained how justices got to the state's court of last resort and the kinds of backgrounds and experiences they brought with them. Now, the concern is with what they did while on the state's high bench. This means an analysis of (1) the workload of the judges; (2) the solutions proposed and accepted to deal with workload problems; (3) the kinds of disputes that confronted the judges; and (4) the variety of litigants involved. An analysis of these aspects of the judges' work will give a rough sketch of the problems that confronted society and the role of the court in solving or exacerbating those problems. Clearly, the state's society and the court are inextricably intertwined.

Three decisional practices have allowed although not dictated the judges' role in the state. Common law construction dominated the judicial and legal systems throughout the United States in the early 1800s, and its influence, although waning, was still felt when Washington entered the Union. As one student of legal history observed, "What dramatically distinguishes nineteenth century law from its eighteenth century counterpart was the extent to which the common law judges came to play a central role in directing the course of social change."[1] Actually, with little confidence shown in the legislatures and with the crying need for "law to meet [the] everyday needs and everyday problems of the people," the judges were not all too reluctantly drawn into the limelight.[2] But the limelight involved economics. The movement from a relatively passive role for the courts in the affairs of state to a leading role closely followed the movement of America from a precommercial and preindustrial society to a market economy and a complex industrial

1. Morton J. Horwitz, *The Transformation of American Law, 1780–1860* (Cambridge: Harvard University Press, 1977), 1.
2. James Willard Hurst, *The Growth of American Law: The Lawmakers* (Boston: Little, Brown, 1950), 186.

system.[3] Judge-made law was instrumental in this movement and common law construction was the method.[4]

However, as legislatures began to intervene in the economic and industrial system, on many occasions common law came into conflict with statutory law. Judges resisted the encroachments of the enactments of the people's representatives, but with the sheer increase in statutes, many of which overlapped the common law, and with the shift in legal education (however slight) away from pure case method to more legislative materials, statutes became the subject of judicial attention.[5] Despite the appearance that legislative enactments were supplanting judge-made law, creative jurists submitted the enactments to close scrutiny as they applied them to issues before them. Many judges were not reluctant to read their own predilections into ambiguous, inadequate, or outdated legislation. Statutory construction became a common judicial practice.

Finally, throughout the nineteenth century, judicial review clearly was a sword in the hands of the judiciary that infrequently but always decisively was drawn to strike down those legislative acts that were in violation of the constitution. Washington's high court has exercised its power of judicial review sparingly but without hesitation since 1890.[6]

The data reported in table 9.1 indicate that although the incidence of judicial review has fluctuated somewhat over the years, the number of times that statutes are declared unconstitutional remains about the same.[7] Only about one out of four challenged laws are voided by the Supreme Court. However, what the data clearly confirm is the power of the state's court of last resort not only to oversee the consistency of legislative acts with the constitution but, when so compelled, to invalidate those acts. Constitutional construction has been a judicial practice since statehood. Into this vortex was

3. Horwitz, *The Transformation*, xv.

4. John W. Johnson, *American Legal Culture, 1908–1940* (Westport, Conn.: Greenwood Press, 1981), 4.

5. *Ibid.*

6. The Territorial Supreme Court also had exercised judicial review at least a dozen times.

7. Table 9.1's earlier estimation of the exercise of judicial review is conservative. The source for the 1890–1901 data is from *Miller's Washington Digest* which covers volumes 1–3 of the *Territorial Reports* and 1 through 24 of the *Washington Reports*. Only when the digest reported a particular statute or ordinance as unconstitutional was it recorded. Some laws, which remained unrecorded, were invalidated or voided because of procedural violations (for example, that the title did not adequately reflect the substance of the law). The 1941–52 data are from Earl L. Darrah, "Judicial Veto of Statutes in Washington State, 1932–1957" (Master's thesis, Washington State University, 1960), 16–17. The 1972–81 figures are from *Washington Reports*.

Table 9.1
Statutes Declared Unconstitutional
and the Exercise and Results of Judicial Review

Years	*Judicial Review Exercised*	*Laws Declared Unconstitutional*	*Percentage Declared Unconstitutional*
1890–1901	112	33	29%
1941–1952	175	36	21
1972–1981	141	41	29

thrust the 1889 Washington Supreme Court. Common law construction as a practice was waning, to be replaced by statutory interpretation. Constitutional construction, however, remained viable from the very beginnings of the state.

The Court's Workload and Reform Measures

To understand the business of the Supreme Court, we must initially understand its workload.[8] What demands have been made for the court's services, by whom, and what have been the judges' responses? Figure 9.1 reports the number of filings with the court, and the number of opinions produced by the judges since 1890, the first full year of the court's work. From nearly the beginning of statehood, the judges were under increasing workload pressures. Although the pressures vary, students of the court are nearly unani-

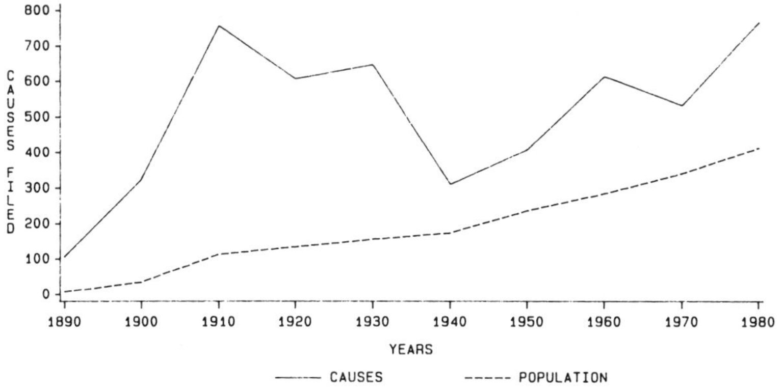

Fig. 9.1. Causes filed and population growth, 1890–1980 (causes filed figures averaged per ten years after 1930; population growth in 10,000s)

8. For a brief historical review of how other courts dealt with the problem of overload, see Hurst, *Growth of American Law*, 88–107.

mous in their opinion that the judges were overworked. Almost immediately after statehood a variety of proposals were suggested to bring the docket of the high court down to manageable levels.

More Judges: From Five to Seven to Nine

Article IV of the State Constitution provided the simplest solution to an overworked court—increase the number of judges sitting on the high bench. The Supreme Court began with five judges, but "The legislature may increase the number of judges from time to time and may provide for separate departments of said court." Taking advantage of this clause, the 1901 legislature initially moved to add two permanent members to the bench, but settled for a temporary increase. The governor was "authorized to appoint one from each of the dominant political parties." Their service would begin March 1901 and terminate in October 1902.[9] Democrat William H. White and Republican Hiram E. Hadley were promptly appointed to assist the court with its increasing and burdening caseload. White had already served a few months on the high court in 1901 and Hadley was an experienced superior court judge from Whatcom County. Both were expected to help the court attack its docket immediately without having to serve an apprenticeship.

In addition to having two additional judges to share the docket overload, the legislature permitted the court to conduct business with a quorum of four of the seven jurists.[10] However, the legislature stipulated that unless four of the judges agreed on the disposition of a case, parties to the dispute, by right, could resubmit the cause to the full court.[11]

Despite the additional help, the crisis remained. In 1905, only three years after the expiration of the temporary appointments, the legislature chose to increase the number of judges again to seven

9. Chapter 148, Session Laws, 1901, p. 345.

10. *Ibid.*

11. A court challenge to the 1901 temporary increase in the size of the court forced the judges to face the constitutionality of the very act that was designed to relieve them of a calendar overload. The issue was whether, according to Article IV, Section 3, of the state constitution, the legislature could increase *only temporarily,* the number of judges and whether, after their appointments expired, the legislature could decrease the court size back to five judges. Additionally, could the judges be appointed and not be required to stand for election at the next general election? The court majority, per Mount, upheld the act on both counts. (Interestingly, Judges Hadley and White agreed.) However, Chief Justice Reavis and Judge Anders went further and argued in dissent that not only were Hadley and White's appointments valid, but their positions could not be terminated. The appointees should have been allowed to run for permanent seats at the next general election, according to the dissenting opinion. See *State Ex Rel. Murphy* v. *McBride* (29 WASH. 335, 1902).

and this time to make the additions permanent.[12] Republicans Milo Root and Herman Crow were appointed by Republican governor Albert Mead. They were nominated at the Republican party convention the next year and overwhelmingly affirmed by the voters in November 1906.

However the persistence of pressures on the court prompted approval of two solutions, all part of a single package provided by the legislature in 1909. The court's membership was expanded to nine, and, in effect, two courts were authorized with the establishment of the departmental system. Section three of Senate Bill 198 provided:

> There shall be two departments of the Supreme Court. . . . The Chief Justice shall assign four of the associate judges to each department. . . . The Chief Justice may sit in either department and shall preside when so sitting. . . . Each of the departments shall have the power to hear and determine causes, and all questions arising therein.[13]

Henceforth, the vast majority of the cases were heard by the two departments, although those of great import, as well as those involving disagreement among the judges, eventually were heard and decided *en banc* (by the entire nine-judge bench.) A court challenge to the 1909 legislation was turned aside by the judges in a not altogether selfless decision. Separate departmental decisions were regarded as a constitutional means of dealing with the anticipated increase in litigation.[14]

As figure 9.1 reports, after 1910 and until the modern era the demands on the court diminished, the pressure on the individual judges lessened (figure 9.2), and the apparent result was a quick dispatch of routine cases in the departments and a more thorough handling of the important legal issues in *en banc* proceedings. Perhaps the 1909 reforms were working to some degree, although

12. Chapter 5, Session Laws, 1905, p. 14
13. Chapter 24, Session Laws, 1909, p. 34
14. *State Ex Rel. Vanderveer* v. *Gormely* (53 WASH. 543, 1909, at 557). That was clearly the intent of Senate Bill 198, passed in February 1909. Actually, the question of the validity of decisions by the departments did not arise in the initial consideration of the case but rather was brought up in a subsequent rehearing *en banc*. Appellant argued that "this court is without right, power, or authority, to render or pronounce a decision unless a majority of the judges constituting the [full] court join and concur therein" (at 553). The wording in Article IV was "A majority of whom shall be necessary to form a quorum and pronounce a decision," which appellant read to mean all nine members of the Court. The Court, per Parker, looking for the intent of the framers, argued that the obvious purpose of the clause in the constitution was to do what the legislature did in fact in 1909—provide two departments to render decisions.

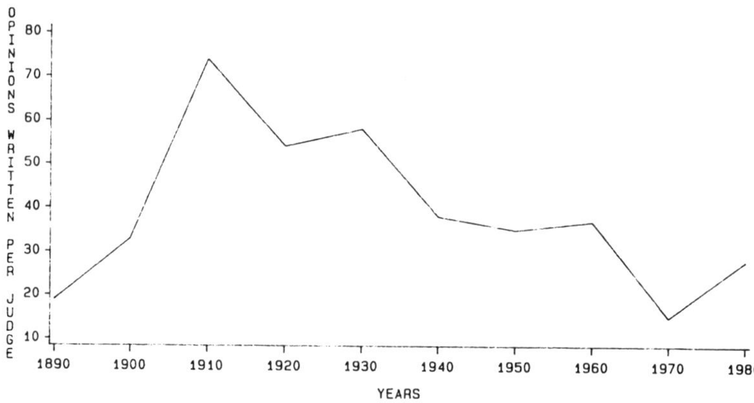

Fig. 9.2. Opinions written per judge, 1890–1980

the reforms were designated primarily to increase the capabilities of the court, not to decrease litigation demands on the judges.

The growth of population and the concomitant complexity of social, political, and economic life accounted for the increase in litigation. Population growth remained the best indicator of the volume of demand on the courts (see figure 9.1).[15] The correlation between increasing population and soaring case loads appeared broken at least for a time after 1912, however. Many other factors help account for the abatement in the number of cases. Precedents gradually developed and thereby a body of law was established which provided guidelines for social and economic relations, allowing for voluntary agreements. Federal law began to intervene, taking some disputes into the federal courts. Statutory law assumed more importance in defining rights and obligations, relieving the courts of part of this all-important legal function. For example, soon after the turn of the century state commissions and boards took over many of the responsibilities for settling disputes that heretofore went to the courts, although some appeals from the rulings of these boards were heard by the court.[16] The prevailing mood of the people also accounted for a lessening of the pressures on courts generally.

15. James Willard Hurst, "The Functions of Courts in the United States, 1950–1980," *Law and Society Review* 15 (1980): 415.

16. Hurst wrote that "thereafter [1900] the competition of administrative decisions and commercial arbitration began to cut the proportion of dispute business that went to court" (Hurst, *Growth of American Law*, 176). For the court's interpretation of the delegation of judical powers to administrative bodies see *Bellingham Bay Imp. Co.* v. *New Whatcom* (20 Wash. 53, 1898).

> The country community had emphasized and insisted on the drama of the country courthouse; city people, rich or poor or middling, looked at their legal problems from a viewpoint that was more impersonal, more cost-conscious, more hurrying and business-result minded.[17]

A feeling of futility also could have discouraged many litigants. The likelihood that the state's high court would affirm the lower court's decision discouraged appeals. Also, the increasing costs of litigation acted as a deterrent, in part due to the fact that the number of attorneys remained behind the population growth until recent times. Finally, the mere fact that the Supreme Court was available to settle disputes and enunciate policy, if necessary, forced many voluntary out-of-court agreements.[18]

The sharp decline of causes brought to the court during the 1940s can be largely attributed to the nation's attention being focused on winning the Second World War. The abrupt decline in the 1970s clearly indicates that the new Court of Appeals was assuming its share of causes. The increase, again, in recent times suggests that the practice of petitioning the high court for review is common, although, as the opinion writing levels indicate, few of these petitions are granted. Nonetheless, the court appears again to be under some docket pressures. Contrary to earlier times, however, the justices today can simply refuse to hear many of the appeals. Whatever the explanation for the declining demands for the services of the nine judges, after 1910 they were still burdened with an inordinate number of cases and a need for reform persisted.

The Judicial Council

Another approach to dealing with the business of the court was to provide the judges with the best advice available and to allow them to experiment with their own decisional procedures rather than imposing long-range and inflexible structural changes by legislation. Upon the insistence of the State Bar Association, with the encouragement of the American Judicature Society, and with the example of a few other states, the 1925 legislature passed a package of legislation designed to turn over some administrative responsibilities to the judges and to provide them with expert advice.

First, the legislators established a Judicial Council with the duties:

17. Hurst, *Growth of American Law*, 176.
18. *Ibid.*, 174.

(1) Continuously to survey and study the operation of the judicial department of the state. . . .
(2) To receive and consider suggestions from judges, public officers, members of the bar, and citizens as to remedies for faults in the administration of justice;
(3) To devise ways of . . . correcting faults in the administration of justice;
(4) To submit . . . suggestions . . . for changes in rules, procedures, or methods of administration;
(5) To report biennially to the governor and the legislature . . . with the council's recommendations.[19]

The membership of the council included representatives from the legislature, the legal profession, and the bench. The Chief Justice was designated the chairman of the new agency, and by April 1926 the council was organized and ready for operation. In its first report the members recommended among other things several rules changes in appellate procedures. The council emphasized that the "sole purpose of these proposed amendments is to shorten the time for appeal."[20]

Accompanying the judicial council legislation in 1925 was a statutory authorization for the Supreme Court to assume responsibility for making the rules for courts.[21] The legislation was entitled: "An act to promote the speedy determination of litigation on the merits and authorizing the Supreme Court to make rules relating to pleading, procedure and practice in the courts of this state." Any statutes in effect then dealing with court procedures would be superseded by these rules.[22]

The substance of the rules now under the control of the high bench concerned administrative rules (judicial assignments, calendars, and scheduling of meetings), practice rules (bar admission, discipline, and ethics), and rules of procedure ("rules that regulate access to the courts, control parties to a lawsuit, the shape of litigation and a range of judicial powers").[23]

By 1927 the council was ready with a significant legislative recommendation to narrow the right of appeal. It was urged that the judges write opinions supporting their decisions only "when in the

19. Chapter 45, Laws Ex. Sess., 1925, pp. 39–40.
20. Judicial Council, "*First Report*" (Olympia, State of Washington, 1927), 11.
21. Chapter 188, Laws Ex. Sess., 1925, p. 187.
22. For an account of the need for and establishment of this act, see Charles H. Paul, "The Rule-Making Power of the Courts," *Washington Law Review* 1 (1926):163. Also for an update and critique of this power see Hugh Spitzer, "Court Rulemaking in Washington State," *University of Puget Sound Law Review* 6 (1982):31.
23. Spitzer, "Court Rulemaking," 31.

judgment of the court the decision is of public importance." It was also recommended that for appeals in civil cases the amount involved be raised from the constitutional limit of $200 to $1,000, and that only felony convictions in criminal cases would have an absolute right of appeal.[24] The proposal was submitted to the bar for discussion and debate, but when a consensus failed to materialize the council dropped the proposal without submitting it to the legislature. The legal profession was reluctant to restrict its near limitless access to the state's court of last resort. Despite this set-back the Judicial Council continued studying other alternatives for bringing some relief to the Supreme Court.

In 1930 the council unveiled its most comprehensive study of the situation and concluded with specific recommendations. The preface to its study isolated the problem and blamed it on population increase and economic growth:

> Unquestionably the most urgent judicial problem of the state of Washington today has to do with the relief of the Supreme Court. The court is now burdened with a volume of work greater than that imposed upon any other court in the nation.[25]

Five possible solutions were suggested, following the recommendations of Alfred J. Schweppe, Dean of the University of Washington Law School. Additional judges could be appointed to the court and a third department created; supreme court commissioners could assume some of the workload of the judges; an intermediate court of appeals could be established; the amount of money involved in a civil dispute could be increased for appeals to be automatic; and changes in the method of appeal could restrict access. From the five alternatives the council recommended that as an immediate solution four commissioners be appointed, and that as a permanent answer an intermediate court of appeals be established.

The council prefaced its recommendation by citing that "Whereas the docket of the Supreme Court . . . is heavily crowded, and said court has insufficient time for dispatch of business," and the people's legal causes "are being delayed thereby and [they are] suffering therefrom," immediate relief was necessary. The legislature should authorize the appointment of four commissioners who would act as *pro tempore* members of the high court, conducting business under the supervision and review of the supreme court judges. In the meantime, a constitutional amendment would be submitted to the

24. State of Washington, *Second Annual Report of the Judicial Council* (1930), 14.
25. *Ibid.*, 10.

people establishing an intermediate court of appeals. However, neither proposal was formally introduced in subsequent legislative sessions since more immediate problems confronted state officials as the dislocations of the Great Depression struck the state.

Also, accompanying the Depression was an unanticipated decline in the demands placed on the high court, removing the urgency that accompanied earlier reform proposals.[26] The pressures on the Supreme Court abated for a time.

The Judicial Council settled for less drastic measures for assisting the judges, and in 1935 recommended a constitutional amendment authorizing a majority of the supreme court judges to commission superior court judges to serve on the high bench during docket emergencies. However, the legislature again failed to act. The council persistently submitted the same proposal to subsequent legislatures, with the same negative result.[27]

The Washington State Bar Association

The legal profession had heretofore played an important role in nearly all the proposed reforms aimed at removing the pressure from the court. In 1933, upon the insistence of most of the leaders in the State Bar, with the support of the Judicial Council and the American Judicature Society, Washington became one of the earliest states to integrate or unify the legal profession. As a result of the State Bar Act, all attorneys had to be dues-paying members of the

26. Alfred J. Schweppe, "Report of the Judicial Council on Expediting the Work of the Supreme Court," *State Bar Journal* 31 (1956): 340. According to the report by Dean Schweppe: "Back in 1929 when the Supreme Court was under a heavy workload, studies were made of methods of expediting the work of the Supreme Court. . . . We went into a very severe depression, however, and the workload and the number of cases that went to the Supreme Court fell off rapidly, so that the emergency has not again presented itself until [much later]."

27. The history of the Judicial Council has varied. It exerted considerable influence in the early years, and many of its recommendations were adopted. During the early sixties enthusiasm for the council's recommendations waned and the "Council was viable in name only" (Quote from Lavern V. Rieke, Executive Secretary of the Judicial Council. Reported in Q. Booker, K. Evans, and S. Skinner, "Support Agencies of the Washington State Supreme Court: Their Influences upon the Judicial Process," Occasional Paper [Division of Governmental Studies and Services, Department of Political Science, Washington State University, 1979], 37). Due to the efforts of Professor Rieke, and chief justices like Robert C. Finley, the council was revitalized in the late sixties and seventies. However, by 1983 the council was again out of business, being effectively shut down by the lack of appropriations from the legislature. Its future remains uncertain.

For an early history of the council in Washington and other states, see Charles H. Paul, "The Judicial Council Movement," *Washington Law Review* 1 (1925):101.

Washington State Bar Association before they could practice law in the state.[28]

It was hoped that by integrating, the profession would have a greater influence with the state legislature in lobbying for bar interests. Also they could direct their concerted attention toward electing and having appointed acceptable judges, institute judicial reforms, and, finally, systematize the admissions to the bar and the discipline of its members. In this latter area it would work closely with the Supreme Court as the high court was given final authority over disbarments and attorney suspensions.[29]

Personal Assistants to the Judges

In 1937, upon the suggestion of Judge William Steinert, the legislature allotted an additional biennial appropriation of $29,800 to the court's budget for the purpose of hiring up to seven recent law school graduates to assist the judges. The appropriation allowed an annual salary of $2,100 for each law clerk. Although Judge Steinert's initial motivation was to gain the assistance of these young minds to help the court with its overload, not all the judges took advantage of the opportunity. Only three were hired at first, but they worked with several of the judges during their year's clerkship. The practice gradually caught on so that by 1950 each judge had one law clerk.[30]

28. Chapter 94, Session Laws, 1933 (House Bill, 239), p. 397.

29. The first gathering of attorneys in Washington was in 1888 when thirty-five lawyers formed the Washington Bar Association. In 1933 twenty-seven hundred lawyers were practicing in the state but only four hundred of these were members of the WBA. The dues for the first year were $5.00. See Joseph H. Gordon, "Our State Bar Associations: The Washington State Bar Association," *American Bar Association Journal* 48 (January 1962):71.

30. John N. Rupp was one of the first three law clerks appointed in 1937. He recalled some of his duties: "As Chief Justice, Judge Steinert was entitled to have a law clerk all to himself, so I worked with him alone. Of course, he had never had a law clerk, and I had never been one, so we ploughed new ground.

"One major part of my job was to read the briefs on the cases that the Court was about to hear and to report to Judge Steinert about them. . . .

"It was particularly difficult for him to prepare adequately for the next day's cases. So he had me read the briefs for him. Each day, then, I would read the briefs in the cases to be argued the next day and write a memorandum on each case telling what the case was about, what the facts were, what appeared to be the important cases in point and what seemed to me should be inquired into at oral argument. . . . Then we would get together in his chambers early in the morning and talk about the cases. . . .

"The other main part of my job was helping with the opinions. . . . I would pretend I was a judge writing an opinion. . . . Never once did he go along. We usually agreed on the results, and we didn't quarrel much about the correct analysis, but he always

The hiring of clerks had an impact on the court's workload. In 1934–36, the three years before clerks were assigned, these judges who subsequently hired law clerks wrote majority opinions that averaged 6.5 pages in length. In 1938–40, the first three years with the assistance of the clerks, these judges wrote majority opinions which averaged 8.5 pages.[31] Also, those judges using clerks were able to complete and file their opinion assignments an average of nearly five weeks ahead of those completed by judges not assisted by law clerks. The addition of the personal assistants did improve the thoroughness and effectiveness of the court.

Administrator for the Courts

After the addition of law clerks, no substantial structural changes were made until 1957 when the office of the administrator for the courts was established. The office was to study the administrative methods of courts at all levels in the state and to examine their dockets for inequities and overcrowding.[32]

The administrator could recommend to the chief justice any changes in the rules needed to rationalize administrative practices throughout the state. Visiting judgeships were coordinated by the office in order to equalize the workload between and among trial jurisdictions. Further, the new office took over budgetary responsibilities heretofore performed by the supreme court clerk, leaving the clerk's office with the more immediate administrative and scheduling duties relating to the Supreme Court's docket.[33]

---

wrote his own opinions" (John N. Rupp, "How It Used to Be: The Supreme Court's Law Clerks," unpublished manuscript, n.d., Department of Political Science, Washington State University).

31. For an analysis of law clerking with the Washington Supreme Court, see C. Sheldon, "Law Clerking with a State Supreme Court: Views from the Perspective of the Personal Assistants to the Judges," *Justice System Journal* 6 (Fall 1981):346–71.

32. Chapter 259, Laws of 1957, p. 1019. Albert C. Bise served as the first administrator for the courts (1957–72), followed by Phillip Winberry (1972–79), Howard S. Primer (1979–81), James Larson (1981–86), and Mary McQueen (1986–present).

33. "The Clerk of the Supreme Court . . . maintains all the Court's rulings and files. The Clerk is also responsible for managing the caseflow of the Court which includes the preparation of the calendar and docket for all cases and papers filed. In addition . . . the Clerk . . . must tax assess on all matters decided by the Court, maintain records of admission of attorneys to practice within the state and arrange for the reproduction and service of the briefs. The Clerk may also rule on various procedural motions" (Administrator for the Courts, "Judicial Administration in the Courts of the State of Washington: Twenty-third Annual Report" [Olympia: State of Washington, 1979], 1–2). Sol Smith was the first clerk to the Supreme Court, serving from 1889 to 1891. C. S. Reinhart served from 1891 until 1934; Benjamin T. Hart, 1934–57; Robert Holstein, 1957–61; William Lowry, 1961–75; John J. Champagne, 1975–81; and Reginald N. Shriver, 1981 to the present.

The act also provided for a Judicial Conference "for the consideration of matters relating to judicial business, the improvement of the judicial system and the administration of justice."[34]

The establishment of the administrator for the courts led to standardization of court data, considerable coordination among the many jurisdictions, and some modernization of court administrative practices. The office clearly relieved the judges and the clerk of many necessary but nonjudicial functions, although the supervisory responsibilities of the chief justice were increased.

Constitutional Reforms

In 1961 another attempt was made to deal directly with the court's workload.[35] That year a coalition of judges, lawyers, and legislators formed behind the Judicial Council's proposal (first suggested in 1935) to allow the Supreme Court to call in *pro tempore* judges to assist during docket emergencies. House Joint Resolution 6 was proposed by the legislature and overwhelmingly approved by the voters in November 1962. The constitutional amendment provided in part:

> When necessary for the prompt and orderly administration of justice a majority of the Supreme Court is empowered to authorize judges or retired judges of courts of record of this state, to perform temporarily, judicial duties in the Supreme Court.[36]

In the following years the concern for an overworked Supreme Court was replaced by an interest in a more general revamping of the state's 1889 constitution and, specifically, rewriting the judicial article. In 1965 the legislature authorized a constitutional advisory council to study the needs of the antiquated basic law and to recommend changes. A separate Joint Committee for the Study of a Revision of Article IV had been formed a year earlier, composed of members of the bar and bench. In addition, the Judicial Council continued its review of the needs of the judiciary. It appeared that the drive for constitutional change was gaining momentum and that very shortly some proposals affecting the Supreme Court would be offered.

34. Chapter 259, Session Laws, 1957, p. 1019.

35. For an analysis of modern reform in the entire Washington judicial system, see Phillip Winberry, "Washington State Court Reform," in Lee Powell, ed., *Court Reform in Seven States* (Chicago: American Bar Association, 1980).

36. Article IV, Section 2(a) (Amendment 38). For further details on Amendment 38, see C. Sheldon and F. Weaver, *Politicians, Judges and the People* (Westport, Conn.: Greenwood Press, 1980), 53–56.

Despite the appearance of consensus, the various groups could only agree on the need for an intermediate court of appeals. Late in 1966 the public was brought into the planning stages for reform of Article IV with the formation of the Citizens' Committee on Washington Courts sponsored by the American Judicature Society with the cooperation of the bench, press, and bar. The general feeling was that the legislature would be reluctant to act, and the voters would not support any substantial constitutional reform of the judicial article without concerted educational and public relations efforts. Perhaps the conference could initiate those efforts. The conference issued a report recognizing the need for reform and recommending consideration of a unified court system under the supervision of the Supreme Court, an intermediate court of appeals, the upgrading of lower courts, the Missouri Plan for selecting judges, and the establishment of a discipline commission for judges.

With the organized bar spearheading the drive, the legislature at least recognized the need for a court of appeals by approving a constitutional amendment (SJR 6) to be submitted to the people to establish an intermediate court of appeals which would clearly and substantially alleviate the workload of the Supreme Court.

The Eleventh Annual Report of the Administrator for the Courts (1967) anticipated a breakdown of the appellate process unless the proposed amendment was passed. By 1985, at the present rate of increase, he projected a backlog of 8,038 cases! Already in 1968 a backlog of ninety-one unresolved appeals would remain even if the court worked at its fullest capacity.

> Without the assistance of an appellate court, the ordinary civil litigant's right for review will not only be eroded by delay—it will be preempted, in a rising tide of appellate work in which only the priority cases will be heard. The majority of the priority cases will be criminal, the remainder will be cases of great public concern.[37]

As during the earlier history of the state, the anticipated increase in appeals and the corresponding pressures on the Supreme Court could be attributed in large part to population increase. The state was growing faster than ever before and led the nation in percentage increase. But other reasons account for the anticipated tide of

37. State of Washington, *Eleventh Annual Report of the Administrator for the Courts* (1967), 17.

appeals.[38] Government regulations were increasing, the number of automobiles was literally exploding, and the densely populated urban areas were contributing to "the abrasions of human relationships."[39] Criminal appeals, encouraged by the expanding rights of the accused as defined by the U.S. Supreme Court, alone would cripple the present system according to the report. "The result is obvious," the administrator concluded: "the state must have an intermediate court of appeals."

An additional explanation for the increased case load at the high court level had been given earlier (1956) by a member of the Supreme Court, Justice Frederick G. Hamley:

> The number of trial court judges in 1909 was thirty-eight. Today (1956) it is sixty-six or seven. In 1909 there was one State Supreme Court judge for every 4.2 trial court judges. Today there is one Supreme Court judge for every 7.4 trial court judges, and that is a rough way of measuring the increase in appellate business.[40]

By 1970 the number of trial judges had increased to eighty-eight, and thus, at the time the Court of Appeals was established, there were 9.8 trial judges per supreme court justice, providing a much broader base from which appeals were made.

The joint efforts of citizen's groups, the bar, bench, press, and state and local officials led to a substantial approval of the court of appeals amendment with a 650,025 (64%) "yes" to 370,059 (36%) "no" vote in November 1968.[41] Amendment 50 (which became sec-

38. Writing in 1968, Justice Hugh Rosellini recognized the effects of population growth and modernization on the court's increasing caseload: "The increase in the number of persons living within the borders of the state does not account entirely for the tremendous expansion of court business. It is the increasing complexity of life which has accompanied this population growth, enhanced by technological developments and industrialization." He isolated several areas of the law that were impacted by population and industrial growth: "Transportation alone, and particularly the automobile, produce a mass of litigation. Other areas of litigation which have expanded with the expanding industrial society include labor relations, eminent domain, the activities of administrative bodies, municipal corporations, business corporations, taxation and construction contracts." Rosellini also added that this complex society contributed to an increase in criminal activity (Hugh Rosellini, "Crisis in the Supreme Court," *Gonzaga Law Review* 3 [1968]:12).

39. *Eleventh Annual Report of the Administrator for the Courts*, 15.

40. Frederick G. Hamley, "Address to the Washington State Bar Association's Annual Meeting, 1956," *State Bar Journal* (1956): 337.

41. The only arguments against the amendment were that it would add another unwarranted level to an already cluttered court system, and that the legislature could easily solve the high court's excessive workload by adding more judges and creating another department. The amendment had received a 47–2 vote in the Senate and an 88–4 approval vote in the House.

tion 30 of Article IV) read in part: "In addition to the courts authorized in section 1 of this article, judicial power is vested in a court of appeals, which shall be established by statute." The court's jurisdiction, its division of labor with the Supreme Court, its membership, the means of selecting its judges, and its administration would all be established by statute or by supreme court rules. It was correctly thought that a complicated constitutional amendment cluttered with such details would detract from its merits. The enabling legislation and the subsequent rules promulgated by the Supreme Court defined the form and content of the new bench.

The Court of Appeals

Three divisions of the Court of Appeals were created by the enabling legislation, one headquartered in Tacoma, another in Seattle, and the third in Spokane.[42] Nearly all appeals previously targeted for the Supreme Court would pass through or end with the new court. Appeals of a particular nature would be made directly to the Supreme Court, and, under some circumstances, appeals by right could be made from the Court of Appeals. Direct appeals by right from the Superior Courts of the state were authorized under the following conditions:

(1) cases involving special court orders directed toward public officials;
(2) death penalty cases;
(3) cases where all or part of a state law had been declared unconstitutional; and
(4) "cases involving fundamental and urgent issues of broad public import requiring prompt and ultimate determination."

Cases involving important issues where panels of the Court of Appeals had disagreed or a decision appeared in conflict with a supreme court ruling, would by right be subject to review by the Supreme Court. In addition, a right of appeal was possible when the Appeals Court reversed a superior court ruling by less than a unanimous decision. In all other cases "appeals . . . to the Supreme Court shall be only at the discretion of the Supreme Court upon the filing of a petition for review."[43] Through its rule-making powers the Supreme Court further refined the relationship between the two

42. Chapter 22, Laws Ex. Sess., 1969, 1653–58.
43. See, for example, *Supreme Court Administrative Rules* (SAR), Rule 6, and Rules on Appellate Procedure (ROA), Rule 15.

levels of the judicial system. Thus, for the first time the state's high court gained considerable control over its own docket. By 1983 the Supreme Court was allowed to exercise complete discretion over appeals from the intermediate court. Henceforth, the court would hear arguments and decide all cases on their merits *en banc*. Departments would be used only for arguments on motions, considerations of petitions for review, or other lesser matters referred to the panels by the chief justice.[44]

After seven decades of frustrating and largely unsuccessful efforts to cope with a burdensome workload, it appeared as though the establishment of the Court of Appeals provided the needed relief. Without question the change in jurisdiction and the sharing of appellate business brought fewer and different concerns to the justices of the Supreme Court.

Supreme Court Commissioner

Although the Court of Appeals initially relieved the Supreme Court of considerable amount of its workload, it added another burden which had gone largely unanticipated. With discretion passing to the nine justices, a necessary duty required that the justices determine which of those appeals coming to them warranted their review. By 1975 it was apparent that some assistance in such screening was necessary. In December of that year the justices through their rule-making powers set up the office of Commissioner of the Supreme Court and authorized it to "screen petitions for review and direct appeals to the Supreme Court and recommend whether . . . review should be granted. . . . [T]he commissioner will also screen motions which are to be decided by the Justices and recommend . . . appropriate disposition."[45] In addition the commissioner could hear motions authorized by the Rules of Appellate Procedure and other motions. The commissioner also helped screen applications for law clerking positions and performed other assignments the justices or chief justice made.[46]

All of these structural changes had been motivated by the desire to free the justices from distracting administrative responsibilities and

44. The 1969 change prompted the members of the high court to distinguish themselves from the judges of the Court of Appeals by designating all members of the Supreme Court as "justices." Heretofore it was only the chief justice who could justifiably utilize the title because of wording of Article IV which refers to "judges" of the Supreme Court and to the "chief justice" of that bench.

45. SAR 15.

46. The first court commissioner was Joan Smith Lawrence, who served from 1976 to 1980. Geoffry Crooks was her successor.

from the pressures of crowded dockets to allow them to concentrate on their constitutionally assigned duty to decide legal controversies. But what kind of cases have they been called upon to resolve over nearly a century of judging?

The Kinds of Cases Confronting the Court

As the political, social, and economic segments of the state developed and changed, so did the kinds of disputes brought to the high court. The Supreme Court's docket was (and is) a reflection of the conflicts in society. Additionally, as the justices gained greater control over their own business (as in 1969 and 1983), the cases heard by the judges tended not only to reflect society but also to reflect somewhat the interests of the judges themselves.

We have seen that the workload of the court was influenced by the structures and procedures of the court as well as by the demands of the citizenry. The kinds of cases it hears should tell us something about what was bothering society. Over the years who has been involved in the litigation that the judges have had to resolve? Table 9.2 breaks down the parties to disputes into those periods noted earlier as the natural breaking points for the analysis of recruitment.[47]

Individuals, as expected, dominate the process through the nearly one hundred years recorded. Over the years the public sector gradually replaced the private, increasing from 15% in the first years to over 33% of the litigants today. Correspondingly, the private sector has dropped from about 25% to 14% in recent years.

The public sector has expanded as litigant largely because of the expansion of regulations, protective legislation, and criminal law. The sharpest increase in the public area was evident in criminal appeals, as public prosecutors have constituted 14% of all litigants in recent years. Much of the decline in private litigation was due to the fact that regulatory agencies and boards assumed responsibilities leading to administrative rules, negotiations, and arbitration, thereby partially replacing courtrooms as the areas of conflict resolution.

The decline of railroads as parties to disputes, and the rise of the

47. Tables 9.2 and 9.3 are based upon a sampling of volumes of the Washington Reports from 1889 to the present. All cases found in every fifth volume of the reports were classified and coded. The coding followed that used by R. Kagan et al., "The Business of State Supreme Courts, 1870–1970," *Stanford Law Review* 30 (November 1977):121–55. The data in table 9.1 were compiled by recording the nature of both major parties to a dispute. For example, a criminal case such as *State* v. *Smith* would be tabulated under the public sector (prosecutors) and under individuals. When more than one litigant was involved on one side, only the first named was recorded.

Table 9.2
Users of the Supreme Court

	1890–1912	*1913–32*	*1933–49*	*1950–68*	*1969–83*
Public Sector					
State executive	0.8%	5.9%	4.5%	6.2%	3.2%
Judiciary	1.4	1.0	1.5	0.6	1.8
Municipalities	6.3	4.3	4.8	4.9	3.2
Counties	3.1	4.0	6.5	3.2	4.1
Prosecutors	3.3	3.2	1.8	5.1	13.6
Education	0.2	0.3	0.8	1.9	1.4
Regulatory agencies	0.2	3.5	6.3	3.2	7.3
Total	15.2	22.8	26.2	25.1	34.6
Individuals	58.0	48.4	50.3	54.3	47.3
Private sector					
Large business	10.0	11.2	11.8	8.5	5.9
Small business	7.0	7.0	1.0	1.5	2.7
Railroads	2.9	4.3	1.3	0.4	0.0
Banks	3.3	4.1	2.3	1.3	0.9
Insurance	1.0	1.1	1.3	1.3	0.9
Bar association	0.0	1.3	1.5	2.6	3.6
Total	24.2	28.9	19.2	15.6	14.0
Other or Unclassified	2.6	2.1	4.3	4.9	4.1
Totals	100.0%	100.0%	100.0%	99.9%	100.0%
Total number	512	374	398	468	220

bar association (involving discipline rulings) and educational units as litigants were reflections of the times. Also in the period up to 1932, banks and lending institutions suffered considerably with bankruptcies and insolvencies during the beginnings of the Great Depression, and regulatory agencies moved in to bring some semblance of order under the state's "Little New Deal" led by Democratic governor Clarence Martin with federal assistance from the Roosevelt Administration.

From what areas of the state have these litigants brought their cases to the high court? Table 9.3 reports the origins of the cases appealed to the justices. King County, the largest and most populous county, has continually generated more than one-third of all the cases since 1890 and accounted for two out of five of the appeals recently. Spokane and Pierce Counties, traditionally the next two largest population centers, declined as instigators of supreme court

Table 9.3
Lower Court Origins of Disputes

Superior Court	*1890–1912*	*1913–32*	*1933–49*	*1950–68*	*1969–83*
King County	30.9%	33.7%	36.2%	36.8%	40.9%
Pierce County	13.7	8.0	10.6	5.1	10.0
Spokane County	13.3	9.1	8.5	5.1	6.4
Other Counties	36.7	33.7	36.7	39.7	32.7
Original jurisdiction	5.1	13.9	8.0	12.8	9.0
Other origins	0.4	1.6	0.0	0.4	0.9
Total %	100.1%	100.0%	100.0%	99.9%	99.9%
Total number	256	187	199	234	110

business until very recently. Again, the county-of-origin data suggest that population is strongly correlated with the instigation of legal disputes.

What results has the Supreme Court provided? Table 9.4 suggests that the responses of the justices to appeals have remained fairly stable, since most appeals were affirmed. One might reasonably have anticipated that, as the court gained greater control of its docket, the reversal rate would increase on the assumption that the justices would tend to select for review only those cases that troubled them, leading to more frequent reversals. Although the reversal rate between 1949 and 1969 decreased nearly 10%, it has remained fairly stable (around 45%) since 1890. The data from the years subsequent to 1983 are needed to confirm or reject the reversal assumption.[48]

A fairly reliable indicator of the condition of the society would be a review of the kinds of disputes which confront the justices.[49] What troubled the citizenry of Washington over the years ultimately would likely be expressed in litigation. Long ago Alexis de Tocqueville recognized that "scarcely any political question arises in the U.S.

48. See R. Kagan et al., "The Evolution of State Supreme Courts," *Michigan Law Review* 76 (May 1978):995. The Washington reversal rate is not out of line when compared to other state supreme courts. Kagan concluded that "Of course, case-selecting discretion does not necessarily mean that supreme courts only take cases they intend to reverse."

49. See, for example, R. Kagan, "Business of State Supreme Courts," 121–56, and Burton M. Atkins and Henry R. Glick, "Environmental and Structural Variables as Determinants of Issues in State Courts of Last Resort," *American Journal of Political Science* 20 (February 1976):97–115.

Table 9.4
Results of Appeals

	1890–1912	*1913–32*	*1933–49*	*1950–68*	*1969–83*
Affirm	56.3%	47.1%	48.2%	51.3%	50.0%
Reverse	40.6	46.0	45.2	36.3	43.6
Affirmed & reversed in part	0.8	2.7	3.5	6.4	0.9
Remanded, modified, or dismissed	2.4	4.4	3.0	5.9	5.4
Total %	100.1%	100.2%	99.9%	99.8%	99.9%
Total number	256	187	199	234	110

that is not resolved, sooner or later, into a judicial question."[50] The state of Washington should be no exception.

Table 9.5 records the kinds of disputes that found their way to the state's court of last resort. Again, as suggested by previous data, trends evident in table 9.5 followed the development of the state from a farming, fishing, shipping, and timber economy to a fairly diversified industrial economic system with urban areas and the problems associated therewith.[51] Kagan observed that, shortly before the turn of the century, courts were

> deeply involved in ordinary commercial disputes—disputes over title to real-estate, foreclosure of mortgages, creditor's rights against defaulting debtors and failed businesses. They decided mostly cases of commercial, contract and property law. Their basic function, at least quantitively, was to settle private disputes arising out of market *transactions*.
>
> In the succeeding 100 years, these courts shifted their focus in a significant way. . . . Now [state supreme courts] are concerned much less with elaborating private law commercial doctrine and much more with non-market problems. Many of these problems arise out of the confrontation between citizens and state . . . between body and machine.[52]

The same pattern is evident in the state of Washington. Torts, public law, and criminal cases increased while issues involving property, estates, corporations, and debt and contracts decreased.

50. Alexis de Tocqueville, *Democracy in America* (New York: New American Library, 1956), 126.

51. The trends isolated in table 9.5 follow Kagan closely, "Business of State Supreme Courts," 133–35.

52. *Ibid.*, 133.

Table 9.5
Percent of Cases by Area of Law

	1890–1912	*1913–32*	*1933–49*	*1950–68*	*1969–84*
I. *Debt & Contract* (Debt collection, contracts for goods and services, insurance, contractual claims, etc.)	30.5	20.9	15.6	6.8	9.1
II. *Real Property* (Ownership, land use, real estate contracts, landlord tenant, damage and impairment, etc.)	16.4	7.0	5.5	6.4	3.6
III. *Corporations & Partnerships* (Control, mismanagement, stockholders and creditors rights, securities fraud, etc.)	4.3	0.5	2.5	0.4	0.0
IV. *Torts* (Negligence, workman's comp., malpractice, false arrest, accidents, etc.)	9.8	17.1	27.1	27.8	13.6
V. *Criminal* (Murder, against persons and property, morality, license, violations, etc.)	7.4	8.0	6.5	14.5	30.0
VI. *Public Law* (Business regulation, taxation, eminent domain, elections, etc.)	18.0	28.9	31.7	33.8	29.1
VII. *Family & Estates* (Divorce, child custody, wills, estates admin., etc.)	6.3	12.3	7.5	8.1	7.3
VIII. *Miscellaneous or Unclassified*	7.4	5.3	3.5	2.1	7.2
Total %	100.1	100.0	99.9	99.9	99.9
Total number	256	187	199	234	110

Debt collection and contracts dominated the cases immediately following statehood, due to the ups and downs of the infant economy. A booming economy was soon struck by the 1893 "panic," and then the discovery of gold in Alaska led to another boom. Seattle became the major shipping center for the rush to the North. An underdeveloped credit system and insecure banking arrangements characterized the economy. Contracts were often based on little else than "handshakes." Business failures and insolvencies were rampant in the early 1890s. All of these developments required that the courts determine the value and transfer of property, the validity and performance of questionable contracts, and the supervision of bankruptcies.[53] As market customs, statutes, and government regulations increased and as case law developed, the debt and contract area of the court's business gradually declined. After constituting nearly one-third of the court's docket in the first twenty years of statehood, such cases now only account for about one-tenth of the total.

Another rapidly shrinking area of concern for the justices was real property. The disputes regarding the transfer of property for payment of debts, as well as the liens on property and valuation of land evident in the debts and contracts area in early Washington suggest that land was the primary form of wealth. Thus, disputes over real-estate transactions, titles to land, and challenges to the use and leasing of the huge public lands were common. Issues over water, mining and logging rights were also characteristic phenomena of western states to which Washington was no exception. The state sold off tracts of its extensive public lands to private parties in order to finance government and to keep taxes nonexistent or low. Land changed hands quickly and profits soared. In the first two decades of statehood, disputes over real property accounted for over 16% of the court's caseload, compared to just under 4% for the decade of the 1970s.

53. A number of the "debt and contract" as well as "real property" cases just after statehood were due to the 1893 depression. The "panic swept west on the mainlines of the railroads like the very spirit of destruction, and for a while it tore at the very foundations of the new and yet incohesive frontier-industrial society. Investors withheld their promised funds. Financiers like John D. Rockerfeller actually withdrew from major enterprises . . . abandoning their sinking companies and corporations and collapsing highly speculative developments. . . . Land companies disintegrated, newspapers failed. Wages, for those who could find them, fell as much as sixty percent" (Norman H. Clark, *Washington, A Bicentennial History* [New York: Norton, 1976], 62). See also Edmond S. Meany, *History of the State of Washington* (New York: Macmillan, 1924), and Cecil Dryden, *History of Washington* (Portland, Ore.: Binfords & Mort, 1968).

An economy moving out of an undeveloped stage near the turn of the century, and a society that relied almost totally on the private market system to allocate values, demanded that courts move in to define relationships.

> Sustained market operations required a social setting in which individuals and firms could act on reasonably assured expectations of other people's behavior affecting commitments of assets. Contract and property law appeared to contribute materially to such a climate of reliance.[54]

However, by 1912 the boom was over, and the economy leveled off to remain relatively stable until the late 1920s. The private market system was gradually modified by more intervention from government.

Because Washington's economy developed behind that of the rest of the country and its exploitation of natural resources was also tardy, corporations and large business organizations were not involved in litigation to any great extent during any of the periods. As Kagan and others have pointed out, however, this does not mean that the legal matters were unimportant to corporations.[55] Rather, the large business entities used their attorneys to negotiate agreements, create broad protective legal theories, and gain legislative favors and influence which largely kept them out of the courtrooms. Additionally, as observed by Hurst:

> [Large businesses] can afford, and are likely to make extensive use of skilled professional help to channel their affairs so as to prevent trouble. Similarly, when trouble emerges, they are likely to be equipped to make sophisticated choices of alternatives to litigation to resolve difficulties through bargaining, mediation or arbitration.[56]

Maintaining good relations with potential adversaries was part of corporate business practice. Large businesses relied upon "good will" and shunned the publicity that litigation brought.[57] Thus, corporations managed to be only a small part of the business of the State Supreme Court.

In Washington as in other states the law of torts paralleled the development of transportation. Issues arising out of railroad and

54. Hurst, "Functions of Courts," 418.
55. Kagan, "Business of State Supreme Courts," 142.
56. Hurst, "Functions of Courts," 422.
57. *Ibid.*

automobile accidents constituted a large number of the cases. Workplace accidents also commonly lead to litigation. Washington was one of the first states to enact its own law, the Workmen's Compensation Act of 1911,[58] requiring that the state carry industrial accident insurance. Appeals from administrative rulings on awards became relatively common concerns of the high bench. In the 1970s tort appeals declined partially due to the court's refusal to hear many of those cases already heard by administrative agencies and reviewed by the Court of Appeals.

The most dramatic increase in cases reported in table 9.5 was in the criminal law area. Two fundamental changes, one in society and one in the law itself, account for this increase: the crime explosion and the Warren Court's criminal law "revolution." In a modern urbanized state crimes against persons and property appear natural concomitants. The upsurge in criminal cases was also attributable to changes in legal doctrine and practice, particularly the "due process revolution" of the late 1950s and the 1960s. The Warren Court's extension of criminal defendant's constitutional rights—including rights to free counsel—facilitated and encouraged criminal appeals and post-conviction relief applications.[59]

The Great Depression brought the realization that government must get involved in the economy and at the very least provide some relief to the thousands who were jobless, homeless, and destitute.[60] The administration of Clarence D. Martin, with its own New Deal, attempted to meet the challenge of the 1930s. The construction of Grand Coulee and Bonneville dams brought jobs to parts of Washington. The Washington State Department of Public Welfare assisted more than 600,000 of the needy early in the 1930s. A revolution in the function of government was thrust upon the state by the Depression that paralleled that taking place in the nation's capitol.

58. Chapter 74, Session Laws, 1911, pp. 345–74. Judge James Geraghty, writing from his many years of experience as corporate counsel for Spokane, described the pressures on city governments during the late twenties and early thirties which, apparently, Spokane avoided: "Fewer claims are filed against the city. This represents a change in the temperature of the community. Many have found it is not profitable to sue the city. Then, too, the improved condition of our streets, sidewalks and sewers is a factor in the situation. The city government has adopted a different attitude toward the people. We haven't had an appeal from a superior court decision in 16 years on local assessment rolls. Industrial insurance has operated to cut down damage suits against the city by employees, once an important feature. Where the city is liable we try to do the right thing to make a settlement" (Geraghty Family Scrapbook, p. 10). Cities not as fortunate as Spokane then contributed to the increases in torts shown in table 9.3.

59. Kagan, "Business of State Supreme Courts," 147.

60. Clark, *Washington*, 155.

Table 9.6
Percentage of Cases Reviewed by Washington Supreme Court Compared to Other State Courts of Last Resort

	1890–1983 Washington	*1870–1970 Other States**
Debt and contract	17.6	25.8
Real property	8.6	15.8
Corporations and partnerships	1.8	2.1
Torts	19.4	16.2
Criminal	11.6	13.6
Public law	27.8	15.0
Family and estates	8.2	9.8
Miscellaneous or unknown	5.0	1.6
	99.7	99.9
	Number: 986	5,904

*Kagan et al., "The Business of State Supreme Courts, 1870–1970," *Stanford Law Review* 30 (Nov., 1977), 133–35.

As government became more involved in business regulation, taxing, licensing, zoning, eminent domain, and the utilities—the very essence of a modern government—the public law cases increased. Accelerating this rise in public law was the nature of the Washington constitution. The state's fundamental law, like so many other state constitutions, was a detailed, restrictive document that defined a great number of relations between state and person, encouraging constitutional litigation.[61] The growth of population and the industrialization of the state also added to the demands on government and, thus, more public law disputes. The acceptance of "substantive due process" as a means of challenging governmental intrusion also made its contribution to the increase in such public law cases.[62] This area of the law remained the most common of all the legal classifications and constitutes nearly one-third of the cases even today, equaling the number of criminal cases.

61. The number of cases involving constitutional issues has remained steady over the years although they have increased slightly as a percentage of all cases heard by the bench. See table 9.1.

62. "Substantive due process" was a concept utilized by the courts to protect private property from government regulation or taxation beginning in the mid-1800s but reaching its apex in the 1920s. The courts applied a "reasonableness" test to such "confiscatory" legislation finding that the intrusion of the legislation in the name of the "public interest" was in fact unreasonable and unconstitutional. See Alfred H. Kelly and Winfred A. Harbison, *The American Constitution* (New York: Norton, 1976), 645–81.

Although the family and estate cases have remained relatively stable throughout the last ninety years, there has been a decline in the latter area with a corresponding increase in the former. Inheritance claims and disputes over estates have been diverted from the courts largely by professional planning and administration. On the other hand, divorce, child custody, alimony, and child support issues have recently added to the case load of the Supreme Court.

The rise and fall of various kinds of cases brought to the Washington Supreme Court followed developments in other states. The trends just reviewed match those found by Kagan and others in their nationwide study of the business of state supreme courts. (See table 9.6.)[63] Also the Court of Appeals not only had an impact on the number of cases heard by the Supreme Court, but its filtering function also accounted for some of the differences between the types of cases coming to the court before and after 1969.[64]

Conclusion

The portrait sketched by the foregoing data is that of a state evolving from an agricultural, fishing, mining, lumber, and shipping society running on a marginal investment basis with a relatively poor and unstable economy, to a highly developed, industrialized, urban, and affluent state. Most of the imaginable social, economic, and political issues accompanying such a developed system eventually find their way to the Supreme Court. This portrait is nearly indistinguishable from that of other states, and what can be said of the business of the Washington Supreme Court can also be said about most of the high courts of other states.

The evidence is fairly clear that after an initial steep rise in the volume of cases, peaking in the 1910s, the court slowly gained control of its docket. By increasing the size of the court, creating departments to strengthen the capacity of the bench, hiring law clerks to assist the judges, and simply encouraging hard work from the jurists, the court's output increased. However, not until the

63. Atkins and Glick, "Environmental and Structural Variables, 97–115. Atkins and Glick's study of forty-eight state supreme courts' dockets discovered a positive correlation between criminal law and such societal factors as degree of affluence, political competitiveness, and welfare coverage. Civil liberty and economic regulation cases were positively correlated with industrialization, professionalism (high pay for public officials, staff, etc.), and high welfare outlay. On the other hand private economic and private noneconomic issues were positively correlated with economic and social policies that diverted government support from persons to highways, natural resources and the like.

64. *Ibid.*, 111–13.

establishment of the Court of Appeals and the constriction of the court's jurisdiction does the Supreme Court's caseload appear to become manageable. The volume of cases declined, and the length of opinions increased, suggesting that the justices were becoming more thorough in their deliberations.

The litigants who brought cases to the court changed over the years. In the beginning the private sector dominated the use of the court, to be replaced during the Great Depression by the public sector. The nature of the parties to the disputes was also reflected in the kinds of issues brought to the high bench. There was a trend toward more noncommercial cases. For example, debt collection, contracts, real property, and corporation cases constituted 51% of all cases in the first two decades of statehood, but in the past dozen years it has been criminal and public law disputes that account for a majority of the court's docket.

There appeared also to be a trend towards supreme court decisions touching

> on the troubles of people further down the social and economic scale than those involved in most commercial and real estate cases. The victims of car and workplace accidents are as likely to be poor as to be rich; burglars and thieves notoriously are drawn from the lower ranks of society.[65]

The court has always been in a position to encourage or veto aspects of public policy through its power of judicial review, but the increase in public law and constitutional cases, exacerbated by the 1969 change in the court's jurisdiction, pointed to the justices' greater involvement in public policy issues. The Supreme Court was not "first among equals" in the state's system of separation of powers, but it was certainly a coequal branch.

Although the Supreme Court remained passive and reactive throughout its history, it eventually became deeply involved in the concerns of the society. The issues were sooner or later brought to them. This is not to say that the history of the court is the history of the state, but only that the court is very much a part of that history.

65. Kagan, "Business of State Supreme Courts," 156.

10

The Behaviors of Representative Courts

The Washington Supreme Court is composed of a number of singular judges, each with his or her particular personal and professional preferences. However, the court renders collective decisions, requiring that at least a majority of these justices agree on outcomes of disputes brought to them. The authority of their decisions, the process through which the decisions are arrived at, and the demands of fairness and reason all depend upon a sharing of responsibilities among the jurists. To understand the character of any particular court, then, means understanding both the views of each jurist and the character of the unique mix of views as the judges render their collective decisions. This requires answers to the following questions: (1) What effects on both the individual and collective behavior can the particular deliberative process have on the judges? (2) What are the views of each jurist regarding the roles of the court and of government in the state's political system? (3) What compromises and coalitions are necessary to gain a majority from the nine judges sitting at any one time? (4) What differences do all of these factors make in the goals sought and achieved by the court? Figure 10.1 represents the framework used to seek answers to these queries.[1]

The *structural* variables involve those institutional factors within which all of the judges must operate. In a broad sense they define how the jurists go about their deliberations. The conference procedures and case assignments are examples of important structures. Also court size, jurisdiction, and division of responsibilities (e.g., between the chief justice and others, or the prerogatives of seniority) have an impact on how the judges make their decisions. For example, prior to 1909 and subsequent to 1969 the court either did not

1. An earlier version of this comparative model was presented in Charles H. Sheldon, "The Washington Supreme Court: What It Was Like Thirty Years Ago," *Gonzaga Law Review* 19 (1983/84):231.

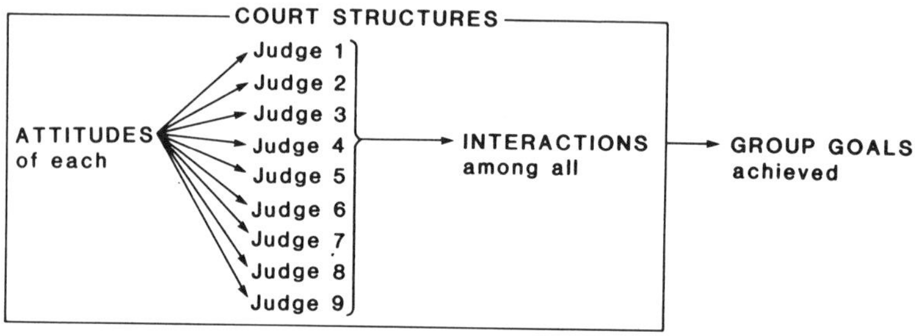

Fig. 10.1. Model of the Supreme Court

use "departments" or used them only for minor decisions. The absence or presence of this "structure," then, would be a factor to weigh in any analysis of the nature of the state's court of last resort.[2]

The *attitudinal* variables refer to particular views held by each of the jurists on the state's high bench. Those who have survived the winnowing forces of the recruitment sequence have retained and gained particular viewpoints. They either possessed these views initially or acquired them in order to survive recruitment, or both. The relevant views fall into two categories and both are derivatives of the accountability-independence conflict. *Values* are reflected in the perspectives held by the judges regarding the proper relationship between government and society. A liberal would invite more government intervention and a conservative would tolerate only that which was unavoidable. *Roles* refer to attitudes concerning the proper relationship between the court and the other political branches of government; namely, the legislature and the executive. A restraintist would bow to the wishes of the politically accountable branches, while the activist would ignore, if not defy, the preferences of the legislature, governor, or even the federal authorities.

Likely, these attitudes have been nurtured through the years of the judge's personal and professional life. As reported in Chapter 8, ascribed, acquired, and affiliated backgrounds vary among the justices as do their role and value orientations. Research has suggested the relevance of a number of these background characteristics, although some of the judges serving on representative benches may present singular combinations of traits. Party identification, region from which the judge came, who appointed him or her, the extent of

2. "Those elements identified with the Supreme Court as an institution (without knowing anything about the members of the court) would be structural variables" (Sheldon, "An Interpretation of the Judicial Process: The Washington Supreme Court as a Small Group," *Gonzaga Law Review* 13 [Fall 1977]: 100).

judicial experience or prosecutorial experience, prestige of college education, and prior elective office all have been shown to be relevant to judicial attitudes.[3] Perhaps other traits such as religion, law school, age, and political activity will be important to the development of attitudes for some jurists.

The *interaction* process involves those variables affecting the personal relations between and among the judges. The interaction process embraces those factors which are associated with the collective deliberations of the court. Circumstances which bring one judge together with another in which each must consider the other are interaction circumstances. Those factors which affect that interaction must be weighed such as the coming together of two judges with disparate backgrounds and attitudes. For example, the high disagreement rate between two judges could be explained by their possessing widely different backgrounds and consequently conflicting attitudes. Judicial biographies can generate suggestions about positive or negative relations between and among judges.

Groups such as courts are, of course, formed for particular purposes. They are organized to achieve certain *goals*, and to remain viable these goals must be achieved or replaced by others that are achievable. By attaining the immediate objectives of resolving disputes and setting public policy, appellate courts are concerned, ultimately, with developing and maintaining cohesiveness, effectiveness, and equilibrium. The continued existence of groups, including courts, depends upon achieving these goals.[4]

Thus, the scheme portrayed in figure 1 is designed to explain the degree of the court's effectiveness, cohesion, and equilibrium in terms of structures, attitudes, and interactions. In the following analysis, five representative courts will be viewed from this perspective in order to understand the development of the Supreme Court since 1889.

The Representative Courts

Five fairly distinct periods in the history of the high court were isolated in our study of recruitment to the Supreme Court. The first period (1889–1912) was characterized by the intense partisanship which brought the judges to the bench. In the second period (1912–

3. See also *ibid.*, 97; S. S. Ulmer, *Courts as Small and Not so Small Groups* (New York: General Learning Press, 1971); Charles H. Sheldon, *The American Judicial Process: Models and Approaches* (New York: Dodd, Mead, 1974); and Walter Murphy, *The Elements of Judicial Strategy* (Chicago: University of Chicago Press, 1964).
4. Sheldon, "Interpretation of Judicial Process," 125.

33), the continuity in recruitment was provided by gubernatorial appointments. From 1933–49 the bar associations asserted themselves in both appointments and elections. The era from 1950 to 1969 was a transition leading to the structured and balanced recruitment system from 1970 to the present. If these differing stages of recruitment have a bearing on the court's behavior, these five periods should be represented by five relatively distinct courts, each behaving in a fairly singular manner. Three standards were used in the selection of the benches representing each period. First, years were chosen in which little or no turnover in the personnel of the bench was experienced. Second, the judges sitting during the years selected were products of the recruitment characteristic of that period. With only two exceptions (Fullerton and Main), no judge sat on more than one of the representative courts. Third, as nearly as possible the two-year cycle of each court from which the information was collected was from its mid-years. A two-year span was used for gathering data in order to arrive at a more reliable one-year average for the data upon which the analysis was based. (See table 10.1.)

Goals: Court Effectiveness

Two dimensions are involved in the measurement of effectiveness—*expeditiousness* and *thoroughness*. Expeditiousness, in turn, has two elements: the time taken to deliberate on a decision and the number of decisions rendered. Of course, if little time elapses between the dates on which the court receives a case and hands down a decision, the judges are being effective. "Justice delayed is justice denied" applies to appellate courts as well as to trial benches. Additionally, if a considerable number of cases are disposed of by the court, the judges are also being effective. Likely the two elements of expeditiousness are mutually supportive.

But if those cases are disposed of quickly with only a few words of explanation, the judges may not be thorough in their deliberations. Not only must the judges decide a number of cases quickly, they must also give reasons why they decide as they do.[5] Charles Evans Hughes explained the values of written opinions for the U.S. Supreme Court, which are no less relevant to the state's court of last resort:

> The practice of fully stating the case in the opinion has contributed in no slight degree to the influence and prestige of the Supreme Court.

5. Article IV, Sec. 2, of the state constitution dictates, "In the determination of causes all decisions of the Court shall be given in writing and the grounds of the decision shall be stated."

Table 10.1
Representative Supreme Courts

Court 1 (1903–4)

Mark A. Fullerton (1899), *C.J.*
Thomas J. Anders (1889)
Ralph O. Dunbar (1889)
Wallace Mount (1901)
Hiram E. Hadley (1903)

Court 2 (1923–24)

*John F. Main (1912), *C.J.*
Mark A. Fullerton (1899)
*Emmett N. Parker (1909)
Oscar R. Holcomb (1915)
*Kenneth Mackintosh (1918)
*John R. Mitchell (1918)
Warren W. Tolman (1918)
*Jessie B. Bridges (1919)
William H. Pemberton (1923)

Court 3 (1939–40)

Bruce Blake (1932), *C.J.*
*John F. Main (1912)
*Walter B. Beals (1928)
*William J. Millard (1928)
*William J. Steinert (1932)
*James M. Geraghty (1933)
John S. Robinson (1937)
*George B. Simpson (1937)
Clyde G. Jeffers (1939)

Court 4 (1952–53)

*E. W. Schwellenbach (1946), *C.J.*
Thomas E. Grady (1949), *C.J.*
*Joseph A. Mallery (1942)
Matthew W. Hill (1947)
*Fred G. Hamley (1949)
*Charles T. Donworth (1949)
Robert C. Finley (1951)
*Frank P. Weaver (1951)
*Ralph O. Olson (1951)

Court 5 (1979–80)

*Robert F. Utter (1971), *C.J.*
Hugh J. Rosellini (1955)
*Charles F. Stafford (1970)
Charles T. Wright (1971)
*Robert F. Brachtenbach (1972)
Charles Horowitz (1975)
*James M. Dolliver (1976)
Floyd V. Hicks (1977)
William H. Williams (1979)

*appointed
Date in parentheses indicates year judge assumed office

> While terseness is a virtue too often lacking in judicial opinions, there is no better precaution against judicial mistakes than the setting out accurately and adequately the material facts as well as the points to be decided. . . . [T]he importance of written opinions as a protection against judicial carelessness and irresponsibility is very great.[6]

Of course, expeditiousness may be sacrified for thoroughness. If judges take more time to research and write opinions, they drop

6. Charles Evans Hughes, *The Supreme Court of the United States* (New York: Garden City Publishers, 1936), 64–65.

behind in the number of cases handled. One dimension of effectiveness yields to another. This dilemma confronts all appellate courts and requires that each aspect of effectiveness be measured separately.

In the following study, effectiveness is measured in several ways, all dictated by the data available. First, the time element of expeditiousness is measured by compiling the average amount of time (months and days) between the date when the trial court entered its decision if the appeal went directly to the Supreme Court or when the Court of Appeals decided, and the date on which the high bench rendered its decision. Although a great number of factors beyond the control of the court can intervene either to expedite or delay an appeal, generally these factors will bear equally on the five representative courts considered. The total number of dispositions by the court will provide a measure of the work-load element of expeditiousness.

Thoroughness, although most often a subjective judgment, can be inferred from (1) the number of majority opinions written; (2) the number of pages devoted to the written opinions; and (3) the number of *en banc* decisions, when the full court decides (as opposed to a departmental decision when only five of the judges participate). The assumption is that fewer opinions allow a more considered effort, and that longer opinions signify more thoroughness on the part of the writer and his colleagues who must sign that opinion. Also, the more cases that are heard and decided *en banc* when all judges are involved, the more scrutiny given these cases.[7]

Table 10.2 reports the effectiveness levels for the representative courts.

Although not entirely clearcut, the 1939–40 and 1979–80 benches appear to have been the most effective. Court 3 got to their decisions quicker, although Court 5 disposed of more filings. The contemporary bench wrote fewer opinions, all of which were *en banc*, but Court 3 wrote longer opinions.

Cohesiveness on the Bench

The Supreme Court's deliberative process has both a collective and an individual phase.

7. An *en banc* hearing signifies one of two things. First, the case has gone to the full court because of some substantial disagreement among the members of a department. Second, it may have gone to the full court because of the importance of the issues involved. In either case, an *en banc* opinion results in more judges giving more consideration to a case than a department hearing would allow. This measure, however, applied only to courts between 1909 and 1969.

Table 10.2
Goal Achievement: Effectiveness (yearly average)

	Court 1	*Court 2*	*Court 3*	*Court 4*	*Court 5*
Expeditiousness					
Time elapse (months, days)	10m,14d	11m,3d	9m,14d	10m,15d	16m,14d
Total dispositions	310	589	323	258	773*
Thoroughness					
Majority opinions	242	548	312	242	173
No. of pages/opinions	5.7	4.7	8.7	5.8	6.4
En banc decisions	242	62	70	44	173
Ranking:	3rd	5th	1st(tie)	4th	1st(tie)

*Includes the following: 476 writs denied, 34 dismissed, 68 transferred and 196 mandated opinions.

> The Supreme Court decides, but each justice separately prepares for and justifies that collegial decision. These two sometimes antithetical phases—collective and individual—are reconciled when a sufficient degree of cohesiveness prevails.[8]

On occasion, the individual phase collides with the collective, and a judge feels compelled to express disagreement with his or her colleagues in the form of a dissenting or a separate concurring opinion.

This American tradition of writing dissenting opinions, which has been so evident at the U.S. Supreme Court level, has also been accepted by the Washington high court. The dissent rate of the state's court falls far behind that of the nation's court of last resort, but, nonetheless, it ranks high among the supreme courts of other states.[9]

Although they are clearly expressions of the lack of cohesiveness, dissenting opinions perform several useful (if not necessary) functions. Challenging the majority is characteristic of a democratic society. The practice carries over into the courts.

> Dissenting is endemic in a country won by blood spilled for conscience and expression. It is natural, essential and inevitable. Its absence

8. Sheldon, "Interpretation of Judicial Process," 125.
9. S. McConkie, "Environmental, Institutional, and Procedural Influences in Collegial Decision-Making" (Ph.D. diss., Department of Political Science, Washington State University, 1974), 227.

> marks the graveyard of conformity, to paraphrase Justice Jackson. And its value and inevitability is no less within the precincts of the law.[10]

Dissents, however futile at the moment, can make an appeal to the future. Charles Evans Hughes expressed this function eloquently:

> A dissent in a court of last resort is an appeal to the brooding spirit of the law, to the intelligence of a future day when a later decision may possibly correct the error into which the dissenting judge believes the Court to have been betrayed.[11]

Dissents may be part of the internal politics of the court. The dissenting judge may write to convince a wavering colleague, to win over another supporter, or perhaps even to gain a majority of signatures. But some dissents are drafted simply to criticize the majority writer or to provoke changes in the original draft of the court's opinion. Often this latter type of dissent is drafted but never filed. It serves its purpose if changes are made in the leading opinion.

Some judges take to heart the admonishments of Article IV of the State Constitution: "in the determination of causes all decisions of the court shall be given in writing and the grounds of the decision shall be stated." Although this pertains to the majority's decisions, a judge may regard it as a constitutional duty to write a dissent.

Dissenting opinions also perform a symbolic function. They

> give assurances to counsel, litigants and the public that the issues received considerable debate, deliberation and discussion, and that the diverse views received attention from the judges. In a symbolic sense, greater legitimacy accompanies the court's decision simply because it is obviously the result of an extended deliberative process.[12]

Finally, some dissents are designed to warn the majority, and the public, of the ramifications of the decision. A "parade of horribles" is drummed out, angrily arguing that what the majority decision has wrought today had in similar decisions in the past led to suffering, and the results will return to haunt us again soon. Justice Hugo Black of the U.S. Supreme Court often adopted this approach to

10. Percival Jackson, *Dissent in the Supreme Court* (Norman: University of Oklahoma Press, 1969), 4. See also Steven A. Peterson, "Dissent in American Courts," *Journal of Politics* 43 (May 1981):412.
11. Hughes, *The Supreme Court of the United States*, 128.
12. Sheldon, "Interpretation of Judicial Process," 128.

dissents.[13] Whatever the motivations of the dissenting judge, the disagreements expressed through the dissenting opinion and vote, or in the separate concurring opinion, are examples of the lack of cohesion on the bench.[14] Although dissents have a long tradition and may actually perform a useful function, and separate concurrences do not alter the final outcome, no court can long tolerate a high level of dissonance over an extended period of time and remain viable. Cohesion is a necessary goal of any stable group and certainly of the State Supreme Court.[15]

The tradition of dissent on the Washington bench began early in its history. The first dissent was filed by Judge Theodore L. Stiles in an 1890 case concerning community property. The majority opinion as expressed by Judge Ralph O. Dunbar swept aside the argument that the law as interpreted would lead to confusion and would remain impractical. Community property issues, according to Dunbar, "are subjects for legislative consideration, and not for judicial determination." But Judge Stiles failed to accept such restraintist arguments and warned of the future impact of the court's ruling: "I cannot believe that it was the intention of the legislature . . . to withdraw all this community real estate from liability. . . . The combinations and confusions are endless, if this doctrine is once announced."[16]

Again, questions of activism and restraint arose in the second dissent filed with the court (in the so-called "Opium Den Case," *Ah Lim* v. *Territory*, 1 WASH. 156, 1890). Dissenter Elmon Scott, joined by Stiles, argued that courts must look into the substance of laws when individual rights were involved. He invoked the U.S. Constitution, several landmark U.S. Supreme Court cases, including *Mar-*

13. See, for example, his dissent in *Noto* vs. *U.S.* (367 U.S. 290, 1961 at 300). Some students of courts regard dissents as forms of civil disobedience written to bring about needed changes. See J. L. Campbell, III, "The Spirit of Dissent," *Judicature* 66 (February 1983):305.

14. This analysis regards separate concurring opinions, and votes cast for those concurring opinions, as examples of dissonance. The cohesion level disintegrates as quickly with an exorbitant number of concurring opinions and votes as with dissents. The outcome remains the same as advocated by the majority, but the reasons for that outcome are different.

15. The U.S. Supreme Court, which in modern times appears to disregard the need for cohesion, had traditionally frowned upon dissenting opinions. Justice Pierce Butler expressed the reluctance as follows: "I voted to reverse. While this sustains your conclusion to affirm, I still think reversal would be better. But I shall in silence acquiesce. Dissents seldom aid in the right development of the law. They often do harm. For myself I say: 'Lead us not into temptation'" (Murphy, *The Elements of Judical Strategy*, 52). The earlier Canons of Judicial Ethics (Canon 1a), representing the moral aspects of judicial traditions, also urge against dissent.

16. *Brotton* v. *Langert* (1 WASH. 73, 1890 at 82 and 86).

bury v. *Madison*, and the social compact theory underlying American constitutionalism. The dissent read like a treatise on constitutional philosophy.

Concurring opinions may reflect dissonance as strongly as dissents. Indeed, to agree in the outcome but for different reasons may place the concurring judge at greater odds with his colleagues because the reasons explained in the opinions constitute the essence of judicial decisions. The first concurring vote was even earlier. Chief Justice Thomas Anders and Judge Elmon Scott concurred only "in the result" in *Andrews* v. *King County* (1 WASH. 46, 1890). They gave no reason for their concurrence but, of course, they were not sufficiently pleased with the majority's opinion.

Table 10.3 reports the disagreement rates among the representative courts.

Table 10.3
Goal Achievement: Cohesiveness (yearly average)

	Court 1	*Court 2*	*Court 3*	*Court 4*	*Court 5*
Total majority and *per curiam* opinions	310	589	323	258	176
*Total written dissents	10	68.5	68.5	45.5	49.5
Total dissenting votes	5.5	37	74.5	33	81.5
Total written concurrences and votes	7.5	37	39.5	33	55
Total cases with disagreement	11.5	89	81.5	50	64
Percentage disagreement	3.7%	15.1%	25.3%	19.4%	36.5%
Ranking:	1st	2nd	4th	3rd	5th

*Includes "I Dissent" without any further explanation.

The levels of cohesiveness vary significantly among the representative courts. The judges on the earlier court were most cohesive, dissenting, or concurring separately, in only 3.7% of the cases. In contrast, the members of the contemporary court expressed some form of disagreement in one out of three cases. Except for Court 4, the judges have displayed an ever increasing dissonance rate.

Several "structural" explanations for the varying levels of cohesiveness reported in table 10.3 are possible. There has been a steady decline in the number of cases heard by the courts, allowing more time for the contemplation and writing of concurrences and dissents. (Court 1 heard only 310 cases, but only five judges were sitting, and thus were responsible for nearly as many cases per member—62 as compared to 65—as in Court 2.) Also, more judges were on the bench after 1907, increasing the probabilities for disagreement. After the elimination of partisan recruitment in 1912, a more diverse group of judges was selected for the court of last resort. As the recruitment process matured and more participants became involved, more disparate qualifications were expected of the judicial candidates, accompanied, of course, by varied attitudes.

These trends both contributed to and were a product of an aura of respectability gradually forming around the dissenter in the American judiciary. The United States Supreme Court, of course, provided the model for state judiciaries, and the practice of dissent was becoming well-established in the nation's highest courts.[17]

Equilibrium or Authority

Courts, more than other public agencies, rely upon their authority to gain compliance with their decisions. If every decision of a court, or for that matter, even a small number of decisions, required enforcement by means of marshals, police, or prosecutors, this likely would signify the breakdown of law. The problem of authority is the problem of a group's reaction to its environment. All groups attempt to adjust to their environment: to achieve an equilibrium between what the environment demands of them and what they are able to provide the environment. Over a period of time courts also must be at peace with other governmental agencies (especially the legislature), with major groups in the political system (usually with other judges and the legal profession), and with the public in order to perform those duties assigned them. They must, in a word, be respected—possess authority.

Authority is a relational concept, involving interactions between persons. It develops through a two-stage process. First, authority is closely associated with power (force). Decisions of those in power are obeyed because of fear, apathy, habit, awe, agreement, or some weighing of the alternative forms of action on the basis of rewards or punishments. Governments exercise power and courts are part of the governmental structure. In the second stage, however, obedience depends upon whether those being ordered to do something (or to refrain from so doing) feel that those who give orders have the *right* to so order. This view of power as being exercised by the appropriate or legitimate person or agency is the core of authority. Rewards and punishments are seldom offered or invoked. Courts

17. See Jackson, *Dissent in the Supreme Court.*

are especially dependent upon compliance based on the acceptance of this version of authority. They must be acknowledged as possessing the right to decide what they decide. They must possess authority, which can be briefly defined as legitimated power. No longer are they directly a part of the power structure but rather should behave independently of that structure.

The authority of courts surges and wanes, for judges are not without means for increasing or decreasing their authority, depending on how they deal with their environment. For example, if judges persist in substituting their view of the law for that of the elected representatives in the legislature, their authority will be jeopardized. Also, if they fail to meet the demands placed on them by the constitution, precedent, or the law, and refuse to deal with pressing legal issues simply because they may have political ramifications, they are shirking their responsibilities. Again, it is the dilemma presented by the tension between public accountability and judicial independence. A balance must be struck.[18]

Measuring a court's authority ideally should involve viewing reactions as well as actions, motives as well as overt behavior. Practically, however, inferences as to the level of authority of any given court must be drawn from several sets of data. First, a comparison of the number of favorable case citations of one court by subsequent judges suggests the degree of authority of that court. Second, the number of *American Law Reports* citations implies the respect given a particular judge or court.[19] Third, the fate of cases appealed to the U.S. Supreme Court (as well as the number of citations) suggests the authority of a particular group of judges. Finally, law review references to cases decided by a court also provide clues as to the attention paid its decisions. By comparing the five representative courts along these four dimensions (subsequent case citation, A.L.R. references, U.S. Supreme Court reactions, and law review citations) a sense for the relative authority of the representative courts is gained.[20]

18. Stephen C. Halpern and Charles M. Lamb, *Supreme Court Activism and Restraint* (Lexington, Mass: Lexington Books, 1982).

19. "The American Law Reports is a selective reporter of appellate court decisions. Its editors scan all current decisions and select those that in their opinion are or will become 'leading' cases" (from J. Jacobstein and R. M. Mersky, *Legal Research Illustrated* [Mineola, N.Y.: Foundation Press, 1977], 77). According to the Introduction to the A.L.R. Digest: "The decisions included represent the best in American case law. . . . The annotations are the famous ALR annotations, universally recognized as the profession's most useful and reliable source of case authorities and analysis" (*Permanent A.L.R. Digest* 1 [1949]:iii).

20. Not all citations and references are favorable, however. Positive indications of deference are cases that subsequent courts have simply cited "followed," "explained," "harmonized," "affirmed," or "cited in dissent." Negative responses include those

Table 10.4
Goal Achievement: Authority (yearly average)

	Court 1	Court 2	Court 3	Court 4	Court 5
*Subsequent citations	1714	3015	1818	1610	2027
A.L.R. references	579	1909	757	409	405
U.S. Supreme Court citations	31	41	18	23	35
Law review references	117	453	290	434	248
Ranking:	5th	1st	2nd	4th	3rd

*Total less the negative citations

Table 10.5
Court Viability (yearly average)

	Court 1	Court 2	Court 3	Court 4	Court 5
Ranking of respective courts on dissonance	1st	2nd	4th	3rd	5th
Ranking on court authority	5th	1st	2nd	4th	3rd
Ranking on effectiveness	3rd	5th	1st(tie)	4th	1st(tie)
Composite ranking on goal achievement	3rd	2nd	1st	5th	4th

The data in table 10.4 indicate that Court 2 (1922–23) is clearly the most authoritative of the five benches. The judgment on Court 5 (1979–80) is still to be rendered, although preliminary reports are encouraging. It had been suggested earlier that these three goals of the Supreme Court were perhaps mutually reinforcing. The data, however, fail to substantiate the suggestion. Court 3 was the most effective, Court 1 the most cohesive, and Court 2 the most authoritative. Perhaps, then, each goal must be achieved separately. One will not substitute for another in maintaining the viability of the court.

A composite view of the respective courts presented in table 10.5

---

cases that have been "overruled," "criticized," "questioned," "superseded," "limited," "vacated," "modified," "reversed," or "distinguished." In table 10.4 the negative responses are subtracted from the total of positive citations. The classification scheme and data are from *Shepard's Washington Citations*. Four of the five courts are allowed ten years to establish their authority in the compilation of subsequent citations. For example, citations from Court 2 (1922–23) are compiled through 1933 only. All the A.L.R., U.S. Supreme Court, and law review references are not so limited. Data on Court 5 cover from 1979 through January 1985. These totals are then multiplied by 1.967 (61 months out of the necessary 120 to cover 10 years) to make them comparable.

suggests that Court 3 (1939–40) was the most viable. Those judges were better able to accomplish the group goals than the judges on other benches. The Court 4 (1952–53) bench was the least viable, although its ability to function was certainly not questioned. Explanations for the individual and composite rankings of the representative courts are to be found in the structures defining the courts, the interactions between and among the judges of each court, and the attitudes held by each of the jurists. In the following analysis each of the representative courts is studied by looking at these variables of the court model portrayed in figure 10.1.

11

The 1903–4 Supreme Court

The Deliberative Process

The decisional process by which the judges resolved the disputes brought to them was designed to enhance the court's effectiveness and the judges' thoroughness. From the beginning it was a blend of individual and collective efforts. Approximately twenty-one cases per week were placed on Court 1's (1903–4) calendar. The briefs filed in these cases were reviewed by all the judges prior to oral argument. Mondays through Thursdays were usually devoted to the oral arguments, often involving questions from the bench. (In a few instances oral presentations were dispensed with and the case decided on the briefs alone.) At the close of each week the judges would give collective attention to that week's cases by meeting in conference, discussing, voting on the disposition of cases, and assigning opinion-drafting responsibilities.[1] Cases were assigned "to the several judges in rotation"; that is, without consideration for the subject matter, the litigants, or the judge's preferences. Thereby, each judge received an equal number of assignments.

If in conference all the judges agreed, the assigned judge assumed the opinion-writing tasks. Most of the cases followed this route. However, if some doubts were expressed or if "no definite opinion" could be formed "from the briefs and arguments alone," the assigned judge examined the record and consulted informally with his colleagues. If there still was "any difference of opinion or disagreement," the other judges examined the record and informal consultations continued until differences were resolved or minds were made up. The opinion was drafted by the assigned judge, and

1. It was unclear if the five members actually took a formal although preliminary vote on the disposition of cases in conference. "Consultation" was their term for these collective deliberations.

its circulation followed, along with any dissent. If, in some instances, the assigned judge reached a

> conclusion adversely to the decision in consultation, after an examination of the record, he makes that fact known to the other members, and a further consultation is held. If a majority of the court still adhere to their former views, the case is reassigned to some member of the court who shares the views of the majority.[2]

The new draft opinion was then circulated for other signatures. Further disagreement required the preparation of a dissenting opinion if the dissenter decided not to "remain silent." If a judge agreed with the outcome of the case but not the reasons given in the draft opinion, further consultation ensued. A concurring opinion or vote might result. After everyone had seen the opinion, and a majority had affixed their signatures thereto it was filed or "spindled" in the clerk's office and became the official decision of the Supreme Court. Dissenting or concurring opinions would have also been filed before the decision became official.

The final phase of the decisional sequence sometimes involved petitions for rehearing. The petitions were reviewed by the individual judges at their leisure. If denial seemed in order, the judge so indicated and passed the petition on to the other judges. When a majority of the court signified denial, the petition was rejected. If, however, "any member of the court" felt that further consideration or investigation was in order, consultation among the judges took place and a final decision was made on the petition. Usually a short *per curiam* opinion, simply stating the denial, closed the matter.

Thus, the collective aspects of the decisional process involved formal consultations and possibly votes in conference, the oral arguments before the full bench, and informal conferring should a consensus be lacking. The individual phases involved the examining judge's review of the record (or review by the others if needed), and the drafting of dissenting, concurring, and majority opinions. The occasional petition for rehearing required, again, both a collective and an individual effort. The collective deliberations contributed to a higher level of cohesion because of the tendency toward com-

2. According to Judge Frank Rudkin, "The names of the judges are written at the top of the fly leaf of each bar docket, and the cases are assigned in the order submitted, each judge placing the name of the case under the name of the judge to whom the assignment is made. In this respect the members of the court take their chances, just like the litigants. If a judge to whom the case falls is for any reason disqualified, or does not concur in the views of the majority, the assignment is made to the next judge against whom no such objection exists" (Frank H. Rudkin, "The Court's Work," *Proceedings of the Washington State Bar Association* [1906], 171).

promise, whereas the individual decisional phase tempted dissent because of the relative isolation of each judge. The circulation of the draft opinions likely constituted a bridge between the two phases. The judges reviewed the drafts individually but affixed their signatures to a common opinion.

The Interaction among the Judges

The judges on the early court wrote an average of ten dissenting opinions per year (two per judge) and cast an additional six (5.5) votes in these ten cases. They wrote only an average of two (1.5) concurring opinions each year but cast an additional 6 concurring votes in these opinions. Hence, they averaged twenty-three forms of disagreement per year. Table 11.1 reports the dissents and concurrences for all five judges. To disagree only twenty-three times in 310 written opinions where the possibilities for disagreement are nearly 1,240 (4 × 310) represents a very high level of cohesion.

Table 11.1
Dissonance Rate: Court 1 (yearly average)

Judge	*Dissenting Opinions*	*Dissenting Votes*	*Concurring Opinions-Votes*	*Total Disagreements*
Fullerton	6.0	2.0	3.0	11.0 (48%)
Anders	2.0	1.5	2.5	6.0 (26%)
Dunbar	1.0	1.5	1.5	4.0 (17%)
Mount	0.5	0.5	0.5	1.5 (7%)
Hadley	0.5	0.0	0.0	0.5 (2%)
Total	10.0	5.5	7.5	23.0 (100%)
Average/Judge	2.0	1.1	1.5	4.6

Another set of statistics could potentially lower the cohesive level, but the data must be viewed with some suspicion. Thirty percent or 143 decisions out of the 483 rendered in the two years were decided by fewer than the full five members of the bench. Judge Frank Rudkin explained what the "abstentions" could have signified:

> If a member of the court does not concur in or dissent from an opinion filed, it is because he dissents and does not care to express that dissent for lack of time or otherwise, or because he does not approve of the reasons assigned for the judgment or because he was disqualified, did not participate, or was absent when the opinion was filed.[3]

3. *Ibid.* at 170.

Judge Hadley did not participate, for whatever reason, in 61 of the 483 cases rendered in 1903–4 (13%); Anders did not sign 38 opinions (8%); Fullerton "missed" 35 (7%); Dunbar absented himself in 16 (3%); and Mount missed only 4 (1%).[4] Because these absences have a variety of explanations (as Judge Rudkin pointed out) and only one of these might have been a dissent, the analysis of cohesion here will be limited to those disasgreements that can be documented.[5]

On those few occasions when members of the bench split on the outcome of a case or on the reasons for that outcome, a pattern of interagreement appeared. Table 11.2 reports the percentage of times in the two years covered that pairs of judges agreed.

The interagreement average for the entire court over the two-year period covered was 50% whenever less than unanimous decisions were handed down. Any agreement level between two judges that exceeds 75% is regarded as statistically significant.[6] Judges Hadley, Mount, and Dunbar agreed with one another in three-fourths (76.7%) of the opportunities presented by all the less than unanimous decisions.

4. The Supreme Court Reporter recorded that Judge Fullerton "did not sit in this case" three times out of his total of thirty-eight. No other judge was so recorded. This likely was to document a disqualification on the basis of a conflict of interest. See, for example, *Graves* v. *Thompson* (35 WASH. 282, 1904).

5. A fairly sensible argument can be made that these absences were exactly that: occasions when a judge chose not to be part of the deliberations. First, it was not uncommon for dissenting judges simply to sign an opinion with "I dissent" without any further explanation. Also, "I concur in the result" was a common response of the judges. Thus, the practice of accompanying a dissent or a concurrence with a written opinion was not yet fully developed. If they actually disagreed with a decision, the judges had a common and acceptable alternative: simply to say so rather than abstaining. Secondly, many of the unrelated cases that were decided by fewer than five judges were filed in sequence, suggesting that the absent judge was ill, unavailable, or busy with other court business at that particular time. With the pressures of writing over two hundred opinions a year, it would not be surprising if from time to time a case would be resolved by only three or four judges while the missing judge worked on other opinions. This would have been a more effective dispersal of judicial manpower. Of course, as Judge Rudkin suggested, on occasion a disagreeing judge could find it easier and more judicious to remain off the record in a decision that was troublesome. However, such motives and action can only be a matter of speculation.

Richard F. Jones, reporter for decisions for the *Washington State Law Reports* for over twenty years, agreed that "the judges whose names are not listed as participating in the decision simply were not present at the time of the argument or were not available for signing the opinion" (Letter to author dated February 24, 1983).

6. John D. Sprague has arrived at a "significance level" for blocs by simply subtracting the court average (in this case 50%) from 100, and dividing this in half (25) and adding it to the court average (75). Any percentage of interagreement over this total is regarded as statistically significant and not due to chance. See J. Sprague, *Voting Patterns of the United States Supreme Court: Cases in Federalism, 1889–1959* (Indianapolis: Bobbs-Merrill, 1968), 54.

Table 11.2
Interagreement Percentages

	Hadley	Dunbar	Anders	Fullerton
Mount	86	65	52	37
Hadley		79	52	29
Dunbar			41	13
Anders				46

Court average: 50%
Sprague criterion: 75%

Fullerton tended to be a bit more moderate to liberal than his colleagues by voting more for the underdog in negligence or criminal cases. Dunbar and Anders tended to be more conservative by supporting the railroads or companies in injury cases and private property in government regulation issues. Mount and Hadley assumed a slightly moderate posture on these issues.

Two trends should be explained. First, why the relatively high cohesion for the entire court (only 3.7% disagreement rate) shown in table 11.1 and, second, why the particular patterns of interagreement displayed in table 11.2.

Several important experiences were held in common by the five members of this early court. All were initially elected rather than appointed to their positions.[7] They presented similar images and qualifications to win at the polls. All were Republicans and all had been placed on the judicial ballot by the votes of party activists at Republican nominating conventions. Four of the five (Dunbar, Mount, Anders, and Fullerton) had served as county prosecutors sometime in their earlier careers. All had been and still were involved in politics, but Dunbar, Hadley, and Mount had been especially active. Dunbar and Mount had served in state or territorial legislatures. All but Hadley (Bellingham) were from the east side of the state. These common political and electoral backgrounds may account for much of the agreement among the judges.

The size of the court tended also to discourage dissent. Apart from the simple mathematical probabilities that in a group involving fewer persons there is less chance of at least one member disagreeing, the pressures for unanimity were great in 1903–4. First,

7. Hadley had been appointed to an earlier temporary position in 1901 but won his permanent seat in 1903 through election.

many of the cases were decided by only three or four judges. A dissent in such a court would bring into question the validity of the decision where a resolution was achieved by less than a majority of the full court. Second, the court was under docket pressure. To dissent or concur only "in the result" implied an obligation (not often assumed, however) for the dissenting judge to write his reasons for the disasgreement. This meant more demands on a judge's time of which he had precious little considering the heavy caseload.

Anders and Fullerton, the dissenters on the bench, and the two who failed to agree significantly with the others (and with each other), had not been as active in partisan politics as their colleagues, although certainly not uninitiated in political matters. Also, Anders and Fullerton were the only two who had not previously sat on the trial bench, although Dunbar's experience was limited to probate judge. Hadley had been a superior court judge for four years and Mount for seven.

Fullerton served as chief justice during the two years studied. The demands of administering the court in 1903–4 were certainly less than in subsequent courts, and Fullerton had nearly as much time to contemplate and act upon disagreements as his colleagues. Perhaps, also, the role of chief justice did not yet include a concern for effectiveness, cohesion, and authority. In the earlier court, the chief was simply one among equals, not first among equals as evolved in later benches.

The "bloc" of Hadley, Mount, and Dunbar in which all three agreed among themselves in over three-fourths of the nonunanimous cases, may be explained, again, by their experiences in highly partisan (Republican) affairs. Dunbar had been a serious Congressional aspirant in the 1889 Republican convention (he missed nomination by 3 votes) and was nominated for the bench as a consolation prize. He had been speaker of the Territorial House of Representatives in 1885 and a delegate to the Constitutional Convention of 1889. Hadley had practiced law with his brother who had served several terms as a U.S. Congressman. Hadley had been active in Garfield's presidential campaign in Illinois, and as Bellingham city attorney was involved in a number of political events that brought the several communities around Bellingham Bay together. He was leader of the Whatcom County delegation to several state conventions. Wallace Mount served as Sprague City Councilman, county prosecutor, and as a member of the state House of Representatives in the 1889 session. Anders and Fullerton, in contrast, had no or little experience in partisan campaigns outside of the legal profession. (Both had been elected as county prosecutors.)

Finally, social and political philosophy, however acquired, likely dictated some of the alignments on the 1903–4 bench. Fullerton may have been a bit too liberal for his colleagues and Anders may have been too conservative. Dunbar, another conservative, however, was more acceptable to the moderates Hadley and Mount. Noting the importance of philosophical leanings is not to suggest that Anders' conservativism and Fullerton's liberalism made them extremists. Quite the contrary, both fit well within the acceptable limits of political attitudes during the early period of the state's history. For example, Anders' conservative outlook meant a clear respect for precedent:

> Were it not for the former rulings of the court I should feel strongly inclined to hold that the judgment ought to be reversed. . . . But in as much as it seems to have been heretofore decided by this court that mandamus is a proper remedy in cases like the one at bar, I am constrained to concur in the opinion written by Judge Hadley.[8]

As the court's liberal, Fullerton did not ignore precedent, but if he felt it out of date and inappropriate, he did not hesitate to replace it:

> While to depart from precedent is always a serious matter, we can do it in this instance with less regret, as we think that there was not much reason for the rule as applied to the former statute.[9]

Fullerton's liberalism was also displayed in his concern for giving full consideration to all appeals. He believed that everyone should have his day in the appellate court as well:

> Courts should not be over zealous in searching for reasons for dismissal of appeals. The purpose of an appeal is to have a review of a cause upon its merits and the construction of the statutes should be with a view to accomplish that end, rather than dispose of them without such review.[10]

An important aspect of the relationships among the judges pertains to leadership—providing the often necessary inspiration or challenge to the brethren, moving them toward effectiveness, cohesiveness, and authority. Table 11.3 provides certain clues regarding the leadership on the early court.

These data suggest several intriguing hypotheses. Each judge was initially assigned the same number of cases. If other judges agreed

8. *State Ex Rel. Hill* v. *Garner* (32 WASH. 550, 1903, at 555–56).
9. *Tozer* v. *Skagit County* (34 WASH. 147, 1904, at 151).
10. *Brown* v. *Davis* (36 WASH. 135, 1904, at 137).

Table 11.3
Interactions of Court 1 (yearly average)

Justice	*Majority Opinions*	*Disagree-ments*	*Absences*	*Pages per Opinion*
Hadley	68	0.5	32	6.2
Mount	56	1.5	2	5.1
Dunbar	56	4.0	8	5.1
Fullerton	50	10.0	18	5.2
Anders	12	6.0	19	10.4
Court averages	49	4.0	16	5.7

with his analysis of the case, he wrote the court's opinion. If not, and a compromise could not be reached, another judge wrote for the court. The data in table 11.3 indicate that Judge Hadley exerted some influence over his colleagues. He absented himself more than any other judge, expressed the fewest number of recorded disagreements, and yet wrote most of the majority opinions.

Judge Anders was far below the court average in opinion assignments. Actually he participated in about as many cases as the others, but wrote only twelve of the majority opinions. Although his opinions were lengthier than the average, he failed either to hold the majority on those cases assigned him or was unable to convince others to join him when a division on the bench occurred.[11] Judge Anders had planned not to run for reelection in 1904, had been on the bench since its inception fourteen years earlier, was sixty-five years old, and had perhaps lost some of his desire for fulfilling the substantial demands of the office. Another aspect of Anders' personality explained part of his inability to keep up with his colleagues' opinion writing level. When he did write for the court or dissented, his opinions were lengthy and thorough. His opinions were nearly twice as long as those of his colleagues. Clerk of the court C. S. Reinhart wrote of Anders that he "was a very conscientious judge, so much so that it was hard for him to come to a decision. He was well grounded in the general principles of law, but he would spend an inconceivable amount of time in looking up authorities in support of even fundamental principles. He seemed to be as anxious to render

11. Although Judge Anders wrote lengthy opinions, Judge Fullerton held the record for the court with a thirty-page unanimous opinion in *Title Guarantee & Trust Co.* v. *McDonnell* (32 Wash. 418, 1903). Anders' longest was twenty-five, Dunbar's seventeen, Mount's and Hadley's fourteen each. There were 137 *per curiam* opinions penned, averaging a little less than four pages (3.9). These opinions had no precedential value, often were denials of rehearings, and were rarely contentious.

his opinions satisfactory to the layman as to members of the bar."[12] For whatever reason Anders was obviously isolated from his brethren.

Summary: The 1903–4 Court

Although the early court experienced some mild dissonance, it must be characterized as a cohesive bench, composed of politically sophisticated and experienced judges who gained their elected positions through partisan activities, favors, or both. The judges were more alike than not, and tended to agree on legal issues and gave moderate to conservative responses to disputes appealed to them.

The small size of the court, the common backgrounds of the judges, and the still-evolving tradition of deliberation explain a number of behavior patterns of the judges. However, the basic issue that haunted the court (and still troubles judges today) was defined but certainly not resolved. It was an issue of public accountability vs. judicial responsibility.[13]

The judges were held accountable by partisan elections, party nominating conventions, and the dominance of the Republicans. This compelled them to avoid direct conflicts with the other elected representatives—the legislators—leading often to a sacrifice of the needs of the rule of law for the demands of public accountability. The issue was most angrily debated among the members of the state's high bench in the first year of the court's existence.

In the so-called "Opium Den Case," Judge Dunbar, writing for the majority, agonized over the role of the court in relation to the legislature and opted for granting deference to the elected representatives:

> The duty of passing upon the constitutionality of a law should be approached by the court with the utmost caution, and demands the most solemn, thoughtful and painstaking consideration. And in view of the consequences to society from the annuling of laws made by the representatives of the people . . . it becomes the gravest question with which courts have to deal; and we believe it has been the uniform conviction of the courts that they ought not and cannot in justice to a coordinate department of the state government, declare a law to be void without a strong and earnest conviction, divested of all reasonable doubt, of its invalidity.[14]

12. C. S. Reinhart, *History of the Supreme Court of the Territory and State of Washington* (Privately published: n.d.), 92.
13. G. Edward White, *The American Judicial Tradition* (New York: Oxford, 1978).
14. *Ah Lim* v. *Territory* (1 Wash. 156, 1890, at 158–59).

However, Judge Elmon Scott would have none of this view. Despite the demands of accountability, he believed that the courts must act upon principle not upon what the legislature thought best.

> A body politic is a social compact by which the whole people covenants with each citizen, and each citizen with the whole people, that all shall be governed by certain laws for the common good. This does not confer power upon the whole people to control rights which are purely an exclusive private. . . .
>
> The power to protect the rights of the citizen from the wrongful effect of such legislation is peculiarly adapted to, and within the province of, the judicial branch of the government.[15]

The rule of law must prevail over majoritarian decisions, according to Scott.

Although the tension between accountability and responsibility was acutely felt by the members of Court 1, the jurists more often than not accepted the demands of accountability.

15. *Ibid.*, 173. For other early examples of the accountability-responsibility issue, see Judge Anders in *Kelly* v. *Stewart* (1 WASH. 98, 1890, at 110); Judge Dunbar in *State Ex Rel. Cann* v. *Moore* (23 WASH. 115, 1900, at 120); and Dunbar in *Brotton* v. *Langert* (1 WASH. 73, 1890, at 82). What was striking about these examples was that they were from the first year of the court and were the first examples of dissent on the court. The judges perceived the issue immediately.

12

The Supreme Court of the 1920s

The 1923–34 court differed from its 1903–4 predecessor in many respects. The structures had changed substantially, and, except for Judge Mark Fullerton, the entire membership of the bench was different.[1] It clearly was a distinct bench.

The Decisional Process

The structural alterations instituted since 1904 were significant. First, the bench was expanded from five to seven and, then, finally, to nine in 1909. In the process of increasing the membership of the state's high court, the legislature authorized decisions to be rendered by departments. The practical effect of the departmental arrangement was to create two supreme courts composed of four judges each and the chief justice who sat in and presided over both panels.[2] However, Article IV of the State Constitution dictated that "The judicial power of the state shall be vested in *a supreme court*" (emphasis added). Although departmental (and thus, court) decisions could be rendered by as few as three judges, the single court rule was observed by extensive coordination between the two de-

1. Judge Fullerton holds the record for years on the Supreme Court. He served a total of thirty-two years, eight months, and twelve days.

2. The enabling legislation authorized the chief justice to appoint four judges to the respective two departments and "from time to time" to reassign the judges. The judges themselves, by mutual consent, also could switch departments. "Each of the departments shall have power to hear and determine causes and all questions arising therein. . . ." Three judges constituted a quorum but if agreement among the three was lacking, the full membership of the department, the judges in the other panel or the entire court (*en banc*) reheard the case. The chief justice could transfer a case to the full court or, with the consent of at least two other judges, he could have a case reheard *en banc*. Any four judges, without the consent of the chief, could also have an *en banc* rehearing. Cases rarely received automatic *en banc* hearings, although the most serious and contentious cases eventually found their way to a hearing by the full court. Five judges constituted an *en banc* quorum. Chapter 24, Sessions Laws, 1909, (Senate Bill 198), 33–36.

partments. According to Judge O. G. Ellis, "There is constant and increasing effort on the part of the judges to make the work of each department the work of the entire court. . . ."[3]

To achieve coordination, the chief justice presided over both departments. Each year a change in the membership of the respective divisions was made with at least two members of each being reassigned. Also the members of one department read and checked every opinion coming out of the other, so that the final decision was reviewed by, if not a product of, the full bench. Finally, under some circumstances, a case originally assigned to one department could be transferred to the other department or brought to the full membership of the court for resolution. Thus, although the Supreme Court was divided into two tribunals to keep up with its growing caseload, it was still a single court.

Chief Justice John Main reviewed the departmental decisional process of the 1923–24 Court:

> During the term the ordinary working day of a judge . . . is from 8:30 or 9:00 in the morning, when he reaches the office until 10:00 or 11:00 o'clock at night when he finishes reading briefs of the succeeding day's work.
>
> [After argument we return to the consultation room the same day.] Here the calendar is called again informally. The first case is taken up and the Chief Justice calls upon the judge whose turn it is to take an assignment for his view. The case is then discussed. . . . The case is then assigned for the writing of an opinion to one of those sitting whose views are those of the majority justices.[4]

The opinion assignments were made in rotation when possible (unless the court was divided) in order to assure an even distribution of work.[5] One of three possible courses of action then followed. Most

3. O. G. Ellis, "The Court's Work," *Proceedings of the Washington State Bar Association* (1914): 179.

4. John Main, *Seattle Daily Times*, September 3, 1924. For another account of the process see John Mitchell, "Address at State Prosecuting Attorneys' Association," *Proceedings* (1921): 172.

5. A contemporary newspaper account described the workings of the court during the oral arguments: "At 10:00 A.M. and 1:30 P.M. the judges enter from chambers in the rear, gowned in the black-silk robes their profession insists upon. As they enter all present rise and remain standing until the bailiff recites his formal announcement that the court is now in session, and the judges are seated. Without further ceremony the chief justice then calls the next case on the calendar. At a table within the bar the attorney concerned in that arises and opens his argument. His formal style of reference to the supreme judges will be 'your honors' and 'may it please the court.'

"Except on occasion, . . . one-half hour is allowed each side for argument. When of the time the judge assigned the drafting responsibilities completed his opinion, put it in circulation, and it was signed by all or most of the judges. It was then filed in the clerk's office and became the opinion of the court. However, if the judge who had been assigned the opinion-writing task, after reviewing the briefs, the abstract of the record, and other relevant materials arrived at a conclusion contrary to the decision of the majority in conference, he informed his brethren, and a reassignment of the draft opinion was made to a judge in the majority who would have his version in circulation for signatures within the appropriate time. If a troublesome case failed to be resolved in conference, the case was assigned to the judge whose turn it was, and he conducted a thorough reexamination of the briefs, record, transcript, and so forth (the other judges may have also reviewed the relevant materials). Then his draft opinion (which likely contained discussions of the concerns of other judges) was circulated among the members of the department and eventually to members of the other department. Either the judges signed the majority opinion, concurred in the result (and, perhaps, wrote a concurring opinion), dissented (and possibly wrote a dissenting opinion), or remained silent. The abstentions, as in the 1903–4 court, meant a judge (1) "dissents and does not care to express that dissent"; (2) "does not approve of the language used"; (3) "was disqualified"; or (4) "was absent when the opinion was filed."[6] Of course, if disagreement among the members of a department was sharp, and informal consultation failed to resolve the conflicts, the case was reheard *en banc* and the same process was followed.

The preliminary resolution of cases in conference relied on the

---

the time limit expires the chief justice announces that fact. . . . The attorney so reminded invariably subsides immediately.

"Counsel here waste little time on witticism, although a smile is not penalized. But the Supreme Court is an extremely busy institution and neither is there any bickering. . . .

"The judges themselves will sound him by careful questioning, if necessary, until they gain a comprehensive idea of what it is he wants to impress. . . .

"The attorney who has thoroughly digested his case and condensed and clarified his argument offers a welcome oasis in the vast area of litigation that stretches behind and before the supreme judges, yet the advocate fated to stumble along his way will be understood eventually if that is possible. . . .

"Attorneys, as a rule, betray no symptoms of irritation at questioning from the bench. Many of them imagine they can catch the drift of the court's ideas on a point involved by his line of inquiry, which supposed indication they are usually prone to interpret as favorable to themselves. Later, when the opinion is filed, they frequently discover that they must have somehow been deluded." *Seattle Daily Times,* Aug. 25, 1918.

6. Ellis, "The Court's Work," 180.

authorities cited in the briefs, the contentions presented in oral arguments, and the facts as outlined in the abstract of the trial record (since 1913 each litigant was required to file an abstract of the record with their briefs).[7] But oral arguments were heavily relied upon. This was stressed by Judge Mitchell in a 1921 address to county prosecutors:

> [We] are often asked if oral arguments are useful. The matter is not even debatable—the emphatic answer is affirmative. . . . [Oral arguments] give . . . the human touch and invest the whole controversy with your faith in your contention, pressing home what you consider the most dominant features as to the facts and the law of the case. In oral argument you are the teachers, we the pupils. You are advising us of something that you have thoroughly and recently studied, and we are engaged in learning it from you.[8]

All judges considered petitions for rehearing but in contrast with 1903–4, the review process was greatly accelerated.

In summary, the structural characteristics of Court 2 included: (1) an increased number of judges; (2) the use of departments; (3) *en banc* consideration only for contentious and important cases; (4) greater responsibilities for the chief justice and; (5) an increased number of causes filed with the court.

Judicial Relationships

The personnel on Court 2, with the exception of Mark Fullerton, had not sat on the earlier bench. The relationships between and among these judges exerted considerable influence over the level of cohesion, authority, and effectiveness displayed by the 1923–24 Court.

The dissonance rate increased with Court 2. The disagreement level for the entire bench was 15.1%. That is, of the 1,178 decisions filed in 1923–24, one or more judges disagreed (dissented or concurred separately) from his colleagues in 178 cases. Table 12.1 tabulates the various categories of dissent among the judges.

7. *Ibid.*, 181. As during the deliberations of Court 1, many of the judges absented themselves from some cases. A department decision was often rendered by only four judges and an *en banc* opinion was filed with only seven or eight signatures. But the patterns of abstentions indicated, as earlier, that motivations other than a "silent dissent" were involved. For example, on one day in January 1923 fourteen cases involving a variety of issues were filed without Judge Main's signatures, suggesting his absence. Also the increased use of "I dissent" without any explanations gave a dissenter a way of expressing disagreement nearly as easy as remaining "silent."

8. Mitchell, "Address at State Prosecuting Attorneys' Association," 175.

Table 12.1
Dissonance Rate: Court 2 (yearly average)

Judge	*Dissenting Opinions*	*Dissenting Votes*	*Concurring Opinions-Votes*	*Total Disagreements*
Pemberton	22.0	6.5	4.0	32.5 (22.8%)
Holcomb	11.0	3.5	3.5	18.0 (12.6%)
Mackintosh	8.5	4.5	4.5	17.5 (12.0%)
Fullerton	7.0	4.5	4.5	16.0 (11.2%)
Parker	6.5	4.0	3.0	13.5 (9.5%)
Mitchell	1.5	4.5	7.5	13.5 (9.5%)
Tolman	6.5	2.5	3.5	12.5 (8.8%)
Bridges	4.0	2.5	3.5	10.0 (7.0%)
Main	1.5	4.5	3.0	9.0 (6.3%)
Total	68.5	37.0	37.0	142.9 (100.0%)
Average/Judge	7.6	4.1	4.1	15.8

According to table 12.1, Judges Pemberton, Holcomb, and Mackintosh were above the average of 15.8 disagreements per judge, and Judges Main and Bridges were below.

The nine jurists heard an average of 589 causes per year, wrote 548 court opinions and rendered forty-two *per curiam* decisions. Despite the effort to rotate the assignments, the sharing of the writing responsibilities varied. The average number of majority opinions per judge for the year was sixty-one (see table 12.2). Judges Tolman, Bridges, and Fullerton wrote more court opinions than the

Table 12.2
Number of Majority Opinions per Judge (yearly average)

Judge	Opinions
Tolman	73.5
Bridges	70.0
Fullerton	69.0
Parker	66.0
Holcomb	63.0
Mitchell	60.0
Mackintosh	57.5
Pemberton	56.0
Main	32.5
Total	547.5
Court average	60.8

Table 12.3
Interagreement Percentages

	Bridges	Mitchell	Parker	Tolman	Fullerton	Mackintosh	Holcomb	Pemberton
Main	85	76	72	69	69	63	52	39
Bridges		71	67	67	56	62	59	33
Mitchell			67	66	65	60	59	33
Parker				60	65	45	55	46
Tolman					60	57	60	46
Fullerton						50	48	24
Mackintosh							52	38
Holcomb								39

Court average: 57%
Sprague criterion: 78%

others, and Judges Main, Mackintosh, and Pemberton tended to write fewer.

Finally, the levels of agreement varied between and among the judges. Table 12.3 reports the percentage of agreements between each pair of judges over the two-year period. Actually, as indicated earlier, the vast majority of the court's cases were decided by a unanimous bench. In only 15% of all the cases was there any disagreement. But in those cases where the judges could not all agree on either the outcome of the cases or the reasons for a particular outcome, a pattern of interagreement developed. Judges Bridges, Mitchell, and Main formed a fairly distinct group agreeing with each other in over 75% of the divided cases. Judges Fullerton and Pemberton agreed in only one-fourth of these contentious cases and Judges Mitchell and Bridges concurred with Pemberton in only one-third of the cases.

These tables suggest several judicial relationships that need explaining. First, why the difference between Judges Pemberton and Main in their levels of dissonance? Why did Judges Tolman and Bridges write more opinions and Pemberton and Main fewer? Finally, why were Judges Main, Mitchell, and Bridges so often in accord and Judge Pemberton isolated from Judges Fullerton, Bridges, and Mitchell?

Some of the behavioral trends can be explained to some degree by the structural characteristics of Court 2. Judge Main served as chief justice during the two-year period studied. As chief he was responsible for a number of administrative tasks (largely involved with coordinating the two departments) and, thus, was relieved of a full decisional load. He was obligated to render only half of the opinions for which each of his colleagues was responsible. (Main's total writing assignments—32.5—were half of the court's average for each judge.) The chief justice also had the lowest dissonance level. As chief he was the presiding officer at departments, *en banc* proceedings, and conference deliberations. He determined the panel membership and assigned the court opinions in the more contentious cases.[9] Thus, he had the prime responsibility for coordination, compromise, and communication. Apparently, he viewed his role as working toward a court that was effective, cohesive, and authoritative. As such, he was compelled to seek compromise and to avoid disagreement as much as possible, and his own behavior reflected that compulsion. Also as chief his tasks were sufficiently time consuming, perhaps preventing him from giving the necessary consideration to the writing of dissents. Much of Main's behavior reported in the tables, then, can be explained by his role as chief justice under the departmental system.

The dissent rate increased over the earlier court for the simple reason that nine rather than five judges constituted the high bench. The probabilities for at least one dissent increased as the number of participants in the deliberations increased. But the increased caseload imposed on the court had its impact on the nature of these dissents. Not only did the length of majority opinions decrease, but more judges dissented with a simple "I dissent," without any explanation. The few dissents that were accompanied by explanations failed to match the previous court's in length. Actually the dissenting opinion had fallen into disuse if not disrepute. Judge Fullerton expressed the prevailing attitude:

> I am compelled to dissent from the conclusion reached by the majority in the foregoing opinion. Since, however, all of my brothers have joined therein, I feel that it would be a useless task to express the reasons for my conclusion at length.[10]

9. The departmental feature permitted the chief to make changes in panel membership that led to better balances within as well as between the departments. For example, the switch of Mitchell and Bridges for Parker and Tolman during the second year studied offset the liberal leanings of Department 2.

10. *Spokane and Eastern Trust Co.* v. *Hart* (127 WASH. 541, 1923, at 557).

Others may have argued that the situation the judge described was exactly one in which reasons for dissent should be recorded.

Judge William Pemberton stood out in Court 2 as the leading dissenter and, apart from the chief justice, as writing the fewest number of majority opinions. Since the drafting assignments were made on a rotation basis in conference but always to a member of the preliminary majority, it must be assumed that Pemberton was simply not persuasive or flexible enough to create or hold a majority of the judges. In 1924 the legal establishment played a significant role in defeating Judge Pemberton at the polls and, again, in 1926 preventing him from returning to the high bench. The organized bar regarded him as "radical" and as representing the extremist elements of the labor movement and leftist "class interests"; a representation wholly unacceptable to the attorneys, and unacceptable to the bench as well.[11]

Pemberton held strong liberal beliefs in support of labor and the working person. In his dissent in a workers compensation decision, these feelings were expressed:

> We have a man in every way physically strong, receiving an injury, and from that time on had undergone four operations and spent a large portion of his time in the hospital and doctors concede that his condition may result from the injury; and in the face of his testimony, the trial court and the Department refuse to recognize his claim. The law takes away a common law right of the working man. It deprives him of the right of trial by jury, and should be liberally construed in the interest of the unfortunate working man who receives an injury.[12]

Given the general attitudes toward labor held by the profession (if not by the general public), due in part to the image of the I.W.W. prior to and during the First World War, it was not surprising that Pemberton appeared to be a threat as a member of the state's court of last resort.

Judges Tolman and Bridges assumed leadership positions on Court 2, along, of course, with Chief Justice Main. Tolman wrote more of the court's opinions (73.5) than any other judge. He was able to keep a majority of his brethren's votes in those cases assigned him as well as to receive most of the reassignments when agreement was missing during the preliminary consideration of a case. Judge Bridges was the "swing man" in contentious cases, voting with the

11. See *The Seattle Daily Times*, August 19, 1924. Also for a discussion of Pemberton's campaign see Chapter 4.
12. *Tomovich* v. *Department of Labor and Industries* (126 WASH. 27, 1923, at 289).

majority, dissenting only occasionally and writing many of the court's opinions.

The ideological tendencies of the judges help explain to some extent the relationships among and between them. The liberals on the bench—Judges Pemberton, Tolman, and Parker—were prone to cast their vote in conference and to write or sign opinions that supported the injured in negligence cases, the accused in criminal matters, the government in regulation issues, the public interest in property disputes, and generally for the "underdog" in cases brought to the court. Judges Fullerton, Mackintosh, and Mitchell tended to adhere to the conservative approach and, consequently, voted in opposition. Judges Main, Holcomb, and Bridges, as moderates, held the balance on the bench. They could often be found agreeing with Tolman in one case and Fullerton in another.

Judge Fullerton appeared to have shifted from his moderate to liberal stance in Court 1. Much of this apparent switch was due to the new membership on the bench representing more liberal stances and the conservative members (such as Mackintosh) actually tending more toward the center than the conservatives on the earlier court. Judge Fullerton was still a team player, however. He did not dissent to any great degree, and he wrote more than his share of the court's decisions.

The concern for private property was often expressed by the entire bench, but certainly by the conservatives. For example, Judge Mackintosh reminded his colleagues that

> The right of every individual to engage in any lawful business cannot be prohibited, unless that prohibition is based on some condition existing in the business which the court finds to be interfering with the public morals, health, safety or welfare.[13]

The danger of such an approach, of course, was that the courts rather than the legislatures were tempted to assume responsibility for defining public morals, health, and so forth.

On the other hand, the liberals tended to accept the regulatory statutes that emerged from a fairly progressive legislature. Judge Parker, for example, in *Spokane I.E.R.* v. *Spokane County,* reflected the court's considerable tolerance of taxing powers, even though the railroad had claimed that the taxes were illegal, arbitrary, and confiscatory.

13. *Northwest National Ins. Co.* v. *Fishback* (130 WASH. 490, 1924, at 493).

> [T]he ascertaining of the value of the property of a railroad for purposes of taxation is so closely akin to the subject of regulation of such public service corporations as to bring this provision within the comprehensive though brief language of the [law].[14]

And, therefore, the taxes were allowable.

Judicial Backgrounds

Perhaps a review of the backgrounds and experiences of judges will provide explanations for some of their behaviors and relationships. Even a quick review of table 12.4 leaves the impression that few of the backgrounds and experiences of the judges on Court 2 account for their behaviors during the years studied. Whether a judge was elected or appointed, had received his legal training from a law school or from having clerked, was politically active or inactive, or had been a former judge at the trial level failed to explain much.

A slight tendency can be discerned regarding the association between political party affiliation and ideology. Except for Judge Mitchell, the Democrats tended to be liberal or moderate; except for Judge Parker, the Republicans tended to be conservative or moderate. Given the wide diversity in backgrounds, the divisiveness of Court 2 is understandable, especially in comparison with the homogeneous membership of the 1903–4 court.

From time to time the judges displayed their disagreements in impatient if not intemperate references in their opinions. For example, Judge Holcomb, who sometimes could be as uncooperative as Judge Pemberton, penned an angry dissent aimed more at chastising his colleagues than convincing them:

> By the majority decision the disintegration of the probate code of 1917 is begun. . . . Their reasoning is wholly inconsistent and illogical. . . . It is positively legislating and creating disqualifications which the statutes did not create. . . . The majority opinion is manifestly wrong.[15]

Or Judge Tolman, in a more conciliatory but still direct one, wrote simply: "It seems to me that the majority opinion overlooks the simple governing points in this case."[16]

14. 75 WASH. 72, 1913, at 85.

15. *In Re Langill's Estate* (117 WASH. 268, 1920, at 270, 274). It is interesting to note that Judge Bridges, who was largely responsible for drafting the 1917 probate code, voted with the majority.

16. *Finch* v. *Sprague* (117 WASH. 650, 1920, at 658).

Table 12.4
Backgrounds of Court 2

Justice	*Elected or Appointed*	*Party*	*Locale*	*Legal Education*	*Political Experience*	*Legal Experience*	*Ideology*
Pemberton	E	D	Bellingham	Clerk	None	Superior Court	Liberal
Holcomb	E	D	Ritzville	Chicago-Kent	Much	Superior Court	Moderate
Fullerton	E	R	Colfax	Clerk	Some	Private practice	Conservative
Mitchell	A	D	Olympia	Clerk	Some	Superior Court	Conservative
Tolman	A	D	Spokane	Northwestern	Much	Private practice	Liberal
Parker	A	R	Tacoma	Cincinnati	None	Superior Court	Liberal
Bridges	A	R	Aberdeen	Clerk	Some	Private practice	Moderate
Main	A	R	Seattle	Michigan	None	Superior Court	Moderate
Mackintosh	A	R	Seattle	Columbia	Some	Superior Court	Conservative

Summary: Court 2 and Cohesion, Effectiveness, and Authority

The most striking characteristic of Court 2 was its low level of cohesion. But for several procedural features (such as transferring troublesome cases to the full court for a more thorough study) and for the efforts of chief justice Main, it might have been lower. The judges met their increased loads, but largely at the expense of less thorough opinions and especially of fewer responsible dissenting opinions.

The diverse backgrounds of the jurists contributed to their often divergent views but also to the public image of the court. Nearly all of the judges were highly regarded even before they came on the bench. Main had been a University of Washington law professor, and a considerable number of his former students now practiced in the state. Mackintosh, as King County prosecutor, had professionalized the office, freeing it from most political considerations. Bridges had been president of the Washington State Bar Association. Mitchell was superior court judge of Thurston County, responsible for presiding over the important cases involving state government. Parker was a charter member of the American Law Institute. Fullerton had served on the high bench before the turn of the century. Holcomb and Tolman had been respected public officials. The former was a member of the governor's cabinet, and the latter a leader in the legislature who was largely responsible for establishing the State Railroad Commission. Pemberton had served with distinction on the trial bench and had the support of labor and the Grange. These were well known and respected members of the legal and political communities. This respect undoubtedly contributed to a favorable public image of the state's court of last resort.

No matter how respected the judges were, however, they inevitably were confronted with the perennial challenge of accountability vs. independence. In the long run, how they met this challenge had more to do with their image than any of their past experiences. In *State Ex. Rel. Reclamation Board* v. *Clausen*, the judges recognized this tension. Judge Parker wrote for the majority that a particular tax was constitutional if designed for the public interest. He realized clearly the policy implications of the decision:

> That such a question, when arising in the courts, has proven so vexatious is, we apprehend, because of its inherent nature in that, in its last analysis, it is not one of exclusive legal logic, but is one more or less of policy and wisdom, properly determinable in the light of public welfare, present and future, in a broad sense; and hence is not a pure judicial law question.[17]

17. 110 Wash. 525, 1920, at 532.

Casting their lot with the legislature and public accountability, the majority accepted the taxing measure as constitutional. However, Judge Mackintosh would have none of it:

> It is needless to prolong a discussion already too ambiguous. On principle, and under the authorities, I cannot agree that a public purpose is being served by this attractive bit of paternalistic legislation, and therefore dissent.[18]

For Mackintosh, judicial independence meant he should decide what he felt was right despite what the representatives of the public—the legislature—claimed was correct.

The judges of Court 2 began to give closer scrutiny to legislation which appeared to be in the public interest. No longer was it assumed that the legislature was always correct. Of course, the court majority was far from a run-away activist bench. Most often the intent of the framers of the legislation was determined and followed. Nonetheless, in comparison to the earlier Court 1, these jurists were more prone to exercise a greater degree of judicial independence. The accountability vs. independence conflict was actually intensified.

An opinion filed at the end of the period represented by Court 2 suggested both sides of the conflict. Some judges had resisted the temptation to act as policy makers, but others had not. Some critics of the court thought litigants were lured to the courts to achieve ends unattainable through the ordinary political processes. Judge Henry E. T. Herman penned a revealing dissent in *Municipal League of Bremerton* v. *Tacoma*:

> It is quite apparent the real purpose of appellant's brief is to persuade this court to . . . accomplish the result which was attempted but not achieved by the proponents of 22 bills introduced in the legislature. . . .
>
> Since then . . . one initiative measure and one referendum act having the same object have been submitted to the people and defeated at the polls. To fail to recognize this case as a fictitious lawsuit and order its dismissal as such . . . is to inspire interested parties to attempt to accomplish in the courts what they could not achieve in the legislature or by a vote of the people.[19]

But Judge Herman's warning had for the moment been ignored.

18. *Ibid.*, 546. Also see his dissenting opinion in *Washington Cranberry Growers Assn's.* v. *Moore* (117 Wash. 441, 1920, at 452).
19. 155 Wash. 82, 1931, at 91.

13

The Court of 1939–40

The 1939–40 Deliberative Process

The decision-making procedures of Court 3 did not differ substantially from the earlier benches. The court was still divided into two panels with the chief justice presiding in both. One department sat for a week and then the other, giving all but the chief a week off from hearing cases. However, these one-week breaks were used to research and draft opinions and to consult informally with colleagues.

One of the first three law clerks to serve with the court, John N. Rupp, recalled the decisional sequence when he worked for the judges in 1937:

> The Court normally heard six cases a day, two in the morning and four in the afternoon. At about 5:00 or 5:30 P.M. the Court would rise, and the judges would go into consultation to discuss the day's cases, arrive at a tentative conclusion and assign cases for opinion. Opinion assignment normally went in rotation, but if the judge to whom the opinion would normally be assigned was not in agreement with the tentative majority, the rotation, would be altered. Along about 7:30 P.M. the day would be over, and the judges would go home for dinner and get ready for the next day's six cases.[1]

The only structural change in the decisional process was the use of law clerks. Three were hired in 1937 as an experiment to assist the judges in their tasks and, thereby, to contribute to the effectiveness of the bench. One was assigned to the chief justice and the other two helped several of the remaining judges. Some judges worked with-

1. John N. Rupp, "How It Used to Be: The Supreme Court's Law Clerks" (unpublished memoir, n.d., Department of Political Science, Washington State University).

out clerks.[2] Although their tasks varied, depending upon the desires and needs of each judge, generally the clerks prepared memoranda on the cases to be heard (prehearing memos) and researched and drafted opinions assigned to their judges.[3] As in Court 2, an opinion from one department was circulated among the members of the other department for their approval. The final opinion was issued as though it were for the entire court, although in fact it was the product of only one panel and went into the *Washington Reports* with only that panel members' signatures affixed.

The Interaction System of Court 3

Judge Main was the only holdover from the 1923–24 Court. Given their varied attitudes and backgrounds, the relations between and among the judges made this court unique.

The judges of Court 3 disposed of fewer cases than the previous court and recorded more disagreements. The yearly average of written opinions (majority and *per curiam*) was 323. Yet seventy-five separate dissenting opinions were filed (including the two-worded "I dissent" without any further explanation). In over one-fourth of all the cases heard, the members of Court 3 expressed some form of dissonance (dissenting opinions, dissenting votes, separate concurring opinions, or concurring votes). Table 13.1 reports the incidents of dissonance attributed to each of the judges.[4] Even though (or perhaps because) he served as chief justice, Bruce Blake had the highest level of dissonance, accounting for over one-fourth of all the disagreements and 38% of the dissenting opinions. Also Judge William Millard, on the bench since 1928, accounted for more than his share of the disagreements.

Except for Chief Justice Blake and Judge James Geraghty, the opinion writing load was shared nearly equally among the judges (see table 13.2).

Table 13.3 indicates that Judges Simpson, Robinson, Jeffers, and

2. The first three clerks were John N. Rupp, Ernest H. Campbell, and Robert Read. For an analysis of law clerks with the Washington Supreme Court see Charles H. Sheldon, "Law Clerking with a State Supreme Court: Views from the Perspective of the Personal Assistants to the Judges," *Justice System Journal* 6 (Fall 1981):346.

3. For a description of the tasks assigned to law clerks, see John Rupp's account of his duties as quoted in chapter 9, note 30, *supra.*

4. Judge Holcomb retired from Court 3 on January 9, 1939, and a few of his cases in which he participated were subsequently filed. Judge Jeffers succeeded him on the same day. Judge Geraghty died on April 29, 1940, to be succeeded by Samuel Driver on May 9, 1940, and, thus, did not participate in the full two years. Figures for Holcomb and Driver are recorded separately but are counted as part of the court total.

Table 13.1
Dissonance Rate: Court 3 (yearly average)

Judge	*Dissenting Opinions*	*Dissenting Votes*	*Concurring Opinions-Votes*	*Total Disagreements*
Blake	28.5	14.0	6.5	49.0 (26.6%)
Millard	10.0	10.5	6.0	26.5 (14.4%)
Main	7.0	15.0	1.5	23.5 (12.8%)
Beals	8.5	5.5	6.5	20.5 (11.1%)
Steinert	8.0	6.0	5.0	19.0 (10.3%)
Simpson	5.5	6.0	2.0	13.5 (7.3%)
Robinson	2.5	9.5	1.5	13.5 (7.3%)
Geraghty	4.0	3.5	2.0	9.5 (5.1%)
Jeffers	0.5	2.5	2.0	5.0 (2.7%)
Holcomb	0.0	1.0	0.0	1.0 (.5%)
Driver	0.5	1.0	1.5	3.0 (1.6%)
Total	75.0*	74.5	34.5	184.0 (100.0%)
Average/Judge	8.3	8.3	3.8	20.4

*Total includes second dissenting opinions in single cases.

Table 13.2
Number of Majority Opinions per Judge (yearly average)

Main	39.0
Millard	39.0
Simpson	39.0
Steinert	38.0
Beals	37.5
Robinson	36.0
Jeffers	35.5
Geraghty	24.0
Blake	20.5
Holcomb	1.0
Driver	2.5
Total	312.0
Court average	35.0

Table 13.3
Interagreement Percentages

	Simpson	Jeffers	Steinert	Geraghty	Beals	Millard	Main	Blake
Robinson	84	76	62	58	51	44	44	22
Simpson		76	80	50	56	53	43	20
Jeffers			71	69	58	52	52	33
Steinert				51	49	47	47	19
Geraghty					75	52	51	45
Beals						42	43	30
Millard							56	38
Main								64

Court average: 51%
Sprague criterion: 74%

Steinert agreed in three-fourths of the cases involving a division among the members, and Judges Beals and Geraghty formed a pair that also went along with each other 75% of the time. Considering that in those split decisions (involving dissent and concurrences as well) the court average was only 51%, the 75% agreement level is impressive.

Several questions are generated by tables 13.1, 2, and 3. First, why the high dissonance level from Chief Justice Blake and why such a low level from Jeffers? Second, why the particular distribution of majority opinion assignments found in table 13.2? Finally, why the high interagreement percentage among Judges Robinson, Simpson, Jeffers, and Steinert, as well as between Judges Beals and Geraghty?

Again, as in Court 2, part of the interaction behavior can be explained by Blake's perception of his role as chief justice. He was assigned only half as many opinions as his colleagues because of the demands placed on him as presiding officer and coordinator of the court's two departments. However, the chief recorded the highest dissonance rate of all courts thus far.

Judge Blake had developed a reputation as a dissenter since his election in 1932. As chief this practice did not abate, suggesting that

Blake failed to accept the role of conciliator and compromiser exemplified by Chief Justice Main on Court 2. Rather than attaching special significance to his role of chief, Blake simply continued or intensified the dissonance practice he so often had displayed previously. Judge Harry Ellsworth Foster provided a telling clue about Blake's behavior:

> He found himself frequently in dissent, but he never dissented for dissent alone and never without clearly stating his reasons. He held many unorthodox views, for, in fact, he was an iconoclast, but was exceedingly tolerant of those who did not share his views. . . .
>
> He firmly believed in Holmes' philosophy that the life of the law has not been logic but experience, and because he did take the pains to state the reasons for his dissents, it may still come to pass that future generations of judges will regard his dissenting opinions as the more persuasive.[5]

Blake saw the dissenting opinion as performing two functions. First, a judge who was unable to convince his colleagues at the moment should make an appeal to the "intelligence of a future day" when some later judge may recognize the wisdom of the dissent. Each important dissent, then, must be accompanied by the appropriate reasoning in order to provide directions to subsequent courts. Second, Blake interpreted the Article IV admonishment that the "grounds of the decision" should be stated in writing to mean dissenting opinions as well. Blake's dissents flowed from his strongly held liberal-activist ideology. Ben Kizer, a leading Spokane attorney and friend of the judge, isolated Blake's ideological stance:

> He had a deep sympathy with the underprivileged that caused him to be liberal in his political convictions, and a strong desire to see their wrongs righted, helping whenever he could, no less in the field of politics, where, as judge, he could not take an active part, than in the halls of justice where he pled their cause, first as a lawyer, then as jurist, with the deepest earnestness and conviction.
>
> If an earlier decision of the Court seemed to him to pay too much deference to the ancient rigidities of the law, he did not hesitate to declare that it should be overruled.[6]

Blake tended to cast his judicial vote for the underdog and for government intervention in order to improve the condition of the

5. Memorial Services, Wn. 2d, xxix–xxx (1957).
6. *Ibid.*, p. xxvi.

ordinary person. Simply because he was largely alone in his view of the law, he was pushed into disagreement with his brethren.

The explanation for the strong accord among Judges Robinson, Simpson, Jeffers, and Steinert lies in their affinity toward a conservative ideology. With the support of one or both of the "swing" judges, Beals and Geraghty, the conservatives usually won on those issues that divided the court, with Blake (and Main) left in isolation.[7]

Figure 13.1 portrays the relative position of the nine members of Court 3 along a liberal-conservative continuum.[8] Illustrative of the

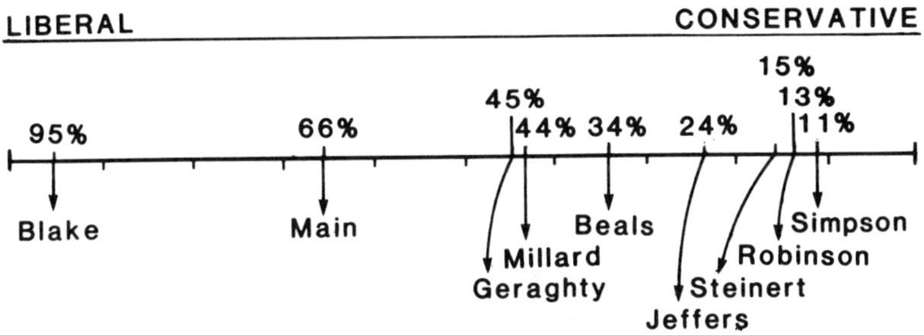

Fig. 13.1. Relative positions of judges on a liberal-conservative continuum, 1939–40

7. Two measures were used to determine the liberal-conservative leanings of the judges. First, the judges' vote in divided cases presenting issues along conservative-liberal lines were compiled. For example, in workers compensation and negligence cases, conservatives would tend to vote against the alleged injured party. In criminal cases conservatives would vote for the state and against the accused. In taxation and government regulation cases conservatives would tend to reject the tax or regulation if it threatened private property. Second, surveys of experienced appellate attorneys and of former law clerks to the judges were conducted, and their reactions to the conservative-liberal leanings of judges solicited. In all cases, except the few mentioned, the lawyers and clerks' appraisal coincided with the author's compilation of the voting behavior of the judges in those split decisions of the court.

8. The compiling of votes on those cases that presented a clear liberal-conservative issue during the two-year period of Court 3 led to the liberal percentages being assigned each judge. The percentages represent the number of times the judge voted in a liberal direction. A 1977 survey of two-hundred appellate attorneys who had presented five or more cases to the state's high bench over the years and a survey of 166 law clerks largely agreed with the above ranking except that Judge Main was regarded as conservative and Millard more liberal. On a scale of 1 to 3 (1 being liberal and 3 being conservative) the following ranking was compiled from the clerk-attorney surveys: Millard, 1.6; Blake, 1.7; Geraghty, 2.2; Beals, 2.5; Robinson, 2.5; Jeffers, 2.5; Steinert, 2.6; Main, 2.7; and Simpson, 2.8. Possible explanations for Millard's liberalism and the placing of Main among the conservatives lie in the fact that the surveys were not limited to where the respondents thought the judges might be placed in 1939–40, but rather their philosophy over their entire careers. Of the two hundred attorneys and 166 law clerks in the surveys, only a few remembered the earlier judges. Only five clerks could respond to the rating of Main while only forty-two attorneys ventured a guess on his ideological leanings.

liberal view of the law was Judge Blake's dissent (joined by the liberal to moderate Main, Millard, and Geraghty) in a workmen's compensation case:

> The ultimate physical facts upon which this case should turn are undisputed: (1) injury sustained in course of employment in extra-hazardous industry, (2) followed by steadily increasing physical impairment which culminates in total disability. To accept in face of these undisputed facts, the opinion of medical experts that there is no causal connection between the injury and the total disability, is to set at naught the rule of law established and applied in cases cited above. I dissent.[9]

In contrast, Judge Simpson represented the conservative approach in such cases. In dissenting on another case (joined by fellow conservatives Robinson, Steinert, and moderate Beals), Simpson wrote:

> To hold that relatives of a deceased employee may secure the benefits of the law when that employee dies on the job because of ordinary exertion and without the happening of an accident, makes for extra hazardous occupations a mecca for all ailing workmen who, by securing employment in occupations covered by the act, may obtain life insurance without the payment of premiums.[10]

The accord between Judges Beals and Geraghty can be attributed to their close location on the ideological continuum and to their positions as buffers between the liberals and conservatives. They often provided the deciding votes in cases that divided the court.

Judge Jeffers had the lowest dissonance rate on Court 3. He had been elected to the high bench in 1938 and assumed his seat on January 9, 1939. Although he had years of experience as county prosecutor and superior court judge, he likely was reluctant to take a separate posture on the court, at least in the beginning. As a new member of the bench, he kept a low profile and behaved somewhat like the "backbencher" in legislative bodies, learning his role and gaining acceptance before acting independently.[11] Also by many accounts, Judge Jeffers' personality lent itself to this accommodating role. Compromise and agreement suited him much more than contention and dissent. Attorney Clifford Moe, who knew Jeffers from the early days in Ephrata, recalled that Jeffers

9. *Hoff* v. *Department of Labor and Industries* (198 WASH. 257, 1939, at 267).
10. *Bergagna* v. *Department of Labor and Industries* (199 WASH. 263, 1939, at 284–85).
11. For similar behavior on the U.S. Supreme Court, see Eloise Snyder, "The Supreme Court as a Small Group," *Social Forces* 36 (March 1952):232.

> was truly a kindly man and was deeply religious. . . . He was blessed with a complete lack of envy, insincerity, or suspicion of actions or motives of others. . . . Many are the times that the quality of his kindness was demonstrated in his Court.

And fellow judge, E. W. Schwellenbach, remembered that he was friendly. He was patient. He was tolerant. He was without guile. He was always without prejudice. He never indulged in personalities.[12]

The distribution of opinion-writing assignments recorded in table 13.2 fails to indicate leadership on the bench.[13] Blake, as chief justice, wrote his share of the majority opinions which was half of those assigned others. Jeffers came on the bench at the beginning of the 1939 term and had not heard oral arguments in a few of the earlier cases. He fell slightly behind his colleagues at first but soon was carrying his share of the assignments. Geraghty's illness and death in April 1940 explained his below-average number of opinions. Neither conservatives nor liberals dominated the assignments. About all that can be inferred from table 13.2 is that perhaps there were few changes of mind after the conference vote, and that the circulation of concurring and dissenting opinions rarely changed minds. The assigning of opinions in rotation after the preliminary vote in conference was designed to equalize the workload. For Court 3 it worked.

Backgrounds

Perhaps some understanding of the ideological leanings of the members of Court 3 can be gained from looking at their backgrounds and experiences. The hypothesis is that similar ideologies flow from similar backgrounds. (See table 13.4.)

What is striking about table 13.4 is that no pattern is discernible that would associate experiences and ideology. Some hidden attributes apparently were responsible for the ideological leanings and behavior of the members of Court 3. Although such a study goes beyond what is summarized here, a careful review of the individual

12. 50 Wn. 2d xxxi and xxxiii (1957).

13. The voting records of the judges suggest leadership. For example, in 1939, Judge Jeffers gained an average of 4.1 votes whenever he wrote an opinion (whether *en banc* or department, dissenting, concurring, or majority). At the other extreme, Chief Justice Blake gathered only an average of 2.2 votes whenever he penned an opinion. The breakdown for the court was as follows: Jeffers, 4.1; Robinson, 3.9; Simpson, 3.8; Geraghty, 3.7; Beals, 3.5; Steinert, 3.4; Main 3.4; Millard, 3.4; and Blake, 2.2.

Table 13.4
Backgrounds of Court 3

Justice	*Elected or Appointed*	*Party*	*Locale*	*Legal Education*	*Political Experience*	*Legal Experience*	*Ideology*
Blake	E	D	Spokane	Michigan	None	Superior Court	Liberal
Main	*E	R	Seattle	Michigan	None	Superior Court	Liberal
Geraghty	A	D	Spokane	Georgetown	Much	City Attorney	Moderate
Millard	A	R	Olympia	Georgetown	None	Law Librarian	Moderate
Beals	A	R	Seattle	U. of Washington	None	Superior Court	Moderate
Jeffers	E	R	Ephrata	U. of Iowa	Some	Superior Court	Conservative
Steinert	A	R	Seattle	Michigan	None	Superior Court	Conservative
Robinson	E	R	Seattle	Columbia	None	Superior Court	Conservative
Simpson	A	D	Vancouver	Willamette	None	Superior Court	Conservative

*Main was appointed after having won a write-in election.

biographies of the nine judges might suggest hypotheses explaining each of their approaches to the law.

Structures

The one structural change wrought on Court 3 was the inclusion of law clerks into the deliberative process in order to increase the effectiveness of the court. Three clerks served the court throughout 1939, and three more were hired for the 1940 term.[14] Judges Blake, Main, Geraghty, and Millard worked without clerks during this period. Thus, a rough test of the clerk's contribution to the court could be gained by comparing the output of these judges with those who used clerks.

The distribution of opinion writing, reported in table 13.2, provides clues as to the impact of law clerking on the effectiveness of the court. The group of judges using clerks wrote an average of thirty-six of the majority opinions and the judges without clerks wrote thirty-seven. Therefore, the addition of clerks appears not to encourage the writing of more majority opinions. Also, as table 13.5 suggests, the judges who wrote the dissents were those who did not have a clerk assigned them.

By tabulating the average number of months and days between the lower courts' ruling and the filing of the high courts' opinions, an indication of the differences in the "expeditiousness" between the two groups of judges is provided. The average number of pages devoted to each opinion suggests the relative "thoroughness" of the two groups. Table 13.5 reports the results.

The law clerks' contribution to court effectiveness was not in expediting the resolution of cases but rather in the thoroughness given the written decisions. The judges with clerks wrote longer opinions which likely were also more thorough opinions.

Public Accountability vs. Judicial Independence

The prevailing issue was still a tension between whether the judges should disregard the agencies representing popular democracy, primarily the legislature, and determine public policy themselves, or

14. The 1939 clerks were William Lowry (who later became the Clerk for the Supreme Court), Ernest Campbell and Robert Reid (both of whom were among the original three in 1937). Reid stayed on in 1940 and Max Kaminoff, Jack H. Jaffee, Lamar N. Ostrander, Frank Foley, and William Blevens joined the court as "elbow clerks" to the judges. The full impact of the clerks on Court 3 was felt in 1940. The data are gathered from the last two volumes of the 1940 term when six clerks were working for the Court (Volumes 5 and 6, Wn. 2d were used).

Table 13.5
Clerks' Contribution to Effectiveness

	Expeditiousness	*Thoroughness*
Nonclerk judges	9 months, 14 days	7.1 pages/opinion
Clerk judges	9 months, 24 days	11.1 pages/opinion

follow the desires of the representatives of the people. It was an issue of judical activism (independence) vs. self-restraint (accountability).

In Court 3 the activists were found on both ends of the ideological spectrum. For example, conservative George Simpson echoed the arguments of the "Four Horsemen" of the U.S. Supreme Court, who fought so hard against the efforts of the New Deal in the 1930s:

> If constitutional, legislation such as now before us presages extension of the police power which bids fair to take from our citizens all the personal liberties and rights of private property hitherto considered to be guaranteed by our state and federal constitutions. This act destroys the ideal of free enterprise which has been the dominant spirit of American progress. It is contrary to the wording and ideas contained in our . . . constitutions.[15]

But in the same case Jeffers remarked that:

> With the wisdom of the policy adopted, with the adequacy or practicability of the law to enforce it, the courts are both incompetent and unauthorized to deal.[16]

Judge Blake, on the other extreme, was most willing to let courts decide issues which others would leave to legislators or other public officials. In one workman's compensation case the answer was clear to him:

> Plaintiff was 39 years old at the time of his injury and weighed between 140–150 pounds. At the time of the hearing in the superior court he weighed 125. . . . That he is suffering from traumatic neurosis and traumatic arthritis seems to me to be established beyond a reasonable doubt. He should long ago have been classified as permanently disabled and placed on the pension rolls.[17]

15. *State* v. *Sears* (4 Wn. 2d, 200, 1940, at 226).
16. *Ibid.*, at 207.
17. *Lalone* v. *Department of Labor and Industries* (3 Wn. 2d, 191, 1940, at 199). See also Blake's dissent in *Eyer* v. *Department of Labor and Industries* (1 Wn. 2d, 553, 1939, at 558).

There were those judges on Court 3 who would grant the utmost deference to the enactments of the legislature and the actions of public officials as well as those who would make policy decisions based upon their view of what was best for the public. Whether a judge was conservative or liberal was not a sure indication that he was an activist or a restraintist. Court 3 can be viewed as a balanced bench regarding the stands taken on public accountability vs. judicial independence.

14

The Court of the 1950s

The Deliberative Process

The 1952–53 court went about its business much in the same manner as preceding benches. The bulk of the decisions were products of five-judge departments only with the troublesome cases going before the full nine-member court. About forty-four of the nearly 260 decisions each year were *en banc* (17%). The chief justice presided over both departments (and was responsible for coordinating them), *en banc* hearings, and all conferences. Because of these added responsibilities, his opinion assignments were half those of his brethren. All members of the bench reviewed and approved a department's decision although it was published in the *Washington Reports* over the names of the panel members only.

As before, cases were assigned by lot by the clerk of court at the beginning of each term. The assigned or "reporting" judge was responsible for reviewing the briefs, record, and authorities for his colleagues prior to oral arguments. A prehearing bench memo was circulated among the judges by the reporting judge. It was usually researched and written by the judge's law clerk. Each of the judges could then be somewhat familiar with the issues during the oral arguments and conference deliberations. At the oral argument stage each side was allowed a half hour to present its case, with the chief extending the time if he felt it useful. Queries from the bench often consumed much of the time in contentious cases. Following oral arguments, the judges moved into secret conference to discuss the cases just heard and to take a tentative vote on the disposition of each. The reporting judge recited first, recommending disposition and giving his reasons, followed by the judge sitting next to him and so on counterclockwise around the table with the chief speaking last.

The opinion drafting assignments were made in conference. If with the majority, the reporting judge wrote the court's opinion. If not with the majority, the judge who first expressed disagreement was given the drafting assignment. Dissents were not assigned although informal agreements were struck. On those few occasions when the reporting judge lost the vote, he usually penned the dissent.

After opinion assignment in conference, the judges returned to chambers to research and draft their opinions. Although the vote could change during the opinion circulation stage, and the dissent could pick up a signature or two and become the majority, rarely did the outcome decided upon in conference change. Judge Weaver, a member of Court 5, described his version of the alternatives available at the opinion drafting and circulation stages:

> When I have been assigned to write an opinion for the Supreme Court when a majority agreed tentatively with my conclusion, I became the constitutional judge to pre-offer a written opinion to the court for consideration.
>
> The other justices had not given up a bit of their judicial power. They still had six alternatives: (1) sign my opinion; (2) write "I concur in the result"; (3) write their own concurring opinion; (4) sign "I dissent"; (5) write their own dissent; [or] (6) sign a dissent written by another.[1]

As suggested by Weaver, little give and take during the circulation stage was evident. When all signatures were accounted for, the opinion was sent to the court reporter's office for headnotes and it, along with any dissents or concurrences, was then "spindled" in the clerk's office, thereby becoming the court's final say on that particular issue—for the time being.

How important to the thinking of the nine members of the court were various decisional "inputs"? According to those law clerks who served over the years with the judges on Court 4 (a total of 77) the judges relied upon the following sources for their final decisions.

Table 14.1 reports that the efforts of the attorneys were clearly important.[2] What they argued and supported in their briefs and how they emphasized the factual situations provided guidance to the

1. An earlier version of this chapter appeared under the title of "The Washington Supreme Court: What It Was Like Thirty Years Ago," *Gonzaga Law Review* 19 (1983/84): 231. The quote is from an undated letter to the author from Judge Weaver.

2. The data in table 14.1 came from a 1977–78 survey of all former law clerks with the Washington Court. (Hereafter cited as Law Clerk Survey.) For an analysis of the data from that survey see Charles Sheldon, "Law Clerking with a State Supreme Court: Views from the Perspective of the Personal Assistants to the Judges," *Justice System Journal* 6 (1981): 346.

Table 14.1
Importance of Decisional Factors

Decisional Factors	*Positive Importance** *(%) (N = 77)*
Written briefs of litigants	76.6
The facts of the case	71.6
Judge's feeling for what is right	70.5
Judge's knowledge of the law	70.2
Research of law clerk	70.2
Judge's own research	63.7
The dictates of precedent	55.9
Research of reporting judge	40.3
The views of the trial court	36.4
Awareness of socio-economic and political environment	32.5
Views of brethren on the bench	28.6
Oral arguments of lawyers	22.0

*"Very important" and "rather important"

judges. But, interestingly, the judges' own skills and attitudes played a nearly equal role. In a very real sense table 14.1 is suggesting that often, when settling issues of public policy, the judges' relied to a significant degree on their own reactions and efforts without reference to the "socio-economic and political environment" even though it was this environment that was affected by many of their decisions.

The decisional process or structures are important to developing an understanding of those influences that bear equally on all members of the bench, but it is the particular mix of individual judges that must be carefully scrutinized.

Interactions on the 1952–53 Bench

In almost one out of five cases (19%) a disagreement was registered by one or more members of the court. In fifty cases out of the total of 258 a dissenting opinion or vote, or a concurring opinion or vote was filed. This 19% dissonance level was lower than the 25% registered by the previous bench. Forty-five separate dissenting opinions were written by the judges (many of the cases included a second and sometimes a third separate dissenting opinion).

This moderate level of cohesion should be viewed as encouraging, considering that the judges had just recently experienced several traumatic years of internal stress and external criticism. The 1947–

48 court was perhaps the most divisive bench to sit in the state's history.[3] The court still suffered from a poor public image and was in the process of rebuilding its authority.[4]

By 1952 Judges Steinert and Jeffers had retired (partially motivated by the internal strife among the judges) and Mallery appeared to have withdrawn somewhat from the public life of the court. Judge Simpson had been removed from the bench by Robert Finley in the 1950 elections. The only carryovers from the 1947–48 crisis years were Judges Mallery, Hill, and Schwellenbach. The court could be characterized, then, as cautiously rebuilding its own confidence and seeking to improve its public image.

The rates of dissonance, as reported in table 14.2, were distributed fairly equally among the jurists. Judge Grady wrote most of the dissents and Weaver the fewest. Judge Schwellenbach had the highest over-all dissonance rate and Mallery the lowest.

Table 14.2
Dissonance Rate: Court 4 (yearly average)

Judge	*Dissenting Opinions*	*Dissenting Votes*	*Concurring Opinions-Votes*	*Total Disagreements*
Schwellenbach	4.5	5.5	7.5	17.5 (15.7%)
Grady	12.0	1.5	3.0	16.5 (14.8%)
Olson	5.5	4.5	5.5	15.5 (13.9%)
Donworth	6.5	4.0	2.5	13.0 (11.7%)
Finley	5.5	3.0	4.0	12.5 (11.2%)
Hill	5.0	4.0	3.5	12.5 (11.2%)
Weaver	1.0	4.5	3.5	9.0 (8.1%)
Hamley	2.5	3.0	2.5	8.0 (7.2%)
Mallery	3.0	3.0	1.0	7.0 (6.3%)
Total	45.5	33.0	33.0	11.5 (100.1%)
Average/Judge	5.0	3.6	3.6	12.4

The average number of written opinions per judge was twenty-seven. As table 14.3 shows, Judge Olson led the court in majority assignments and Judges Grady and Schwellenbach wrote the fewest.

The fairly unusual behavior of Grady and Schwellenbach (high

3. Briefly the legal issue was private vs. public power, but the judicial issue was personal and ethical. See *Wash. St. B. News* 1 (August 1947): 21–23 and 1 (October 1947): 29. See also Chapter 5.

4. Chief Justice Edward Schwellenbach assumed personal responsibility for raising the reputation of the court. He organized a statewide automobile tour in 1952 for the judges and their wives in which they visited with the public, newspaper editors, other judges, and members of the legal profession.

Table 14.3
Number of Majority Opinions per Justice (yearly average)

Olson	34.5
Hamley	30.0
Donworth	30.5
Weaver	30.5
Finley	28.0
Hill	26.0
Mallery	23.5
Grady	22.0
Schwellenbach	16.5
Per curiam	16.0
Total	257.5
Court average	26.8

dissonance and low opinion writing averages) reported in tables 14.2 and 14.3 can be partially attributed to their having shared the responsibilities of chief justice. Schwellenbach was chief in 1952 and Grady took over the position the next year. Thus, both were assigned fewer opinions than their colleagues. Grady wrote twenty-two and Schwellenbach seventeen, nearly half of the court average. (Grady's total exceeded his colleague's simply because many of the opinions from which he was excused would be filed later in 1954 and are not included in the tables). Although they contributed their own particular style to the chief justiceship they behaved to some degree similarly. Both acted in the tradition of Chief Justices from earlier courts. Given the relief from the regular assignment of opinions and given the task of sitting in both panels, they were able to take a broader perspective of the Court's work. They appeared to assume a "devil's advocate" role. By challenging the majority, the court's ultimate output could be strengthened, something about which a chief should be concerned.

Schwellenbach's version of the role was to disagree but to avoid writing a separate dissenting opinion. Dissenting votes and concurring opinions and votes were more appropriate to him. The conference room debate and informal consultation seemed the best forum for the articulate, gregarious, and persuasive Schwellenbach.[5] In contrast, Grady favored the dissenting opinion. Part of Grady's attraction to writing dissents was due to his exceptional ability to pen

5. One of Schwellenbach's law clerks recalled that the judge did not rely on the draft circulation and opinion revision to persuade, but rather "all attempts to 'win over' were in personal contact." Law Clerk Survey.

a quick and concise opinion and get it in circulation rapidly. The extra time and effort involved in writing dissents were not a burden for him. Judge Hill recalled Grady's drafting style: "Almost invariably when a case was assigned to him there was an opinion in circulation within a relatively short period of time, frequently within three or four days."[6]

Judge Grady's son explained how his father's opinions were drafted:

> He would write his own in his own way in long hand. . . . He would write them short. He felt that you shouldn't make a monument out of a case. . . . You should decide the case on its merits and then quit. . . .
> [He wrote] short concise opinions and to the point.[7]

Perhaps, also, Grady recognized that he was put on the bench in 1948 by the legal profession and he owed them conciseness in his opinions.[8]

Judge Weaver had the lowest dissent rate and nearly the lowest dissonance ranking. His attitude toward dissent was that unless a judge felt he was absolutely right on a matter of deep concern he should abstain. One of Judge Weaver's law clerks also noticed the judge's reluctance to pen a dissent:

> I could not understand why he didn't write more dissents. It was more important to him to carry and sway the others than to record his disagreement. He would write a dissent if the majority infringed on one of his prior opinions.[9]

Mallery's view, in contrast, was that dissents had a political purpose. They were "to win over the majority or to win more votes" or "to keep the majority 'honest.'" When he had little chance to convince his brethren he usually dissented without explanation.[10]

6. Memorial Services, 83 Wn. 2d XXIV (1973–74).
7. Author's interview with Thomas E. Grady, Jr., September 21, 1982.
8. Grady's concern for the legal profession was also derived from his presidency of the Washington State Bar Association, from his years as a member of the bar association's admissions committee, and as a person who always took time to help counsel. This concern often found its way into his opinions. For example, in *Paulson* v. *Higgins*, 43 Wn. 2d 81, 1953, at 84, he reminded his colleagues, "We must not overlook the fact that many members of the bar have not yet adjusted themselves to the changes made in our rules."
9. Law Clerk Survey. Of course, by 1953 Weaver had been on the bench only two years and had not yet penned a great number of prior opinions.
10. Author's interview with Judge Mallery, July 8, 1976. One of Judge Mallery's law clerks commented on the judge's reluctance to dissent as follows: "My recollection is that he dissented infrequently and that, when he dissented, he did so briefly and

The interagreement rate between the judges was not altogether low as a court but conversely not significantly high between pairs of judges. Judges Weaver and Olson had the highest rate of agreement, but even their 70% was below what should be regarded as statistically significant. Judge Weaver's explanation for even this level of agreement was that he and Olson "had a lot [of interests] in common. We were rather kindred souls. . . . We never really discussed law very much." The agreement was not a coordinated effort, it just happened.[11]

It apparently was not an accident that Weaver tended to agree with most of his colleagues. A former law clerk for Weaver recalled that:

> The Judge always took notes in conferences of the other judges' feelings and opinions, and, when possible, attempted to persuade and win them over and threw them crumbs in the opinion to satisfy them.[12]

Despite Weaver's efforts, the other members of court simply were not sufficiently drawn together politically, ideologically, or personally to register a significant level of agreement (over 75%) in the problematic cases.

Tables 14.3 and 14.4 suggest that, with the possible exception of Judges Olson and Weaver, no one provided substantial leadership that could pull the court together. Olson wrote more than his share of the court's opinions and apparently won a few cases that were not initially assigned to him. Weaver's leadership was reflected in having the highest interagreement index (see table 14.4). Another view of leadership can be gained by simply dividing all of a judge's opinions by the total number of votes for those opinions. The assumption is that when a judge averages more votes for his decisions than the rest, he was providing some leadership. Table 14.5 records the total number of votes each judge received (department and *en banc*), the total number of opinions he wrote, and the average number of votes per opinion throughout the two-year period of Court 4.

---

sometimes cryptically, but this should not be interpreted as reluctance or disinclination to dissent. He expressed the view on several occasions that most appellate court opinions were too long, that this made for too many volumes of appellate court reports and that frequent and lengthy dissents contributed to this regrettable volume. Accordingly, my impression is that he chose to write a reasoned dissent only when he could get other judges to join him and when the dissent stood a fair opportunity of affecting ultimately a rule of law." One of Mallery's "sayings," and he had many, was "I feel a dissent coming on" (Law Clerk Survey).

11. Interview with Judge Weaver, May 9, 1983.

12. Law Clerk Survey.

Table 14.4
Interagreement Percentages

	Olson	Mallery	Donworth	Hamley	Schwellenbach	Hill	Finley	Grady
Weaver	70	65	65	58	57	54	48	44
Olson		54	55	46	63	57	35	30
Mallery			58	65	55	60	54	51
Donworth				58	42	46	41	40
Hamley					55	61	68	51
Schwellenbach						41	46	37
Hill							49	52
Finley								47

Court average: 52%
Sprague criterion: 75%

What leadership was evident on the court appeared to be provided by Donworth, Schwellenbach, and Olson. However, none stood out as the inspiration for the others. Perhaps this lack of a strong leader helps explain the low effectiveness rating for the court. Actually, the foregoing tables suggest: (1) a highly independent bench with no coalitions or outstanding leadership; and (2) a fairly cohesive group with few serious disagreements. Explanations for the apparently contradictory behavior of the judges may lie in a more detailed look at their individual backgrounds, ideologies, and writing styles.

Backgrounds of Members of the 1952–53 Court

Judges Weaver, Olson, Donworth, and Hamley were all appointed by Governor Langlie and all were Republicans. However, there the similarities ended. Weaver came from a background of private practice in Spokane and from law school teaching. He was on the Gonzaga Law School faculty for twenty-three years and served as dean. He had been somewhat active in Republican affairs. Olson was a former Republican, but had not participated in partisan politics since his election to the Superior Court in 1936. He had been president of the Superior Court Judge's Association. Donworth came from a prominent legal family in Seattle, and his activities had been largely professional, having been president of the Seattle Bar Association in 1934. Hamley was politically active early in his career.

Table 14.5
Leadership Index

Justice	*Total Votes*	*Number of Opinions*	*Average Votes/Opinion*
Donworth	328	61	5.38
Schwellenbach	174	33	5.27
Olson	359	69	5.20
Hamley	309	60	5.15
Weaver	313	61	5.13
Hill	266	52	5.12
Finley	286	56	5.11
Mallery	235	47	5.00
Grady	220	44	5.00

He was a close associate and friend of Governor Langlie since the latter's term as Seattle mayor, serving in both his city and state administrations. He had left the state to accept an appointment as assistant solicitor general for the National Association of Railroad and Utilities Commissioners in 1943, but returned to the state six years later.

Judges Mallery, Schwellenbach, Grady, Hill, and Finley won their seats through elections (although Mallery and Schwellenbach were initially appointed to serve a short term before they began their elected terms). Hill, Grady, and Finley defeated incumbents in fairly hard-fought campaigns. Schwellenbach and Finley were Democrats, and Mallery, Hill, and Grady were Republicans. Finley's experience had been with the federal government and the New Deal of President Roosevelt. Schwellenbach came from a prominent political family in eastern Washington and had been on the superior court bench. Hill had been superior court judge and head of the University of Washington Alumni Association for years. He was fairly active in partisan affairs. Mallery, from Tacoma, had several partisan activities to his credit and had been superior court judge prior to his election. What these details suggest is a highly diverse court, each member bringing to the bench something unique.

Ideologically, the members of the court were also quite diverse. They represented nearly all aspects of two important ideological dimensions of judging: liberal-conservative and activist-restraintist.[13] A conservative judge was apt to view the law as a restraint on,

13. The ideological ratings were compiled from a 1977–78 survey of 166 former law clerks who served the judges, and of two hundred experienced appellate lawyers who over the years had presented five or more cases before the high bench.

rather than an opportunity for, human action. The free enterprise system would be favorably viewed, and a strong "law and order" line toward criminals was regarded as necessary. A liberal judge would tend to adopt contrasting viewpoints. Along the other dimension, a restraintist judge would tend to decide cases on narrow grounds, follow precedent closely, grant deference to the other political branches of government, and avoid controversial economic, social, and political issues as well as eschewing moral judgments. An activist would not be so reluctant to intervene in the political process.

Figure 14.1 shows that the judges tended to cluster around the center of the two ideological spectrums. Finley, Hill, and Donworth, however, represented the extremes in both of the continua. The conservative-restraintists dominate the 1952–53 bench. This domination could help account for the court's average cohesion level. (See table 14.2.)

What figure 14.1 fails to show is that for many judges a conflict between the two ideological dimensions often pushed them further toward the center. For example, Judge Hill's conservatism could have conflicted with his belief that public policy should be left to the political branches of government. Judge Finley could also find himself on the same horns of the dilemma. He might be tempted to act restraintist in order to protect liberal policies enacted by the legislature. He would then argue that courts must follow the dictates of the elected representatives. But he would make this argument most often when these dictates remained fairly consistent with his liberal views. For example, in his dissent in the *Price* case, he stressed the

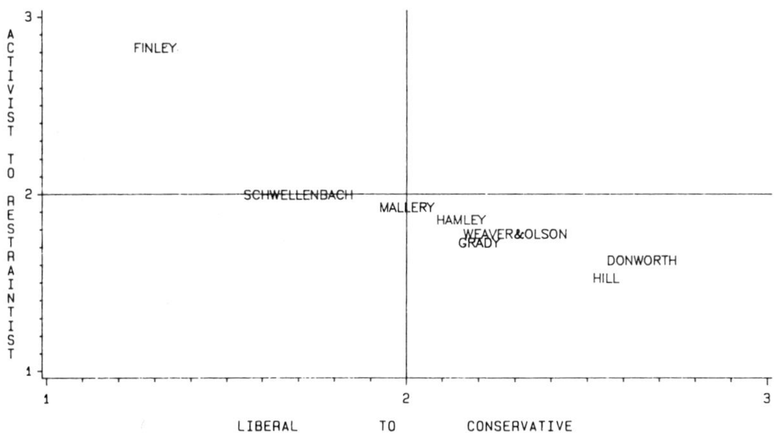

Fig. 14.1. Philosophical positions of judges on Court 4 (Source: Survey of former law clerks and appellate attorneys)

desirability of judicial restraint when the judges were reviewing laws enacted under the police powers of the state. Of course, the liberal intent of the statute made Finley's restraint more acceptable to him. The law read: "It shall be unlawful for any cemetery . . . to refuse burial to any person because such person may not be of the Caucasian race." The majority had upheld the denial of the burial of a small Black child in an all-white "Baby-land" section of a private cemetery. Finley argued:

> When our state legislature has taken action in such a significant area of social policy, such action should not be frustrated by the judicial branch of government unless the grounds therefore are crystal clear. . . . [I]t is my opinion that an exercise of judicial self-restraint is indicated.[14]

In the celebrated "Seat of Government" case of 1954, Hill and Donworth were caught in the restraintist-conservative dilemma. The issue was whether several state agencies headquartered in Seattle violated the state constitution by, in effect, moving the seat of government away from Olympia. A restraintist would argue, as Judge Hill did, that the decision should be left to the legislature, not the courts. In dissent he concluded: "Under our form of government, the location of these offices is a political, not a constitutional, question" (at 115). However, Donworth ignored his restraintist tendencies and choose to intervene. But in the process he displayed a conservative style by researching the "intent of the framers" of the constitution rather than attempting to determine whether moving the agencies was good or effective public policy. For the majority, Donworth wrote:

> In deciding this case, we have interpreted the state constitution in the only manner which appears to us to be reasonable in light of the historical background which its framers and the people who adopted it necessarily must have had in mind at the time.
>
> Some suggestion was made in the oral argument that the constitution should be interpreted liberally in light of present day condition. . . .
>
> The vice of this reasoning is that it destroys the usefulness and the very purpose of a written constitution.[15]

14. *Price* v. *Evergreen Cemetery Co.*, 57 Wn. 2d 352, 1960.
15. *State Ex Rel. Lemon* v. *Langlie*, 45 Wn. 2d 82, 1954, at 109–10.

The "Seat of Government" case illustrated Hill's sacrifice of a conservative approach for restraint and Donworth's rejection of restraint for a conservative application of judicial review.

What is being argued here is that ideological categories were appropriate for understanding some decisions, but that ideological viewpoints often worked at cross-purposes, creating a conflict for the judges. Thus the judges' positions represented in figure 14.1 were not as far apart as they initially appeared. The extreme on one issue tended often to be canceled by the extreme on another. The result was a court of moderation, diverse in background, styles, and ideologies, but moderate when all of these characteristics blended in the decisional process. The several statistical tables reflect this moderation.

Of course, whether the reaction of a jurist was restraintist or activist depended to a great extent upon the kinds of laws that were coming out of the legislature. For example, Donworth would have felt uneasy about refusing to review liberal legislation while Finley would have hesitated to intervene in the same statutes.

Conclusion: Accountability vs. Independence

Issues of public policy and the role of courts in making that policy often confront judges with the question of whether to substitute their ideas of "good" public policy for that of the legislature's or the executive's. Should judges exercise restraint and defer to the other branches of government or be activist and make policy?[16] It is a question of public accountability vs. judicial independence.[17]

One landmark case handed down in 1953 confronted the jurists squarely with the fundamental question of how independent or accountable should they be. A review of this case will give us a sense of the respective approaches of the judges and of the actual dilemma expressed in a concrete dispute.

In *Pierce* v. *Yakima Valley Memorial Hospital Association* (43 Wn. 2d 162, 1953), the court was faced with deciding whether a charitable, non-profit hospital should retain its exemption from liability for the negligence of its employees. A nurse had allegedly injected a foreign substance into a patient's arm, causing pain and injury. The patient sued. Nearly sixty years of practice, a number of precedents, legislative acquiescence, and a recent (1943) supreme court case all reaf-

16. S. Halpern and C. Lamb, *Supreme Court Activism and Restraint* (Lexington, Mass.: Lexington Books, 1982).
17. G. E. White, *The American Judicial Tradition* (New York: Oxford, 1978).

firmed the immunity of such hospitals. The court majority opinion as written by Hamley (supported by Finley, Schwellenbach, Mallery, Weaver, and Olson) reviewed precedent and concluded that the court had already made a public policy decision possibly as early as 1893. Thus,

> The fact that the immunity rule . . . is based upon a declaration of public policy made by our court thirty-five years ago has significance in determining whether we should now reexamine the rule. The factors upon which any public policy is based—the relevant factual situation and the thinking of the times— are not static. They change as conditions change, and as ways of looking at things change. . . .
>
> We therefore believe it to be appropriate, after this lapse of time . . . , to reexamine the public policy there announced, in light of present conditions and present-day thinking.[18]

Hamley admitted that "the public policy upon which our rule is based is legislative in character. It pertains not to the functioning of courts . . . but to broad economic and social considerations." Nonetheless, the majority felt that since the court had originally established the policy, they could disestablish it. "We closed our courtroom doors without legislative help, and we can likewise open them."[19] The majority, then, overruled precedent and withdrew immunity from liability for charitable, nonprofit hospitals in the state.

Judge Grady concurred. He recognized that they had no business substituting their judgment for that of the legislature, but this time, because of his rather arbitrary judicial notice of legislative politics, he would acquiesce. "When immunity from liability is involved, legislatures are faced with strong opposition to change by those who are beneficiaries of such rule, and proponents of a change find efforts to secure corrective legislation futile."[20] Consequently, the court must act.

Judge Hill, in dissent, insisted that "a change in a doctrine which has become fixed as a matter of public policy should be sought from the legislature, regardless of the reason upon which the rule is made

18. 43 Wn. 2d 162 (1953), at 166. In weighing the changes over time, Hamley perhaps inadvertently juxtaposes the implications of considering a "policy" decision with a "legal" decision. The fact that the hospital had liability insurance was, from the legal perspective, irrelevant. "The taking of liability insurance could create no liability where none before existed." But, since it was public policy with which the court was concerned, the fact that "liability insurance is now available . . . is appropriate for consideration."

19. *Ibid.*, 178.

20. *Ibid.*, 180.

to rest."[21] Further, the legislature had not interfered with the rule, resulting in "its acceptance as a public policy."[22] He accused the majority of regarding the immunity policy as "bad policy" and therefore of being intent upon changing it.

Hill recognized the dilemma in which the judges in the majority were caught. They settle disputes but in the process establish policy. Restraintist Hill would have had them withdraw from the former to prevent the latter.

> The instant case presents, . . . an excellent example of why the courts should leave public policy to the legislature. After hearing only the litigants on a matter which affects, directly or indirectly, hundreds of charitable organizations and of which they have had no notice, the majority does what the legislature would not be permitted to do, i.e., change the public policy of the state *ex post facto*.[23]

Judge Donworth, true to his restraintist and conservative views, also took issue with the majority. As a restraintist he decried the majority's rejection of sixty years of practice "encouraging the operations of charitable, non-profit corporations" and of ignoring that the court had "on five separate occasions during the past thirty years"[24] refused to change the policy. Practice and precedent should prevail. However, Donworth's conservatism tended to push him into the legislative role he decried when he asserted:

> [T]he majority opinion bases its determination to abandon our long established policy upon the proposition that private charity has been displaced by a paternalistic government which will furnish free charitable services (as long as the taxpayers are financially able), and that hospitals, Y.M.C.A.s, Boy Scouts, Red Cross chapters, and other similar organizations do not any longer need encouragement. In my opinion, this proposition is without any factual support in this state at the present time.[25]

He remained unconvinced that the "theory of charity is a relic of the horse-and-buggy days." The theory need not be supplanted with the "welfare state."

> The majority's opinion provides an excellent example of the inability of any court to intelligently function on a matter of public policy in

21. *Ibid.*
22. *Ibid.*
23. *Ibid.*, 181.
24. *Ibid.*, 182.
25. *Ibid.*, 182–83.

a case of this kind because of its lack of facilities for ascertaining the necessary factual background.[26]

Again, all the judges were more concerned with accountability and independence than with the factors directly associated with the merits of the case. Hamley and the majority found a number of sources which indicated to them that the public was not only ready for the change but was beginning to demand it. They asserted that public policy, when emanating from the courts, "must be based upon a thorough, developed, persistent, and united state of public mind."[27] In other words, the judges must be accountable to the public. However, at the same time, the court should be independent enough to move ahead without waiting for action from the legislature. Grady had pointed out that such a wait may be long in duration, however.

The dissenters also were cognizant of the tension between accountability and independence. They argued that courts should remain independent from the pressures for a change because of the doctrine of *stare decisis* and "long adherence to the rule." However, courts should also remain accountable to the people by leaving the change for the legislature, where the correct legislative facts can be submitted.

The judges of the 1952–53 court were aware of the legal and political burdens placed on them. True, the vast majority of their cases were simple exercises in dispute settlement. But in those few cases involving public policy and constitutional issues, the judges as a group were in the business of attempting to bring about a balance between the two antagonistic but essential considerations of accountability and independence. They also were fairly successful in their efforts.

26. *Ibid.*, 184.
27. *Ibid.*, 172.

15

The Modern Court

Court 5 represents the end product of nearly a century of evolution. As the types of disputes change, personnel are replaced, and different structures imposed, the Supreme Court will certainly take on a different form in coming years. Nonetheless, its inheritance will be rich, and the 1979–80 Court is to be regarded, for the moment, as the most developed version of the state's court of last resort. Interestingly, some of the new features of Court 5 are really the old features of Court 1.

Structural Changes since 1953

The single most important structural change recently instituted which had broad implications for the Supreme Court was the establishment of the Court of Appeals. In June 1969, Governor Evans appointed five attorneys and seven superior court judges to the Court of Appeals, and it was ready for business by late summer 1969.[1]

The establishment of the intermediate appeals bench meant that, first, a division of labor between it and the Supreme Court had to be drawn; and, second, a readjustment in the high court's decisional process was needed in order for the justices to devote more time to the fewer and more contentious issues that would ultimately confront them.[2]

1. Amendment 50 of Article 4 of the State Constitution reads in part: "Art. 4, Sec. 30. *Court of Appeals*—(1) Authorization, in addition to the courts authorized in section 1 of this article, judicial power is vested in a court of appeals, which shall be established by statute." The statute establishing the Court of Appeals was Chapter 221 of Laws 1st Ex. Sess., 1969. The membership, jurisdiction, and location were spelled out by the statute.

2. Although the state constitution uses the term "judge" of the Supreme Court (except for "chief justice"), the legislature designated members of the high court as "justices," reserving "judge" for the new court.

The question of a division of appellate labor was addressed by the legislature in the implementing statute and in subsequent rules of court written by the justices. The Supreme Court retained original appellate jurisdiction in cases declaring a statute to be unconstitutional, death penalty convictions, the overruling of prior cases by the Supreme Court and other conflicts of law, actions against state officials, and those cases "involving a fundamental and urgent issue of broad public import which requires prompt and ultimate determination."

The court exercised discretionary review of the decisions of the Court of Appeals unless its reversal of the trial court's decision was less than unanimous. In that event, the Supreme Court was required to review the reversal. The justices could transfer an appeal pending in the Court of Appeals for their consideration and could also send cases to the appeals judges.[3]

The business of the court was altered significantly by the jurisdictional division of labor worked out by the courts and the legislature. Six avenues of access to the justices were defined. First, the justices were required to accept *notices of appeal* filed with the court, if the issues fell within categories defined in the Rules of Appellate Procedure. In 1979–80, an average of 159 appeals were filed with the court. Second, *petitions for review* were filed with the court when a losing party at the Court of Appeals level felt that the case warranted further consideration. The members of the high court determined whether the petitions deserved their attention, and most (nearly 85%) were either denied or dismissed. Third, *personal restraint petitions* were registered with the court by individuals who argued that they were being unlawfully confined or restrained. The earlier petitions for writs of habeas corpus and postconviction relief now followed this route. Most of the personal restraint petitions were transferred to the appeals bench. Fourth, *motions for discretionary review* also were presented to the court and accepted if the justices deemed a particular case as presenting an issue not covered by the requirements for notices of appeal but important enough for their review. These motions came directly from the losing parties at the superior court level and from litigants at the appeals court who desired a review of some interim ruling. Next, appeals from *disciplinary proceedings* against members of the legal profession (imposed by the board of governors of the Washington State Bar Association) were also reviewed by the justices. (Recently the chief justice assumed responsibility for the initial review of these proceedings.)

3. See *Rules of Appellate Procedure* (RAP).

Table 15.1
Washington Court System: 1980

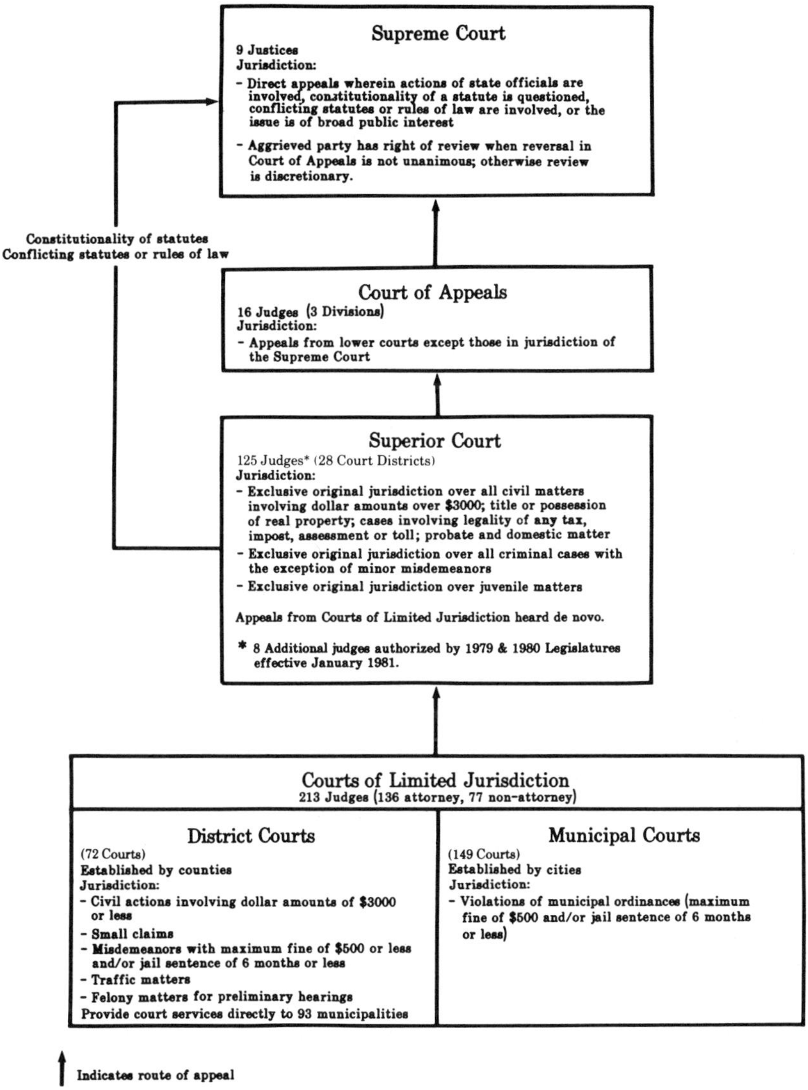

Table 15.2
Access to Court 5

	Numbers Filed	%	*Numbers Disposed of*	%
Appeals	159.0	20.5	171.0	63.8
Petitions for review	406.0	52.4	59.5	22.2
Personal restraint petitions	41.0	5.3	7.0	2.6
Motions for discretionary review	160.5	20.7	22.0	8.2
Disciplinary proceedings	8.5	1.1	8.5	3.2
Total	775.0	100.1	268.0	100.0

SOURCE: Administrator for the Courts, *Annual Reports* (1980)
*Yearly average for 1979–80

The justices were also responsible for ruling on the recommendations of the Judicial Qualifications Commission regarding judicial discipline and ethics. Finally other matters such as petitions for expenditures of public funds, certifications from federal courts, and actions against state officers also found their way to the Supreme Court. The high court also was responsible for the adoption and promulgation of procedural rules for all courts. Court 5's time was dispersed among the various categories of access as reported in table 15.2 (1979–80 yearly average).

Although the justices considered similar categories of disputes prior to 1969, the petitions for review, notices of discretionary review, and the transferring of cases between the high court and the Court of Appeals were new procedures. In sum, what the 1969 changes in jurisdiction meant was that the high court was confronted with fewer but more important cases. Except for those few direct appeals from the trial court, the justices soon had nearly complete control of their own business. They heard only those cases they (a department or a majority *en banc*) chose to hear.

The new jurisdictional responsibilities required a new set of decisional procedures. Again, as in 1903–4, the justices heard cases *en banc*. Motions, petitions for review, notices of discretionary review and petitions for certain writs were still heard in departments (or by the court commissioner). The decisional process for Court 5 can be conveniently divided into the preparatory, hearing, conference, and opinion stages, and each of these stages involved to some degree both individual and collective deliberations. Whether deciding alone or together, the justices had available a variety of sources

Table 15.3
Importance of Decisional Stages and Sources

Stages and Sources	*Positive Importance* (%)*	*Number of Justices Responding*
Preparatory Stage		
Written briefs	100	9
Pre-hearing memos and research of reporting judge	78	9
Hearing Stage		
Oral arguments	44	9
Queries during oral argument	25	8
Conference Stage		
Conference discussion, vote and views of other justices	78	9
Opinion Stage		
Opinion circulation	63	8
Written briefs	100	9

*"Very" or "fairly important" or above 5 on a 1 to 10 scale.

which made contributions to their final decisions. But some sources were more important than others. (See table 15.3.)[4]

Although none of the factors was unimportant, the written briefs (used both during the preparatory and opinion stages by the reporting judge and by others), the prehearing efforts of the reporting judge, and the conference deliberations were the most important inputs to the decisional process. A closer look at each of the four stages of the decisional process used by Court 5 provides insights into these structural influences on the justices.

Preparatory Stage

Petitions for review and notices for discretionary review were initially assigned the court commissioner for research and recom-

4. Table 15.3 was constructed from responses to interview schedules and mailed surveys conducted by the author. (Hereafter referred to as "Judicial Surveys.") The questions posed to the justices were: "Please rate the importance to your final decision of each of the following steps in the decisional process," and "Although each case is unique, generally speaking, how important is each of the following to your final decision?"

mendation.[5] The justices, often with the assistance of their law clerks, reviewed the recommendations of the staff attorneys attached to the commissioner's office. A vote by justices in a department conference could have changed these recommendations. With the high court having gained nearly complete control over its own docket, these preliminary decisions whether to hear a case or not became crucial. Far more requests for review were filed than the justices accepted.[6]

If a case was accepted for review, the judge who was initially assigned the request for review became the "reporting" judge. He or she assumed responsibility for researching the case prior to oral argument and for recommending disposition in conference. The reporting judges (and their law clerks) worked on the assigned cases in isolation from the other judges, researching and writing prehearing memoranda for the entire bench:

> the assigned judge's law clerk prepares a pre-hearing summary of the briefs and may or may not (depending on his own judges' instructions) give an evaluation of the case. This summary is distributed to each judge about a week prior to argument so that each member of the court not only has all the briefs, but also a well prepared synopsis of the contentions on both sides.[7]

In preparing and circulating the memos not only did the reporting judges add to their knowledge on the issues gained from the

5. Rule 15 of the Supreme Court Administrative Rules (SAR) reads: The "commissioner will screen petitions for review and direct appeals to the Supreme Court and recommend whether Supreme Court review should be granted." Motions for discretionary review and transfer considerations also were reviewed and recommended by the commissioner's office. Recently, because of the great number of petitions filed with the commissioner, law clerks attached to the chief justice have assisted in screening the petitions and requests for review or appeal. The staff attorneys with the commissioner's office made three recommendations which were reviewed by the justices; "grant," "deny," and "suggested deny." About one-third to one-fourth of the petitions fall into this "suggested deny" category. Although most requests for review were clearly within or outside the rules for granting review, some were sent to the justices because of the important public interest involved. Generally the commissioner's staff would recommend review in these cases if the issue was a recurring issue, if the issue was often argued in previous cases, or if transactions depended upon a resolution by a court. If "sooner or later the Court is going to have to deal with [the issue]," a review was recommended.

6. In the 1979–80 two-year period, 812 petitions for review were filed with the court but only 119 (15%) were granted. See the statistics in Office of the Administrator for the Courts, *Annual Report of the Caseloads and Operations of the Courts of Washington* (Olympia, 1980). Accepting or denying review was decided upon in department. But if one member of the department had doubts, the request went to the full court for resolution.

7. Robert F. Brachtenbach, "Mechanics of Supreme Court Decision-Making," *Washington State Bar News* (April 1973): 9.

study of requests for review, but the other justices also became more informed. Although regarded as a "hot bench" because of their preparation prior to the oral arguments, the reporting judges had prime responsibility for thoroughly reviewing the briefs, consulting the record, and investigating other authorities, most often with the assistance of their law clerks. (Some judges even prepared draft opinions in some "obvious" cases prior to the oral stage.) The preparation for oral arguments was largely an individual endeavor. With the circulation of the pre-hearing memo the collective efforts began.

Oral Arguments

Although not as important to the justices as, for example, the briefs and the conference deliberations, the oral arguments had always been an integral part of appellate deliberations. Few have talked seriously of dispensing with them. Justice Robert F. Brachtenbach of Court 5 confirmed the immediacy of arguments:

> Oral arguments can be of substantial assistance to the court. Remember it is the last event occurring before the court makes at least a tentative decision on disposition of the matter. . . . Also, the argument or questions from the court may make significant facts which seem unimportant in the initial reading of the briefs or the record. . . . Questions from the court may indicate concern or doubt on points of law, factual issues or broad philosophical implications of the case.[8]

The oral arguments were a balanced mixture of individual and collective efforts. All the judges heard the same presentation, but the hour session (usually a half-hour for each side) was often interrupted by queries from the bench. Both individual and collective functions were performed. For example, justices may have had specific questions to pose to counsel on facts or issues that troubled them. Other justices might wish to bring certain points to the attention of their colleagues through the responses of counsel. The reporting judge, probably having already arrived at a tentative disposition of the case, could use counsel to clarify facts, issues, or authorities that would prove useful in conference and during opinion drafting. Oral arguments, then, perform a variety of functions.

Seven of the justices on Court 5 tended to agree on the importance of the several possible uses of oral arguments. (See table 15.4.)[9]

8. *Ibid.*, 10.

9. The questions posed to the justices, as shown in table 15.4, were: "Following are several functions of oral arguments. Please rate each of them in terms of degree of importance to you," or "Please weigh the importance of each to your deliberations."

Table 15.4
Justices' Views of the Functions of Oral Arguments*

Function	%
To force attorneys to focus on most important matters	100
To prepare for conference deliberations	57
To legitimate the decisional process	57
To clarify facts	44
To persuade colleagues	33
To communicate with colleagues	29
To reinforce prehearing memos	14
To show that briefs have been carefully read	0

*"Very important" or above 5 on a 1 to 10 scale.
SOURCE: The table was constructed from interviews and surveys of Court 5 justices.

Of course, focusing on important matters, clarifying facts, reading briefs, and reinforcing prehearing memos were most likely of concern to individual judges, while persuading and communicating with colleagues and legitimating the court's deliberative process were collective concerns.

Conference Stage

The most important collective decisional stage for the court was and is the conference deliberations. Following the morning oral arguments, the justices moved into secret conference to consider the cases (usually two) heard that morning. The reporting judge gave a detailed and comprehensive report on the case and the recommended disposition. According to Justice William Williams, the reporting judge:

> reports to the entire court on the facts and the applicable law and what he thinks the decision should be with the supporting rationale. If a majority of the court concurs with his views, he is assigned to write the decision. . . . At the time I report on the case, I have pretty well thought it out and have concluded how it should be decided. Absent some unusual circumstances that convince me I'm wrong, I write it that way or else write a dissent.[10]

The time spent by each judge in "reciting" varied in conference and rarely did the chief have to interrupt to direct the discussion. It was largely an informal process where ideas were exchanged, and

10. Letter to the author dated April 22, 1983.

now and then it was as Felix Frankfurter described conference deliberations at the U.S. Supreme Court—like "scorpions in a bottle." Troublesome cases resulted in a give-and-take among the justices while easy cases were quickly disposed of without much discussion after the reporting judge's review and recommendation. One justice on Court 5 gave this account of the conference. He remembered telling his colleagues:

> "I need your collective judgment on these things. Here are the issues. You can wind this one whatever way you want. I just want the collective judgment." Occasionally I say "the issue is very simple. It's a 'yes' or 'no' question and I frankly in my own mind can't write it 'no.' I've got to write it 'yes.' So if you don't want to write it that way that's fine with me. No offense." . . . The best cases . . . are those that we do sit and go back and forth, back and forth, as we try to mesh some kind of logical solution . . . lots of our problems up here are insoluble. They really are. We shouldn't be in the business. One of those that belong across the street [with the legislature] but they dump it here. . . . That's where a consensus is very important. . . . Whatever their backgrounds are and whatever their input is, to listen to everybody. That kind of case [is the best case].[11]

After the reporting judge's recitation and recommendation, the other justices, counterclockwise around the table with the chief justice last, commented and indicated how they would dispose of the case. As in earlier courts, the reporting judge was assigned the opinion if a member of the majority. If the reporting judge was not with the majority, the chief would assign the drafting tasks ordinarily to the first judge who expressed disagreement with the recommendation of the reporting judge and who had gained four other votes. Then the reporting judge who lost the majority would likely draft a dissent.

Opinion Drafting and Circulation

The justice responsible for drafting the court's opinion (the "assignment judge") would have the opinion in circulation within a few weeks or months. The task of drafting an opinion for the court varied with the practices of each of the justices. For all the jurists on Court 5, the law clerks played some role in the opinion-drafting stage.[12] Some were instructed as to the desired outcome with a few

11. Judicial Survey.
12. A former law clerk had observed the wide diversity in judge–law clerk relationships: "Each judge has different work patterns, different handicaps, different

remarks on the reasons therefore and sent off to research and draft an opinion. Then the justice and the clerk would go over the draft carefully, editing, changing, adding, and deleting until both were satisfied. Other jurists would draft the initial opinion and then use the clerk as critic, editor, and researcher until agreeing on the final version to be put into circulation.[13]

The drafting of the dissenting opinion followed the same course as the majority, although there was a tendency on Court 5 for the dissenting judge to draft his own opinion with less help from the law clerk. Again, however, the use of the clerk varied with each of the justices.

Although the conference deliberations constituted the most important stage in the decisional process, the circulation of draft opinions now and then led to changes. According to Justice Charles Horowitz:

> All judges, including the reporting judge, may, of course, change their minds when the majority opinion is written and circulated for signature. A judge who changes his mind may choose to concur with the results only, or to dissent. Ordinarily this will be done by separate opinion, although a judge may concur in the result or dissent without opinion.[14]

The opinions in noncontentious cases were put into "fast circulation" by the chief justice, while those needing closer scrutiny were put in a colored folder and circulated.[15]

---

skills. The individual propensities and limitations of the individual judge should and always will be the major factors that determine how a judge utilizes his clerk. For example, Judge Steinert suffered from a loss of sight that limited his reading of records, transcripts and briefs. He relied on his clerk to do much of his reading for him. Judge Mallery was extraordinary (canny) in his ability to analyze facts, to apply to them what he thought the law was or ought to be and to articulate key issues. He seemed to be short on tedious, legal scholarship and exhaustive legal research. He had to lean heavily on his clerk to furnish this essential ingredient. Other judges were considered by the clerks, including me, to have been too wordy, ungrammatical, and generally clumsy and obscure in their written work. Properly utilized, their clerks improved substantially the quality of their written opinions" (Law Clerk Survey).

13. See Charles H. Sheldon, "Law Clerking with a State Supreme Court: Views from the Perspective of the Personal Assistants to the Judges," *Justice System Journal* 6 (Fall 1981): 346.

14. Charles Horowitz, "Values and Decision-Making: Some Observations on the Role of Non-legal Factors in the Appellate Process," *Washington Appellate Practice Handbook* (Seattle: Continuing Legal Education Committee, Washington State Bar Association, 1980), 3.2.

15. Because of his increased responsibilities for administration and decisional matters, the chief justice was not assigned any of the cases for review or for opinion, although he wrote a number of opinions for the court and a dissent now and then.

When all signatures were accounted for, the opinion was headnoted by the reporter's office, checked by the opinion writer, and returned to the chief who passed it (along with concurring or dissenting opinions) to the supreme court clerk. The clerk filed them and they were available for public scrutiny and officially designated as the final say of the jurists on the issues therein.[16]

In summary, the unique structural features of Court 5 were (1) sharing of appellate review with the Court of Appeals; (2) gaining nearly complete control over its own docket; (3) acquiring assistance on requests for review from the court commissioner; (4) hearing cases *en banc*; (5) wider use of law clerks; and (6) no opinion assignments for the chief justice.

Cohesion on Court 5

The overall dissonance level of Court 5 was considerably higher than in any of the previous Courts (36.5%). However, as reported in table 15.3, the disagreements were dispersed fairly evenly among the justices.

Perhaps the single most important structural change which accounted for the higher dissonance rate for Court 5 was the sharing of appellate responsibilities with the Court of Appeals. The justices had nearly complete control over their own docket. They reviewed those cases they felt it necessary to review because they presented "a fundamental and urgent issue of broad public import which requires prompt and ultimate determination." These tended to be contentious policy issues which had ordinarily divided groups and public officials even before they reached the justices.

Further, when cases were appealed from the Court of Appeals, they were nonunanimous decisions when the trial judge was reversed. Serious disagreement had existed among members of the appeals bench as well as between the court and the trial judge. These were already troublesome cases. Also, the decisions appealed directly from the superior court benches were, by definition, the more important cases involving contentious issues.

By the 1980s, politicians, the public, and judges had accepted, although perhaps reluctantly, the proposition that state courts of last resort did make public policy. The concommitant tendency, then, was for the public to take more policy questions to courts and

16. For an account of the inner workings of the Washington Supreme Court see Justice Weaver's chapter "The Pro Tempore Supreme Court" in C. H. Sheldon and F. P. Weaver, *Politicians, Judges and the People: A Study in Citizens' Participation* (Westport, Conn.: Greenwood, 1980), 53.

for politicians to pass on to courts political issues they felt unable or unwilling themselves to resolve. The U.S. Supreme Court, through its precedent-setting authority, had created both an atmosphere of acceptability for judicial activism and policy making in addition to leaving to the state courts the task of consolidating its revolution in civil rights and criminal procedures based upon the due process and equal protection clauses of the Fourteenth Amendment to the U.S. Constitution.

Finally, the Washington Supreme Court's membership came from diverse backgrounds and experiences, thereby contributing to their differing views of politics and the law. All things considered, it is surprising that the justices disagreed in only a bit more than one out of three cases. However, beyond the pressures on Court 5 as a whole, some differences between the justices were evident as reported in table 15.5.

Table 15.5
Dissonance Rate: Court 5 (yearly average)

Judge	*Dissenting Opinions*	*Dissenting Votes*	*Concurring Opinions-Votes*	*Total Disagreements*
Rosellini	10.0	8.0	8.0	26.0 (13.9%)
Dolliver	14.5	6.5	4.0	25.0 (13.4%)
Brachtenbach	4.0	14.0	7.0	25.0 (13.4%)
Utter	6.5	9.5	8.0	24.0 (13.4%)
Stafford	5.0	6.0	9.0	20.0 (10.7%)
Hicks	2.5	11.0	6.0	19.5 (10.4%)
Wright	2.5	11.5	4.5	18.5 (9.9%)
Horowitz	2.5	12.0	3.0	17.5 (9.4%)
Williams	2.0	3.0	5.5	10.5 (5.6%)
Total	49.5	81.5	55.0	186.0 (100.0%)
Average/Judge	5.5	9.0	6.1	20.6

Justices Dolliver and Rosellini dissented most, Justice Brachtenbach voted most often in dissent, and Justices Horowitz and Williams disagreed with their colleagues the least. Thus, table 15.5 poses several questions which must be addressed regarding individual behavior.

As we have observed, dissenting opinions and votes perform a variety of functions. Drafting dissenting opinions and casting dissenting votes are clearly part of the deliberative process. As with that process, the functions or roles of dissent fall into collective or individual modes. When a dissent is written to stimulate some reaction

Table 15.6
Functions of Dissent from the Perspectives of the Justices of Court 5

Functions	*% Positive**
Collective Mode	
To win over the majority or to win more "votes"	100
To point out the impact of the majority's opinion on society	100
To keep the majority "honest"	57
To improve the majority opinion	29
Individual Mode	
To lay groundwork for the future	86
To "write it as I see it," despite the majority or concurrences	43
To provide a forum for minorities, the discouraged, and ignored	29
To participate in freedom and democracy requires occasional dissent	14

*Above 5 on a 1 to 10 scale and "Very Important" or "Important."
SOURCE: Judicial survey.

from other members of the bench, it is in a collective mode. When the dissent is inner-directed to satisfy some personal compulsion, it is in the individual mode. Table 15.6 reports the dissenting preferences of seven of the nine members of Court 5.

Justices Dolliver and Rosellini, the members of Court 5 with the highest dissonance level and greatest dissenting rate, tended to accept the individual form of the dissenting functions. Although they regarded dissents as useful in winning a majority and for criticising the court's opinions, the individual mode appealed to them more.

After having served a year on the court, Dolliver held an open mind regarding the uses of dissent and was yet unsure of his own motivations. He admitted he was not reluctant to write dissents, but

> It may be as I serve on the Court longer, . . . either a) the fire will go out of me, or b) I'll say, "Now look, are you really writing something important or are you just sort of trying to stroke your own ego." I'm not suggesting I think that's what I'm doing now but the thought has occurred to me.[17]

17. The judge reflected further: "As a person is on the Court longer, maybe you don't see the need for dissent quite as much as you see the greater need to try to get everybody on the same side and are willing to give and take, perhaps compromise more and I'll learn more about the law. Maybe some of my dissents are rather foolish but as I learn more about what's going on I may change" (Interview with Dolliver, April 5, 1977).

Six years later his individual mode was still pronounced and again, he was introspective concerning his role:

> If it looks like an 8-1 dissent I'm going to look very carefully but if I've got one or two on the passing sheet that look like they're going with me and maybe a chance to pull some others in, why, I'll [try]. But dissent is an entirely different way of writing. [In] the typical dissent you've got one issue. You can see it right there and you just press that one button and if that doesn't persuade them, well, ok . . . I guess I haven't figured out my real motivation in dissent and I'm not sure I'm doing it just to prefigure the future. I think that's a little bit pompous somehow.[18]

Justice Rosellini, perhaps reflecting his long tenure on the bench (twenty-five years in 1980), wrote his dissents with future courts in mind. In reflecting on the uses of dissent he confided: "I hope that I can convince someone to go along and also with the idea that it may become law later on. It has happened to me before so . . . [it's worth a try]."[19]

Justice Brachtenbach's relatively high dissonance level was the result of a large number of dissenting votes rather than opinions. His orientation was clearly toward the collective mode for dissent, which suggests that he reserved dissenting opinions for those occasions when he had an opportunity to persuade his colleagues and perhaps win a majority. He expressed it this way:

> You have to ask yourself what the purpose of it is if eight of the people on the Court have agreed that the majority is correct. I question my own analysis at that stage. . . . So then what are you trying to accomplish, parading your own ideas out? . . . I think I write them to try to persuade four other people and that sometimes happens even after the vote in conference. . . . My prime purpose is to win over the majority.[20]

The fewer number of written dissents from Brachtenbach and some of the others may also have indicated relative success in the collective uses of dissent.[21] Also Brachtenbach assumed the administrative

18. Interview with Dolliver, April 13, 1983.
19. Interview with Rosellini, April 5, 1977.
20. Interview with Brachtenbach, April 5, 1977.
21. Brachtenbach had presented this alternative as an interpretation of his dissenting behavior: "[M]y lack of dissents, for example, more likely indicates that I was in a dissenting position, wrote a dissenting opinion which then obtained enough votes to become a majority position. This is not a unique situation so that the final opinion does not always reflect the initial consideration and conclusion of the Court" (Letter to the author dated August 12, 1975).

tasks of acting chief justice without the relief from opinion assignments that regularly accompanied the assumption of the chief justiceship. His many dissenting votes rather than opinions may have been the result of these extra responsibilities.

Justices Williams and Horowitz tended more than the other justices to resist the temptations of a written dissent or concurrence.[22] Both saw the collective mode as the most viable approach to dissents, and neither was reluctant to pen them. Initially, Williams avoided disagreement. The collective approach to dissents which he adopted, would be ineffective to someone newly arrived at the court until some credibility with the other justices had been established. Apparently his approach proved successful, as subsequently he established himself as one of the leaders on the bench.

Justice Horowitz, on the other hand, was an experienced hand at appellate review, having served on the Court of Appeals before election to the Supreme Court in 1975. Although he accepted the collective approach to dissent, Horowitz looked beyond the immediate politics of opinion writing to the long-range impact of the law. According to one of Horowitz's former law clerks:

> The judge would always write a dissent, I think, when he disagreed with the majority, unless, a) the issue's importance did not merit the large amount of time, and b) there was no chance of obtaining a majority to his side.[23]

Horowitz's particular approach to collective decision-making also could explain to a significant degree his low dissonance level. He would not dissent unless able to convince others to agree. His appeal to wavering colleagues was to a commonly shared policy perspective. Just before retirement from the high bench Justice Horowitz wrote about his approach to the decisional process:

> What should a multi-judge court do when its members differ in their respective schemes of values, or differ in the contents of individual values . . . or differ in the priorities in which the values are held by the respective judges?
>
> It should be remembered that judges are engaged in a practical

22. Court 5 had instituted a unique system of "credits" in order to equalize the workload. If the reporting judge was assigned the opinion as a member of the majority in conference but lost the vote upon circulation of the drafts and chose not to change the opinion, he or she lost a "credit." The dissenting judge who won and penned the Court's final opinion was awarded a "credit." He or she was, then, responsible for one less assigned opinion in the future. A judge could only use two credits a term, however.

23. Law Clerk Survey.

> calling. Their decisions may influence the conduct of thousands. . . . Judges may seek to iron out their differences by treating the decision reached as one required by considerations of public policy, or what they believe to be in the public interest.[24]

Apparently, if others could not be convinced of the public interest involved, he would not venture a dissenting opinion.

Interactions among the Justices

Of course, part of the explanation for dissonance must be found in the particular mix of justices on the bench. If, as on previous courts, a particular judge's view of the legal and political world isolated him from his colleagues, his dissonance level would be high. For example, Judges Blake and Pemberton were in such positions on earlier courts. Both had much higher dissonance rates than any of the judges on Court 5, however. The knowledge of the interaction among the judges on this most recent court would add to an understanding of dissonance behavior. Table 15.7 reports the degree to which the justices agreed with one another in those cases where a dissenting opinion or vote or a concurring opinion or vote was registered.

Only Justices Horowitz's and Utter's agreement rate reached a significant level (81%), which meant that they agreed in four out of five of the contentious cases. At the other extreme, Justice Wright and Utter agreed in only one out of three of these cases. Although they both registered the highest dissonance levels, Justices Dolliver and Rosellini agreed with each other in only 42% of these split decisions, suggesting that their many dissents and concurrences were not for the same reasons.

Ordinarily, explanations for the varying dissonance levels and the particular interagreement patterns can be found in the philosophical perspectives of the justices. It could be anticipated that Rosellini and Dolliver, because of their dissonance level, would hold contrasting views from their colleagues (but for different reasons), that Utter and Horowitz would be in close agreement philosophically, and that Utter and Wright would be at opposite ends of the philosophical spectrum.

According to the experienced appellate attorneys and the former law clerks, the justices on Court 5 were dispersed widely across the liberal-conservative and activist-restraintist axes. Figure 15.1 portrays the relative positions of each of the members of Court 5.

24. Horowitz, "Values and Decision-Making."

Table 15.7
Interagreement Percentages: Court 5

	Utter	Dolliver	Williams	Brachtenbach	Hicks	Wright	Stafford	Rosellini
Horowitz	81%	59	58	51	48	51	49	39
Utter		57	58	45	50	32	43	34
Dolliver			53	50	49	43	39	42
Williams				49	70	51	58	58
Brachtenbach					51	54	50	47
Hicks						51	50	50
Wright							51	64
Stafford								43

Court average: 50.7%
Sprague criterion: 74.6%

Justice Williams was dead center on both dimensions and Utter was at one extreme and Wright at the other. Generally, the court was dominated by liberals and moderates with slightly activist tendencies. However, Dolliver and Rosellini were not as isolated from the others as their dissonance rates suggest. Utter and Wright were poles apart as anticipated. Williams' and Horowitz's center positions help to explain their low dissonance rate. Being in or near the philosophical centers allowed alignment with either side without

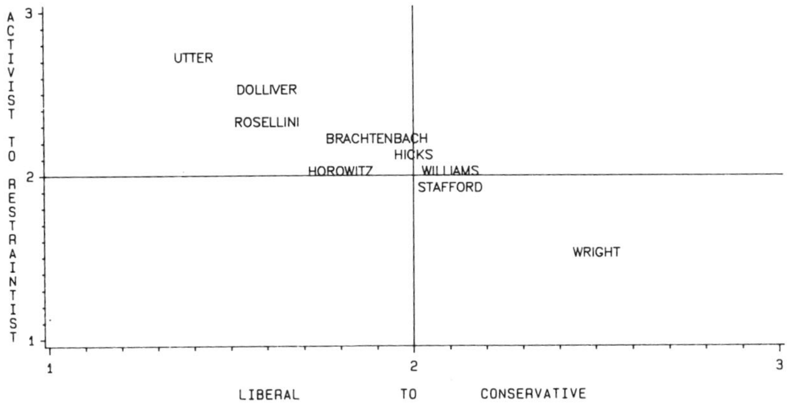

Fig. 15.1. Philosophical positions of judges on Court 5 (Source: Survey of former law clerks and appellate attorneys)

damage to their own perspectives. However, Horowitz and Utter, although certainly not at opposite ends of the scales, were not aligned as closely as their agreement level suggested. Explanations for their behavior lay elsewhere.

Justice Williams' center position regarding the role of courts in the state's political system was expressed clearly in *State* v. *Fain*, (94 Wn. 2d 387 at 402, 1980). For the majority he wrote:

> We hasten to repeat that we must and do defer to the legislative branch decision to impose an enhanced penalty on recidivists. . . . Yet legislative authority is ultimately circumscribed by the constitutional mandate forbidding cruel punishment. Our duty to determine whether a legislatively imposed penalty is constitutionally excessive is not one which we assume eagerly, but we do not shrink from our responsibility.

On the other hand, restraintists Stafford and Wright (and Brachtenbach) concurred with Rosellini's dissent in *Fain* (at 407).[25]

> The majority approach does not accord to the people, acting through their legislature, the deference that is due their judgment upon this matter, which is at the very least one upon which reasonable minds may differ. Thus the majority substitutes its judgment for that of the legislature, and casts that judgment in constitutional cement.

Horowitz, along with Dolliver and Utter, dissented in *Buchanan* v. *International Brotherhood of Teamsters* (94 Wn. 2d 508 at 518, 520, 1980) criticizing the majority's assumption that legislative inaction meant acquiescence in a previous court decision. They suggested that such reasoning would be an unacceptable form of restraint.

25. In 1979–80 it appears that Justice Rosellini was not as activist nor as liberal as the clerks and attorneys had suggested. The survey from which the data were taken was designed to isolate the judges' perspectives over their full careers on the bench, not just one or two years. Actually, the law clerks sensed that Rosellini had indeed moved from his liberal-activist stances toward the center. Of those clerks who served the judges between 1955 and 1969, 61% regarded Rosellini as liberal and 37% thought he was activist. However, of those clerks who served between 1969 and 1978 only 27% regarded the judge as liberal and 30% as activist. Three explanations for this shift are plausible. First, Rosellini may have moderated his views in recent years. Second, the judge may have remained consistent with his previous stands but, through new elections and appointments, the membership of the court had moved toward the activist-liberal ends of the spectrum. Rosellini, then, only "appears" to have changed. Third, and perhaps most likely, both of these two explanations are at play. The judge has become slightly more moderate and the court has become slightly more liberal-activist.

> [L]egislatures express intent by enacting statutes, not by remaining silent. The majority's presumption is that the legislature is aware of its past enactments, and judicial interpretations thereof. . . .
>
> . . . This court should not attempt to avoid its interpretative duties by relying on the legislature's inaction in light of a decision, . . . which is now revealed to be clearly erroneous.

Although registering a high interagreement rate, Justices Utter and Horowitz remained somewhat apart on the philosophical scales. Some other coincidence of interests held them together. They had served together on the Court of Appeals in Division 1 and were appointed to the court by Governor Evans. An intellectual affinity soon developed which was reaffirmed when Horowitz joined Utter on the high court in 1975. Horowitz, a former Rhodes Scholar, had received numerous academic honors and had played a significant role in fashioning Washington law both from the bench and the bar. He provided a role model for many of the younger members of the court (Horowitz was forced to retire under the mandatory age statute when he became 75 in 1980). Dolliver, who sat across from him in conference, recalled the impact Horowitz had on his colleagues:

> [I]t was in the conference room where the lesson really took place. . . . [H]e would stand, sometimes in back of his chair, grasping the top of the high back, sometimes in front, taking his glasses off and putting them on as he read a passage or made a point. These recitations were neither cursory nor brief. They were extended, detailed, scholarly—and simply marvelous. Whatever the subject case, there was always the same careful preparation, the same measured, articulate recitation. A scrupulously fair presentation was given in the same low, unhurried voice as had asked questions from the bench. To savor a recitation of Justice Horowitz was to understand what continuing judicial education was all about.[26]

The Utter-Horowitz relationship on the court resembled a mentor-student relationship, but between equals. The intellectual excitement of appellate decisionmaking drew them together. Both had inquiring and flexible minds willing to pursue new or different lines of thought and to consult creative and often remote sources of law.[27]

26. James M. Dolliver, "Charles Horowitz: A Memoir," *Washington Law Review* 56 (1981): 168–69.

27. For example, see Utter's opinion in *In Re Bowman* (94 Wn. 2d 407, 1980). At issue was a legal standard for when death occurs.

Influence or Leadership on Court 5

The ability to bring others around to one's way of thinking in political circumstances has been variously termed "leadership," "power," "politics," "authority," or "influence." For the purposes of documenting this aspect of the interactions among the members of Court 5, the more inclusive term of "influence" will be adopted.

The deliberations among the nine justices must ultimately result in some agreement involving at least a majority of five. Among competent, committed and contentious judges, all steeped in the adversarial tradition of legal training and practice, forging such an agreement is not easily achieved and may take a variety of forms.[28] One judge might assume leadership in particular cases under certain circumstances, while another judge might take over in different cases and situations.[29] Over the long haul, however, the general direction of the court likely will be chartered by one or two from among the judges. Apart from the many forms influence may take, how can the results of its exercise be measured? The clues to influence on the bench are provided by an analysis of judicial votes and written opinions.

Although the justices on Court 5 had adopted a rule granting "credits" for penning majority opinions in order to equalize the assignment load, several justices did not take full advantage of their credits, and it was the practice that not more than two credits could be "turned in" per term. Thus, one indication of influence is provided by a comparison of the number of majority opinions written by each of the justices.[30] The assumption is that the jurists who wrote

28. Walter F. Murphy, *The Elements of Judicial Strategy* (Chicago: University of Chicago Press, 1963).

29. David J. Danelski, "The Influence of the Chief Justice in the Decisional Process," in Walter F. Murphy and C. Herman Pritchett, eds., *Courts, Judges and Politics* (New York: Random House, 1979), 695.

30. According to a former law clerk, other factors may explain the number of assigned opinions. For example, a judge may have a backlog of cases from the previous term, "got himself a good law clerk that year and managed to catch up." However, the same clerk admitted some validity to the scale: "The slight variation in the number of majority opinions published I would attribute to the fact that judges, being human, sometimes change their minds. If a case is very controversial (and most of the cases that come to the court are controversial to some extent) a judge may vote with the reporting judge at conference but change his mind when he reads the opinions. That would turn what was the original majority opinion into a dissent when published. I doubt that these changes of heart take place as a result of leadership qualities of the writer, but rather the persuasiveness of his argument. The persuasiveness of arguments depends a great deal on the controlling principles that govern the case and the clarity with which they are presented in the proposed opinion; and of course, it may have been a law clerk who wrote the opinion, so you can't judge leadership from that."

more of the court's majority opinions were likely to have had more success in persuading colleagues to their views. As reported in table 15.8 (first column), Justices Hicks, Dolliver, and Rosellini were responsible for more majority opinions than their brethren.

Similarly, when a justice gathers more signatures on his opinion drafts (majority, concurring, or dissenting), the more likely he is influential. Again, table 15.8 (second column) suggests that Justices Williams, Brachtenbach, and Horowitz attracted more votes for their opinions than other members of the bench.

In close cases, the single vote of a judge can decide the issue. When a judge tends to be located near the middle of the Court's ideological spectrum, he likely casts many of these deciding votes. Persistent swing voting places him in a strategic position.[31] He makes the difference in close decisions. Justices Hicks, Williams, and Rosellini provided this dimension of influence as reported in table 15.8 (third column).

Another view of leadership is suggested by the subsequent impact of opinions written by each of the justices. A counting of the number of positive citations by later courts (Supreme Court and Court of Appeals) implies influence. That judge who is cited most often would have exercised more influence than the judge whose opinions are ignored by future courts.[32] Again, table 15.8 (fourth column) indicates that Justices Stafford, Horowitz and Williams have had a greater impact on the law as viewed by subsequent courts.[33]

Because of the wide variety of legal issues confronting courts of last resort, a division of labor among the justices tends to evolve. As a result of interest, training, experience, or coincidence, members of the bench become experts in particular areas of the law. In conference deliberations they lead the discussions on those issues on which

31. The "swing vote" score was arrived at by awarding those among a 5-4 majority one-fifth of the total or .20; each of those in a majority of six received one-sixth of the total or .167; a majority of seven .143; and those in a majority of eight received .125. The totals were then calculated for the two years covered in Court 5. See L. S. Shapley and Martin Shubik, "A Method for Evaluating the Distribution of Power in a Committee System," *American Political Science Review* 48 (1954), 787. Its application to courts was first used by Glendon Schubert, *Judicial Behavior: A Reader in Theory and Research* (Chicago: Rand McNally, 1964).

32. The totals for citations were taken from Shepard's *Washington Citations*. The total includes all the positive citations from subsequent decisions of both the Washington Supreme Court and Court of Appeals from 1980 to 1985. (Such negative citations as "overruled," "questioned," "distinguished," etc., were excluded.) The index was calculated by simply dividing the total by the number of majority opinions written by that judge.

33. For a similar analysis of the Michigan Supreme Court see S. Sidney Ulmer, "Leadership in the Michigan Supreme Court," in Glendon Schubert, ed., *Judicial Decision-Making* (New York: Free Press of Glencoe, 1963), 13.

Table 15.8
Influence Indices

Justice	*Number of Majority Opinions Written*	*Rank*	*Average Number of Votes per Opinion*	*Rank*	*Swing Vote Scores*	*Rank*	*Average Number of Subsequent Citations*	*Rank*	*Law Professors Rating*	*Rank*	*Composite Ranking*
Williams	20.0	4	7.0	1	11.7	2	8.5	4	4.0	2	1
Hicks	24.5	1	6.4	5	12.8	1	8.5	3	1.7	8	2
Horowitz	19.5	7	6.8	3	10.5	4	8.5	2	3.5	3	3
Stafford	18.5	8	6.3	6	10.5	5	12.7	1	2.8	5	4
Brachtenbach	20.0	4	6.8	2	10.2	8	7.9	5	2.1	7	5
Utter (C.J.)	20.0	4	5.7	7	10.2	7	6.2	8	4.2	1	6
Rosellini	20.5	3	5.3	9	11.5	3	7.3	6	2.6	6	6
Dolliver	22.0	2	5.4	8	10.4	6	5.4	9	3.4	4	8
Wright	12.5	9	6.6	4	9.3	9	6.8	7	1.4	9	9
Court averages	19.7		6.3		10.8		7.9		2.9		

they have expertise. Their votes are closely watched, their opinion drafts seldom challenged, and their advice often sought. This division of labor is evident in the 1979–80 bench, and it makes its contribution to the leadership relations among the judges.

According to law professors teaching tort law, contracts, environmental law, criminal law, and constitutional law at the state's three law schools (University of Puget Sound, University of Washington, and Gonzaga University), members of Court 5 varied significantly in their contribution to the development of these specific areas of the law.[34] The next to last column in table 15.8 reports the mean scores (1 = "little impact" to 5 = "significant impact") over the five areas of the law according to law professors familiar with the justices and their rulings. Chief Justice Utter, followed closely by Williams, and then Horowitz and Dolliver provide expert leadership to the court. Utter's influence was predominantly in the constitutional area. Williams contributed to the court's criminal law rulings as did also Horowitz and Dolliver.

As previously suggested, influence can take many forms and be exerted by more than one or two judges. However, eventually, leaders tend to emerge. By forming a composite influence index through averaging the rankings on each of the above individual influence measures, a clue is provided about which justices generally were a bit more effective in swaying their colleagues. The last column in table 15.8 reports the composite ranking of the nine justices. Justices Williams, Hicks, and Horowitz appeared to be the more influential members of Court 5.

One form of influence not measured by the indices in table 15.8 is exercised by the chief justice, a position rotated among the justices and occupied by Justice Utter on Court 5. Because of administrative and public responsibilities, the chief accepts only a few opinion assignments and, consequently loses influence in the opinion writing and voting categories during his term. However, his influence is felt elsewhere.

A chief's leadership on the bench can be appraised by ascertain-

34. Each of the law professors was asked the following question: "On a scale of 1 to 5 (1 = 'little impact' and 5 = 'significant impact'), please rate the following members of the 1979–80 Supreme Court on their impact on those areas of the law with which you are familiar. Having an 'impact' could mean writing the leading opinion in a particular area, being responsible for changing the law, writing opinions used in classes and casebooks, arriving at creative resolutions to disputes, penning opinions that clearly reflect a thorough understanding of the law and are well researched and written, etc." The other justices strengths were Stafford—constitutional law; Rosellini—constitutional law; Brachtenbach—contracts; Hicks—torts; and Wright—environmental law. Hamilton was also recognized for his contributions to environmental law.

ing the goals he sets for his two-year term and determining whether these goals were met. Also the chief's traditional role is to keep the court's calendar as current as possible.

Chief Justice Utter took special interest in the campaign for the Judicial Qualifications Commission which would be responsible for investigating and recommending to the Supreme Court disciplinary actions against violators of the Code of Judicial Conduct. Some of the chief's own brethren opposed the commission as a threat to judicial independence, but Utter prevailed. After an extended struggle within the judiciary, the legal profession, and the legislature, the measure was submitted to the people, and the voters approved the constitutional amendment establishing the commission in the 1982 general election.

The chief's responsibility for keeping the court current did not meet with equal success. Although the number of terminated matters increased, the court fell further behind in 1979, largely because of the greater number of filings. However, the next year the justices increased their output, began chipping away at the backlog, and filed a greater number of written opinions.

The turn-around in matters facing the court was to some degree due to Chief Justice Utter's efforts, both as manager of the court's business and as a member. He continued to carry his full share of case assignments during his tenure.

The influence indices are susceptible to another interpretation, however. No one justice dominates the bench in all categories, nor should he. Members of a court of last resort must confront a vast number of complicated issues involving often creative solutions to be recorded in authoritative rulings. To accomplish this, each of the nine members of a diverse bench should make his or her own unique contribution. While one possesses leadership abilities in one endeavor, another justice adds elsewhere. Perhaps this mix of talents is the most striking attribute of the modern court.

Table 15.9
Calendar Pressures: Court 5

	1978	*1979*	*1980*
Total filings	654	785	767
Total terminated	734	755	791
Total pending	262	342	276
Total opinions written	150	189	203

Backgrounds of Members of Court 5

Some possible explanations for the variations in agreement rates, for the similarities or differences in philosophical outlooks, and for levels of influence can be found in a review of the backgrounds and experiences of the members of Court 5. Four sets of background variables are relevant to understanding a judges' subsequent behavior.[35]

Justices Utter and Wright were at opposite ends of both philosophical continua reported in figure 15.1. Utter was appointed at the age of forty-one and Wright elected when he was sixty. Utter was a Republican from Seattle but Wright maintained an independent affiliation and was from Shelton, near Olympia. Both were Protestants and religion played an important role in their lives. Wright was an Episcopalian and Utter a Baptist. The two justices shared prior judicial experiences. Both had served on the Superior Court, Wright for twenty-two years and Utter for five. Utter also had been a member of the Court of Appeals as well as a juvenile court commissioner and judge in King County for nearly six years. Utter earned his academic degrees from the University of Washington. Wright received his Bachelors degree from the University of Puget Sound and attended the University of Washington Law School for a time before clerking in his father's office and passing the bar in 1937.

Wright served as prosecuting attorney for two years and Utter was a deputy prosecutor for a year and a half. Wright had had his own law practice in Thurston County for nearly twelve years, while Utter's practice had been for only about two years before he became juvenile court commissioner in 1959.

Both of Wright's parents were professionals. His father had practiced law in Washington since the turn of the century and was elected superior court judge in 1914. He retired from that bench in 1949 to be replaced by his son. Wright's mother was one of the first women in the state to pass the bar. Utter's father was an insurance executive and his mother was a housewife. Although interested in politics, neither justice was very active in partisan affairs. Justices Utter and Wright shared some backgrounds, but they had accumulated a number of contrasting experiences to give them different

35. See, for example, John Schmidhauser, *The Supreme Court: Its Politics, Personalities and Procedures* (New York: Holt, Rinehart and Winston, 1960), and C. N. Tate, "Personal Attribute Models of the Voting Behavior of U.S. Supreme Court Justices: Liberalism in Civil Liberties and Economic Decisions, 1946–1978," *American Political Science Review* 75 (1981): 355.

perspectives concerning the role of the courts in a democratic society (activist-restraintist) and the place of law in people's lives (liberal-conservative).

Although apparently sharing a liberal and activist philosophy, Justices Dolliver and Rosellini failed to achieve a high level of interagreement in the 1979–80 period. (See table 15.7.) They were both political activists, although Dolliver was a Rockefeller Republican and Rosellini a New Deal Democrat. Rosellini was a native of Tacoma and the son of Italian Catholic immigrants. He worked in lumber mills in the area to help support his family during the Depression. He attended St. Martin's preparatory school and the College of Puget Sound. In 1933 he graduated from the University of Washington Law School and practiced law in Tacoma from 1933 to 1948. Dolliver grew up in Iowa, the son of a U.S. Congressman. He graduated from Swarthmore College in Pennsylvania and from the University of Washington Law School in 1952. He clerked his first year after graduation for Justice Fred Hamley and then practiced law in Port Angeles and Everett for a few years.

Rosellini began his political career as a state legislator (1939–45) and was appointed to the superior court bench in 1948, serving until elected to the Supreme Court in 1954. Dolliver served as administrative assistant to Congressman Jack Westland (1955–61) and then as assistant to Governor Dan Evans from 1965 until his appointment to the high bench in 1976.

Actually, with the exception of a shared legal education, Dolliver and Rosellini had little in common. Consequently, their liberalism and activism failed to coincide to any significant degree.

Justices Williams and Hicks lived parallel experiences which tended to give them similar outlooks on the law and politics. Both were long-time Democrats, born and raised in eastern Washington. Williams was a Spokane native, educated at the University of Idaho, where he excelled in athletics. His studies were interrupted by duty with the Air Force in World War II. Returning from the military, Williams finished his undergraduate work and entered the University of Idaho Law School. He transferred to Gonzaga Law School after a year and was awarded his LL.B. in 1951. Hicks was born in Prosser and graduated from Central Washington Teachers' College in 1938 followed by several years of teaching and coaching in high schools in eastern Washington. He served with the Air Force during the war, returning to the University of Washington School of Law and graduating in 1948.

Williams began his legal practice as deputy prosecutor, and after three years he entered private practice in his home town. In 1958, at the age of thirty-five, he was appointed to the superior court bench where he served for twenty-one years before winning election to the Supreme Court. Hicks entered private practice in Tacoma following graduation. In 1961 he was appointed to the superior court bench and then successfully ran for the U.S. Congress in 1964, where he served for thirteen years before election to the state's highest bench. Both judges received labor endorsement for all of their campaigns, judicial and congressional.

Justice Horowitz shared few common experiences with his brethren. He was born in Brooklyn, N.Y., of immigrant Jewish parents. His father was a tailor. Horowitz moved to Seattle while still young, attended public schools in that city, and graduated from the University of Washington with honors. He worked at several odd jobs as a youth to help pay for his education. Horowitz received his law degree from the University of Washington Law School in 1927, again with honors, and was awarded a Rhodes Scholarship to Oxford University, earning first class honors in 1929. He joined a prestigious law firm in Seattle upon returning from England, practicing until his appointment to the Court of Appeals in 1969. He also taught briefly at the University of Washington Law School.

Horowitz was active in professional affairs, serving as president of the Seattle Bar Association and as a member or chairman of several law commissions. He was also a member of the American Law Institute and the American Judicature Society. Horowitz was also active in civic affairs and in several charitable groups. Although not extremely active in partisan politics, Horowitz was a lifelong New Deal Democrat and a supporter of labor unions. He accepted appointment to the Court of Appeals and won a seat on the Supreme Court at an age when most of his contemporaries had retired. A devotion to the law and to public service prompted Horowitz to move to the judiciary.

Although the differences in backgrounds between Horowitz and his colleagues might partially explain differing outlooks regarding the law, they fail to shed light on the agreements on law and policy that he shared with others. Perhaps his scholarship and powers of persuasion won over others who might not initially have viewed issues as he did.

Perhaps Justice Brachtenbach had more shared experiences with the others on the bench, but his experiences did not coincide with any one of the other judges. For example, his Catholic upbringing was similar to that of Rosellini but in contrast with the Protestant backgrounds of Utter and Dolliver. His small but successful law practice in Yakima was similar to Hicks's in Tacoma and unlike Horowitz's in Seattle. Like Rosellini, he served in the state legislature (1962–66), but across the aisle as a Republican. Like Dolliver, he had had no prior judicial experience. He was appointed by Governor Evans as were fellow Republicans Utter, Stafford, and Dolliver. Like Horowitz, he also taught law school for a short time. Brachtenbach was not a native Washingtonian, although he graduated from Yakima High School, Yakima Valley College, and the University of Washington. He received his law degree, like most of his colleagues, from the University of Washington Law School. He had written several scholarly works on the law, served on several public service commissions, and was somewhat active in bar affairs. He practiced law for sixteen years in Selah, near Yakima. Community property and the commercial code were his specialities.

Given these diverse but overlapping experiences, Brachtenbach was in an excellent position to appreciate the perspectives of nearly all the justices. He tended to advocate a common ground upon which agreement could be reached in some divisive cases.

Justice Stafford was born and raised in Northwest Washington. He attended public schools in Anacortes and graduated with honors from Whitman College in 1940. After duty with the Signal Corps, Stafford attended Yale Law School, graduating in 1946. Until 1953, he served as chief deputy prosecutor for Skagit and Island Counties and was relatively active in Republican affairs in the area. Stafford had the distinction of being the first judge to serve on three levels of the state system. He was a judge of the Superior Court for over sixteen years and on the Court of Appeals for five months until his appointment to the Supreme Court in 1970. Stafford was involved in a number of community service and professional groups, such as the Boy Scouts, Y.M.C.A., American Judicature Society, and the National College of Trial Judges.

Stafford's moderate to conservative restraint may have been encouraged by his sixteen years as a trial judge and six years as county prosecutor. Although Yale Law School had a reputation for training policy-oriented attorneys, Stafford's experiences before and after law school apparently balanced what activism he might have absorbed while at New Haven.

An understanding of the backgrounds of the judges has only limited utility, as we have seen. However, some clues are provided about why a judge's view of important legal and policy issues might vary somewhat from that of his brethren.

Court 5 as the Modern Court

The Supreme Court of 1979–80 represented the culmination of nearly a century of evolution from the beginnings of the Supreme Court of Washington. The modern court had assumed greater responsibilities, which, if quickly and thoroughly discharged, would have clearly enhanced the authority of the high bench and, indeed, it is now held in higher regard than its predecessors.[36]

The contemporary court displayed lower cohesion than that reached by earlier courts. Actually, considering the responsibilities assumed by the justices, the variety of their backgrounds and experiences, and the number of important issues confronting them, this low cohesion is not altogether that striking.[37]

Although a few judges who served their constitutionally mandated two years as chief justice "merely occupied" the chair and carried on largely as before, others experimented with administrative innovations and procedures. Some innovations in communications among the justices enhanced indirectly the decisional process. Any task or social leadership on the court provided by the chief was almost exclusively the product of the incumbent's personality rather than of the prerogatives attached to the position.[38]

The modern court has increased its authority despite the low cohesion level. The justices have been somewhat more thorough in their research and opinions, but have not been entirely expeditious with their decisions. However, the structures surrounding the court explain these variations in achieving court goals.

The existence of the Court of Appeals had thrust these changes upon the justices. Recruitment had changed so that an apprenticeship on the intermediate court appeared to be a highly desirable,

36. Gregory A. Caldeira ranks the Washington Supreme Court eighth among all the fifty states and District of Columbia courts of last resort. In 1920 the court was ranked eighteenth. The top ten, according to Caldeira, are: California, New York, New Jersey, Pennsylvania, Massachusetts, Wisconsin, Illinois, *Washington*, Iowa, and Michigan. See G. A. Caldeira, "On the Reputation of State Supreme Courts," in D. Danelski, ed., "Judicial Behavior: Theory and Method," *Political Behavior* (1983): 83–108.

37. The differences between and among the justices on substantive legal issues appeared not to go beyond the conference room. Several of the judges regularly shared coffee time and had lunch together. Lasting friendships had developed. Some judges went their own way but as a matter of personal preference rather than pique. All the judges spoke respectfully of their colleagues and of the congeniality of their relationship in the interviews conducted by the author. This was not the case in earlier courts.

38. For an analysis of task and social leadership at the U.S. Supreme Court, see Danelski, "The Influence of the Chief Justice," 695.

if not necessary, qualification. (Six of the present [1986] members had served on the Court of Appeals.) Also because of the appeals bench, the justices had assumed a greater policy role. They controlled their own docket and thus selected out those important and contentious cases.[39] The rules require that "If the [case] involves an issue of substantial public interest that should be determined by the Supreme Court," the justices will grant review.[40] Consequently, the court had become a more active participant in affirming or making public policy for the state. This, of course, bears directly on the issue of public accountability and judicial independence.

39. Even in a number of cases that can be appealed directly and by right from the superior courts, the justices can transfer them to the Court of Appeals. See RAP 4.2.
40. RAP 13.4.

16

Prospects for the Second Century

Courts are both products of and have an impact on society. The disputes brought to the Washington Supreme Court are a reflection of the problems confronting persons and groups in the state (and since states do not exist in isolation, confronting the nation). Because legal disputes are generated by what troubles society, what is normal, acceptable, and the result of consensus most often fails to be docketed on the court's calendar. Nonetheless, the consensus is found in the standards applied by the jurists, as they attempt to reconcile the differences according to law. Law that prevails, whether enacted by the legislature, defined by judges, or practiced by public agencies, reflects those values that hold the community together.

But courts also have their say about the nature of society. This is only to recognize that what judges decide is important. Courts in general, and the Washington Supreme Court in particular, settle disputes, and as a result, on occasion, they will make, affirm, and change public policy. Whenever the justices contemplate the consequences to the community of alternative resolutions to any dispute before them, they are contemplating issues of public policy.

There is no suggestion that the Washington Supreme Court will not continue to assume a significant role in the life of the state during the state's second century. The highly mobile, diversified, and interdependent populace will complicate the state's political, economic, and social sectors, generating conflicts. Many will be resolved by courts. A citizen's legislature will invariably be under pressure of time, attracted to interest politics, and confronted by highly technical issues, increasing chances for oversights and mistakes. A state constitution with antiquated details will need to be adjusted to the demands of contemporary society. Judicial corrections, interpretations, and vetoes appear inevitable. Judicial review shows no signs of atrophying in the foreseeable future. The issues of the 1900s will fade, but new problems will arise which ultimately will be brought to the court. It is only in Utopia that law becomes obsolete and lawyers and judges are no longer needed.

Because it can be anticipated that the Supreme Court will continue to resolve disputes generated by disagreements within society (many among them involving public policy issues), it is quite clear that the prevailing tension between public accountability and judicial independence will persist. The present and future members of the court will be called upon to tender their varying preferences for one or another of these antithetical demands.

What the first century of the court's history has shown is that the law is not simply what is printed in the *Revised Code of Washington*, and the Supreme Court is more than what is spindled in the clerk's office in the Temple of Justice and ultimately printed in the *Washington Reports*. The court and its law are the result of a prolonged and personal give and take among competent, committed, and contentious justices. The court is people.

The Washington Supreme Court comprises nine singular judges; each with his or her own particular background and perspective. But, these judges are charged with rendering collective decisions, requiring collective deliberations, through which at least five of the total agree. These individual judges are compelled to interact with one another, and this compulsion shapes their individual preferences. Thus, whatever dispute gets to the state's court of last resort must be submitted to the views of nine judges, and a majority of these jurists must arrive at some consensus.

To understand the dynamic process by which disputes are brought to the court, processed by the judges, and, again, returned to the community, is to understand a number of forces. Foremost among these forces would be the judges themselves, individually and collectively. In this study no claim is made that we have exhausted the sources for understanding judges. However, several tentative conclusions can be introduced.

The shape of recruitment of the justices to the state's high court has evolved from partisanship to nonpartisanship; from convention nomination to open primary election; from a passive to an active appointment role for the governor; from a relatively simple low- to a dynamic high-articulation recruitment system. Recruitment began as a political process and remains political; only the participants and the degree of their involvement have changed. But what are the consequences of the more structured and crowded selection process evident today?

First, different judges are brought to the bench; although it must be recognized that through the process of legal training and professionalization in legal practice and apprenticeship on lower courts, those who survive the process are actually more alike than not. They have shared experiences and traits that have allowed them to survive the often trying experience of electoral recruitment or gubernatorial appointment. Although it could be argued that the appointed judges tend to be a bit different from their elected counterparts, the difference is soon lost as those appointed must also suffer the labors of election. Certainly after several submittals to the electorate, an appointed judge soon absorbs the attributes of his or her elected counterpart, acquiring expectations learned during the selection process. The meaningful difference which can be attributed to recruitment is, of course, the difference between those who survive and those who fall by the wayside.

Recruitment also has a profound impact on the role courts assume in a democratic society. Judges must be held accountable for their policy decisions but, at the same time, must be free from the passions of the moment and the conflicting interests of the parties to the dispute. To render objective decisions, judges must be independent. The tension between public accountability and judicial independence is eased as recruitment becomes more structured with more persons and groups involved through the initiation, screening, and affirmation sequence. The authority of the bench deepens. More actors are involved in selecting the jurists, more standards are applied, more expectations communicated to the judges, and more satisfaction with the results of recruitment are apparent from the contemporary high articulation recruitment system. A pluralistic equilibrium develops.

Recruitment also brings to the bench judges with diverse but balanced views. Rarely in recent times has the court been dominated by activists or restraintists or liberals or conservatives. Justices appointed (or elected) in earlier times tend to blend with those recently appointed (or elected), preventing extremes. The court's philosophical leanings shift, but rarely suddenly, and almost never drastically.

Despite the periodic demands for a change in the formal method by which supreme court justices are selected, the informal and sometimes hidden recruitment processes are of far greater importance. What happens within the apparent or formal methods is what makes the difference, and the difference is felt in how the balance between accountability and independence is struck.

But another lesson is to be learned from the study of recruitment. The justices (and the legal profession) have the obligation to go among the public to educate, to listen and to conduct a public seminar on the issues facing the judges, on the workings of the court, on its decisions, and its personnel. Judges make public policy, and they ought to be seen among the public, not necessarily to justify but rather to explain and to learn. Only then is it likely that the attentive among the public will increase, and correspondingly the tolerance for independence and accountability will widen.

Fortunately, judicial elections blended with the short term appointments give to the jurists considerably more credibility than granted the remote and sometimes arrogant federal judiciary. If judges are to play a role in state politics, then they need the aura of respectability that accompanies their election after a sometimes hard-fought struggle with another competent but competitive aspirant.

To maintain their authority, the justices must be sufficiently cohesive, effective, and responsive to their environment. Important policy decisions require concentrated attention from judges, and, after considerable deliberations, the reasons for the decision must be thorough, convincing, and comprehensible. It is the public, or at least the attentive public among them, that must be addressed. They must be convinced of the soundness of the decision. The forum for convincing is the written opinion. But to appeal successfully to the reason of the citizenry, judges must have a sense for those common attitudes, values, and beliefs that hold society together. Not only is it to these that the justices turn for standards of judgment, but it is to these that they appeal as they justify their decisions.

To be a judge is far more difficult than to be a legislator. No less than legislators, judges must divine what is in the public interest. Unlike legislators, however, judges cannot go to their constituents for guidance, they cannot poll their voters, they cannot refer to the mandate given them from the last election, nor can they consult with representatives of special interests or of party leaders. Nonetheless, they are not without access to the prevailing mood of the public. The most salient if not sole opportunity for developing this access is through judicial election campaigns.

Two serious problems confront the justices if they are successfully to discover the public's interest. First, the ever-spiraling number of causes filed with the court must be brought under control. Nine justices can barely adequately, but rarely superbly, deal with the nearly one thousand cases filed with them each year. Of course, with their discretionary docket, they can quickly winnow this one thousand down to less than two hundred causes for their full attention. Even with the assistance of court commissioners and law clerks (who, we must often remind ourselves, are not directly accountable to the public), only cursory attention can be devoted to the study of these thousand requests for the court's attention. Even with the nearly two hundred which are finally selected, how much contemplation can be given each? What this requires is that each justice assume responsibility for at least twenty written decisions a year. Even apart from the work needed for dissenting and concurring opinions and for critiquing colleague's drafts, can the judges give the needed research, contemplation, and consultation to their assigned cases? The written opinions are the judge's legacy, and they must be convincing. But if the docket pressures increase, the judges will be hard pressed to produce the well-reasoned opinions needed to retain their respect with the public. Of course, implied in this plea is a charge to the media to give more attention to the court generally and, certainly to the reasoning of its decisions particularly. Supreme court decisions ought to be written and read as literature; political and legal literature, but nonetheless literature.

Additionally, submitting themselves to the appraisal of the electorate at least every six years extracts from the judges a considerable physical, mental, and financial toll. To teach and learn from the public during campaigning, the candidates are required to spend more money and more time in order to survive the screening and affirmation tests. The point at which a high articulation system is able to maintain a balance between independence and accountability may be passed by when the costs of campaigning become prohibitive. A candidate becomes reliant upon a few large contributors, and independence is threatened. But if campaigning is ignored, accountability is sacrificed. Perhaps increasing judicial pay, placing limits on contributions, or some form of public financing of elections are in order. In any case, the costs, both in time and money, of judicial elections must be debated and alternatives brought forth and thoroughly weighed (not alone by just the judicial and legal profession) before some experimentation is conducted.

The Washington court, of course, is not solely responsible for the course charted by the state in its second century. What the court does is to a great extent shaped by what the legislature, lower courts, and public officials do, and how the citizenry reacts. Equally important is what the U.S. Supreme Court does. The clear lesson from a review of constitutional issues during the 1930s, 1960s and 1980s is that what happens with the U.S. Supreme Court in the nation's capital often dictates what happens at the Temple of Justice in Olympia. Judge Millard's majority opinion in *West Coast Hotel* v. *Parrish* (300 U.S. 379, 1937) is perhaps a special but important example. Until this "switch in time that saved nine," the U.S. Supreme Court's reading of the due process clause of the Fourteenth Amendment to the U.S. Constitution largely tied the hands of state courts.

In the 1960s the Warren court's innovations in equal protection, due process, and First Amendment freedoms shaped many of the decisions of the Washington Supreme Court. Again, in the 1980s, the Burger court's conservative views compelled some state courts, the Washington Supreme Court included, to turn to their state constitutions for guidance. As long as the applications of the state's Declaration of Rights expand the freedoms of the nation's Bill of Rights and remain a matter of state law, federal judges cannot intervene. This form of "new federalism" appears to have captured the mood of the times and could dominate the resolution of a number of constitutional issues in the years to come. But again such resolution depends upon the views of those who are sitting on the state's court of last resort. The importance of the recruitment process is, again, emphasized.

For a fruitful recruitment process the electorate must insist upon candidates, opposed and unopposed, expressing their views on matters such as election costs, state vs. federal constitution, activism vs. restraint, liberalism vs. conservatism, and accountability vs. independence. The public must also tell the candidates their preferences. Working together, the Washington State Supreme Court will remain viable for another one hundred years.

Appendix 1

The Constitution of the State of Washington
Article IV: The Judiciary

§–1–JUDICIAL POWER, WHERE VESTED. The judicial power of the state shall be vested in a supreme court, superior courts, justices of the peace, and such inferior courts as the legislature may provide.
Court of appeals: Art. 4 § 29.

§–2–SUPREME COURT. The supreme court shall consist of five judges, a majority of whom shall be necessary to form a quorum, and pronounce a decision. The said court shall always be open for the transaction of business except on nonjudicial days. In the determination of causes all decisions of the court shall be given in writing and the grounds of the decision shall be stated. The legislature may increase the number of judges of the supreme court from time to time and may provide for separate departments of said court.

§–2(a)–TEMPORARY PERFORMANCE OF JUDICIAL DUTIES. When necessary for the prompt and orderly administration of justice a majority of the supreme court is empowered to authorize judges or retired judges of courts of record of this state, to perform, temporarily, judicial duties in the supreme court, and to authorize any superior court judge to perform judicial duties in any superior court of this state. [AMENDMENT 38, 1961 House Joint Resolution No. 6, p. 2757. Approved November, 1962.]

§–3–ELECTION AND TERMS OF SUPREME JUDGES. The judges of the supreme court shall be elected by the qualified electors of the state at large at the general state election at the times and places at which state officers are elected, unless some other time be provided by the legislature. The first election of judges of the supreme court shall be at the election which shall be held upon the adoption of this Constitution and the judges elected thereat shall be classified by lot, so that two shall hold their office for the term of three years, two for the term of five years, and one for the term of seven years. The lot shall be drawn by the judges who shall for that purpose assemble at the seat of government, and they shall cause the result thereof to be certified to the secretary of state, and filed in his office. The judge having the shortest term to serve not holding his office by appointment or election to fill a vacancy, shall be the chief justice, and shall preside at all sessions of the supreme court, and in case there shall be two judges having in like manner the same short term, the other judges of the supreme court shall determine which of them shall be chief justice. In case of the absence of the chief justice, the judge having in like manner the shortest or next shortest term to serve shall preside. After the first election the terms of judges elected shall be six years from and after the second Monday in January next succeeding their election. If a vacancy occurs in the office of a judge of the supreme court the governor shall appoint a person to hold the office until the election and qualification of a judge to fill the vacancy, which election shall take place at the next succeeding general election, and the judge so elected shall hold the office for the remainder of the unexpired term. The term of office of the judges of the supreme court, first elected, shall commence as soon as the state shall have been admitted into the Union, and continue for the term herein provided, and until their successors are elected and qualified. The sessions of the supreme court shall be held at the seat of government until otherwise provided by law.

§–3(a)–RETIREMENT OF SUPREME COURT AND SUPERIOR COURT JUDGES. A judge of the supreme court or the superior court shall retire from judicial office at the end of the calendar year in which he attains the age of seventy-five years. The legislature may, from time to time, fix a lesser age for mandatory retirement, not earlier than the end of the calendar year in which any such judge attains the age of seventy years, as the legislature deems proper. This provision shall not affect the term to which any such judge shall have been elected or appointed prior to, or at the time of approval and ratification of this provision. Notwithstanding the limitations of this section, the legislature may by general law authorize or require the retirement of judges for physical or mental disability, or any cause rendering judges incapable of performing their judicial duties. [AMENDMENT 25, 1951 House Joint Resolution No. 6, p. 960. Approved November 4, 1952.]

§–4–JURISDICTION. The supreme court shall have original jurisdiction in habeas corpus, and quo warranto and mandamus as to all state officers, and appellate jurisdiction in all actions and proceedings, excepting that its appellate jurisdiction shall not extend to civil actions at law for the recovery of money or personal property when the original amount in controversy, or the value of the property does not exceed the sum of two hundred dollars ($200) unless the action involves the legality of a tax, impost, assessment, toll, municipal fine, or the validity of a statute. The supreme court shall also have power to issue writs of mandamus, review, prohibition, habeas corpus, certiorari and all other writs necessary and proper to the complete exercise of its appellate and revisory jurisdiction. Each of the judges shall have power to issue writs of habeas corpus to any part of the state upon petition by or on behalf of any person held in actual custody, and may make such writs returnable before himself, or before the supreme court, or before any superior court of the state or any judge thereof.

§–5–SUPERIOR COURT—ELECTION OF JUDGES, TERMS of, etc. There shall be in each of the organized counties of this state a superior court for which at least one judge shall be elected by the qualified electors of the county at the general state election: *Provided,* That until otherwise directed by the legislature one judge only shall be elected for the counties of Spokane and Stevens; one judge for the county of Whitman; one judge for the counties of Lincoln, Okanogan, Douglas and Adams; one judge for the counties of Walla Walla and Franklin; one judge for the counties of Columbia, Garfield and Asotin; one judge for the counties of Kittitas, Yakima and Klickitat; one judge for the counties of Clark, Skamania, Pacific, Cowlitz and Wahkiakum; one judge for the counties of Thurston, Chehalis, Mason and Lewis; one judge for the county of Pierce; one judge for the county of King; one judge for the counties of Jefferson, Island, Kitsap, San Juan and Clallam; and one judge for the counties of Whatcom, Skagit and Snohomish. In any county where there shall be more than one superior judge, there may be as many sessions of the superior court at the same time as there are judges thereof, and whenever the governor shall direct a superior judge to hold court in any county other than that for which he has been elected, there may be as many sessions of the superior court in said county at the same time as there are judges therein or assigned to duty therein by the governor, and the business of the court shall be so distributed and assigned by law or in the absence of legislation therefor, by such rules and orders of court as shall best promote and secure the convenient and expeditious transaction thereof. The judgments, decrees, orders and proceedings of any session of the superior court held by any one or more of the judges of such court shall be equally effectual as if all the judges of said court presided at such session. The first superior judges elected under this Constitution shall hold their offices for the period of three years, and until their successors shall be elected and qualified, and thereafter the term of office of all superior judges in this state shall be for four years from the second Monday in January next succeeding their election and until their successors are elected and qualified. The first election of judges of the superior court shall be at the election held for the adoption of this Constitution. If a vacancy occurs in the office of judge of the superior court, the governor shall appoint a person to hold the office until the election and qualification of a judge to fill the vacancy, which election shall be at the next succeeding general election, and the judge so elected shall hold office for the remainder of the unexpired term.

§–6–JURISDICTION OF SUPERIOR COURTS. The superior court shall have orginal jurisdiction in all cases in equity and in all cases at law which involve the title or possession of real property, or the legality of any tax, impost, assessment, toll, or municipal fine, and in all other cases in which the demand or the value of the property in controversy amounts to three thousand dollars or as otherwise determined by law, or a lesser sum in excess of the jurisdiction granted to justices of the peace and other inferior courts, and in all criminal cases amounting to felony, and in all cases of misdemeanor not otherwise provided for by law; of actions of forcible entry and detainer; of proceedings in insolvency; of actions to prevent or abate a nuisance; of all matters of probate, of divorce, and for annulment of marriage; and for such special cases and proceedings as are not otherwise provided for. The superior court shall also have original jurisdiction in all cases and of all proceedings in which jurisdiction shall not have been by law vested exclusively in some other court; and said court shall have the power of naturalization and to issue papers therefor. They shall have such appellate jurisdiction in cases arising in justices' and other inferior courts in their respective counties as may be prescribed by law. They shall always be open, except on nonjudicial days, and their process shall extend to all parts of the state. Said courts and their judges shall have power to issue writs of mandamus, quo warranto, review, certiorari, prohibition, and writs of habeas corpus, on petition by or on behalf of any person in actual custody in their respective counties. Injunctions and writs of prohibition and of habeas corpus may be issued and served on legal holidays and nonjudicial days. [1977 Senate Joint Resolution No. 113. Approved November 8, 1977.]

§–7–EXCHANGE OF JUDGES—JUDGE PRO TEMPORE. The judge of any superior court may hold a superior court in any county at the request of the judge of the superior court thereof, and upon the request of the governor it shall be his duty to do so. A case in the superior court may be tried by a judge, pro tempore, who must be a member of the bar, agreed upon in writing by the parties litigant, or their attorneys of record, approved by the court and sworn to try the case.

§–8–ABSENCE OF JUDICIAL OFFICER. Any judicial officer who shall absent himself from the state for more than sixty consecutive days shall be deemed to have forfeited his office: *Provided*, That in cases of extreme necessity the governor may extend the leave of absence such time as the necessity therefor shall exist.

§–9–REMOVAL OF JUDGES, ATTORNEY GENERAL, ETC. Any judge of any court of record, the attorney general, or any prosecuting attorney may be removed from office by joint resolution of the legislature, in which three-fourths of the members elected to each house shall concur, for incompetency, corruption, malfeasance, or delinquency in office, or other sufficient cause stated in such resolution. But no removal shall be made unless the officer complained of shall have been served with a copy of the charges against him as the ground of removal, and shall have an opportunity of being heard in his defense. Such resolution shall be entered at length on the journal of both houses and on the question of removal the ayes and nays shall also be entered on the journal.

§–10–JUSTICES OF THE PEACE. The legislature shall determine the number of justices of the peace to be elected and shall prescribe by law the powers, duties and jurisdiction of justices of the peace: *Provided*, That such jurisdiction granted by the legislature shall not trench upon the jurisdiction of superior or other courts of record, except that justices of the peace may be made police justices of incorporated cities and towns. Justices of the peace shall have original jurisdiction in cases where the demand or value of the property in controversy is less than three hundred dollars or such greater sum, not to exceed three thousand dollars or as otherwise determined by law, as shall be prescribed by the legislature. In incorporated cities or towns having more than five thousand inhabitants, the justices of the peace shall receive such salary as may be provided by law, and shall receive no fees for their own use. [1977 Senate Joint Resolution No. 113. Approved November 8, 1977.]

§–11–COURTS OF RECORD. The supreme court and the superior courts shall be courts of record, and the legislature shall have power to provide that any of the courts of this state, excepting justices of the peace, shall be courts of record.

§–12–INFERIOR COURTS. The legislature shall prescribe by law the jurisdiction and powers of any of the inferior courts which may be established in pursuance of this Constitution.

§–13–SALARIES OF JUDICIAL OFFICERS——HOW PAID, ETC. No judicial officer, except court commissioners and unsalaried justices of the peace, shall receive to his own use any fees or perquisites of office. The judges of the supreme court and judges of the superior courts shall severally at stated times, during their continuance in office, receive for their services the salaries prescribed by law therefor, which shall not be increased after the election, nor during the term for which they shall have been elected. The salaries of the judges of the supreme court shall be paid by the state. One-half of the salary of each of the superior court judges shall be paid by the state, and the other one-half by the county or counties for which he is elected. In cases where a judge is provided for more than one county, that portion of his salary which is to be paid by the counties shall be apportioned between or among them according to the assessed value of their taxable property, to be determined by the assessment next preceding the time for which such salary is to be paid.

§–14–SALARIES OF SUPREME AND SUPERIOR COURT JUDGES. Each of the judges of the supreme court shall receive an annual salary of four thousand dollars ($4,000); each of the superior court judges shall receive an annual salary of three thousand dollars ($3,000), which said salaries shall be payable quarterly. The legislature may increase the salaries of judges herein provided.

§–15–INELIGIBILITY OF JUDGES. The judges of the supreme court and the judges of the superior court shall be ineligible to any other office or public employment than a judicial office, or employment, during the term for which they shall have been elected.

§–16–CHARGING JURIES. Judges shall not charge juries with respect to matters of fact, nor comment thereon, but shall declare the law.

§–17–ELIGIBILITY OF JUDGES. No person shall be eligible to the office of judge of the supreme court, or judge of a superior court, unless he shall have been admitted to practice in the courts of record of this state, or of the Territory of Washington.

§–18–SUPREME COURT REPORTER. The judges of the supreme court shall appoint a reporter for the decisions of that court, who shall be removable at their pleasure. He shall receive such annual salary as shall be prescribed by law.

§–19–JUDGES MAY NOT PRACTICE LAW. No judge of a court of record shall practice law in any court of this state during his continuance in office.

§–20–DECISIONS, WHEN TO BE MADE. Every cause submitted to a judge of a superior court for his decision shall be decided by him within ninety days from the submission thereof; *Provided*, That if within said period of ninety days a rehearing shall have been ordered, then the period within which he is to decide shall commence at the time the cause is submitted upon such a hearing.

§–21–PUBLICATION OF OPINIONS. The legislature shall provide for the speedy publication of opinions of the supreme court, and all opinions shall be free for publication by any person.

§–22–CLERK OF THE SUPREME COURT. The judges of the supreme court shall appoint a clerk of that court who shall be removable at their pleasure, but the legislature may provide for the election of the clerk of the supreme court, and prescribe the term of his office. The clerk of the supreme court shall receive such compensation by salary only as shall be provided by law.

§–23–COURT COMMISSIONERS. There may be appointed in each county, by the judge of the superior court having jurisdiction therein, one or more court commissioners, not exceeding three in number, who shall have authority to perform like duties as a judge of the superior court at chambers, subject to revision by such judge, to take depositions and to perform such other business connected with the administration of justice as may be prescribed by law.

§–24–RULES FOR SUPERIOR COURTS. The judges of the superior courts, shall from time to time, establish uniform rules for the government of the superior courts.

§–25–REPORTS OF SUPERIOR COURT JUDGES. Superior judges, shall on or before the first day of November in each year, report in writing to the judges of the supreme court such defects and omissions in the laws as their experience may suggest, and the judges of the supreme court shall on or before the first day of January in each year report in writing to the governor such defects and omissions in the laws as they may believe to exist.

§–26–CLERK OF THE SUPERIOR COURT. The county clerk shall be by virtue of his office, clerk of the superior court.

§–27–STYLE OF PROCESS. The style of all process shall be, "The State of Washington," and all prosecutions shall be conducted in its name and by its authority.

§–28–OATH OF JUDGES. Every judge of the supreme court, and every judge of a superior court shall, before entering upon the duties of his office, take and subscribe an oath that he will support the Constitution of the United States and the Constitution of the State of Washington, and will faithfully and impartially discharge the duties of judge to the best of his ability, which oath shall be filed in the office of the secretary of state.

§–29–ELECTION OF SUPERIOR

COURT JUDGES. Notwithstanding any provision of this Constitution to the contrary, if, after the last day as provided by law for the withdrawal of declarations of candidacy has expired, only one candidate has filed for any single position of superior court judge in any county containing a population of one hundred thousand or more, no primary or election shall be held as to such position, and a certificate of election shall be issued to such candidate. If, after any contested primary for superior court judge in any county, only one candidate is entitled to have his name printed on the general election ballot for any single position, no election shall be held as to such position, and a certificate of election shall be issued to such candidate: *Provided,* That in the event that there is filed with the county auditor within ten days after the date of the primary, a petition indicating that a write in campaign will be conducted for such single position and signed by one hundred registered voters qualified to vote with respect of the office, then such single position shall be subject to the general election. Provisions for the contingency of the death or disqualification of a sole candidate between the last date for withdrawal and the time when the election would be held but for the provisions of this section and such other provisions as may be deemed necessary to implement the provisions of this section, may be enacted by the legislature. [AMENDMENT 41 1965 ex.s. Substitute Senate Joint Resolution No. 6, p. 2815. Approved November 8, 1966.]

§–30–COURT OF APPEALS. (1) *Authorization.* In addition to the courts authorized in section 1 of this article, judicial power is vested in a court of appeals, which shall be established by statute.

(2) *Jurisdiction.* The jurisdiction of the court of appeals shall be as provided by statute or by rules authorized by statute.

(3) *Review of Superior Court.* Superior court actions may be reviewed by the court of appeals or by the supreme court as provided by statute or by rule authorized by statute.

(4) *Judges.* The number, manner of election, compensation, terms of office, removal and retirement of judges of the court of appeals shall be as provided by statute.

(5) *Administration and Procedure.* The administration and procedures of the court of appeals shall be as provided by rules issued by the supreme court.

(6) *Conflicts.* The provisions of this section shall supersede any conflicting provisions in prior sections of this article. [AMENDMENT 50, 1967 Senate Joint Resolution No. 6. Approved November 5, 1968.]

Article V: Impeachment

§–1–IMPEACHMENT—POWER OF AND PROCEDURE. The house of representatives shall have the sole power of impeachment. The concurrence of a majority of all the members shall be necessary to an impeachment. All impeachments shall be tried by the senate, and, when sitting for that purpose, the senators shall be upon oath or affirmation to do justice according to law and evidence. When the governor or lieutenant governor is on trial, the chief justice of the supreme court shall preside. No person shall be convicted without a concurrence of two-thirds of the senators elected.

§–2–OFFICERS LIABLE TO. The governor and other state and judicial officers, except judges and justices of courts not of record, shall be liable to impeachment for high crimes or misdemeanors, or malfeasance in office, but judgment in such cases shall extend only to removal from office and disqualification to hold any office of honor, trust or profit, in the state. The party, whether convicted or acquitted, shall, nevertheless, be liable to prosecution, trial, judgment and punishment according to law.

§–3–REMOVAL FROM OFFICE. All officers not liable to impeachment shall be subject to removal for misconduct or malfeasance in office, in such manner as may be provided by law.

Article XXVII: Schedule

In order that no inconvenience may arise by reason of a change from a Territorial to a State government, it is hereby declared and ordained as follows:

§–1–EXISTING RIGHTS, ACTIONS AND CONTRACTS SAVED. No existing rights, actions, suits, proceedings, contracts or claims shall be affected by a change in the form of government, but all shall continue as if no such change had taken place; and all process which may have been issued under the authority of the Territory of Washington previous to its admission into the Union shall be as valid as if issued in the name of the state.

§–2–LAWS IN FORCE CONTINUED. All laws now in force in the Territory of Washington, which are not repugnant to this Constitution, shall remain in force until they expire by their own limitation, or are altered or repealed by the legislature: *Provided*, That this section shall not be so construed as to validate any act of the legislature of Washington Territory granting shore or tide lands to any person, company or any municipal or private corporation.

§–3–DEBTS, FINES, ETC., TO INURE TO THE STATE. All debts, fines, penalties and forfeitures, which have accrued, or may hereafter accrue, to the Territory of Washington, shall inure to the State of Washington.

. . . .

§–5–CRIMINAL PROSECUTIONS AND PENAL ACTIONS. All criminal prosecutions and penal actions which may have arisen, or which may arise, before the change from a territorial to a state government, and which shall then be pending, shall be prosecuted to judgment, and execution in the name of the state. All offenses committed against the laws of the Territory of Washington, before the change from a territorial to a state government, and which shall not be prosecuted before such change, may be prosecuted in the name and by the authority of the State of Washington, with like effect as though such change had not taken place; and all penalties incurred shall remain the same as if this Constitution had not been adopted. All actions at law and suits in equity which may be pending in any of the courts of the Territory of Washington, at the time of the change from a territorial to a state government, shall be continued, and transferred to the court of the state having jurisdiction of the subject matter thereof.

§–6–RETENTION OF TERRITORIAL OFFICERS. All officers now holding their office under the authority of the United States, or of the Territory of Washington, shall continue to hold and exercise their respective offices until they shall be superseded by the authority of the state.

§–7–CONSTITUTIONAL OFFICERS, WHEN ELECTED. All officers provided for in this Constitution including a county clerk for each county when no other time is fixed for their election, shall be elected at the election to be held for the adoption of this Constitution on the first Tuesday of October, 1889.

§–8–CHANGE OF COURTS—TRANSFER OF CAUSES. Whenever the judge of the superior court of any county, elected or appointed under the provisions of this Constitution shall have qualified the several causes then pending in the district court of the territory except such causes as would have been within the exclusive jurisdiction of the United States district court had such court existed at the time of the commencement of such causes, within such county, and the records, papers and proceedings of said district court, and the seal and other property pertaining thereto, shall pass into the jurisdiction and possession of the superior court for such county. And where the same judge is elected for two or more counties, it shall be the duty of the clerk of the district court having custody of such papers and records to transmit to the clerk of such county, or counties, other than that in which such records are kept the original papers in all cases pending in such district court and belonging to the jurisdiction of such county or counties together with transcript of so much of the records of said district court as relate to the same; and until the district courts of the Territory shall be superseded in manner aforesaid, the said district courts and the judges thereof, shall continue with the same jurisdiction and powers, to be exercised in the same judicial districts respectively, as heretofore constituted under the laws of the Territory. Whenever a quorum of the judges of the supreme court of the state shall have been elected and qualified, the causes then pending in the supreme court of the Territory, except such causes as would have been within the exclusive jurisdiction of the United States, circuit court had such court existed at the time of the commencement of such causes, and the papers, records and proceedings of said court and the seal and other property pertaining thereto, shall pass into the jurisdiction and possession of the supreme court of the state, and until so superseded, the supreme court of the Territory and the judges thereof, shall continue with like powers and jurisdiction as if this Constitution had not been adopted.

§–9–SEALS OF COURTS AND MUNICIPALITIES. Until otherwise provided by law, the seal now in use in the supreme court of the Territory shall be the seal of the supreme court of the state. The seals of the superior courts of the several counties of the state shall be, until otherwise provided by law, the vignette of General George Washington with the words "Seal of the Superior Court of __________ county" surrounding the vignette. The seal of municipalities, and of all county officers of the Territory, shall be the seals of such municipalities, and county officers respectively under the state, until otherwise provided by law.

§–10–PROBATE COURT, TRANSFER OF. When the state is admitted into the Union, and the superior courts in the respective counties organized, the books, records, papers and proceedings of the probate court in each county, and all causes and matters of administration pending therein, shall, upon the expiration of the term of office of the probate judges, on the second Monday in January, 1891, pass into the jurisdiction and possession of the superior court of the same county created by this Constitution, and the said court shall proceed to final judgment or decree, order of other determination in the several matters and causes, as the territorial probate court might have done, if this Constitution had not been adopted. And until the expiration of the term of office of the probate judges, such probate judges shall perform the duties now imposed upon them by laws of the Territory. The superior courts shall have appellate and revisory jurisdiction over the decisions of the probate courts, as now provided by law, until such latter courts expire by limitation.

§–11–DUTIES OF FIRST LEGISLATURE. The legislature, at its first session, shall provide for the election of all officers whose election is not provided for elsewhere in this Constitution, and fix the time for the commencement and duration of their term.

§–12–ELECTION CONTESTS FOR SUPERIOR JUDGES, HOW DECIDED. In case of a contest of election between candidates, at the first general election under this Constitution, for judges of the superior courts, the evidence shall be taken in the manner prescribed by the Territorial laws, and the testimony so taken shall be certified to the secretary of state; and said officer, together with the governor and treasurer of state, shall review the evidence and determine who is entitled to the certificate of election.

. . . .

§–15–ELECTION ON ADOPTION OF CONSTITUTION, HOW TO BE CONDUCTED. The election held at the time of the adoption of this Constitution shall be held and conducted in all respects according to the laws of the Territory, and the votes cast at said election for all officers (where no other provisions are made in this Constitution), and for the adoption of this Constitution and the several separate articles and the location of the state capital, shall be canvassed and returned in the several counties in the manner provided by Territorial law, and shall be returned to the secretary of the Territory in the manner provided by the Enabling Act.

§–16–WHEN CONSTITUTION TO TAKE EFFECT. The provisions of this Constitution shall be in force from the day on which the president of the United State shall issue his proclamation declaring the State of Washington admitted into the Union, and the terms of all officers elected at the first election under the provisions of this Constitution shall commence on the Monday next succeeding the issue of said proclamation, unless otherwise provided herein.

Appendix 2

Justices and Chief Justices of the Supreme Court of Washington, 1889–1985

Abel, Don G. Term of Office: November 7, 1946 (temporary appointment pursuant to Laws of 1941, ch. 201, 2), to September 10, 1947.

Anders, Thomas J. November 11, 1889, to January 10, 1905. Chief Justice: November 11, 1889, to January 9, 1893.

Andersen, James A. July 24, 1984 (appointed), to (presently serving).

Askren, William D. January 12, 1925, to November 30, 1928.

Bausman, Frederick. October 26, 1915 (appointed), to November 20, 1916 (resigned).

Beals, Walter B. April 16, 1928 (appointed), to October 1, 1946 (war service); September 10, 1947, to September 10, 1951 (retired). Chief Justice: January 9, 1933, to January 14, 1935; January 8, 1945, to December 18, 1945; May 7, 1946, to October 1, 1946.

Beeler, Adam. September 30, 1930 (appointed), to May 23, 1923 (resigned).

Blake, Bruce. December 1, 1932, to August 31, 1946 (resigned). Chief Justice: January 9, 1939, to January 13, 1941.

Brachtenbach, Robert F. November 20, 1972 (appointed), to (presently serving). Chief Justice: January 12, 1981, to January 10, 1983.

Bridges, Jessee B. June 1, 1919 (appointed), to April 14, 1927 (died).

Callow, Keith M. January 5, 1985 (appointed), to (presently serving).

Chadwick, Stephen J. December 3, 1908 (appointed), to June 1, 1919 (resigned). Chief Justice: January 13, 1919, to June 1, 1919.

Connelly, Edward M. April 22, 1946 (appointed), to January 13, 1947.

Crow, Herman D. January 19, 1905 (appointed pursuant to Laws of 1905, ch. 5, permanently increasing the number of judges), to October 22, 1915 (died). Chief Justice: January 13, 1913, to January 11, 1915.

Dimmick, Carolyn R. January 2, 1981 (appointed), to January 12, 1985 (resigned).

Dolliver, James M. May 6, 1976 (appointed), to (presently serving). Chief Justice: January 14, 1985, to January 10, 1987.

Donworth, Charles T. September 12, 1949 (appointed), to December 31, 1967 (retired). Chief Justice: July 6, 1956, to January 14, 1957.

Dore, Fred H. January 2, 1981 (appointed), to (presently serving).

Driver, Samuel M. May 9, 1940 (appointed), to November 21, 1942 (war service); December 1, 1945, to April 22, 1946 (resigned). Chief Justice: December 18, 1945, to April 22, 1946.

Dunbar, Ralph O. November 11, 1889, to September 19, 1912 (died). Chief Justice: January 9, 1893, to January 14, 1895; June 1, 1900, to January 14, 1901; January 9, 1911, to September 19, 1912.

Durham, Barbara. January 12, 1985 (appointed), to (presently serving).

Ellis, Overton G. May 10, 1911 (appointed), to May 11, 1918 (resigned). Chief Justice: January 8, 1917, to May 11, 1918.

Finley, Robert C. January 8, 1951, to March 23, 1976 (died). Chief Justice: January 9, 1961, to January 14, 1963; January 9, 1967, to January 13, 1969.

Foster, Harry Ellsworth. July 8, 1956 (appointed), to December 6, 1956; January 14, 1957, to December 5, 1962 (died).

French, Walter M. January 10, 1927, to September 13, 1930 (died).

Fullerton, Mark A. January 9, 1899, to September 21, 1931 (died). Chief Justice: January 12, 1903, to January 9, 1905; April 16, 1928, to January 14, 1929.

Geraghty, James M. August 15, 1933 (appointed), to April 29, 1940 (died).

Goodloe, William C. January 14, 1985, to (presently serving).

Gordon, Merritt J. January 14, 1895, to June 1, 1900 (resigned). Chief Justice: January 9, 1899, to June 1, 1900.

Gose, Mack F. January 11, 1909 (appointed), to January 11, 1915.

Grady, Thomas E. November 25, 1942 (temporary appointment pursuant to Laws of 1941, ch. 201, sec. 2), to November 30, 1945; January 10, 1949, to January 10, 1955. Chief Justice: January 12, 1953, to January 10, 1955.

Hadley, Hiram E. March 20, 1901 (temporary appointment pursuant to Act of March 18, 1901), to October 7, 1902; January 12, 1903, to January 11, 1909. Chief Justice: January 14, 1907, to January 11, 1909.

Hale, Frank. January 14, 1963 (appointed), to January 13, 1975. Chief Justice: January 8, 1973, to January 13, 1975.

Hamilton, Orris L. January 22, 1962 (appointed), to January 8, 1979. Chief Justice: January 11, 1971, to January 8, 1973.

Hamley, Frederick G. September 6, 1949 (appointed), to July 6, 1956 (resigned). Chief Justice: January 10, 1955, to July 6, 1956.

Herman, Henry E. T. September 23, 1931 (appointed), to December 1, 1932.

Hicks, Floyd V. January 10, 1977, to January 17, 1982 (resigned).

Hill, Matthew W. January 13, 1947, to December 31, 1969 (retired). Chief Justice: January 14, 1957, to January 12, 1959.

Holcomb, Oscar R. January 11, 1915, to January 10, 1927; April 22, 1927 (appointed), to January 9, 1939. Chief Justice: June 1, 1919, to January 10, 1921.

Horowitz, Charles J. January 13, 1975, to December 31, 1980 (retired).

Hovey, C. R. September 14, 1921 (appointed), to January 8, 1923.

Hoyt, John P. November 11, 1889, to January 11, 1897. Chief Justice: January 14, 1895, to January 11, 1897.

Hunter, Robert T. October 11, 1957 (appointed), to January 10, 1977. Chief Justice: January 13, 1969, to January 11, 1971.

Jeffers, Clyde G. January 9, 1939, to August 8, 1949 (retired). Chief Justice: January 10, 1949, to August 8, 1949.

Mackintosh, Kenneth. March 30, 1918 (appointed), to April 16, 1928 (retired). Chief Justice: January 10, 1927, to April 16, 1928.

Main, John F. September 27, 1912 (appointed), to October 13, 1943 (died). Chief Justice: May 11, 1918, to January 13, 1919; January 8, 1923, to January 12, 1925.

Mallery, Joseph A. November 9, 1942 (appointed), to January 15, 1962 (retired). Chief Justice: January 13, 1947, to January 10, 1949.

McGovern, Walter T. January 8, 1968 (appointed), to May 13, 1971 (resigned).

Millard, William J. December 1, 1928 (appointed), to January 10, 1949; December 6, 1956, to January 14, 1957. Chief Justice: January 14, 1935, to January 11, 1937; October 17, 1946, to January 13, 1947.

Mitchell, John R. May 11, 1918 (appointed), to January 11, 1937. Chief Justice: January 14, 1929, to January 12, 1931.

Morris, George E. February 26, 1909 (appointed pursuant to Laws of 1909, ch. 24, permanently increasing the number of judges), to March 30, 1918 (died). Chief Justice: January 11, 1915, to January 8, 1917.

Mount, Wallace. January 14, 1901, to September 4, 1921 (died). Chief Justice: January 9, 1905, to January 14, 1907; September 27, 1912, to January 13, 1913.

Neill, Marshall A. April 24, 1967 (appointed), to November 16, 1972 (resigned).

Olson, Ralph O. September 10, 1951 (appointed), to January 15, 1955 (died).

Ott, Richard B. January 24, 1955 (appointed), to March 31, 1967 (retired). Chief Justice: January 14, 1963, to January 11, 1965.

Parker, Emmett N. February 26, 1909 (appointed pursuant to Laws of 1909, ch. 24, permanently increasing the number of judges), to August 15, 1933 (retired). Chief Justice: January 10, 1921, to January 8, 1923.

Pearson, Vernon R. January 18, 1982 (appointed), to (presently serving). Chief Justice, January 10, 1987, to present.

Pemberton, William H. January 8, 1923, to January 12, 1925.

Reavis, James Bradley. January 11, 1897, to January 12, 1903. Chief Justice: January 14, 1901, to January 12, 1903.

Robinson, John S. January 11, 1937, to May 21, 1951 (retired). Chief Justice: January 13, 1941, to January 11, 1943.

Root, Milo A. January 19, 1905 (appointed pursuant to Laws of 1905, ch. 5, permanently increasing the number of judges), to December 2, 1908 (resigned).

Rosellini, Hugh J. January 10, 1955, to November 26, 1984 (died). Chief Justice: January 11, 1965, to January 9, 1967.

Rudkin, Frank H. January 10, 1905, to February 14, 1911 (resigned). Chief Justice: January 11, 1909, to January 9, 1911.

Schwellenbach, E. W. September 3, 1946 (appointed), to September 22, 1957 (died). Chief Justice: January 8, 1951, to January 12, 1963.

Scott, Elmon. November 11, 1889, to January 9, 1899. Chief Justice: January 11, 1897, to January 1, 1899.

Sharp, Morell E. May 28, 1970 (appointed), to January 11, 1971; May 13, 1971 (appointed), to December 17, 1971 (resigned).

Simpson, George B. September 20, 1937 (appointed), to January 8, 1951. Chief Justice: January 11, 1943, to January 8, 1945; August 8, 1949, to January 8, 1951.

Stafford, Charles F. January 1, 1970 (appointed), to July 3, 1984 (died). Chief Justice: January 13, 1975, to January 10, 1977.

Steinert, William J. May 23, 1932 (appointed), to September 12, 1949 (retired). Chief Justice: January 11, 1937, to January 9, 1939.

Stiles, Theodore L. November 11, 1889, to January 14, 1895.

Tolman, Warren W. May 11, 1918 (appointed), to September 20, 1937 (retired). Chief Justice: January 12, 1925, to January 10, 1927; January 12, 1931, to January 9, 1933.

Utter, Robert F. December 20, 1971 (appointed), to (presently serving). Chief Justice: January 8, 1979, to January 12, 1981.

Weaver, Frank P. May 21, 1951 (appointed), to May 21, 1970 (retired). Chief Justice: January 12, 1959, to January 9, 1961.

Webster, J. Stanley. November 20, 1916 (appointed), to May 11, 1918 (resigned).

White, William H. June 1, 1900 (appointed), to January 14, 1901; March 20, 1901 (temporary appointment pursuant to Act of March 18, 1901), to October 7, 1902.

Williams, William H. January 8, 1979, to January 14, 1985 (resigned). Chief Justice: January 10, 1983, to January 14, 1985.

Wright, Charles T. January 11, 1971, to November 6, 1980 (died). Chief Justice: January 10, 1977, to January 8, 1979.

Bibliography

Territorial Period, Constitutional Development, and the Early Years

Books

Airey, Wilfred J. "A History of the Constitution and Government of Washington Territory." Ph.D. dissertation, University of Washington, 1945.

Aumann, Francis R. *The Changing American Legal System*. New York: Da Capo Press, 1969.

Bagley, Clarence. *History of Seattle from the Earliest Settlement to the Present Time*. Chicago: S. J. Clarke, 1916.

Beckett, Paul L. *From Wilderness to Enabling Act: The Evolution of the State of Washington*. Pullman: Washington State University Press, 1968.

Bond, Carroll T. *The Court of Appeals of Maryland: A History*. Baltimore: Barton-Gillett Co., 1928.

Clark, Norman H. *Washington, a Bicentennial History*. New York: Norton, 1976.

———. *The Dry Years: Prohibition and Social Change in Washington*. Seattle: University of Washington Press, 1965.

Cole, Robert L. "The Democratic Party in Washington, 1919–1933." Ph.D. dissertation, University of Washington, 1972.

Dodds, Gordon B. *The American Northwest: A History of Oregon and Washington*. Arlington Heights: Forum Press, 1986.

Dryden, Cecil. *History of Washington*. Portland: Binfords & Mort, 1968.

Deutsch, Herman J. *History and Government of the State of Washington*. Pullman: State College of Washington, 1941.

Dimond, Allan J. *The Superior Court of Massachusetts, Its Origin and Development*. Boston: Little, Brown, 1960.

Easton, David. *The Political System*. New York: Knopf, 1953.

Edwards, G. Thomas, and Carlos A. Schwantes, eds., *Experiences in a Promised Land: Essays in Pacific Northwest History*. Seattle, University of Washington Press, 1986.

Ekirch, Arthur A. *Progressivism in America: A Study of the Era from Theodore Roosevelt to Woodrow Wilson*. New York: New Viewpoints, 1974.

Friedman, Lawrence M. *A History of American Law*. New York: Simon and Schuster, 1973.

Frisch, Richard. "A History of the Democratic Party in the State of Washington, 1854–1956." Ph.D. dissertation, University of Oregon, 1975.

Gilmore, Grant. *The Ages of American Law.* New Haven: Yale University Press, 1974.

Gould, Lewis L., ed. *The Progressive Era.* Syracuse, N.Y.: Syracuse University Press, 1974.

Guice, John D. *The Rocky Mountain Bench: The Territorial Supreme Courts of Colorado, Montana, and Wyoming, 1861–1890.* New Haven: Yale University Press, 1972.

Halpern, Stephen, and Charles Lamb. *Supreme Court Activism and Restraint.* Lexington, Mass.: Lexington Books, 1982.

Harris, Silas A. *Appellate Courts and Appellate Procedure in Ohio.* Baltimore: Johns Hopkins Press, 1933.

Hawley, Lowell S., and Ralph B. Potts. *Counsel for the Damned.* New York: Lippincott, 1953.

Hawthorne, Julian, ed. *History of Washington, the Evergreen State.* New York: American Historical Publishing Company, 1893.

Haynes, Evan. *The Selection and Tenure of Judges.* Newark: The National Conference of Judicial Councils, 1944.

Hines, H. K. *An Illustrated History of the State of Washington.* Chicago: The Lewis Publishing Company, 1894.

Holman, Frank E. *The Life and Career of a Western Lawyer, 1886–1961.* Baltimore: Port City Press, 1963.

Horwitz, Morton J. *The Transformation of American Law, 1780–1860.* Cambridge: Harvard University Press, 1977.

Hurst, James W. *The Growth of American Law: The Lawmakers.* Boston: Little, Brown, 1950.

———. *Law and the Conditions of Freedom in the Nineteenth Century United States.* Madison: University of Wisconsin Press, 1956.

Johnson, John W. *American Legal Culture, 1908–1940.* Westport, Conn.: Greenwood Press, 1981.

Meany, Edmond. *The History of the State of Washington.* New York: Macmillan, 1924.

Miles, Charles, and O. B. Sperlin. *Building a State: Washington, 1889–1939.* Tacoma: Washington State Historical Society, 1940.

Morgan, Murray C. *Puget's Sound: A Narrative History of Early Tacoma and the Southern Sound.* Seattle: University of Washington Press, 1979.

———. *Skid Road: An Informal Portrait of Seattle.* Rev. ed., Seattle: University of Washington Press, 1982.

Mullen, W. Frank, John C. Pierce, Charles H. Sheldon, and Thor Swanson. *The Government and Politics of Washington State.* Pullman, Wash.: Washington State University Press, 1978.

Nelson, Margaret V. *A Study of Judicial Review in Virginia: 1789–1928.* New York: Columbia University Press, 1947.

Pollard, Lancaster. *A History of the State of Washington.* Portland: Binfords & Mort, 1941.

Pomeroy, Earl S. *The Territories of the United States, 1862–1890.* Philadelphia: University of Pennsylvania Press, 1947.

Pound, Roscoe. *The Lawyer from Antiquity to Modern Times*. St. Paul: West, 1953.

Reinhart, C. S. *History of the Supreme Court of the Territory and State of Washington*. Olympia: Private printing, n.d.

Rosenow, Beverly Paulik. *The Journal of the Washington Constitutional Convention, 1889*. Seattle: Book Publishing Company, 1962.

Sale, Roger. *Seattle: Past to Present*. Seattle: University of Washington Press, 1976.

Sheldon, Charles H. *The American Judicial Process: Models and Approaches*. New York: Dodd, Mead, 1974.

Smith, Franklin A. *Judicial Review of Legislation in New York, 1906–1938*. New York: Columbia University Press, 1952.

Spencer, Lloyd, and Lancaster Pollard, eds. *A History of the State of Washington*. New York: The American Historical Society, 1937.

Taylor, C. W., Jr. *Eminent Judges and Lawyers of the Northwest: 1843–1955*. Palo Alto: C. W. Taylor, Jr., 1954.

Tocqueville, Alexis de. *Democracy in America* (1834). New York: New American Library, 1956.

White, G. Edward. *The American Judicial Tradition*. New York: Oxford, 1978.

Wilkins, William J. *The Sword and the Gavel*. Seattle: The Writing Works, 1981.

Woodward, Walter C. *The Rise and Early History of Political Parties in Oregon, 1843–1868*. Portland: J. K. Gill, 1913.

Wunder, John R. *Inferior Courts, Superior Justice*. Westport, Conn.: Greenwood, 1979.

Articles

Blackford, Mansel G. "Reform Politics in Seattle during the Progressive Era," *Pacific Northwest Quarterly* 59 (1968):177.

Booker, Quinten, Kathy Evans, and Shannon Skinner. "Support Agencies of the Washington State Supreme Court: Their Influences upon the Judicial Process." Occasional Paper, Division of Governmental Studies and Services, Department of Political Science, Washington State University (1979).

Brown, Theodore J. "The Tennessee County Courts under the North Carolina and Territorial Governments: The Davidson County Court of Pleas and Quarter Sessions, 1783–1796, as a Case Study." *Vanderbilt Law Review* 32 (1979):349.

Chadwick, Stephen F., ed. "The Recollections of Stephen James Chadwick." *Pacific Northwest Quarterly* 55 (1964):111.

Clark, Cornelia Anne. "Justice on the Tennessee Frontier: The Williamson County Circuit Court, 1810–1820." *Vanderbilt Law Review* 32 (1979):413.

Collins, Ronald K. L. "Forward: Reliance on State Constitutions—Beyond the 'New Federalism.'" *University of Puget Sound Law Review* 8 (1985):vi.

Conklin, Frank J., and James M. Vache. "The Establishment Clause and the

Free Exercise Clause of the Washington Constitution—A Proposal to the Supreme Court." *University of Puget Sound Law Review* 8 (1985):411.

Countryman, Vern. "Why a State Bill of Rights?" *Washington Law Review* 45 (1970):453.

Ellis, Overton G. "The Court's Work." *Proceedings of the Washington State Bar Association* (1914):179.

Field, Oliver. "Unconstitutional Legislation in Indiana." *Indiana Law Journal* 17 (1941):101.

———. "Unconstitutional Legislation in Minnesota." *American Political Science Review* 35 (1941):898.

Friedman, Lawrence M., et al. "State Supreme Courts: A Century of Style and Citation." *Stanford Law Review* 33 (1981):773.

Gordon, Joseph H. "Our State Bar Associations: The Washington State Bar Asssociation." *American Bar Association Journal* 48 (January 1962):71.

Hall, Kermit L. "Hacks and Derelicts Revisited: American Territorial Judiciary, 1789–1959." *Western Historical Quarterly* 12 (July 1981).

———. "Progressive Reform and the Decline of Democratic Accountability: The Popular Election of State Supreme Court Judges, 1850–1920." *American Bar Foundation Research Journal* (1984):345.

———. "The Judiciary on Trial: State Constitutional Reform and the Rise of an Elected Judiciary, 1846–1860." *The Historian* 44 (1983):337.

———. "The 'Route to Hell' Retraced: The Impact of Popular Election on the Southern Appellate Judiciary, 1832–1920." David Bodenhamer and James Ely, Jr., eds. *Essays on Legal History of the South.* University: University of Mississippi Press, 1984.

Heiberg, Robert A. "Social Backgrounds on the Minnesota Supreme Court Justices, 1858–1968." *Minnesota Law Review* 53 (1969):901.

Hickman, Martin B. "Judicial Review of Legislation in Utah." *Utah Law Review* 5 (1954):50.

Hurst, James W. "The Functions of Courts in the United States, 1950–1980." *Law and Society Review* 15 (1980):415.

Johnson, C. O. "The Initiative and Referendum in Washington." *Pacific Northwest Quarterly* 36 (1945):29.

Kagan, Robert, et al. "The Business of State Supreme Courts, 1870–1970." *Stanford Law Review* 30 (1977):121.

———. "The Evolution of State Supreme Courts." *Michigan Law Review* 76 (1978):961.

Kagan, Robert, Bobby D. Infelise, and Robert R. Detlefsen. "American State Supreme Court Justices, 1900–1970." *American Bar Foundation Research Journal* (1984):371.

Kerr, William T., Jr., "The Progressives of Washington, 1910–12." *Pacific Northwest Quarterly* 55 (1964):16.

Kimball, Edward. "Criminal Cases in a State Appellate Court, 1839–1959." *American Journal of Legal History* 9 (1965):95.

Knapp, Lebbeus J. "Origin of the Constitution of the State of Washington." *Washington Historical Quarterly* 4 (1913):227.

Linde, Hans. "E Pluribus—Constitutional Theory and State Courts." *Georgia Law Review* 18 (1984):165.

McIntosh, Wayne V. "150 Years of Litigation and Dispute Settlement: A Court Tale." *Law and Society Review* 15 (1981):823.

Mitchell, John. "Address at State Prosecuting Attorneys' Association." *Proceedings of the Washington State Bar Association* (1921):172.

Murray, Keith A. "The Movement for Statehood in Washington." *Pacific Northwest Quarterly* 32 (1941):349.

———. "Issues and Personalities of Pacific Northwest Politics: 1889–1950." *Pacific Northwest Quarterly* 41 (1950):213.

Nelson, William E. "Changing Concepts of Judicial Review: The Evolution of Constitutional Theory in the States, 1760–1860." *University of Pennsylvania Law Review* 120 (1972):1169.

Paul, Charles H. "The Rule-Making Power of the Courts." *Washington Law Review* 1 (1926):163.

———. "The Judicial Council Movement." *Washington Law Review* 1 (1925):101.

Post, Frank Truman. "Effect of the Direct Primary Law upon the Character, Ability and Independence of the Judiciary." *Oregon Bar Association Proceedings* (1908–10).

Price, Charles. "The Initiative: A Comparative State Analysis and Reassessment of a Western Phenomenon." *Western Political Quarterly* 28 (1975):243.

Prosch, Thomas W. "Washington Territory Fifty Years Ago." *Washington Historical Quarterly* 4 (1913):96.

Rudkin, Frank H. "The Court's Work." *Proceedings of the Washington State Bar Association* (1906):171.

Rupp, John N. "How It Used to Be: The Supreme Court's Law Clerks." Unpublished manuscript, n.d., Department of Political Science, Washington State University.

Schlag, Pierre. "Framers' Intent: The Illegitimate Uses of History." *University of Puget Sound Law Review* 8 (1985):283.

Schreiber, H. N. "Public Rights and the Rule of Law in American Legal History." *California Law Review* 71 (1984):217.

Schweppe, Alfred J. "Report of the Judicial Council on Expediting the Work of the Supreme Court." *State Bar Journal* 31 (1956):340.

Sheldon, Charles H. "The Recruitment of Judges to the Washington Supreme Court: Past and Present." *Willamette Law Review* 22 (Winter 1986):85.

———. "Judicial Review and the Supreme Court of Washington, 1890–1986." *Publius* 17 (Winter 1987):69.

Stiles, Theodore L. "Legislative Encroachments upon Private Rights." *Proceedings of the Washington State Bar Association* (1889).

———. "The Constitution of the State and Its Effect upon the Public Interest." *Washington Historical Quarterly* 4 (1913):281.

Tripp, J. F. "Progressive Jurisprudence in the West: The Washington

Supreme Court, Labor Law, and the Problem of Industrial Accidents." *Labor History* 24 (1983):242.

Utter, Robert F. "Freedom and Diversity in a Federal System: Perspectives on State Constitutions and the Washington Declaration of Rights." *University of Puget Sound Law Review* 7 (1984):491.

Vernier, C. G., and Philip Selig, Jr. "The Reversal of Criminal Cases in the Supreme Court of California." *Southern California Law Review* 2 (1928):21.

Judicial Recruitment

Books

Ashman, A., and J. Alfini. *The Key to Judicial Merit Selection: The Nominating Process.* Chicago: American Judicature Society, 1974.

Beman, Lamar T. *Election vs. Appointment of Judges.* New York: H. W. Wilson, 1926.

Carpenter, William S. *Judicial Tenure in the United States.* New Haven: Yale University Press, 1918.

Chinn, Nancy, and Larry Berkson. *Literature on Judicial Selection.* Chicago: American Judicature Society, 1980.

Danelski, David J. *A Supreme Court Justice Is Appointed.* New York: Random House, 1964.

Dubois, Philip. *From Ballot to Bench.* Austin: University of Texas Press, 1980.

Escovitz, S. S., F. Kurland, and N. Gold. *Judicial Selection and Tenure.* Chicago: American Judicature Society, 1975.

Greer, James, Ronald Hedluns, and James Gibson. *Accountability in Urban Society.* Beverly Hills: Sage, 1978.

Haynes, Evan. *The Selection and Tenure of Judges.* Newark: The National Conference of Judicial Councils, 1944.

Maddi, Dorothy. *Judicial Performance Polls.* Chicago: American Bar Foundation, 1977.

Martin, Edward M. *The Role of the Bar in Electing the Bench in Chicago.* Chicago: University of Chicago Press, 1936.

Nagel, Stuart. *Comparing Elected and Appointed Judicial Systems.* Beverly Hills: Sage, 1973.

Philip, Cynthia Owen, Paul Nejelski, and Arie Press. *Where Do Judges Come From?* New York: Institute of Judicial Administration, 1976.

Richardson, Richard, and Kenneth Vines. *The Politics of Federal Courts.* Boston: Little, Brown, 1970.

Stolz, Preble. *Judging the Judges: The Investigation of Rose Bird and the California Supreme Court.* New York: Free Press, 1981.

Winters, Glenn R., ed. *Judicial Selection and Tenure: Selected Readings.* Chicago: American Judicature Society, 1973.

Articles

Adamany, David, and Philip Dubois. "Electing State Judges." *Wisconsin Law Review* (1976):734.

Alarcon, Arthur S. "Political Appointments and Judicial Independence: An Unreasonable Expectation." *Loyola of Los Angeles Law Review* 16 (1983):9.

Barber, Kathleen. "Ohio Judicial Elections: Nonpartisan Premises with Partisan Results." *Ohio State Law Journal* 32 (1971):762.

Baum, Lawrence. "The Electoral Fates of Incumbent Judges in the Ohio Court of Common Pleas." *Judicature* 66 (1983):420.

Berkson, Larry. "Selecting State Judges: Election or Appointment." Larry Berkson, Steven Hays, and Susan Carbon, eds. *Managing the State Courts: Text and Readings*. St. Paul: West, 1971.

Canon, Bradley C. "The Impact of Formal Selection Processes on the Characteristics of Judges—Reconsidered." *Law and Society Review* 6 (1972):579.

Carbon, Susan B. "Judicial Retention Elections: Are They Serving Their Intended Purpose?" *Judicature* 64 (1980):210.

Crowe, John E. "Subterranean Politics: A Judge Is Chosen." *Journal of Public Law* 11 (1963):275.

Czudnowski, Moshe. "Political Recruitment." Fred Greenstein and Nelson Polsby, eds. *Handbook of Political Science*. Reading, Pa.: Addison-Wesley, 1975.

Dubois, Philip. "The Significance of Voting Cues in State Supreme Court Elections." *Law and Society Review* 13 (1979):757.

———. "Public Participation in Trial Court Elections." *Law and Policy Quarterly* 2 (1980):133.

———. "The Influence of Selection Systems and Region on the Characteristics of the Trial Court Bench: The Case of California." *Justice System Journal* 8 (1983):59.

Dunn, Patrick W. "Judicial Selection in the States: A Critical Study with Proposals for Reform." *Hofstra Law Review* 4 (1976):267.

Flango, Victor, and Craig Ducat. "What Difference Does Method of Judicial Selection Make: Selection Methods in State Courts of Last Resort." *Justice System Journal* 5 (Fall 1979):25.

Goldman, Sheldon. "Judicial Selection and the Qualities That Make a 'Good' Judge." *The Annals* 462 (1982):112.

Griffin, Kenyon N., and Michael J. Horan. "Patterns of Voting Behavior in Judicial Retention Elections for Supreme Court Justices in Wyoming." *Judicature* 67 (1983):68.

———. "Merit Retention Elections: What Influences the Voters?." *Judicature* 63 (1979):78.

———. "Judicial Retention Election Decisions: A Search for Correlates." *Social Science Journal* 19 (1982):93.

Hall, Charles H. "The Choosing of Public Officials." *Proceedings of the Washington State Bar Association* (1925):44.

Jacob, Herbert. "The Effects of Institutional Differences in the Recruitment Process: The Case of State Judges." *Journal of Public Law* 13 (1964):104.

———. "Judicial Insulation: Elections, Direct Participation and Public Attention to Courts in Wisconsin." *Wisconsin Law Review* (1966):1.

Jenkins, William, Jr. "Retention Elections: Who Wins When No One Loses?." *Judicature* 61 (1977):79.

Johnson, Charles A., Roger Schaefer, and R. Neal McKnight. "The Salience of Judicial Candidates and Elections." *Social Science Quarterly* 59 (September 1978):371.

———. "Judicial Selection in Texas." Symposium. *Texas Bar Journal* 45 (1982):1513.

Klots, Allen T. "The Selection of Judges and the Short Ballot." *Journal of the American Judicature Society* 38 (February 1955):134.

Ladinski, Jack, and Allen Silver. "Popular Democracy and Judicial Independence: Electorate and Elite Reactions to Two Wisconsin Supreme Court Elections." *Wisconsin Law Review* 1967 (Winter):128.

Levin, Martin A. "Urban Politics and Judicial Behavior." *Journal of Legal Studies* 1 (1972):193.

Lovrich, Nicholas P., Jr., and Charles H. Sheldon. "Voters in Contested, Non-partisan Elections: A Responsible Electorate or a Problematic Public?" *Western Political Quarterly* 36 (June 1983):241.

———. "Assessing Judicial Elections: Effects upon the Electorate of High and Low Articulation Systems." *Western Political Quarterly* 38 (June 1985):276.

———. "Voters in Judicial Elections: An Attentive Public or an Uninformed Electorate?" *Justice System Journal* 9 (Spring 1984):23.

McKnight, R. Neal, Roger Schaefer, and Charles A. Johnson. "Choosing Judges: Do the Voters Know What They Are Doing?" *Judicature* 62 (August 1978):94.

May, Janice C., and N. Goldman. "Judicial Selection: An Analysis." *Texas Bar Journal* 46 (1983):316.

Mikva, Abner J. "Judicial Selection: Casting a Wider Net." *The Annals* 462 (1982):125.

Nejelski, Paul. "The Tension of Popular Participation." *State Court Journal* 1 (Fall 1977):1.

Nichols, R. J. "Elections vs. Appointments: Time for a Change." *Michigan Bar Journal* 60 (1981):761.

"Politicization of the Courts: Balancing the Need for Judicial Independence against the Need for Judicial Accountability." Symposium. *Harvard Journal of Law and Public Policy* 6 (1983):295.

Post, Frank Truman. "Effect of the Direct Primary Law upon the Character, Ability and Independence of the Judiciary." *Oregon Bar Association Proceedings* (1908–10):90.

Rosenman, Sam. "A Better Way to Select Judges." *Judicature* 48 (1964):88.

Samuels, Alec. "Appointing the Judges." *New Law Journal* 134 (1984):85.

Scheb, John M. "Is Anyone Listening? Assessing Bar Influence on Merit Retention Elections in Florida." *Judicature* 67 (1983):112.

Schneider, Ronald, and Ralph Maughan. "Does the Appointment of Judges Lead to a More Conservative Bench?" *Justice System Journal* 5 (1979):45.

Schotland, Roy A. "Elective Judges' Campaign Financing: Are State Judges' Robes the Emperor's Clothes on American Democracy?" *Journal of Law and Politics* 2 (1985):57.

Seis, Dennis E. "Selecting Judges in the States: A Brief History and Analysis." *Northern Kentucky Law Review* 9 (1982):459.

Sheldon, Charles, and Nicholas P. Lovrich, Jr. "Judicial Accountability vs. Responsibility: Balancing the Views of the Voters and the Judges." *Judicature* 65 (May 1982):470.

———. "Knowledge and Judicial Voting: The Oregon and Washington Experience." *Judicature* 67 (1983):234.

———. "Do Bar Polls Affect the Voters?" *Seattle–King County Bar Bulletin* 3 (1984):6.

———. "Voters' Attitudes toward Elections." *Judiciary: Quarterly for the Washington Courts* (October 1981):1.

———. "Polls: Are They Valid Tools?" *Oregon Bar Bulletin* 43 (1982):10.

———. "A Profile of the Oregon Judicial Electorate." *Ibid.* 45 (1985):23.

Sheldon, Charles H. "Influencing the Selection of Judges: The Variety and Effectiveness of State Bar Activities." *Western Political Quarterly* 30 (1977):397.

———. "Bar Endorsement of Judicial Candidates." *Washington State Bar News* 28 (1974):8.

———. "The Recruitment of Judges to the Washington Supreme Court: Past and Present." *Willamette Law Review* 11 (1986):85.

Spaeth, Edmund B., Jr. "Reflections on a Judicial Campaign: Should Judges Ride a Political Bandwagon?" *Judicature* 60 (1976):10.

Swidorski, C. "Judicial Selection: Reform and the New York Court of Appeals: Illusion or Reality?" *New York State Bar Journal* 55 (1983):10.

Vandenberg, Donna. "Voluntary Merit Selection: Its History and Current Status." *Judicature* 66 (1982/83):265.

Volcansek, Mary L. "An Exploration of the Judicial Elections Process." *Western Political Quarterly* 34 (1981):572.

———. "The Effects of Judicial Selection Reform: What We Know and What We Do Not." Philip L. Dubois, ed. *The Analysis of Judicial Reform.* Lexington, Mass.: Lexington Books, 1982.

———. "Money or Name? A Sectional Analysis of Judicial Elections." *Justice System Journal* 8 (1983):45.

Wasby, Stephen. "Accountability of Courts." Scott Greer, Ronald Hedlund, and James Gibson, eds. *Accountability in Urban Society*. Beverly Hills: Sage, 1978.

Williams, G. Mennan. "Selecting Michigan's Judges." *Detroit College of Law Review* (1983):1489.

Wormuth, Francis, and S. Grover Rich. "Politics, the Bar, and the Selection of Judges." *Utah Law Review* 3 (1953):459.

Court Deliberations and Judicial Behavior

Books

Boyum, Keith O., and Lynn Mather, eds. *Empirical Theories about Courts.* New York: Longman, 1983.

Cramer, James A., ed. *Courts and Judges.* Beverly Hills: Sage, 1981.

Ducat, Craig R., and Victor E. Flango. *Leadership in State Supreme Courts: Roles of the Chief Justice.* Beverly Hills: Sage, 1976.

Dwyer, William L. *The Goldmark Case: An American Libel Trial.* Seattle: University of Washington Press, 1985.

Fetter, Theodore J., ed. *State Courts: A Blueprint for the Future.* Williamsburg: Center for State Courts, 1978.

Glick, Henry. *Supreme Courts in State Politics.* New York: Basic Books, 1970.

Glick, Henry, and Kenneth Vines. *State Court Systems.* Englewood Cliffs: Prentice-Hall, 1972.

Goldman, Sheldon, and Thomas P. Jahnige. *The Federal Courts as a Political System.* New York: Harper and Row, 1971.

Grossman, Joel, and Joseph Tanenhaus, eds. *Frontiers of Judicial Research.* New York: John Wiley, 1969.

Halpern, Stephen, and Charles Lamb. *Supreme Court Activism and Restraint.* Lexington, Mass.: Lexington Books, 1982.

Howard, J. Woodford. *Courts of Appeals in the Federal Judicial System.* Princeton: Princeton University Press, 1981.

Hughes, Charles Evans. *The Supreme Court of the United States.* New York: Garden City Publishers, 1936.

Jackson, Percival. *Dissent in the Supreme Court.* Norman: University of Oklahoma Press, 1949.

Jonas, Frank H. *Western Politics.* Salt Lake City: University of Utah Press, 1961.

———, ed. *Politics in the American West.* Salt Lake City: University of Utah Press, 1969.

Llewellyn, Karl. *The Common Law Tradition: Deciding Appeals.* Boston: Little, Brown, 1960.

McConkie, Stanley. "Environmental, Institutional, and Procedural Influences in Collegial Decision-Making." Ph.D. dissertation, Political Science Department, Washington State University, 1974.

Morris, Thomas R. *The Virginia Supreme Court: An Institutional and Political Analysis.* Charlottesville: University of Virginia Press, 1975.

Mullen, W. Frank, et al. *The Government and Politics of Washington State.* Pullman: Washington State University Press, 1978.

Murphy, Walter F. *The Elements of Judicial Strategy.* Chicago: University of Chicago Press, 1964.

Murphy, Walter F., and C. Herman Pritchett. *Courts, Judges and Politics.* New York: Random House, 1979.

Nagel, Stuart S. *The Legal Process from a Behavioral Perspective.* Homewood: Dorsey Press, 1969.

Neely, Richard. *How Courts Govern America.* New Haven: Yale University Press, 1980.

Oakley, John B., and Robert S. Thompson. *Law Clerks and the Judicial Process.* Berkeley, University of California Press, 1980.

Powell, Lee, ed. *Court Reform in Seven States.* Chicago: American Bar Association, 1980.

Richardson, Richard J., and Kenneth N. Vines. *The Politics of Federal Courts.* Boston: Little, Brown, 1970.

Ryan, John P., et al. *American Trial Judges.* New York: Free Press, 1980.

Schmidhauser, John. *The Supreme Court: Its Politics, Personalities and Procedures.* New York: Holt, Rinehart and Winston, 1960.

Schubert, Glendon. *Judicial Behavior: A Reader in Theory and Research.* Chicago: Rand McNally, 1964.

———, ed. *Judicial Decision-Making.* New York: Free Press of Glencoe, 1963.

———. *Quantitative Analysis of Judicial Behavior.* Glencoe, Ill.: Free Press, 1959.

———. *The Judicial Mind Revisited.* New York: Oxford, 1974.

———. *Judicial Policy Making.* Glenview: Scott Foresman, 1974.

———. *The Judicial Mind.* Evanston: Northwestern University Press, 1965.

Shapiro, Martin. *Courts: A Comparative and Political Analysis.* Chicago: University of Chicago Press, 1980.

Sheldon, Charles H. *The American Judicial Process: Models and Approaches.* New York: Dodd Mead, 1974.

Sheldon, Charles H., and Frank P. Weaver. *Politicians, Judges and the People: A Study in Citizens' Participation.* Westport, Conn.: Greenwood Press, 1980.

Sprague, John. *Voting Patterns of the United States Supreme Court: Cases in Federalism, 1889–1959.* Indianapolis: Bobbs-Merrill, 1968.

Swanson, Thor K., et al. *Political Life in Washington.* Pullman: Washington State University Press, 1985.

Ulmer, S. Sidney. *Courts as Small and Not So Small Groups.* New York: General Learning Press, 1971.

Articles

Adamany, David. "The Party Variable in Judges' Voting: Conceptual Notes and a Case Study." *American Political Science Review* 63 (1966):57.

Atkins, Burton M. "Decision-Making Rules and Judicial Strategy on the United States Court of Appeals." *Western Political Quarterly* 25 (1972):626.

Atkins, Burton M., and Henry R. Glick. "Environmental and Structural Variables as Determinants of Issues in State Courts of Last Resort." *American Journal of Political Science* 20 (1976):97.

Aynes, Richard L. "Evaluation of Judicial Performance: A Tool for Self-Improvement." *Pepperdine Law Review* 8 (1981):225.

Baum, Lawrence. "Judicial Politics: Still a Distinctive Field." Ada W. Finifter, ed. *Political Science: The State of the Discipline.* Washington, D.C.: American Political Science Association (1983):189.

Becker, Theodore. "A Survey Study of Hawaiian Judges: The Effects of Judicial Role Variations." *American Political Science Review* 60 (1966):677.

———. "Surveys and Judiciaries or Who's Afraid of the Purple Curtain." *Law and Society Review* 1 (1966):133.

Beiser, Edward N., and Jonathan Silberman. "The Political Party Variable: Workmen's Compensation Cases in the New York Court of Appeals." *Polity* 3 (1971):521.

Berg, Larry L., et al. "The Consequences of Judicial Reform: A Comparative Analysis of California and Iowa Appellate Systems." *Western Political Quarterly* 28 (1975):263.

Brachtenbach, Robert F. "Mechanics of Supreme Court Decision-Making." *Washington State Bar News* 8 (April 1973):8.

Campbell, J. L., III. "The Spirit of Dissent." *Judicature* 66 (1983):305.

Canon, Bradley C., and Dean Jaros. "External Variables, Institutional Structure and Dissent on State Supreme Courts." *Polity* 3 (1970):175.

Danelski, David J. "The Influence of the Chief Justice in the Decisional Process." Walter F. Murphy and C. Herman Pritchett, eds. *Courts, Judges and Politics.* New York: Random House, 1979.

———. "Judicial Behavior: Theory and Method." *Political Behavior* 5 (1983).

Dolliver, James M. "Charles Horowitz: A Memoir." *Washington Law Review* 56 (1981):168.

Fair, Daryl R. "State Intermediate Appellate Courts: An Introduction." *Western Political Quarterly* 24 (1971):423.

Gibson, James L. "Judges' Role Orientations, Attitudes and Decisions: An Interactive Model." *American Political Science Review* 72 (1978):911.

———. "The Role Concept in Judicial Research." *Law and Policy Quarterly* 3 (1981):291.

Groot, Roger D. "The Effects of an Intermediate Appellate Court on the Supreme Court Work Product: The North Carolina Experience." *Wake Forest Law Review* 7 (1971):548.

Horowitz, Charles. "Values and Decision-Making: Some Observations on the Role of Non-legal Factors in the Appellate Process." *Washington Appellate Practice Handbook.* Seattle: Continuing Legal Education Committee, Washington State Bar Association (1980):3.2.

Jaros, Dean, and Bradley C. Canon. "Dissent on State Supreme Courts: The Differential Significance of Characteristics of Judges." *MidWest Journal of Political Science* 35 (1971):324.

Krislov, Samuel. "Theoretical Attempts at Predicting Small Group Behavior." *Harvard Law Review* 79 (1966):1580.

Merryman, John H. "Toward a Theory of Citations: An Empirical Study of the Citation Practice of the California Supreme Court in 1950, 1960 and 1970." *Southern California Law Review* 50 (1977):381.

Murphy, Walter F. "Leadership, Bargaining, and the Judicial Process." Glendon A. Schubert, ed. *Judicial Behavior: A Reader in Theory and Research.* Chicago: Rand McNally, 1964.

———. "Marshalling the Court: Leadership, Bargaining, and the Judicial Process." *University of Chicago Law Review* 29 (1962):640.

Rohde, David. "Policy Goals and Opinion Coalitions in the Supreme Court." *Midwest Journal of Political Science* 36 (1972):197.

Rosellini, Hugh. "Crisis in the Supreme Court." *Gonzaga Law Review* 3 (1968):12.

Sheldon, Charles H. "Law Clerking with a State Supreme Court: Views from the Perspective of the Personal Assistants to the Judges." *Justice System Journal* 6 (Fall 1981):346.

———. "The Washington Supreme Court: What It Was Like Thirty Years Ago." *Gonzaga Law Review* 19 (1983/84):231.

———. "An Interpretation of the Judicial Process: The Washington Supreme Court as a Small Group." *Gonzaga Law Review* 13 (1977):97.

———. "Perceptions of Judicial Roles in Nevada." *Utah Law Review* (1966):355.

———. "The Uniqueness of State Legal Systems." *Judicature* 53 (1970):333.

Snyder, Eloise. "The Supreme Court as a Small Group." *Social Forces* 36 (March 1952):232.

Spitzer, Hugh. "Court Rulemaking in Washington State." *University of Puget Sound Law Review* 6 (1982):31.

Tate, C. Neal. "Personal Attribute Models of the Voting Behavior of U.S. Supreme Court Justices: Liberalism in Civil Liberties and Economic Decisions, 1946–1978." *American Political Science Review* 75 (1981):355.

———. "The Methodology of Judicial Behavior Research: A Review and Critique." *Political Behavior* 5 (1983):51.

Ulmer, S. Sidney. "Leadership in the Michigan Supreme Court." Glendon A. Schubert, ed. *Judicial Decision-Making*. New York: Free Press, 1963.

———. "The Analysis of Behavior Patterns in the United States Supreme Court." *Journal of Politics* 22 (1960):629.

———. "The Political Party Variable in the Michigan Supreme Court." *Journal of Public Law* 11 (1962):352.

———. "Toward a Theory of Sub-Group Formation in the United States Supreme Court." *Journal of Politics* 27 (1965):133.

Ungs, Thomas D., and Larry R. Bass. "Judicial Role Perceptions: A Q-Technique Study of Ohio Judges." *Law and Society Review* 6 (1972).

Utter, Robert F. "The Right to Speak, Write, and Publish Freely: State Constitutional Protection against Private Abridgement." *University of Puget Sound Law Review* 8 (1985):157.

Vines, Kenneth. "The Judicial Role in American States: An Exploration." Joel B. Grossman and Joseph Tanenhaus, eds. *Frontiers in Judicial Research*. New York: John Wiley, 1969.

Name Index

Case Index

Subject Index